Volume 6

MODERN CHRISTIANITY TO 1900

AMANDA PORTERFIELD
Editor

FORTRESS PRESS
Minneapolis

REFORMATION CHRISTIANITY
A People's History of Christianity, Volume 6

Cover image: *Portrait of a Black Woman* [*Portrait d'une négresse*] (1800) by Marie-
    Guilhelmine Benoist (1768–1826). Louvre, Paris. © Scala/Art Resource, N.Y.
Cover design: Laurie Ingram
Book design: James Korsmo/Zan Ceeley, Trio Bookworks

Further materials on this volume and the entire series can be found online at
www.peopleshistoryofchristianity.com.

Library of Congress Cataloging-in-Publication Data

Modern Christianity to 1900 / Amanda Porterfield, editor.
    p. cm. — (A people's history of Christianity ; v. 6)
    Includes bibliographical references and index.
    ISBN-13: 978-0-8006-3416-2 (alk. paper)
    ISBN-10: 0-8006-3416-0 (alk. paper)
    1. Church history—Modern period, 1500– I. Porterfield, Amanda
    BR290.M62 2007
    270.8'1—dc22
                                                         2007006548

Manufactured in Canada
11   10   09   08   07   1   2   3   4   5   6   7   8   9   10

MODERN
CHRISTIANITY
TO 1900

FURTHER PRAISE FOR THIS SERIES:

"The concept of this 'people's history' represents a virtual revolution in the writing of Christian history, a change that means something dynamic, something that should draw the attention of many who do not think of themselves as likers of history. . . . These stories may come up from the basement of church history, but news about their existence deserves to be shouted from the housetops."

MARTIN E. MARTY, *University of Chicago Divinity School*

"Hidden for centuries by their anonymity and illiteracy, the people of God—the body of Christ, the church!—are finally having their story told, and by some of today's finest historians of the church. The saints, bishops, and theologians of traditional histories can now be placed against the panoramic and fascinating backdrop of the lived religion of ordinary men and women of faith. Highly recommended."

MARK U. EDWARDS JR., *Harvard Divinity School*

A PEOPLE'S HISTORY OF CHRISTIANITY

Denis R. Janz
General Editor

Editorial Advisory Board

Sean Freyne, *Trinity College, Dublin* **Elizabeth Clark,** *Duke University*
Susan Ashbrook Harvey, *Brown University* **Bernard McGinn,** *University of Chicago*
Charles Lippy, *University of Tennessee, Chattanooga* **Steven E. Ozment,** *Harvard University*
Rosemary Radford Ruether, *Pacific School of Religion*

Volume 1
CHRISTIAN ORIGINS
Richard Horsley, editor

Volume 2
LATE ANCIENT CHRISTIANITY
Virginia Burrus, editor

Volume 3
BYZANTINE CHRISTIANITY
Derek Krueger, editor

Volume 4
MEDIEVAL CHRISTIANITY
Daniel E. Bornstein, editor

Volume 5
REFORMATION CHRISTIANITY
Peter Matheson, editor

Volume 6
MODERN CHRISTIANITY TO 1900
Amanda Porterfield, editor

Volume 7
TWENTIETH-CENTURY GLOBAL CHRISTIANITY
Mary Farrell Bednarowski, editor

excluded, the heretics, those defined by conventional history as the losers? Can a face be put on any of them?

Today, even after half a century of study, answers are still in short supply. It must be conceded that the field is in its infancy, both methodologically and in terms of what remains to be investigated. Very often historians now find themselves no longer interrogating literary texts but rather artifacts, the remains of material culture, court records, wills, popular art, graffiti, and so forth. What is already clear is that many traditional assumptions, timeworn clichés, and well-loved nuggets of conventional wisdom about Christianity's past will have to be abandoned. When the Christian masses are made the leading protagonists of the story, we begin to glimpse a plot with dramatically new contours. In fact, a rewriting of this history is now getting under way, and this may well be the discipline's larger task for the twenty-first century.

A People's History of Christianity is our contribution to this enterprise. In it we gather up the early harvest of this new approach, showcase the current state of the discipline, and plot a trajectory into the future. Essentially what we offer here is a preliminary attempt at a new and more adequate version of the Christian story—one that features the people. Is it comprehensive? Impossible. Definitive? Hardly. A responsible, suggestive, interesting base to build on? We are confident that it is.

Close to a hundred historians of Christianity have generously applied their various types of expertise to this project, whether as advisers or editors or contributors. They have in common no universally agreed-on methodology, nor do they even concur on how precisely to define problematic terms such as "popular religion." What they do share is a conviction that rescuing the Christian people from their historic anonymity is important, that reworking the story's plot with lay piety as the central narrative will be a contribution of lasting value, and that reversing the condescension, not to say contempt, that all too often has marred elite views of the people is long overdue. If progress is made on these fronts, we believe, the groundwork for a new history of Christianity will have been prepared.

This volume, *Modern Christianity to 1900*, takes as its subject popular Christianity's encounter with modernity. In this meeting, the Christianity (Christianities?) of the people came up against realities hitherto undreamt of, significantly altering inherited worldviews; geographical expansion led to diversification along regional lines; and issues such as race and gender now rose to the fore, cutting across all boundaries. "Encounter" can of course mean many things: confrontation, reaction, accommodation, transformation, adjustment, sublation, and so forth. All of these processes occurred, often simultaneously. Thus it would be foolish to underestimate the complexity of our theme. And yet we should not be daunted by it. To orient our entrée into this labyrinth, I could not have chosen a more reliable guide than Amanda Porterfield, the editor of this volume. Neophytes and experts alike have much to learn from her comprehensive grasp of the whole and her remarkable expertise on the details. Her wise judgment, unfailing professionalism, efficiency, and good cheer have made my job easy. I am honored to have had the opportunity to work with her.

Denis R. Janz, General Editor

CONTENTS

CONTRIBUTORS

H. B. Cavalcanti, Professor of Sociology and Anthropology, James Madison University

Ava Chamberlain, Associate Professor of Religion, Wright State University

John Corrigan, Edwin Scott Gaustad Professor of Religion, Florida State University

Carlos Eire, Riggs Professor of History and Religious Studies, Yale University

Peter Gardella, Professor of World Religions, Manhattanville College

Cheryl A. Kirk-Duggan, Professor of Theology and Women's Studies, Shaw University

Charles H. Lippy, LeRoy A. Martin Distinguished Professor of Religious Studies, University of Tennessee, Chattanooga

Ronald L. Numbers, Hilldale and William Coleman Professor of the History and Science and Medicine, University of Wisconsin, Madison

Amanda Porterfield, Robert A. Spivey Professor of Religion, Florida State University

Vera Shevzov, Associate Professor of Religion, Smith College

Marilyn J. Westerkamp, Professor of History, University of California, Santa Cruz

Douglas L. Winiarski, Assistant Professor of Religion, University of Richmond

ILLUSTRATIONS

Color Plates (following page 146)

FOREWORD

This seven-volume series breaks new ground by looking at Christianity's past from the vantage point of a people's history. It is church history, yes, but church history with a difference: "church," we insist, is not to be understood first and foremost as the hierarchical-institutional-bureaucratic corporation; rather, above all, it is the laity, the ordinary faithful, the people. Their religious lives, their pious practices, their self-understandings as Christians, and the way all of this grew and changed over the last two millennia—*this* is the unexplored territory in which we are here setting foot.

To be sure, the undertaking known as people's history, as it is applied to secular themes, is hardly a new one among academic historians. Referred to sometimes as history from below, or grassroots history, or popular history, it was born about a century ago, in conscious opposition to the elitism of conventional (some call it Rankean) historical investigation, fixated as this was on the "great" deeds of "great" men, and little else. What had always been left out of the story, of course, was the vast majority of human beings: almost all women, obviously, but then too all those who could be counted among the socially inferior, the economically distressed, the politically marginalized, the educationally deprived, or the culturally unrefined. Had not various elites always despised "the people"? Cicero, in first-century BCE Rome, referred to them as "urban filth and dung"; Edmund Burke, in eighteenth-century London, called them "the swinish multitude"; and in between, this loathing of "the meaner sort" was almost universal among the privileged. When the discipline called "history" was professionalized in the nineteenth century, traditional gentlemen historians perpetuated this contempt, if not by outright vilification, then at least by keeping the masses invisible. Thus when people's history came on the scene, it was not only a means for uncovering an unknown dimension of the past but also in some sense an instrument for righting an injustice. Today its cumulative contribution is enormous, and its home in the academic world is assured.

Only quite recently has the discipline formerly called "church history" and now more often "the history of Christianity" begun to open itself up to this approach. Its agenda over the last two centuries has been dominated by other facets of this religion's past, such as theology, dogma, institutions, and ecclesio-political relations. Each of these has in fact long since evolved into its own subdiscipline. Thus the history of theology has concentrated on the self-understandings of Christian intellectuals. Historians of dogma have examined the way in which church leaders came to formulate teachings that they then pronounced normative for all Christians. Experts on institutional history have researched the formation, growth, and functioning of leadership offices, bureaucratic structures, official decision-making processes, and so forth. And specialists in the history of church–state relations have worked to fathom the complexities of the institution's interface with its sociopolitical context, above all by studying leaders on both sides.

Collectively, these conventional kinds of church history have yielded enough specialized literature to fill a very large library, and those who read in this library will readily testify to its amazing treasures. Erudite as it is, however, the Achilles' heel of this scholarship, taken as a whole, is that it has told the history of Christianity as the story of one small segment of those who have claimed the name "Christian." What has been studied almost exclusively until now is the religion of various elites, whether spiritual elites, or intellectual elites, or power elites. Without a doubt, mystics and theologians, pastors, priests, bishops, and popes are worth studying. But at best they altogether constitute perhaps 5 percent of all Christians over two millennia. What about the rest? Does not a balanced history of Christianity, not to mention our sense of historical justice, require that attention be paid to them?

Around the mid-twentieth century, a handful of scholars began, hesitantly and yet insistently, to press this question on the international guild of church historians. Since that time, the study of the other 95 percent has gained momentum: ever more ambitious research projects have been launched; innovative scholarly methods have been developed, critiqued, and refined; and a growing public interest has greeted the results. Academics and nonacademics alike want to know about this aspect of Christianity's past. Who were these people—the voiceless, the ordinary faithful who wrote no theological treatises, whose statues adorn no basilicas, who negotiated no concordats, whose very names themselves are largely lost to historical memory? What can we know about their religious consciousness, their devotional practice, their understanding of the faith, their values, beliefs, feelings, habits, attitudes, and their deepest fears, hopes, loves, hatreds, and so forth? And what about the troublemakers, the

EXPANSION AND CHANGE

AMANDA PORTERFIELD

After 1600, new technologies and forms of industry revolutionized the lives of people around the world. Emerging nation-states, international commerce, modern warfare, and growing demands for democracy led to new forms of social organization affecting people's relationships to one another and to the material world. New ideas about the spiritual world, and new ways to engage its forces, explained these relationships and helped people manage them. Volume 6 of A People's History of Christianity explores the beliefs and practices of Christian people during the tumultuous period of modern transformation prior to 1900. Focusing on the expanding reach of Christian cosmologies, on Christianity as a vehicle of modern individualism, and on Christian missionaries as catalysts of social criticism and reform, the volume examines some of the ways that Christian beliefs and practices mediated changes in the lives of ordinary people.

The meaning of the term "modernization" has often been discussed and its implications for religion hotly debated.[1] This introduction defines modernization broadly as enthusiasm for rational explanations of life that privilege individualism, nationalism, scientific enterprise, and strategic planning. While modernization played out differently in different parts of the world, people everywhere utilized religious beliefs and practices to define and shape it. And while modernization posed many challenges for religious belief and traditional forms of religious practice, people often turned to religion (especially Christianity) to work through these challenges. In Europe, where the driving forces of modern social change first took hold, Christian beliefs and practices figured prominently in people's efforts to negotiate the revolutionary social changes associated with individualism, nationalism, scientific enterprise, and other aspects of modernization. As Europeans moved deeper into other parts of the world, more and more people took up Christianity, sometimes in bits and pieces, and always in the context of their own situations. In many different places around the world, Christian symbols, stories, and practices helped people negotiate the forces of modernization.

Modern conversions to Christianity differed in important respects from earlier conversions. During the first centuries of Christian expansion, the political and economic power of the Roman Empire waned, and local customs often engulfed imperial interpretations of Christianity. Although subversive interpretations of Christianity as a religion of the poor never disappeared, traditions of skeptical inquiry and secular reasoning associated with Greek culture declined as Christianity expanded in ancient and early medieval worlds. For all the maiming and killing associated with conversion after Christianity became the established religion of the Roman Empire in the fourth century, conversion left familiar assumptions about the nature of spiritual forces and their relation to the material world unquestioned. In the modern era, by contrast, the spread of Christianity coincided both with the expanding power of Western political and economic influence and with an upsurge in new questions about divine reality and new ways of conceptualizing spiritual authority. Many people took hold of Christian beliefs and practices in modern efforts to maintain or reconstruct their worlds.

As Christians from Europe reached into the Americas, Asia, and Africa in the seventeenth and eighteenth centuries, people indigenous to those regions encountered Christianity, in many cases, through its connections to imperial power. Representatives of Spanish, Portuguese, British, French, Dutch, and German princes invoked the authority of Christ to assert the divine right of their princes to rule over new people and new land, or at least pacify them for purposes of trade and extraction of natural resources. People in the Americas, Asia, and Africa also encountered Christianity through strategic missionary operations designed to spread the gospel and offer the blessings of salvation to those perceived to need them.

Catholic religious orders sent some of their most talented members to foreign fields to support the work of European expansion and bring Christianity to native peoples. Catholic missionaries reintroduced Christianity to parts of India, Persia, and China where it had died out, and brought it to the Americas and to places in Asia and Africa where it had never been. Beginning in the seventeenth century, English, Scottish, German, Dutch, and Danish Protestants also established mission societies, and in the course of the nineteenth century, commitment to foreign missions became a hallmark of evangelical religion in Europe, Britain, and the United States. Through these extensive missionary efforts, and through the expansion of Western influence more generally, people outside of Western Christendom encountered the Christian God, along with the ships, weapons, tools, costumes, manners, books, food and drink, gender roles, sexual habits, and diseases of Westerners who viewed Christianity and Western culture as coextensive and interdependent.

People outside of Europe also had to come to terms with some of the revolutionary changes rocking Western Christendom, revolutionary changes that were destabilizing Western cultures even as those cultures expanded their borders. These changes included challenges to the divine rights of Christian princes, the union of church and state, the legitimacy of monarchical rule, the truth of religious beliefs, and the efficacy of traditional religious practices. The destabilization of traditional cosmologies began inside of Western Christendom and moved outward from there to many parts of the world. Beginning in the reformation movements of the sixteenth century, Protestant attacks on superstition carried devastating messages about the impotence of saints, sacraments, priests, relics, and icons. As Christianity expanded throughout the world, the destabilization of traditional cosmologies spread to other peoples, upsetting traditional family structures, economic patterns, and religious beliefs about authority.

Challenges to religious authority, and defenses of that authority, became increasingly far reaching in their social implications. In North America, English Protestants justified their desire for independence from British rule by refusing to accept the divine right of George III (or any other king) to rule over them. Extending a line of thought that can be traced back through Puritan revolutionaries in seventeenth-century England, American revolutionaries in the eighteenth century portrayed their right to political independence as a logical extension of Protestant refusal to accept the authority of Rome. In January 1766, a corset maker named Thomas Paine made this connection clear in *Common Sense*, the pamphlet that galvanized popular support for the American Revolution. "For monarchy in every instance is the Popery of government," Paine announced in *Common Sense*. Appealing to the supreme authority of God, he exclaimed, "But where says some is the King of America? I'll tell you Friend, he reigns above. . . ."[2]

Such revolutionary appeals to God did not go undisputed. In America, Paine's reputation plummeted as evangelicals sought to rein in democratic claims to reason and natural rights and to define Christianity in terms of emotional experiences of new birth. Partly in reaction against the revolutionary philosophy and violence of the French Revolution, American culture became more conservative. When Paine defended the French Revolution in *The Age of Reason* (1797) and attacked the belief in miracles associated with Christianity, evangelicals tarred him as an atheist.

Revolutionary tendencies and backlashes against them reached people in Asia, Africa, and the Americas, compounding other unsettling aspects of Western intrusion. Christianity provided language for new and revolutionary demands for political freedom in many parts of the world, as well as language that called for return to social order. Christianity was often the language of democracy; it was also a language of social control, manifest in systems of belief and practice that channeled people's feelings and exploited their labor more rationally, efficiently, and systematically than ever before.

Appealing to the Bible to Denounce Monarchy

Government by kings was first introduced into the world by the Heathens, from whom the children of Israel copied the custom. It was the most prosperous invention the Devil ever set on foot for the promotion of idolatry. The Heathens paid divine honors to their deceased kings, and the Christian world hath improved on the plan by doing the same to their living ones. How impious is the title of sacred majesty applied to a worm, who in the midst of his splendor is crumbling into dust.

As the exalting one man so greatly above the rest cannot be justified on the equal rights of nature, so neither can it be defended on the authority of scripture; for the will of the Almighty, as declared by Gideon and the prophet Samuel, expressly disapproves of government by kings.

—Thomas Paine, Common Sense (1776; New York: Penguin, 1976), 71–72.

COSMOLOGY

As millions of people outside of Europe became acquainted with Christian beliefs and practices and Christians in the West became acquainted with non-European peoples, the stories in the Bible offered an overarching schema to accommodate people's expanding awareness of human diversity. Stories from Genesis traced the origin of all human beings to a first set of parents, Adam and Eve, whose disobedience of God's law led to their expulsion from paradise and transmission of sinfulness to all their progeny. With humanity plagued by sin and in dire need of assistance, God sent his Son to earth as the redeemer. Through his perfect life and sacrificial death, Christ atoned for the sins of people who placed faith in his power to save them from death, sin, and hell.

The biblical story of fall and redemption was not new; Christians had been telling much the same story for centuries. But after 1600, when Christianity was expanding and people everywhere were constructing new forms of social organization, the biblical story of fall and redemption provided a narrative framework that encompassed all the people in the world and suggested explanations for the expansion of Christianity and Western culture in the modern era. As far as many Christians in the West were concerned, the Bible supported their conquest of the earth's people and resources and explained their apparent superiority over other people as deriving from their knowledge of God and the Bible. While some cited the Bible as inspiration for building a new era of civilized tolerance and human equality, others cited it to justify extensive systems of social differentiation that included slavery. But even as they disagreed about the implications of biblical teaching with respect to the organization of modern life, and about how equal God intended people to be, modern Christians drew inspiration from the biblical story of fall and redemption to promote new plans for the reorganization of human society, new technologies of communication, and new forms of industry and commerce.

Especially among Protestants in the Calvinist tradition who felt part of God's initiative going forward in history and transforming the world, confidence in God's transcendent oversight coincided with religious ideas about Christian stewardship of the earth, in which true Christians lived righteously in the world, managing its resources peaceably and in conformity with God's will. Protestants often reached out to others to explain the rational order of nature, the providential history of human civilization, and the need to live in a right relationship with God. As champions of literacy and education, they established schools all over the world and produced many translations of the Bible and many books, magazines, and pamphlets to promote their points of view. At the same time, however, literacy and education also stimulated new interpretations of the Bible, new constructions of history, and new religious movements over which Western Protestants had little control.

As part of their rejection of the authority of the Roman Catholic Church, Protestants laid great emphasis on the Bible as a dynamic source of social criticism and reform, downplaying the clergy's role in administering salvation, and challenging some of the traditions that had accrued to Christianity over the centuries. In their appeals to the Bible as the ultimate authority, and in their shift away from priestly authority and church tradition, Protestants looked backward to the primitive origins of Christianity described in the Bible and often tried to align their lives with the primitive church. Many believed that God's plan for redemption was finally unfolding in their own day and that Christian life was awakening after the long dark ages of medieval oppression. Protestant emphasis on the activist message of the Bible helped stimulate expectations of change that justified and even helped propel innovations in technology, commerce, and economic production.

While Protestants were often at the forefront of modern social change between 1600 and 1900, people involved with other branches of Christianity were also modernizing. Catholic adventurers, soldiers, and merchants from Spain, Portugal, and France established colonies, extracted resources, utilized labor, and introduced Western beliefs and practices to many people around the world. The spread of Catholicism in the modern era not only amplified the meaning of Catholic universalism but also encouraged more systematic efforts on the part of the church authorities in Rome to regulate Catholic devotions and Catholic teaching, centralize church government, and elevate papal authority. In strategic forms of outreach, Catholic missionaries acquainted millions in Asia, Africa, and the Americas with modern Christianity through their work as educators, nurses, representatives of papal authority, and priests. Generally more tolerant of indigenous religious practices than Protestant missionaries, and more willing to allow non-Western beliefs about the spirit world into Christianity, Catholic missionaries contributed significantly to the growth, vitality, and indigenization of Christianity.

In North America, some native peoples incorporated biblical symbols and stories into their own cosmologies while resisting conversion. In more than a few cases, Natives employed Christian symbols in banding together to oppose colonial and American aggression. In eastern North America in the eighteenth and early nineteenth centuries, for example, Natives allied with the Delaware chief Pontiac invoked their knowledge of biblical stories against British interpretations, claiming that God intended Indians to retain rightful sovereignty over American land. Later in the nineteenth century, in western North America, Native American Ghost Dancers led by the Paiute

Fig. 0.1. Native Americans (Modoc or Ottawa) at the Quapaw Mission, Indian Territory, Oklahoma, 1870.

prophet Wovoka incorporated Christian ideas about the restoration of paradise and the resurrection of the dead into an indigenous movement based on visions of the purification of their land and the expulsion of white people.[3]

INDIVIDUALISM

The globalization of Christianity in the modern era often involved new expectations of individual self-discipline that diminished the authority of traditional rites of social consensus and communal discipline. In the city of Urmiyah in nineteenth-century Persia, for example, American Protestant missionaries subjected Nestorian children to frightening experiences of isolation and self-recrimination that missionaries found conducive to repentance and conversion. At the school for Nestorian girls in Urmiyah, the missionaries insisted that each child spend time alone in a closet praying about her sins, thinking about hell, and begging God for forgiveness. Unused to such forced solitude—especially when it came to religious life, which in traditional Nestorian culture was more communal than private—the children became terrified of God and of their own sinfulness. The missionaries regarded this terror as a good thing. Most of the girls at the school accepted the missionary regimen, not only because their parents had sent them there, but also because of their learning to read and write, important advantages linked to new forms of individualized piety and to new economic opportunities developed through missionary contacts.[4]

The emotional distress associated with modern conversion derived partly from the breakdown of familiar forms of solidarity and from the anxieties associated with expectations of personal autonomy. In many cases, the personal trauma of conversion involved a disconcerting sense that an old world of miracles and signs from heaven could not be taken for granted and a new and more impersonal world of evidence, power, and industry was arising. Claims about miraculous events did not disappear, however. In many cases, Christians were more insistent than ever about supernatural reality as highly personalized experiences of Christ and other superhuman entities flourished against a background of growing skepticism, rationalism, and modern political and economic change.

Christians in the modern era often believed that individual religious expression was conducive to social order. The evangelical movement, with which most Protestant missionaries identified, was defined by the belief that social order was best achieved through internalized self-discipline and the personal transformation of new birth, and not through the imposition of religious conformity by clerics acting on high. While evangelicals disagreed on questions about the nature of free will and sanctification, the role of education in conversion, and the meaning of the gospel with respect to race and gender, underlying commitments to personal transformation and self-discipline defined evangelicalism as a broad movement within modern Protestant Christianity.

One of the early formulators of modern evangelicalism, the Anglican pastor and preacher John Wesley, developed "methods" for facilitating conversion and holiness. Designed to enhance the individual's internal sensitivity to feelings of remorse, forgiveness, and love, these methods of nurturing piety encouraged individuals to build virtuous lives anchored around such feelings. In highlighting the importance of personal piety and individual religious experience, evangelicals promoted strict standards for virtuous behavior that emphasized personal discipline and close emotional ties between husbands and wives, and between parents and children, that supported the construction of cohesive middle-class cultures. Although it did encourage experimentation and diversity in many cases, evangelical pietism could be a means to social conformity, particularly when linked to clear-cut rules of feeling and behavior.

Nagging problems of hypocrisy moved to the fore as a consequence of Christian investment in religious subjectivity. Hypocrisy was not a new issue for Christians, but it became more subjectivized as ordinary Christians worried that they might not have received saving grace after all. While medieval Christians had also voiced concerns about salvation and hypocrisy, their concerns often revolved around episodes of bad behavior. Distress about behavior did not disappear, but signs of internal anxiety about the paradoxical nature of religious assurance and the slipperiness of Christian humility became increasingly widespread. The profound uncertainty that many modern Christians felt about their spiritual status reflected anxieties associated with feelings of lost innocence and alienation from traditional communities. Pervasive doubt also stimulated growing demands for new sources of religious certainty.

For many Catholics, belief in the objective presence of Christ in the sacraments held fear of hypocrisy and uneasiness about religious authenticity at bay, and the Roman Catholic Church did its best to regularize the sacraments and bolster the authority of the priests who celebrated them. But Catholics had to deal with complaints about the hypocrisy of the church and its priests, as well as with the cultural diversity of Catholic expression that, in many regions, was outpacing priestly efforts to regularize the faith. Despite top-down efforts to impose religious uniformity, converts to Catholicism in many different regions of the world fused their enthusiasm for the sacraments and saints with adherence to native traditions. In many instances, the indigenization of Christian belief and practice contributed to the revitalization of native traditions and communities. In more than a few cases, indigenous people embraced Christian ideas and symbols only

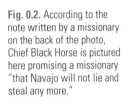

Fig. 0.2. According to the note written by a missionary on the back of the photo, Chief Black Horse is pictured here promising a missionary "that Navajo will not lie and steal any more."

to set themselves apart from European Christians and from missionaries, who were not infrequently perceived as wolves in sheep's clothing.

As European Christians claimed dominion over other lands and people, they often found their claims to moral superiority challenged and even in some cases their identity as Christians questioned. In seventeenth-century North America, for example, more than a few Huron and Iroquois people suspected Jesuit missionaries of causing deadly epidemics through witchcraft. In the eighteenth and nineteenth centuries, Native prophets emerged claiming that God had created both Indians and whites and that Indians could find happiness in the afterlife if they avoided the white man's ways and found their own path to salvation. While many converted and brought beliefs about the presence of spirits in the mountains, winds, waters, and seasons with them into Christianity, other Native Americans incorporated Christian beliefs about resurrection and the restoration of paradise into Nativist movements of religious and political resistance separate from Christianity. (See plate B in gallery.)

The high-handed and inhumane treatment often dispensed by demanding Christians helped to fuel modern preoccupations with Christian hypocrisy. Critics of established churches and external forms of religious authority focused on the disparity between Christian idealism and the behavior of people who called themselves Christian, and complained about their hypocrisy, as the Puritan writer Roger Williams did in 1643 when he compared the spiritual status of English people in the Puritan colony of Massachusetts Bay to that of Native Americans. The natural gifts God bestowed on Adam and Eve could be found in every land and tribe, Williams believed. So could the taint of Adam and Eve's original sin. Indian and English stood on the same precarious moral footing; if anything, English people were worse off since they had often heard but not always heeded the gospel message.

As founder and president of the colony of Rhode Island, Williams established religious freedom and secular government for Christian reasons, arguing that Christ had established a new covenant of grace with individual saints and that God no longer worked his will through nations as he had in ancient times through the nation of Israel. Williams challenged the idea that kings had any divine right permitting them to take over Indian lands or to act in other ways that presumed God stood behind their political authority. Resisting the notion that Christianity could be connected to any nation or government, Williams argued that Christians were scattered throughout the nations of the world. Citing the parable of wheat and tares, he maintained that God intended Christians to live hidden among others until the judgment day.

A century and a half after Williams declared religious freedom in Rhode Island, the First Amendment to the United States Constitution guaranteed religious liberty to all citizens and prohibited the federal government from singling out any religion for official recognition or taxpayer support. The principal author of the amendment, James Madison, argued that people should worship the Creator as directed by individual conscience, that entanglement in politics corrupted Christianity, and that people who chose Christianity freely were less passive and more sincere in their religious lives than people who had religion imposed upon them. Like Williams, Madison understood secular government to be a logical and necessary corollary of religious freedom, and religious freedom to be an equally logical and necessary corollary of Christian humility.

A Christian Warning against Ethnic Pride

Boast not proud English, of thy birth & blood.
Thy brother Indian is by birth as Good.
Of one blood God made Him, and Thee & All
As wise, as faire, as strong, as personall.

By nature wrath's his portion, thine no more
Till Grace his soule and thine in Christ restore.
Make sure thy second birth, else thou shalt see
Heaven ope to Indians wild, but shut to thee.

—Roger Williams, in A Key into the Language of America, ed. John J. Teunissen and Evelyn J. Hinz (1643; Detroit: Wayne State University Press, 1973), 135.

Although the transformation of Christian life from an enveloping world to an available choice was halting and often incomplete, it affected people almost everywhere and coincided with the development of secular realms of commerce, government, and science. Many Christians embraced burgeoning market economies, greater separation between church and state, and the freedom to pursue scientific investigations, presuming that they did so under the ultimate supervision of a creator who predestined everything or, alternatively, allowed human beings to work out their destinies in this world and learn from their own mistakes and sinfulness. Expanding realms of secular enterprise free of institutional religious oversight provided arenas for people of different, conflicting, and even no religious faiths to interact productively, complementing the widespread tendency to define religious faith more privately and individualistically.

Christianity mediated a worldwide transformation after 1600, a transformation that brought different peoples and cultures into contact with one another in unprecedented ways. The geographical spread of Christian ideas and symbols to China, India, Africa, and the Americas coincided with the expansion of market economies; new industrial technologies; more systematic exploitation of natural resources, including human labor; and new forms of transportation and communication that brought people and goods together across distances more frequently than before, disrupting the stability of traditional societies based on face-to-face consensus. In the hands of new interpreters, Christian ideas, symbols, and stories played a major role in carrying forward this global process of modernization, contributing to the criticism of established social structures and forms of religious authority, to the creation of new institutions and forms of social authority, and to increasing communication between different groups within particular societies as well across cultures around the world.

SOCIAL CRITICISM AND REFORM

Christian missionaries contributed to new religious movements as people around the world incorporated elements of the missionaries' worldview into their own cosmologies, revising some aspects of their own traditions to accommodate change, or resisting its incursions. Beginning with their encounters with Catholic missionaries, people outside of Europe appropriated Christian language and behavior as means of constructing new relationships between their local cultures and the modernizing and universalizing forces of Western expansion.

Important as the connection between Christianity and modernization has been, however, the relationship between the two was never seamless or uncomplicated, with Christianity functioning simply as a means of support for modern individualism, economic development, or political reform. As a medium for negotiating change in the modern era, Christianity was not simply a reflection of larger forces of social change but a collection of beliefs, stories, symbols, and practices that people used in many different ways to construct their feelings, thoughts, and behaviors. As a multidimensional cosmology and flexible medium of response to the world, Christianity inspired revolutionary fervor in some situations, new forms of allegiance to traditional authority in others, and tolerance, open-mindedness, and honest self-appraisal in still others. Because people interpreted Christianity in their own terms, missionaries and converts did not always understand one another or agree about what Christianity meant. And because the spread of Christianity after 1600 coincided with the spread of modernization, people turned to Christianity to resist and control modernization as well as to embrace it. Christians were often outspoken in criticizing aspects of modernization that seemed to undermine their moral values and ideals. Catholics were especially sensitive to the problems involved in linking Christianity to nationalism, religious liberty, and free markets, and often suggested that Protestants had forsaken Christianity for the modern world.

Protestants also worried about the problems that nationalism, religious liberty, and free markets posed for human existence and found themselves struggling to rein in forces of modernization that they had helped set in motion. Protestants encouraged doubts about miracles and challenges to religious authority that stimulated avalanches of popular doubt and resistance to authority that extended far beyond what the architects of Protestant faith had intended. The rapid growth of Protestant Christianity in many parts of the world coincided with full-scale industrial development in the West and with strategic exploitation by Western businesses of mineral, agricultural, and labor resources in less developed parts of the world. Protestant missionaries challenged the most egregious forms of economic and political exploitation, often taking the part of natives against harsh policies that removed people from tribal lands and transformed them into a modern underclass of poor and dispossessed workers. While challenging the worst brutalities associated with these aspects of modernization, missionaries also engaged in modern forms of social interaction and modern ways of conceptualizing human society that changed the fabric of life almost everywhere.

In the Middle East, Protestant missionaries established Christianity as an agent of modernization prior to 1900 by promoting Western education, female literacy, and new standards of personal piety among Christian minorities. Muslims in the Ottoman Empire generally tolerated Christians as minority peoples who recognized God, but relegated them to second-class status because of their perceived impurity and religious ignorance with respect to Islam. As Protestant missionaries from Europe and North America worked to educate Eastern Christians to become missionaries to their Muslim neighbors, these efforts exacerbated tensions between Eastern Christians and Muslims and gave Muslims the impression that Western Christians and their Eastern allies meant to conquer the Islamic world, an impression that contributed to the resentment of Western culture evident in much of the Muslim world today.

In southern Africa prior to 1900, American Protestant missionaries worked not only to convert Africans to Christianity but also to bring them into the modern world as educated property owners. To that end, missionaries from North America and Europe established schools, created industrial farms for growing and processing sugar cane, and developed plans for African land ownership, entrepreneurial business, and political participation. Nineteenth-century missionaries often found themselves at odds with the British colonial government, which thwarted many of these plans through laws and policies deliberately aimed at excluding Africans from land and business ownership and from political participation.

Few of the efforts missionaries made to orchestrate Christian modernization in southern Africa worked out as missionaries hoped. Africans experienced the worst effects of modernization, and for all their good intentions, missionaries contributed directly to those negative outcomes. Intending to better women's lot, missionaries attacked polygamy, marriage customs linking exchanges of women and cattle, and women's responsibility for manual labor, all of which missionaries found offensive. But efforts to elevate the status of women disrupted the kinship structures, sexual customs, and traditional gender roles in terms of which people understood their social responsibilities and derived respect from one another. The breakdown of tribal structures, erosion of traditional forms of sociability, and transition to an urban industrial economy left many women more isolated, impoverished, and subject to abuse than before.

In nineteenth-century India, missionaries also worked to improve the living conditions of people, and these efforts often met with greater success than those in southern Africa but were not necessarily accompanied by conversion. Protestant missionaries challenged the Hindu caste structure, in some instances forcing converts from higher castes to share in the Lord's Supper with converts from lower castes in violation of ritual prohibitions designed to prevent members of high castes from being polluted by contact with inferior people. Criticism of the caste system was not new—Buddhism emerged in sixth-century BCE India as an alternative to the caste system and its priestly establishment—but the arrival of Protestant Christianity in nineteenth-century India coincided with the influence of modern Western theories of government and individual rights. Partly in conjunction with Christian evangelicalism, liberal political theories taken up by Indian reformers from writings by John Locke and John Stuart Mill challenged hierarchical divisions of society based on status at birth.

If Christianity mediated democracy in India, it did so more through Christianity's association with Western education and political theory than by demonstrations of egalitarian behavior on the part of missionaries. In many cases, British and American missionaries honored a double standard, challenging certain aspects of the caste system while addressing themselves to members of the priestly, educated Brahmin caste and considering Christians to be members of a spiritual elite. To the extent they presented conversion to Christianity as an initiation into an elect corps of spiritually purified beings, Protestant missionaries also followed in the path of the early seventeenth-century Italian Jesuit missionary in India, Roberto Nobili, who dressed and ate like a Brahmin and used language from the Vedic scriptures read by Brahmins to offer salvation in Christ. The special efforts missionaries made to establish good relationships with Brahmins often dovetailed with British colonial rule and with the class system to which British missionaries themselves belonged. In their self-identification as leaders of an elite religious class superior to Brahmins, nineteenth-century Protestant missionaries could also be compared to Christians in south India who traced their religious ancestry to the apostle Thomas, believed to have arrived on the Malabar coast of the Indian peninsula in the first century CE. Thomas Christians in India took pride in their high caste status, patronized Hindu temples, and held to standards of ritual purity that separated them from people in lower castes.

In nineteenth-century India, despite strenuous efforts on the part of missionaries to bring Brahmins into the Christian fold, Christianity appealed more to people of lower castes than to Brahmins, and mass conversions among low caste groups during the later decades of the century significantly increased the number of Christians in Asia. Contributing in many instances to the dignity and empowerment of poor people,

Fig. 0.3. Missionary view of Christian instruction in Burma, ca. 1850. © CORBIS.

evangelical Christianity encouraged experiences of being saved and loved by God that carried over into growing consciousness of the injustice of the caste system and more egalitarian ideas about social order. In addition, European and American pietism dovetailed with some of the mystical aspects of Hindu devotionalism, contributing to popular forms of mystical piety in both India and the West.

Meanwhile, others in India embraced democratic ideas associated with liberal British and American political thought but found it unnecessary, and even unreasonable, to convert to Christianity. In the eastern region of Maharashtra, Hindu reformers borrowed ideas about women's education and social welfare from Christian missionaries working in the region. In the northwest city of Calcutta, Hindus educated in British-run schools called for a transformation in Indian society and spoke out against religious superstition, the caste system, and the practice of *suttee*, or widow burning, which seemed to them, as it did to Protestant missionaries, to epitomize the denigration of women in traditional religion. The social reform movements led by religious Hindus in Maharashtra and by more secular intellectuals around Calcutta laid important groundwork for the political movement for independence from British colonial government in the twentieth century and for the establishment of India as a democratic nation.

In the complex history of Christianity's direct and indirect impact in India, Protestant missionaries played a crucial role. But the social changes they helped to ignite passed quickly out of their control. More often than not, the response to the Christianity that missionaries represented and taught was not what missionaries intended. In the region around Bombay, devotees of Krishna embraced Jesus as a form of their god and sang kirtans, or hymns, based on Bible stories about Jesus and delighted in Jesus as a new avatar of Krishna. In addition to revealing Christian influence within Hinduism, these kirtans reflected the power of Hindu religiosity to absorb that influence in new, hybrid expressions of belief and practice.

In India as elsewhere, people interpreted Christian ideas, symbols, and stories in the context of their own cultures, drawing their own conclusions about the identity of Jesus and the implications of Christian virtue and salvation and taking aspects of missionary teaching in directions missionaries did not anticipate. At the same time, the universalizing thrust of Christianity created new pathways of interchange among people of different cultures and new ways of thinking about human society. In India, the universalizing elements of Christian missionary ideas contributed to new linkages between India and the West and to new ways of thinking about India as a modern society in which people of different regions and religious backgrounds might live together as a politically independent, democratic nation.

In nineteenth-century China, the impact of modern Christianity was narrower but no less revolutionary. Although Christians had lived in China for centuries, their biggest impact on Chinese culture occurred in the context of modernization. In ancient times, Nestorian Christians traveled the Silk Road as traders, physicians, and missionaries, and in 638 CE the T'ang emperor paid for the construction of a Christian church in the capital city of Chang'an, the most populous city in the world at the time. Franciscan missionaries arrived in the thirteenth century and oversaw the building of the first Catholic church. But when Jesuit missionaries entered China in the sixteenth century, they found no sign of any remaining Christians. In the eighteenth and nineteenth centuries, in the context of growing demand for trade with China in the West and military efforts to force China to open its ports, first Catholic and then Protestant missionaries encountered considerable suspicion and regulation. When Protestant missionaries pressed for admittance in the early nineteenth century, the government assigned them to designated areas, restricted their travel, and confined their efforts to narrow corridors of activity.

In 1832, the first Chinese Protestant, Liang Afa, published an account of creation and God's rule over the world in which he explained Noah's ark, the covenant between God and Israel, the life of Jesus, and John's vision of the coming kingdom of God in the book of Revelation. Liang distributed his tract outside the gates of the Canton, where young men from the surrounding region passed by on their way into the city to take qualifying exams for civil service. In 1836, Liang's book passed into the hands of Hong Xiuquan, a candidate for civil service who had just failed his qualifying exams for the second time. Inspired with a new vision of his destiny as a result of reading Liang's description of biblical history, Hong proclaimed himself the younger brother of Jesus, baptized many followers, and preached abut his Father's coming kingdom. Combining Christian ideas with resistance against both the oppression of the dynastic feudalism of the Chinese government and the intrusion of modern Western capitalism and military force, Hong promoted biblical images of apocalyptic warfare in his drive to bring the heavenly kingdom to earth. He also preached about Jesus' love of the poor and his warnings against wealth, proclaiming this gospel message as a mandate for a new social order in which all families formed one family of God.

Amid the destabilization of the Qing Dynasty after the Opium War ended in 1842, Hong's religion of God Worshippers mushroomed into a mass movement that dominated central and southern China over the next decade. Hong established the Taiping Kingdom, based on a fusion of Christian, Confucian, and socialist principles. When the imperial troops representing Manchu rulers destroyed the Taiping capital in 1864 and ended the God Worshippers' reign, forty million people had died during the revolution as victims of combat, execution, and starvation.

Hong's effort to bring about a new social order based on religious equality reflected modern ideas about the politics of religion derived from Protestant Christianity, recast in a distinctively Chinese mode. Although Hong's God Worshippers were crushed by the Manchu army, echoes of their ideas persist into the present; as many historians argue, Hong's movement laid some of the groundwork for the development of the revolutionary political ideology that came to expression in Chinese communism.

Protestant and Catholic missionaries founded numerous churches in China, some of which still exist today. American Protestants also invested heavily in women's education in China and in the establishment of hospitals and medical and nursing schools. In the late nineteenth century, Protestants opened the first hospitals and medical schools in many provinces and also established nursing schools that altered the practice of medicine in China and created new opportunities for women's education and professional development. The Chinese incorporated Western medicine on their own terms, however, disregarding American beliefs that Protestant Christianity and scientific medicine were more or less coextensive, and dashing missionary hopes that doctors and nurses would draw Chinese people to Christ. Accepting Western medicine as one among a variety of complementary arts, the Chinese found it relatively easy to take Western medicine without Christianity. When Christianity was outlawed during the Communist Revolution, the Communists took over many of the medical and nursing facilities founded by Protestant missionaries as a part of a pluralistic system of health care that included traditional forms of Chinese medicine as well as scientific medicine imported from the West.[5]

Although the conversion of Chinese people did not succeed as missionaries hoped, Christian missionary efforts contributed significantly to modernization in China. With an infrastructure of rational bureaucracy and political art already in place, and predating modern

Western influence by many centuries, modern Western ideas about education, science, and social reform stimulated new interest in democratic ideas, along with an expansion of bureaucratic institutions and further systematization of knowledge. If the Chinese rejected the individualism and capitalism of the West, and relatively few people converted, the ideas and activities of Christians nevertheless contributed to the development of modern political thought in China as well as to the development of modern science and technology.

MORE TO COME

The essays that follow explore the global expansion and modern transformation of Christianity prior to 1900, taking up in greater detail the changing aspects of people's Christianity surveyed in this introduction. The next three essays by Carlos Eire, Peter Gardella, and John Corrigan examine the most basic aspects of people's lives—death, sex, and capitalism—and show how Christian people relied on religious beliefs and practices to manage them. These essays advance our understanding of the importance of Christianity in people's lives as a medium for negotiating the social transformations associated with modernization.

Carlos Eire calls attention to the prominence of death, afterlife, and heaven in the period before 1600, and to the powerful role that Christian beliefs and practices associated with death played in establishing social order and controlling people's behavior. Eire describes the shattering impact of Christian reform efforts to clear away the superstition, corruption, and enormous wealth generated by Catholic cults of communication with, and intercession for, the dead, and the reactionary efforts to preserve them. Although reformers intended to strengthen Christianity by purifying its practices surrounding death, their efforts had the unintended effect of calling basic assumptions about life after death into question and opening the way for modern doubt and skepticism. Even those committed to reform found themselves engaged in battles to preserve Christianity from doubt and skepticism.

Peter Gardella's essay identifies several dynamics at work in the historical development of sexual practices and attitudes toward sex among Christian people after 1600. As Gardella shows, church authorities in the modern era policed sexual behavior more closely than before and devoted new efforts to classifying sexual deviancy and stamping it out. Partly in reaction against these repressive efforts, many Christians affirmed their rights to sexual expression, celebrating romantic love and marital happiness as Christian ideals and embracing birth control as a practice consistent with Christian life. Amid this struggle between Christian repressors and Christian liberators of modern sexuality, new efforts to understand sex in scientific terms attracted popular interest and led many Christians to think about sex in more mechanical and impersonal terms than before.

Turning to the basic human activities of economic productivity and exchange, John Corrigan's essay considers the emotional impact of capitalism for Christian people in different parts of the world, arguing that the depersonalization of economic exchange characteristic of capitalism affected all aspects of life. As relationships between people and things became more consumer oriented and removed from communal life, people's experience of God became more private, individualized, and subject to negotiation. With capitalism, Corrigan writes, "everything is a commodity, everything is negotiable, and negotiation becomes cultural practice relevant to every aspect of life, including religion." Christians in different places handled this transformation differently, finding many various ways to manage capitalism through their own cultural interpretations of Christian feeling. Identifying several Christian strategies for negotiating transitions to modern capitalism, Corrigan explains how some Christians developed emotional cultures of self-deception, others developed cultures of self-assurance, and still others developed cultures of self-control.

Following these essays on modernizing trends in Christian death, sex, gender, and capitalism, the chapter on popular Christian ideas about science by Ronald L. Numbers shows how people's attachment to biblical narratives about creation made it difficult to grasp the implications for religion of modern discoveries in science. Examining the influence of modern science on popular Christianity prior to 1900, Numbers shows that, when they thought about science at all, Christians relied on religion to interpret it and make judgments about its worth. Most Christians remained confident about the supremacy of Christianity and its harmony with science. Popular resistance to the idea that human beings descended from apes did not come to a boil until the second decade after 1900, and it was only then that many Christians began to realize that modern science did not support biblical revelation. Even Christians willing to grant that their religion did not hold all the answers tended to believe in the reality of spiritual forces and their eventual validation by science.

The next four essays are case studies highlighting regional variants in modern Christianity prior to 1900. In their more detailed analyses of particular cultures in different parts of the world, the essays by H. B. Cavalcanti, Vera Shevzov, Douglas Winiarski, and Ava Chamberlain show how the larger themes associated with Christianity and modernization played out in Brazil, Russia, and New England.

Cavalcanti's essay on Christianity in Brazil focuses on the impact of Christian missionaries on the peoples and cultures of Brazil. Cavalcanti describes the strong linkages between Catholicism and Iberian culture in Brazil, the gradual infusion of Catholicism into Native and African Brazilian cultures, and the historical process by which Brazil became a Catholic country. He contrasts the strategies of Catholic missionaries with those of Protestants and highlights the close connections between Protestant missionary strategies in nineteenth-century Brazil and the importation of American business practices and strategies for economic development.

Vera Shevzov's essay on Russian Orthodoxy focuses on the production of icons and the practice of venerating icons as representatives of Christ and his saints. Shevzov examines particular styles of iconography as they developed in Russia during the period 1600–1900, focusing on new technologies that led to the mass production of icons and to the proliferation of icons and icon veneration in homes, shops, stations, and trains. Shevzov also examines the special veneration of icons celebrating local people and their life stories, and some of the ways that the religious practices of ordinary men and women shaped the discourse of debates about iconographic style and veneration.

For centuries prior to 1600, trade in religious art served as an important means of exchange between Christians in the West and those in Eastern Europe and the Middle East. In the period between

1600 and 1900, the development of modern expressions of pietism and mysticism across Europe and the Middle East helped to stimulate the mass production of icons in the East, and vice versa. Despite official animosity between Eastern churches and Rome, artists in different regions drew from one another to portray Christ and his saints, especially Mary, in increasingly lifelike ways. The profusion of humanistic iconography in Eastern churches paralleled the growing attention to internal stages of religious discernment among Catholics and growing attention to internal processes of conversion among Protestants. Modern notions of personality and selfhood took shape through the media of these new forms of religious and emotional expression.

Turning to North America, essays by Douglas Winiarski and Ava Chamberlain focus on the religious lives of New England Congregationalists. Both Winiarski and Chamberlain pay close attention to individuals whose personal lives changed through Christian practice and whose practice of Christianity reflected larger forces of social change. Using letters, diaries, and church records, Winiarski traces important shifts in the meaning of conversion for New England Protestants between 1640 and 1850, identifying changes in practices of recording and describing conversion, as well as in what people seem to have experienced. Expectations about conversion became more finely tuned and well defined over time, reflecting growing interest in human subjectivity as a realm for exploration, analysis, and self-discipline.

Ava Chamberlain's essay zeroes in even more closely on a particular group of eighteenth-century Protestants in New England to show how unrest among laypeople led to challenges of established forms of religious authority and new demands for personal autonomy. Analyzing the parish rebellion in Northampton, Massachusetts, that led to Jonathan Edwards's dismissal as pastor in 1750, Chamberlain argues that Edwards epitomized an older form of patriarchal religious authority that a new generation of eighteenth-century Christians found haughty and offensive. Chamberlain also finds that new patterns of romantic flirtation played a part in the Northampton conflict and that a younger generation of more modern Christians, backed up by their parents, resented the repression of heterosocial amusement that their pastor took it upon himself to impose.

The concluding essays in this volume focus on gender and race, two of the most contentious, problematic, and rapidly changing aspects of modern Christian life prior to 1900. Marilyn Westerkamp's chapter describes conflicting forces associated with women and gender. Modern attention to interiority and the individual's private relationship to God played a role in diminishing the age-old Christian prejudice against women for being inherently more carnal and less spiritual than men and helped to put women on a similar spiritual footing as men. The abolition of a male priesthood in some churches and sects also contributed to greater gender equality, enabling more women to preach and pray in public and even administer the sacraments. On the other hand, Westerkamp shows how expectations about women's natural capacity for emotional piety made them vulnerable to manipulation by male authorities. The disproportionate number of female Christians between 1600 and 1900 may reflect women's susceptibility to guilt, shame, and intimidation as much as the new opportunities for spiritual equality and leadership that Christianity offered. As Westerkamp explains, Christian women gained new powers and influence during this period but also experienced new forms of restriction as a result of their adherence to religious life, as well as vulnerability to religious control.

Essays by Charles H. Lippy and Cheryl A. Kirk-Duggan describe how slavery was part of an international economic strategy in the eighteenth and nineteenth centuries that revolved around investment for profit, acquisition of property, and systematic exploitation of human labor. As investment properties, chattel slaves were commodities that could be bought and sold like other pieces of property and put to work and bred as if they were livestock. On plantations in the Caribbean and in the American South, slave owners and overseers utilized slave labor in extensive systems of agricultural production fueling the textile mills in industrial cities.

As Lippy explains in his essay, this modern form of slavery polarized Christian nations and missionary endeavors; the brutal but lucrative slave trade that developed in the Atlantic world around the production of sugar, rum, and cotton led to unprecedented conflict over the question of whether or not Christians could own slaves in good faith. Many slaveholders believed that God intended human society to be hierarchical and patriarchal, and they cited numerous passages from the Bible to support their position that slavery was part of the natural order of human society ordained by God. Other Christians read the Bible differently, arguing that Christ had come to earth to set human beings free, that Christianity was entirely incompatible with slavery, and that slaveholders could not be regarded as Christians. New forms of social and political activism grew out of their Christian idealism and moral revulsion at the perceived hypocrisy of Christian slaveholding.

Meanwhile, new forms of Christian practice developed among Africans captured and sold as slaves, many of whom interpreted biblical stories and loved Jesus on their own terms. As Kirk-Duggan argues in her essay on spirituals, many slaves identified with the sufferings of Jesus and with his dignity in the midst of suffering. In chants packed with references to biblical stories, slaves played with the ironic relationship between their plight as slaves on one hand and their human dignity and spiritual superiority to the owners who lorded earthly power over them on the other. Kirk-Duggan argues that

Fig. 0.4. Family worship in a plantation in South Carolina. Image © Schomburg Center / Art Resource, N.Y.

slaves chanted spirituals as a means of uplifting people from despair and exorcising the demonic forces that surrounded them. In a final comment on the importance of Christian symbols in the context of modern life, Kirk-Duggan writes, "We will never know how many people's lives were saved by singing spirituals. We do know that these chants inspired endurance, resistance, and hope of freedom."

Rich and informative as these essays are, many important developments in the modern history of people's Christianity have been overlooked in this volume and left unexplored. Because no single volume could possibly comprehend all that occurred in Christian practice prior to 1900, we have tried to create more of an impressionistic picture of this history than a panoramic one. We hope our picture will inspire readers to fill in some of the gaps in our coverage with further study.

As all of the essays in this volume show, the changes occurring in Christian life between 1600 and 1900 were dramatic. In many different ways, people drew on Christian symbols, stories, and practices to humanize their worlds and manage the forces of modernization. The global expansion of Christianity in the modern era fueled interlocking developments in politics, economics, literacy, and emotional life that altered people's religious experience in profound ways. As the authors in this volume show, many people alive between 1600 and 1900 turned to Christian symbols and stories to make sense of their encounters with new people, to cope with the disintegration of traditional societies, and to construct modern worlds.

FOR FURTHER READING

Chidester, David. *Christianity: A Global History.* New York: HarperCollins, 2000.

Porterfield, Amanda. *Healing in the History of Christianity.* New York: Oxford University Press, 2005.

———. *Mary Lyon and the Mount Holyoke Missionaries.* New York: Oxford University Press, 1997.

Robert, Dana L. *American Women in Mission: A Social History of Their Thought and Practice.* Macon: Mercer University Press, 1997.

Saler, Michael. "Modernity and Enchantment: A Historiographic Overview." *The American Historical Review* 111, no. 3 (June 2006): 692–716.

Walls, Andrew. *The Missionary Movement in Christian History.* Maryknoll, N.Y.: Orbis Books, 1996.

RECONFIGURING CHRISTIAN COSMOLOGIES

Part 1

NEW WAYS
OF CONFRONTING DEATH

CARLOS EIRE

CHAPTER ONE

> Logically, beliefs could exist without rituals; rituals, however, could not exist without beliefs.
>
> —Edward Shills[1]

That death demands rituals and beliefs became very evident in the period 1600–1900 as skepticism and doubt increased in those societies that had once made up Christendom. The reason for this is quite simple. Up until the seventeenth century, Christian beliefs and rituals were part and parcel of the civic culture of Europe and its colonies, where unbelief and heresy were seldom tolerated. This meant that Christian burial rites were required for everyone and that the beliefs expressed through these rites were unquestionable. Even in cases of those who were barred from Christian burial, such as heretics or suicides, the exclusion from ritual was itself a ritual and an affirmation of belief for the society at large. As the questioners and skeptics grew in number after 1600, and as the choice of *not* having a Christian burial became possible, the nature and meaning of Christian burials became ever more significant among believers, for the mere existence of an "other"—especially one with diametrically opposed beliefs—necessarily sharpens all identities. Moreover, the very fact that the unbelievers continued to have rites of some sort made it clearly evident to everyone, including the unbelievers themselves, that death rituals are a social necessity and that all such rituals—even those that mock Christian beliefs—always express attitudes and beliefs, by necessity.

When it comes to attitudes toward death, the period 1600–1900 could easily be called an age of questioning, or, as some French historians like to say, a period of de-Christianization. At the beginning of this era, around 1600, Christians everywhere were still caught up in the violent disagreements of the Reformation era and, in addition, were beginning to feel the ascendancy of rational skepticism and science, all of which cast doubt in one way or another, either from within the Christian religion itself because of theological differences, or from outside of it because of new ways of thinking and discoveries that seemed to contradict long-held assumptions. Over the next three centuries, the challenges to Christianity multiplied at a very fast pace. By the end of the nineteenth century, the Christian religion had lost its hegemony over Western culture, thanks to the secularizing effects of the doubt and skepticism that had first begun to take hold around 1600, and thanks also to the scientific and industrial revolutions.

Atheism as a Modern Option

What reason do atheists have to say that one cannot rise from the dead? Which is more difficult, to be born or to be reborn? That that which has never existed should exist, or that that which has existed should exist again? . . . Custom makes the one seem easy, absence of custom makes the other seem impossible: a vulgar way of judging!

—Blaise Pascal, "Pensees," in The Oxford Book of Death, ed. D. J. Enright (New York: Oxford University Press, 1987), 156–57.

To understand fully how Christians dealt with death during this period, one must go back to the cataclysmic events of the sixteenth century, for the process of change unleashed in that period was still very much in progress by 1600, as part of what is now called "the long Reformation" or "the second Reformation" or "early modern Catholicism." One must also go back further to the Middle Ages, and even to ancient times, for what the Protestants rejected in their Reformation is as important as what they affirmed, and much of what they rejected had to do with ancient or medieval rituals they deemed to be of pagan origin.

The Protestant Reformation began in 1517 over the issue of death rituals. The flash point was the doctrine of purgatory and the practice of performing certain rituals to alleviate the suffering of the dead in the afterlife. It could be argued, then, that differing attitudes toward death are a crucial difference between Protestants and Catholics and a key to the battles they were still waging against one another around 1600.

DEATH IN CHRISTIAN TRADITION

The practice of praying for the dead and of offering masses for them had ancient origins. By the fourth century, it was already so widespread that Saint Augustine (354–430) not only accepted it without question but also promoted it. By the sixth century it was also commonplace to believe that purgation, or a painful cleansing of the soul, could take place in the afterlife and that the living on earth could alleviate the suffering of those souls. As Pope Saint Gregory the Great (540–604) put it: "Each one will be presented to the Judge exactly as he was when he departed this life. Yet, there must be a cleansing fire before judgment, because of some minor faults that may remain to be purged away." It matters very little that Gregory spoke of purgatory as a fire, or condition, or state, rather than as a specific place, or locus: this was the doctrine of purgatory, plain and simple. Purgatory provided a realm of spiritual activity for the dead, a realm into which the church extended and on which the living could have an impact. Equally important was the way in which Gregory promoted the redemptive power of the Eucharist over this realm, as when he says, "The holy sacrifice of Christ, our saving Victim, brings great benefits to souls even after death, provided their sins can be pardoned in the life to come. For this reason, the souls of the dead sometimes beg to have Masses offered for them."[2] Here, in a nutshell, was the rationale behind saying masses for the dead. Gregory went even further, providing a formula for salvation that would become immensely popular throughout Western Christendom: thirty masses said for a soul over a span of thirty days, one each day, guaranteed release from purgatory for that soul. This cycle of masses, which came to be known as a trental, or as "the masses of St. Gregory," became immensely popular in the Middle Ages and would later become an emblem of Catholic identity in the period 1600–1900, in defiance of the Protestant challenge, thanks to its promotion by the Council of Trent.

Medieval Catholics would hold firm to five basic beliefs, all neatly summarized by Gregory. After 1517, Martin Luther and all Protestants would reject much of this as un-Christian, and Catholics would embrace all of it with even greater fervor in response. In due course, greater skeptics would later ridicule all of these beliefs as unreasonable: (1) that the human person is made up of two basic components:

body and soul; (2) that the soul separates from the body at death and is immediately judged at that moment; (3) that the soul is then immediately sent to one of three destinations: heaven, purgatory, or hell; (4) that purgatory is a temporary destination where the soul is cleansed and where it can be aided by the sacrifice of the Mass offered by the living through the church; (5) and that there will be a final judgment at the end of history, when purgatory will be abolished and all souls will be reunited with resurrected bodies for eternity, some to enjoy eternal bliss and others to endure eternal torments. All five of these tenets were neatly summarized in the Latin adage *Salus hominis in fine consistit*, which loosely translated means "One's eternal fate is decided at the moment of death." Within this theological framework, each soul's eternal destiny depended on its behavior—on performing good works and avoiding sin—and also on whether or not the church had forgiven its sins. Furthermore, each soul's fate in the afterlife depended on its state at the moment of death, which meant that if one wanted to avoid hell, one needed to die a "good death." By far the most important element of a "good death" was the presence of a priest who could administer the sacraments of penance, Eucharist, and extreme unction. Medieval Christians believed that confessing one's sins and receiving absolution, communion, and the last rites were so essential that they looked upon sudden, unexpected death as one of the most awful things in the world or, worse, as a clear sign of God's wrath.

Fig. 1.1. Allegory of Death (In Ictu Oculi) by Juan de Valdes Leal (1622–1690). Hopital de la Caridad, Seville, Spain. Photo: Scala/Art Resource, N.Y.

One more set of medieval beliefs and practices that developed after Gregory's time looms large over the Reformation and the entire early modern period. In its official teaching, the medieval church made it clear that while all sins were forgiven by its sacrament of penance, what one gained from priestly absolution was not a totally clean slate but rather a commuted sentence, a reduction of eternal penalties into temporal ones. This is why the priest always imposed *penances*, so one could make *satisfaction*: prayers, fasts, pilgrimages, almsgiving, and other such good works that ostensibly made up for one's failings. If one sinned very infrequently, like the saints, then penances were manageable and one could ostensibly go straight to heaven at death. But if one sinned with regularity, like most people, then penances could never be made up before one died. And this meant that the penances had to be completed in the afterlife. This is why ending up in purgatory was the best outcome that most Christians could hope for, and why purgatory was always so crowded.

One of the most salient characteristics of the late medieval Western church—reaffirmed and strengthened by early modern Catholicism—was the way in which its living members constantly acted as intercessors for the dead. This means that by the late Middle Ages, masses were always being offered for the dead, everywhere, at all times, on a much larger scale than ever before, with the support of a highly sophisticated theology. One significant component of this theology gave rise to yet another link between the living and the dead, and between the church and the afterlife, a link that made purgatory ever closer to earth: the issuing of indulgences.

An indulgence was a favor, or privilege, granted by the church that remitted the punishment one still owed God for sin after being absolved in the sacrament of penance. Indulgences came into widespread use in the eleventh century, in connection with the Crusades, when Pope Urban II granted all warriors who would fight to regain the Holy Land a plenary indulgence; eventually, they would be extended to the souls in purgatory, whose fate became the responsibility of the living. In the long run, this concern with the dead would become the proverbial straw that broke the camel's back, for it was because of one priest's bad sermon on indulgences and another priest's response to it that the papacy lost its hegemony in Europe and that the unity of the Western church was forever undone. Exposing a yawning abyss between official theology and popular piety, and dredging up nearly every guilt-inducing, pocket-picking pitch through which he could hawk indulgences to an anxious laity, Johann Tetzel unleashed the Protestant Reformation by preaching these words to many a Saxon crowd in 1517, on behalf of Pope Leo X and his new Basilica of St. Peter in Rome:

> Listen now, God and St. Peter call *you*. Consider the salvation of *your* souls and those of *your loved ones* departed. . . . Listen to the voices of *your dead relatives* and friends, beseeching *you* and saying, 'Pity us, pity us. We are in dire torment from which *you* can redeem us for a pittance.' Do *you* not wish to? Open *your* ears. . . . Remember *you* are able to release them, for *as soon as the coin in the coffer rings, the soul from purgatory springs*. Will *you* not then for a quarter of a florin receive these letters of indulgence through which *you* are able to lead a divine and immortal soul into the fatherland of paradise?[3]

PROTESTANT ATTACKS ON TRADITION

When Martin Luther challenged Tetzel with ninety-five theses in which he questioned the theology behind indulgences, Pope Leo X dismissed the controversy as a "monkish squabble," not realizing the true magnitude of the struggle that would follow. Between 1517 and 1521, Luther's challenge would evolve very rapidly into a wholesale rejection of the pope and his church and of much of Catholic theology and piety. Luther's attack on the medieval Catholic Church was best summarized in his two battle cries: *sola scriptura* (by scripture alone) and *sola fide* (by faith alone). The *sola scriptura* principle allowed Luther to scrutinize all theology and piety according to his interpretation of the Bible and to reject anything he judged as nonbiblical, such as the doctrine of purgatory. The *sola fide* principle, which Luther claimed was the true, biblically centered way of understanding how Christ saves from sin and death, was complex and paradoxical, but reduced to its simplest elements, it boiled down to this: salvation is never earned; it is simply and freely granted by God to those who have faith in the saving sacrifice of Jesus Christ. As Luther saw it, largely through his interpretation of Paul's theology in the New Testament, sin is totally inescapable. One is saved not by one's own good works, or by penances, but rather by Christ's sacrifice on the cross, through which God chose to overlook the sins of the human race. This meant that the Catholic Church was dead wrong in asserting that individuals could not go to heaven until their souls were spotless, for sinlessness was impossible to attain and they could never hope to make satisfaction to God for their sins. It also meant that purgatory was not only an unbiblical invention but also totally unnecessary, along with masses and prayers for the dead.

In one fell swoop, Luther did away with purgatory and severed the connection between the living and the dead. "The Scriptures forbid and condemn communication with the spirits of the dead," he argued, citing Deuteronomy 18:10-11 ("No one shall be found among you who . . . consults ghosts or spirits, or who seeks oracles from the dead"). Moreover, Luther also demonized all of the medieval apparition tales that undergirded belief in purgatory, saying, "Whatever spirits go about, making a noise, screaming, complaining, or seeking help, are truly the work of the devil."[4] Masses for the dead, then, were nothing but demonically inspired sorcery and necromancy.

The essence of Protestantism was the conviction that the medieval church was corrupt and that piety had become intolerably unbiblical. Martin Luther had sparked a revolution with that insight, but his attempt to purify church and society according to scriptural guidelines was somewhat limited in comparison with those of other Protestant reformers such as Andreas Bodenstein von Karlstadt (1480–1541) and Ulrich Zwingli (1483–1531). Luther was never too worried about idolatry or pagan holdovers as he was about "works righteousness," that is, the idea that one's acts can gain God's favor. When he drove the iconoclasts out of Wittenberg, he did so because they thought that destroying the idols would please God, not because of their hatred of idolatry. Changes in attitudes mattered much more to Luther than changes in

> **The Endurance of Ghosts**
>
> Anno 1670, not far from Cyrencester, was an Apparition: Being demanded, whether a good Spirit, or a bad? Returned no answer, but disappeared with a curious Perfume and most melodious Twang.
>
> —John Aubrey, "Miscellanies," in The Oxford Book of Death, ed. D. J. Enright (New York: Oxford University Press, 1987), 208.

ritual; idolatry is in the heart of the worshiper, he insisted, not in the worship itself. Consequently, his reform of ritual was somewhat moderate, and Lutheran funeral practices retained some of the external trappings of Catholic ritual, such as the singing of hymns and the tolling of bells. Among those Protestants who came to be known as Reformed, the heirs of Karlstadt and Zwingli, however, much more of medieval funeral piety was rejected as idolatry and superstition.

It would be up to John Calvin (1509–1564), a second-generation reformer, to articulate and widely disseminate this aggressive war against the "idols" of medieval popular religion. Calvin thought in binary terms, seeing a great dichotomy between "true" and "false" religion and finding the source of all falsehoods deep within the human heart, where idolatry was a basic instinct. As he once said, "Every one of us is, even from his mother's womb, a master craftsman of idols."[5] Over and against such instincts stood the "true" revealed religion of the Bible, made manifest by well-trained and correctly inspired clergymen like himself. The Catholic clergy were liars and thieves, he claimed, not just for teaching false doctrine and encouraging idolatry, but also for saying useless masses for the dead. Scolding a former friend who had become a Catholic bishop, Calvin thundered, "You do not own a single piece of land that has not been placed in your hands by purgatory."[6] Nowhere did his disgust with idolatry shine through more clearly than in his contempt for the Catholic ritual of the Eucharist and its role in the cult of the dead:

> Satan has attempted to adulterate and envelop the sacred Supper of Christ as with thick darkness, that its purity might not be preserved in the Church. But the head of this horrid abomination was, when he raised a sign by which it was not only obscured and perverted, but altogether obliterated and abolished, vanished away and disappeared from the memory of man; namely, when, with most pestilential error, he blinded almost the whole world into the belief that the Mass was a sacrifice and oblation for obtaining the remission of sins . . . for the living and the dead.[7]

The social and cultural repercussions of this redefinition of death and the afterlife were immense but have never been the subject of much sustained study. Only very recently has it been proposed that this severing of the bond between the living and the dead should be viewed as a major change in the daily lives of Christian Europeans. On a personal and social level, the shift from a communally shared responsibility for each death to a very personal and private one signified a turn toward individualism—a turn that has been identified as the key to "modernity." This individualistic turn was perhaps most intense for Protestants at the moment of death, and Martin Luther was well aware of it:

> The summons of death comes to us all, and no one can die for another. Every one must fight his own battle with death by himself, alone. We can shout into each other's ears, but everyone must himself be prepared for the time of death: I will not be with you then, nor you with me.[8]

The psychological and cultural impact of this individualism has yet to be adequately analyzed by historians. Suddenly, death and the afterlife stopped being a communal experience. Barred from aiding the poor souls in purgatory, and also from praying to the saints in heaven and from seeking the suffrages of their relatives and neighbors, Protestants now faced the divine tribunal and their eternal destiny alone, at the end of *this* life. Gone was the communion of saints, and gone too was the chance to earn salvation in the world to come. *This* life and *this* world, then, became the sole focus of religion. In his classic study *The Protestant Ethic and the Spirit of Capitalism*, Max Weber argued that Protestants gained an economic edge over Catholics because they shifted their attention away from the hereafter to the here and now, developing a piety he dubbed "this-worldly asceticism." Though he did not focus on death rituals per se in order to defend his thesis, perhaps he should have, for the economic repercussions of this individualistic, "this-worldly" turn were profound and very easy to discern. Societies that had previously invested heavily in the cult of the dead suddenly redirected a substantial amount of money and resources to other ends. The significance of this major difference between Protestant and Catholic cultures seems even larger when one takes into account that the Catholic Church responded to the

Protestant rejection of purgatory by stressing the value of masses for the dead more than ever before, and that Catholics everywhere intensified their investment in the afterlife.

By 1650, the difference between Protestant and Catholic investment in death was immense. One example alone speaks volumes about the place of the dead in a Catholic economy. In Spain, in the cities of Madrid and Cuenca, investments in funerals and especially in masses for the dead spiraled upward between 1560 and 1650, at a time when the price of a mass continually increased, along with the price of everything else, because of the inflation caused by the so-called price revolution of that period. This meant that the residents of Madrid and Cuenca not only requested more and more masses with each passing year but also spent more and more for each of them. Since most masses were paid for by gifts of land to the church or by rents to be collected on land, this meant that the church accumulated more and more real estate as the demand for masses increased. The end result was the same in Madrid and Cuenca—and it is safe to assume also in most Spanish towns: by 1750, the church had become the chief landlord in the realm. In Cuenca, for instance, the church owned over half of the city's properties and nearly half of all of the surrounding land. It also employed about two-fifths of the total population. In stark contrast, in Protestant societies such as those of England, the Netherlands, Scandinavia, and Germany, the church had been stripped of most of its real estate and all of its income from masses for the dead during the earliest days of the Reformation. Historians need to ask, how was that capital redirected in Protestant societies, and what difference did it make?

Placing a higher value on masses for the dead was only one of the ways in which Catholics reacted to the Protestant challenge. We have plenty of evidence that in France, Italy, and Spain, Catholics also began to stage larger and ever more elaborate funerals, a trend that peaked around the middle of the seventeenth century. In addition, the Catholic Church did all it could to renew interest in every aspect of the cult of the dead that had been rejected by Protestants. What we find, then, is a renewed emphasis on prayer to the saints and veneration of their relics, on the establishment of shrines with wonder-working relics and holy corpses that do not decompose, on the use of traditional *ars moriendi* ("art of dying") texts, and on sermons focused on Catholic eschatology.

In addition, of course, we find the continuation of many traditional practices, such as the celebration of anniversary masses, the ringing of bells, the use of votive lights, and the holding of memorial banquets. We also find a strengthening of the role of confraternities, those lay associations that had developed in the Middle Ages to engage in many different kinds of charitable and devotional activities. Above all, confraternities that focused on funeral devotions enjoyed a great resurgence among Catholics. To ensure the right kind of preparation for the last rites and the moment of death and also to ensure a good funeral, Catholics joined confraternities that aided the dying and buried the dead. Belonging to a confraternity was a lot like taking out spiritual life insurance: it was a pooling of resources that eventually would benefit each member. Confraternity membership enabled one to prepare for one's own death, through repeated visits to other's deathbeds and burials, and when one's turn came to die, one was then assured the presence and intercession of one's confraternity at one's own deathbed and funeral. If one did not belong to any such confraternity, one could still be summoned, for a fee. In some cases, the dying became members on their deathbeds. By the end of the Middle Ages, such confraternities numbered in the tens of thousands all over Europe. In the sixteenth and seventeenth centuries, Catholics would throng to them.

In contrast, what we find among Protestants of all types is an all-out assault on the Catholic cult of the dead and the Catholic idea of the communion of saints and anything that smacked of "popish" idolatry or superstition, such as elaborate ceremonies, the use of bells and candles, the presence of confraternities, or even the use of traditional funeral vestments by the clergy. Whether or not those who lived through this immense change adjusted quickly remains a matter of debate. There is certainly plenty of evidence that in places such as Sweden and England, where Protestantism was imposed from above on everyone by the monarch, resistance flared up. In Durham, England, Bishop James Pilkington found it hard to break his flock's attachment to the dead, issuing many a reprimand between 1561 and 1576, such as the one contained in his rules for funerals. In one brief paragraph,

Bishop Pilkington neatly catalogued all of the Catholic rituals that the faithful continued to observe. His list gives us a clear picture of the differences between a Catholic and a Protestant funeral:

> . . . that no superstition should be committed in them, wherein the papists infinitely offend, as in masses, dirges, trentals, singing, ringing, holy water, hallowed places, years's days and month-minds, crosses, pardon letters to be buried with them, mourners de profundis [psalms] by every lad that could say it, dealing of money solemnly for the dead, watching of the corpse, bell and banner, with many more that I could reckon.[9]

But there is also plenty of evidence that some gave up their ancient customs willingly, or at least without resistance. One story alone, from a remote corner of England, illustrates the process of change vividly. During the reign of Henry VIII (1491–1547), a priest serving a farming community that was barely beyond subsistence level needed new funeral vestments, so he spent years and years collecting funds for this purpose, penny by measly penny. Finally, after begging and scrimping for twenty long years, he purchased the much-needed black vestments. Then, less than a month later, he received a royal order to stop using such vestments and to surrender them to the king's agents. He recorded this without a hint of emotion in his churchwarden's diary and surrendered to the crown his vestments and everything else that went with them: the images, the lights, the altars, the rituals. He continued to minister to his flock and to bury the dead with no less dedication, though in ways unfamiliar to him and to them. He saw his sources of income dry up and vanish and saw the parish brought to financial ruin, since the change in rituals also meant an end to the funding that made them possible.

COMMON CONCERNS

Another dramatic change wrought by the religious turmoil of the early modern age was an increase in violence and the sudden resurgence of martyrdom, as Catholics and Protestants both struggled to obliterate each other and to crush all heretics in their midst. Catholics, of course, gathered new relics from their newly minted martyrs and enshrined them grandly whenever possible. Although Protestants rejected the cult of relics, they still found a way to enshrine and revere their martyrs, in texts that recounted their faith and heroism. Two of the most popular books of the early modern age were John Foxe's *The Acts and Monuments of the Christian Church,* also known as the *Book of Martyrs*, and Jean Crespin's *History of the Martyrs*, both of which went through numerous editions and translations and served for generations as companion volumes to the Bible in many a Protestant home. Both texts also made an effort to trace the persecution of the "true" church from Roman times down to their own day in order to legitimize the Protestant Reformation. Among the Anabaptists, who were persecuted by both Catholics and Protestants, martyrdom was elevated to an even higher theological status as one of the marks of the true church.

Martyrdom was not the only thing shared by Catholics and Protestants. As one might expect, many other beliefs and customs continued to be shared, despite obvious differences. In general, most of the similarities had to do with ethics, which, given the Ten Commandments, is not too surprising. This sharing of a common ethical code has led some historians to argue that Protestantism and Catholicism were much more alike than different and that the early modern period is best understood as a time when religion became a tool in the hands of the elite, a means to strengthen the process of state building. Some historians see this era as one when the social and church elites worked hand in hand to promote a more vigorous Christian identity among the lesser folk. Some historians speak of this as *confessionalization* or *social disciplining*. Among Protestants it is also spoken of as the Second Reformation or the Long Reformation. Some historians have gone so far as to argue that both the Catholic and Protestant Reformations need to be seen as attempts to really *Christianize* Europe, which up until then had only had a really thin Christian veneer.

If one searches for similarities between Catholics and Protestants, one can indeed find them. When it came to funeral customs, Catholics and Protestants continued to practice burial rather than cremation, and they carried it out in hallowed ground, either in the church or in an adjacent or nearby cemetery. As one would expect, funeral rites could vary tremendously, not just between the different churches, but also according to class and status. On the whole, Protestants aimed at a greater simplicity, though this could also be true of Catholics, within limits. Their different approaches to prayer and ritual always made Catholic funerals quite unlike Protestant ones, even the simplest of ones, and the Catholic linking of death to the Mass continued to be one of the more striking differences. For some clergy on both sides, excess pomp on the part of the rich and mighty became a constant source of irritation and something they often railed against. Despite their theological differences, Protestant and Catholic clergy shared another trait in common. This was their common emphasis on the ever-present danger of death and of the need to be ready for it. It is no surprise, then, that *ars moriendi* treatises remained popular among the laity of both religious camps, especially throughout the seventeenth century. On the surface, the emphasis on a "good death" was remarkably similar. These words written by a Protestant would have made perfect sense to a Catholic: "It is the art of all arts, and science of all sciences, to learn to die."[10] As one might expect, of course, that is as far as the similarities extended: Catholic and Protestant *ars moriendi* texts were very different in content. Whereas Protestants were encouraged to face God alone by placing their faith in Christ, without any purgatory on the horizon, Catholics were instructed to rely on every kind of intercession and sacrament they could find, with purgatory in mind as the most likely entry point into the afterlife.

Yet another similarity between Protestants and Catholics was their clergy's apparent fascination with hell, especially in the seventeenth century, when highly detailed meditations on the subject flourished. Apparently, many among the laity liked the subject too, for devotional texts focusing on death and the afterlife in which hell figured prominently were a popular, best-selling genre. Hellfire sermons rang out in both Protestant and Catholic churches. The warning was always clear: sin leads directly to hell. As one Spanish Jesuit put it: "Watch your step. Why do you mock eternity, why don't you fear the eternal death, why do you love this temporal life so much? You are on the wrong track; change your life."[11] If such warnings were not enough, graphic descriptions of hell might do the trick:

> I wish you could open a window through which you would view what happens in hell, and see the torments inflicted on the rich who live in ease and have no compassion for the poor. Oh, if you could see how their flesh is boiled in those cauldrons and how they are baked in those inexorable flames, where every single devil will sear them with firebrands. . . . And it will be very good to imagine how those who can't stand the summer heat outside of their roomy cellars will suffer in the blaze of the eternal fire.[12]

According to some historians, literature and sermons on hell proliferated in this period, principally as part of the common processes of "confessionalization," "social disciplining," and "state building" shared by Protestants and Catholics. Scaring the hell out of people, literally, was a strategy of the early modern state, say many historians: it was a way of creating a more fearful and law-abiding citizenry, with the help of the church.[13] Whether or not this reductionist interpretation of the place of hell in the early modern mentality will stand the test of time remains to be seen.

SKEPTICISM

In the long run, it was religion itself that fell victim to all the violence and the hellish imagery, for the higher the human cost of religious warfare, and the more intense the scare tactics on the part of the clergy, the more urgent it became for Europeans to question their ultimate values. Moreover, the more Christians battled each other in print, developing ever-sharper arguments with which to demolish one another's positions, casting doubt ever more skillfully, the easier it became to take the next logical step toward skepticism, and the more acceptable unbelief became. So in the same way that Protestants rejected purgatory and much of Catholic eschatology in the sixteenth century, skeptics cast doubt on the afterlife and all of religion in the following two centuries. The change was one in scale and intensity rather than one of doubt suddenly appearing. Unbelief had been there all along, even in the most fervently religious societies: the files of the Inquisition and Calvinist consistories prove that skeptics existed and that the ruling elites had a way of silencing them or forcing them into hiding. In sixteenth- and seventeenth-century Spain, the Inquisition handled hundreds of cases of individuals who denied the existence of heaven and hell, and even of God, and who ended up as martyrs for their unbelief. Simple agnosticism was probably more widespread than church authorities would have liked. François Rabelais (1494–1553), a contemporary of Martin Luther, Ignatius Loyola, and John Calvin, may have given voice to a fairly common attitude when he joked on his deathbed, "I go to seek a great Perhaps."[14]

Critiques of religion and of Christianity in particular grew in intensity throughout the seventeenth and eighteenth centuries, gaining ever more ground among educated elites who trusted reason rather than faith and considered themselves "enlightened." First came the dismantling of the traditional cosmos, in which heaven and hell were not other dimensions but physical locations. In that cosmos, the earth was at the center of the universe, surrounded by seven heavenly spheres: the heaven where God and the blessed souls dwelled was the highest place of all, the empyrean or seventh heaven; hell was the lowest place of all, inside at the center of the earth. Thanks to the astronomical discoveries of Nicholas Copernicus (1473–1543) and Galileo Galilei (1564–1642), the traditional geography of the cosmos and the afterlife was blown away, and questioning increased. If the new invention of the telescope and new mathematical calculations could prove that the Bible was mistaken about the visible universe, why not also doubt its accuracy about an unseen cosmos, the afterlife? Among the first to take issue with Christian notions of the afterlife were thinkers heavily influenced by the new science, such as John Locke (1632–1704), John Toland (1670–1722), and Isaac Newton (1642–1727) in the British Isles, Pierre Bayle (1647–1706) in France, and Gottfried Wilhelm Leibniz (1646–1716) in Germany. What their critiques shared in common was the assumption that reason alone should govern all thinking. Arguing that reason is superior to revelation, then, many began to deny the existence of hell, principally because the idea of a just and merciful God tormenting his creatures for eternity seemed thoroughly contradictory and unreasonable. Though many of these early critics of hell thought that it was a useful teaching for the simpler folk, who might become even more immoral without the fear of hell, some nonetheless began to deny hell openly and aggressively.

Denying hell and the afterlife was also one step closer to denying the existence of the soul and even the existence of God. It is no surprise, then, that by the mid-eighteenth century full-fledged atheists were not too hard to find, at least among the educated elites. In 1747, for instance, Julien Offroy de la Mettrie published a treatise entitled *L'homme machine* ("Man the Machine"), in which he argued that it was impossible to prove through reason the existence of anything beyond the material universe, and that God and the soul were irrational concepts. We human beings are nothing more than our bodies, he argued, and nothing more than an organic apparatus. The same is true of the entire universe, which is devoid of spirit and is merely one vast machine. After midcentury, atheism became à la mode in the brightest circles of the "enlightened," and hostility toward Christianity and religion became popular as did hostility toward Christianity and religion in general. For instance, in 1761, Paul Heinrich Dietrich, the Baron D'Holbach, a good friend of Benjamin Franklin, published a book entitled *Le Christianisme dévoilé* ("Christianity Unveiled"), in which he denounced Christianity as contrary to reason and nature. In 1770, he issued an even more popular attack, *Systeme de la nature* ("The System of Nature"), in which he not only denied the existence of God but denounced the Judeo-Christian concept of a bloodthirsty, capricious, and vengeful deity as the source of humankind's worst ills. Writing in 1794, the American revolutionary Thomas Paine summarized an entire century of anti-Christian polemic:

> **Hell as an Unacceptable Idea**
>
> Heaven and hell suppose two distinct species of men, the good and the bad. But the greatest part of mankind float betwixt vice and virtue. Were one to go round the world with an intention of giving a good supper to the righteous and a sound drubbing to the wicked, he would frequently be embarrassed in his choice. . . . The chief source of moral ideas is the reflection on the interests of human society. Ought these interests, so short, so frivolous, to be guarded by punishments, eternal and infinite? The damnation of one man is an infinitely greater evil in the universe, than the subversion of a thousand millions of kingdoms.
>
> —David Hume, "Of the Immortality of the Soul," in The Oxford Book of Death, ed. D. J. Enright (New York: Oxford University Press, 1987), 201.

Of all the systems of religion that ever were invented, there is none more derogatory to the Almighty, more unedifying to man, more repugnant to reason, and more contradictory in itself, than this thing called Christianity. Too absurd for belief, too impossible to convince, and too inconsistent for practice, it renders the heart torpid, or produces only atheists and fanatics. As an engine of power, it serves the purpose of despotism; and as a means of wealth, the avarice of priests; but so far as respects the good of man in general, it leads to nothing here or hereafter.[15]

Committed to replacing religion with rational "enlightment," men like Paine found themselves facing the age-old question of how societies can motivate their members to act ethically without any notion of reward or punishment in an afterlife. Without the fear of hell, what is there besides brute force to prevent wrongdoing? The great *philosophe* Voltaire (1694–1778) was skeptical enough of reason to say that "if God did not exist, it would be necessary for men to invent him." Governments, he concluded, always needed God and hell: "I do not believe that there is in the world a mayor or any official power . . . who does not realize that it is necessary to put a god into their mouths to serve as a bit and bridle." Voltaire's friend Denis Diderot (1713–1784), the editor of the venerable *Encyclopedia*, was less cynical and more representative of the optimism shared by many Enlightenment thinkers. For Diderot, reason itself seemed enough. "Philosophy makes men more honorable than sufficient or efficacious grace," he argued. Seeing no need for God or hell, he replaced them with a vague yet powerful entity:

Posterity is for the philosopher what the next world is for the religious man. . . . O posterity, O holy and sacred support of the oppressed and the unhappy, you who are just, you who are incorruptible, you who will revenge the good man and unmask the hypocrite, consoling and certain ideal, do not abandon me.[16]

Needless to say, as such views gained an ever-larger following, particularly in Western Europe and the Americas, centuries-old attitudes toward death and the afterlife began to change at a relatively quick pace.

THE SECULARIZATION OF DEATH

Overall, the greatest change was the increasing secularization of death. One of the first signs of this development was the detachment of cemeteries from churches. Partly for reasons of public health, but also partly because of secularizing pressures, graveyards began a gradual migration from the vaults beneath churches or churchyards to lots no longer adjacent to the churches, and eventually to much larger areas outside cities and towns. By the time Thomas Paine wrote his *Age of Reason,* the migration of the cemeteries to neutral space was well under way, and so was the development of the nonreligious funeral. A century later, the process was irreversible almost everywhere in the Christian world.

Another change that can be measured in last wills and testaments is the gradual decline and disappearance of any mention of the soul in these legal documents. In Protestant societies, where it had become illegal to offer masses for the dead, the change is subtler, but in Catholic societies, where masses for the dead dwindle and disappear, the shift in attitudes is so immense that some scholars view it as conclusive proof of the "de-Christianization" of Europe.

French historians who speak of "de-Christianization" usually have the French Revolution in mind, of course, when that specific term had a very concrete meaning as part of the revolutionary vocabulary. "De-Christianization" referred quite specifically to the dismantling of the church and the replacement of Christianity by the ideals of the Revolution. This bloody upheaval, the first in human history to industrialize killing on a mass scale with its guillotines, could not help but focus on death, for, as everyone quickly discovered, a counterreligion needed its own inverted ceremonies. First, the brand-new

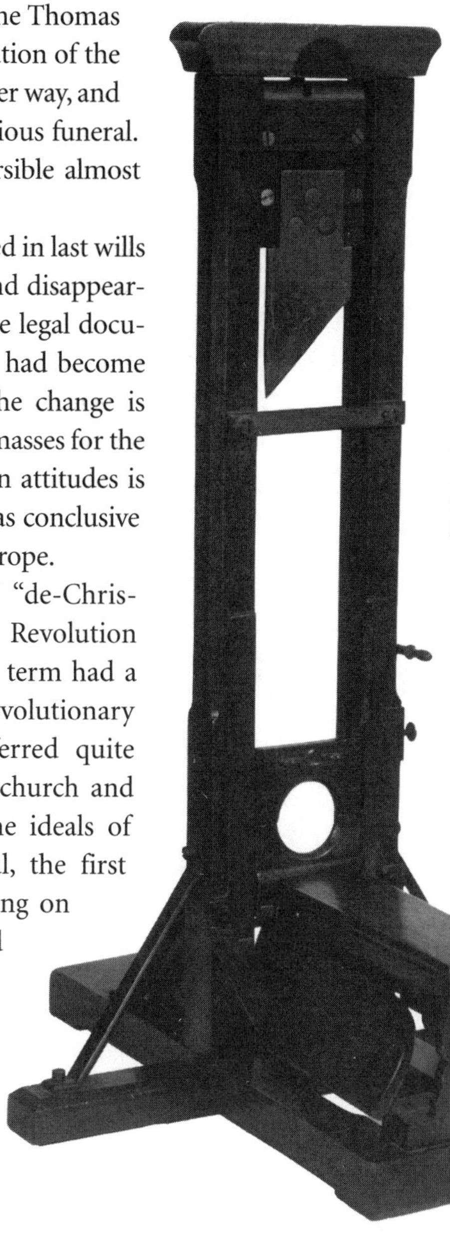

Fig. 1.2. The guillotine, a modern instrument of death used in the French Revolution to behead agents of monarchy. Photo: © Bridgeman-Giraudon / Art Resource, N.Y.

church of Saint Geneviéve in Paris was turned into a mausoleum for the great heroes of the new republic; renamed the Panthéon, after the ancient Roman temple that ostensibly served all the gods, this monument to *enlightened men* underscored the Revolution's triumph over religion and superstition. In 1791, the great cynic Voltaire's remains were transferred there and interred with a surplus of Revolutionary pomp and ritual. Not much later, in 1792, active de-Christianization began in earnest with the killing of priests. In Angers, for instance, clerics were bound in pairs, packed into leaking boats, and set adrift to sink and drown. Mocking baptism, the revolutionaries boasted of this "de-Christianization by immersion." In total, it is esti-

Fig. 1.3. Interior view of Panthéon, Paris (1764), by Jacques Germain Soufflot (1713–1780). Photo: © Bridgeman-Giraudon / Art Resource, N.Y.

mated that about twenty thousand priests agreed to voluntarily "de-Christianize" themselves by simply abjuring their posts and their faith, but thousands of others refused and were slaughtered. During this time, naturally, death rituals were transformed through a hypersecularization that reversed the sacred and the profane. In addition to vandalizing and destroying churches, or turning them into "temples of reason," revolutionary mobs desecrated cemeteries and did all they could to ritually dishonor the remains of their dead enemies. Those brought to the guillotine were humiliated first by ritual insults and then by having their decapitated remains disposed of as trash or carrion, with ritual disrespect. At the abbey church of Saint Denis, which housed the tombs of the royal family, the corpses of kings and queens were dug up and ravaged. Rumor had it that some of the well-preserved remains, such as the heart of King Louis XIV, were actually eaten. Conversely, the heart of the revolutionary Jean Paul Marat (1743–1793), who had been assassinated in his bathtub, was enshrined in a reliquary. Immediately, a cult of the great Marat developed, encouraged by the ever-changing Revolutionary leadership.

RESURGENT CHRISTIAN FERVOR

All of these excesses, which were well publicized around the world, could not help but have their effect. Once the terror subsided and order was restored, nothing could be the same, either in France or in the rest of the Christian world. A great rift had opened in Western culture: unbelief seemed poised to gain the upper hand. Yet as secularization increased, so did Christian fervor. In Europe and the Americas, the age of Enlightenment and revolutions was also a period marked by renewed, intense devotion to the beliefs that were being challenged. One need only turn to the many apparitions and divine messages that Catholics embraced as genuine during this period, which gave rise to immensely popular devotions, such as that to the Sacred Hearts of Jesus and Mary in the seventeenth to eighteenth centuries and to the Miraculous Medal in the nineteenth century. One of these devotions, the wearing of the scapular of Our Lady of Mount Carmel, better known as the Brown Scapular, had to do with death. According to pious tradition dating back to the thirteenth century, the Virgin Mary had promised in an apparition that anyone who died while wearing this small piece of cloth around their neck would not "suffer everlasting fire." In other words, simply wearing this scapular could earn even the worst sinner an entrance into purgatory rather than hell—a promise undoubtedly anchored in the ancient Catholic belief that monastic garb could guarantee salvation, since the scapular was a small replica of the outermost part of the monastic habit. In the middle of the seventeenth century, thanks to the efforts of the Carmelite order, devotion to this scapular blossomed throughout the Catholic world, and the lure of its promises became so attractive that between 1650 and 1900, fourteen other scapulars associated with other religious orders and confraternities would be approved by Rome, each related to some apparition and some large promise. At the very same time, throughout the world, many Catholics continued to be buried in monastic habits purchased from religious orders for the express purpose of dressing the corpse.

Among Protestants, there was plenty of fervor too, and some of it very traditionalist. In Germany, Pietism led to a religious revival that transcended political and national borders. Eventually, this renewed fervor would give rise to even grander revivals, as charismatic preachers took the Christian message to the world at large, beyond church walls. In North America, the Great Awakening would take place alongside the Enlightenment, and the Second Great Awakening alongside the Industrial Revolution. Belief in heaven and hell did not vanish but intensified among the thousands who heard Jonathan Edwards (1703–1758), John Wesley (1703–1791), and George Whitefield (1714–1770) preach, or who sang the inspiring hymns of Charles Wesley (1707–1778). Keeping in mind that Jonathan Edwards was a well-educated Yale graduate and a contemporary of hell-deniers such as D'Holbach, Voltaire, Diderot, Franklin, and Paine, one can only be amazed at the dissonant challenge offered by his sermon "Sinners in the Hands of an Angry God," which terrified many who heard it in 1741, leading them to fits of despair and sudden conversions:

> The God that holds you over the pit of hell, much as one holds a spider, or some loathsome insect over the fire, abhors you, and is dreadfully provoked: his wrath towards you burns like fire; he looks upon you as worthy of nothing else, but to be cast into the fire. . . . It is nothing but his hand that holds you from falling into the fire every moment. . . . Yea, there is nothing else that is to be given as a reason why you do not this very moment drop down into hell. . . . O sinner! Consider the fearful danger you are in: it is a great furnace of wrath, a wide and bottomless pit, full of the fire of wrath, that you are held over in the hand of that God, whose wrath is provoked and incensed as much against you, as against many of the damned in hell. You hang by a slender thread,

with the flames of divine wrath flashing about it, and ready every moment to singe it, and burn it asunder.[17]

Great revivals could not stop secularizing trends from increasing in the nineteenth century, however, as industrialization and urbanization changed much of the Christian world. On an intellectual and spiritual level, doubt and unbelief intensified in the nineteenth century, not just among the intelligentsia, but also among the new working class, and especially among those who embraced socialist and materialist ideology, which tended to view all religion as a means of oppression by the elite. On a very basic practical level, burying the dead became a business like any other. As society grew more complex, it was only natural that the handling of the dead be turned over to professional morticians who gradually took over many of the tasks previously handled by families and their clergy. Along with the morticians came their funeral homes, which also transferred much of the ritual that had previously taken place at the home of the deceased or at the church, further severing the ties that bound the dead to their families and their churches.

At the very same time, as cemeteries moved beyond the crowded cities, their landscaping evolved in new directions, changing the relationship between the dead and the living. Unfettered by space limitations, great necropolises sprang up all over the Christian world, where individuals and families now had the chance to erect the kinds of memorials that had once been reserved for nobility and royalty. In great cities such as Paris, the dead suddenly had their own suburbs, replete with mausoleums great and small, festooned with sculptures, crosses, obelisks, epitaphs, and plaques, all in a parklike setting: an enduring image and symbol of the world of the living, where the social hierarchy was reified most permanently in stone. Some of these nineteenth-century suburbs of the dead aimed at closeness with nature and were designed as parks rather than cities, with carefully planned landscapes that offered tranquil, scenic views. Many of these new cemeteries were open to all who could buy space within, regardless of religion, but the practice of maintaining specific cemeteries for each church or religious group endured and even expanded in the nineteenth century. In death, as in life, the poor ended up in the equivalent of slums, segregated from the paying clientele, often in mass graves or unmarked plots. Most of the urban areas of Europe and the Americas are dotted with these necropolises, which were swallowed up by expanding cities and are now not only very crowded, or totally full, but also smack-dab in the middle of densely congested areas. Smaller cities and towns also followed suit, and by the end of the nineteenth century, the world where most Christians lived was one in which the dead and the living were segregated, and one in which the cemetery became the focal point of all piety for the dead.[18]

SPIRITUALISM

Beautiful cemeteries were not the only place to commune with the dead, however. As secularization intensified and traditional Christianity lost its once-dominant place in Western culture, ancient occult beliefs and practices began to resurface in the nineteenth century,

Fig. 1.4. Mount Auburn Cemetery, Cambridge, Massachusetts, nineteenth-century engraving. From W. H. Bartlett, *Bartlett's Classical Illustrations of America: All 121 Engravings from American Scenery, 1840* (Mineola, N.Y.: Dover, 2000), plate 115.

under new guises, as if to fill the vacuum created by unbelief. Ghosts began to reappear with a vengeance, as did people who believed they could communicate with the dead, when an immensely popular phenomenon known as "spiritualism" quickly gained public attention and won many adherents. Freewheeling and prone to contention—despite the existence of professional associations such as the Society for Psychical Research—it was very far from a cohesive movement. At bottom, spiritualism was a great resurgence of belief in the existence of the soul and in its immortality, for all "spiritualists" believed or hoped that the spirits of the dead lingered on earth and that they could communicate with the living. Ghosts and hauntings had long been part of popular culture, even though Protestant and Catholic clergy alike had tried to suppress such beliefs. Many historians often refer to belief in ghosts as one of those enduring bits of "popular religion" that the elites could never erase. Chances are that the afterlife described by the ghost of Hamlet's father in Shakespeare's play bring us closer to popular beliefs than nearly anything else, and what we find him describing to a Protestant Elizabethan audience is a perfect blend of very *wrong* un-Christian folklore and Catholic beliefs about purgatory:

> I am thy father's spirit,
> Doomed for a certain term to walk the night;
> And for the day confined to fast in fires,
> Till the foul crimes done in my days of nature
> Are burnt and purged away.[19]

Ghosts had never ceased to exist—nor could they stop talking or complaining about grudges and unfinished business, it seems. But beginning in the mid-nineteenth century, reports of ghosts and haunted places began to proliferate, as did so-called experts, or "mediums," who claimed that they had special knowledge or powers that allowed them to speak to the dead and relay their messages to the living. Most churches condemned these beliefs and practices outright, as they had always done, denouncing them as delusions or, worse, as demonic in origin. While some Christians rejected spiritualism or were ambivalent, some clearly embraced it, turning it into part of their Christian faith. The wall between such beliefs and Christian culture had always been somewhat permeable, so it was not too uncommon to even find Christian clergy—especially outside of the mainline churches—engaging in some sort of spiritualism or acting as mediums.

Among the spiritualist beliefs and practices that took root in the nineteenth century, none was more common than that of the séance, a gathering at which mediums would question the dead and seek replies from them. Mediums could claim all sorts of special powers that had once been the preserve of medieval mystics or of witches and demoniacs, that is, those who were in touch with the spiritual dimension: telepathy, clairvoyance, levitation. Some claimed they could make objects materialize out of thin air or, more commonly, that they could heal the sick.

Fig. 1.5. Spirit photograph, 1872, by Fredrick Hudson. © Wm. B. Becker Collection /American Museum of Photography.

After the invention of photography, other "experts" appeared on the scene who claimed to be able to photograph ghosts, ostensibly giving them scientific credibility. Spiritualism cut across class lines and circled the globe: its appeal seemed universal and as boundless as the public's credulity. None other than Sir Arthur Conan Doyle, the creator of the hyperlogical detective Sherlock Holmes, was a firm believer in spiritualism and toured the world, speaking to sell-out crowds, showing them photographs of ghosts. A lasting survival of the spiritualist craze can be found in almost any toy store nowadays: the Ouija board, a "game" once taken very seriously by spiritualists in which two people act as mediums, deciphering messages from the dead. Spiritualism would peak in popularity in the 1920s and 1930s as millions of distraught families sought to cope with the loss of their young men between 1914 and 1918 in the Great War.

An outgrowth of spiritualism that flourished in the late nineteenth century was *theosophy*, a movement founded by Helena Blavatsky in the 1870s. Under her leadership, the Theosophical Society disseminated a combination of spiritualism, ancient Indian philosophy, Gnostic teachings, and several other occult beliefs and practices. By reintroducing belief in reincarnation to the West and by claiming to provide access to memories of past lives, theosophists had some impact on Christians. As in the case of spiritualism, the fact that all of the mainline churches condemned theosophy did not deter all Christians from believing in some of its teachings, especially in reincarnation and the remembering of past lives.

CONCLUSION

Increased secularization caused a few other changes in Christian attitudes and practices in the course of the nineteenth century, most notably in regard to suicide, cremation, and mourning customs. Until the seventeenth century, suicide was considered a sin, and Christian burial was routinely denied to anyone who died at their own hand. Gradually, Christian attitudes toward suicide began to change, especially among Protestants, as the medical profession grew increasingly aware of the connections between mental illness and despair. By 1900 the balance of opinion had begun to shift in most Christian churches toward compassion and a greater acceptance of the physiological and psychological causes of suicide, among both Protestants and Catholics, although the Catholic Church continued to pronounce it a mortal sin. Similarly, the previously banned practice of cremation gained greater acceptance outside the Catholic Church, among Protestants, as burial space became increasingly difficult to find and burials became ever more costly. Mourning customs, which had always varied widely among Christians but had always been an essential part of dealing with the dead, also began to decline by 1900, especially in the industrialized world, where nonproductive behavior and outward signs of sadness tended to be frowned upon.

Changes such as these were but more recent versions of the adjustment that Christians have always made to their cultural environments. Social, cultural, and political developments, coupled with advances in science, technology, and medicine, began to speed up the process of change so much by 1900 that when the history of nineteenth-century Christian attitudes toward death is viewed in the light of traditions that lasted for centuries, the shifting seems abrupt. But the fact remains that even in situations in which Christians had to make decisions on the basis of opinions that came from the secular environment outside of their faith, or from other religious traditions, those who defined themselves as Christians continued to bring their faith into play. Whether they cremated their dead or buried them in secular cemeteries, or whether they dabbled in spiritualism or not, or whether they prayed for the dead or not, Christians confronted death and the disposal of their remains within an ancient framework of belief in an afterlife and a resurrection. Around 1900, death continued to pose the greatest challenge of all to Christians, as to all people, and within that challenge lay another: how best to Christianize the attitudes and rituals of the secularizing societies in which they lived, where death was becoming an unsightly inconvenience and where the dead were already being shuffled off the face of the earth quickly, with out-of-sight, out-of-mind industrial efficiency, with no apparent care for their immortal souls and no hereafter as their ultimate destination, other than perhaps some Ouija board or a séance.

> **Mourning the Afterlife**
>
> Those—dying then,
> Knew where they went—
> They went to God's Right Hand—
> That Hand is amputated now
> And God cannot be found—
>   —Emily Dickinson, "Those—dying then," in The Oxford Book of Death, ed. D. J. Enright (New York: Oxford University Press, 1987), 188.

FOR FURTHER READING

Ariès, Philippe. *L'homme devant la mort.* Paris: Seuil, 1977. Translated by Helen Weaver as *The Hour of Our Death* (New York: Knopf, 1981).

Chéroux, Clément, and Andreas Fischer, eds. *The Perfect Medium: Photography and the Occult.* New Haven: Yale University Press, 2005.

Cressy, David. *Birth, Marriage, and Death: Ritual, Religion, and the Life-Cycle in Tudor and Stuart England.* Oxford: Oxford University Press, 1997.

Eire, Carlos. *From Madrid to Purgatory: The Art and Craft of Dying in Sixteenth-Century Spain.* Cambridge Studies in Early Modern History. Pages 28–31. Cambridge: Cambridge University Press, 1995.

Gregory, Brad S. *Salvation at Stake: Christian Martyrdom in Early Modern Europe.* Harvard Historical Studies. Cambridge: Harvard University Press, 1999.

Harding, Vanessa. *The Dead and the Living in Paris and London, 1500–1670.* Cambridge: Cambridge University Press, 2002.

Koslofsky, Craig M. *The Reformation of the Dead: Death and Ritual in Early Modern Germany, 1450–1700.* New York: Palgrave Macmillan, 2000.

Marshall, Peter. *Beliefs and the Dead in Reformation England.* Oxford: Oxford University Press, 2002.

McManners, John. *Death and the Enlightenment: Changing Attitudes to Death among Christians and Unbelievers in Eighteenth-Century France.* Oxford: Oxford University Press, 1981.

Pearsall, Ronald. *Table-Rappers: The Victorians and the Occult.* Stroud, U.K.: Sutton, 2004.

Reinis, Austra. *Reforming the Art of Dying: The* ars moriendi *in the German Reformation (1519–1528).* Burlington: Ashgate, 2007.

Walker, D. P. *The Decline of Hell: Seventeenth-Century Discussions of Eternal Torment.* Chicago: University of Chicago Press, 1964.

CONTROLLING AND CHRISTIANIZING SEX

PETER GARDELLA

CHAPTER TWO

A Syrian dancer called Fatima and Frances Willard, president of the Women's Christian Temperance Union, performed in the same setting at the end of the nineteenth century. Addressing the World's Parliament of Religions at the Columbian Exposition in Chicago in 1893, Willard declared that "the reciprocal attraction of two natures, out of a thousand million, for each other . . . alone makes possible the true Home, the pure Church, the righteous Nation, the great, kind Brotherhood of Man."[1] With conviction equal to that of Sigmund Freud or Albert Kinsey, Willard saw sex at the heart of everything. She worked to raise the legal age of consent of girls for sexual intercourse from ten years of age to eighteen, to end licensed prostitution, to win the vote for women, to prohibit sales of alcohol, and to hold men to the same ethical standards expected of women. She called her speech "A White Life for Two," and in the twentieth century much of her program came to pass.

As Willard spoke, the sensuality excluded from her ideal flowed through a theater on the Midway of the same Columbian Exposition, where Fatima (whose real name was Fahreda Mahzar) introduced fairgoers to the belly dance, which had been performed at private parties in the Middle East for centuries. In colonial times, the dance began to attract tourists, then migrated to Paris during the Eiffel Tower World's Fair of 1889. The replica of a street in Cairo where Fatima danced attracted two million visitors from May to October and brought in more revenue than any other feature of the fair, surpassing the world's first Ferris wheel. Fatima became the predecessor of "Little Egypt," who danced in Chicago for years, and the ancestor of music videos; Thomas Edison filmed her in 1896. Other theaters on the Midway had Algerian, Moorish, and Turkish themes and featured dancers from those countries and cultures. Replicas of villages allowed visitors to see natives of Samoa and Dahomey, brought from the South Pacific and West Africa, who did their rituals and dances wearing far less clothing than was normal in Chicago. An international beauty contest ran all summer. In August, the *Chicago Herald* called the international theaters "disreputable dives." Under pressure from Willard's W.C.T.U. and others, the "Persian" theater—which featured Parisian women who pretended to be Persian and who danced more explicitly than the Middle Eastern women—was temporarily closed until its dancers changed their routine; but most of the theaters stayed open. The Exposition continued to offer both a White City with temples to human progress (including a Women's Building), where Frances Willard challenged men to ascend the heights of love through sexual purity, and a Midway where women evoked a colonized version of sensual pleasure. A similar relation between sexual purity and sensuality has persisted in Christian civilizations into the twenty-first century. This chapter will explain how that modern combination came together.

Fig. 2.1. The Women's Building, Chicago World's Fair, 1893.

Between the seventeenth and twentieth centuries, Christian theory and practice on sex went through three transformations. First, Catholic and Protestant clergy worked through public discourse and courts of law to tighten the rules and mechanisms of control applied to sex, both in Europe and in new Christian empires of the Americas and Asia. Next, these rules and institutions were made to accommodate the pleasures of secular patriarchs who took power from clergy in the mature empires and revolutionary states of the eighteenth century. Then, while patriarchy and colonialism continued in the 1800s and beyond, reforming Christians of the nineteenth century brought evangelical perfectionism, feminism, medical theology, and psychology into the center of modern discourse on sex.

Scholars since Simone de Beauvoir and Michel Foucault have established the premise that sex is not a natural but a cultural category, shaped by social power. Recent historians of Christianity have concentrated their research on showing how sex was constructed at particular times in specific Christian groups. Reviewing their research, one may conclude that it is more accurate to speak of sex in various Christianities than of Christianity and sex. All those who call themselves Christians do not admit the right of all others to that name. Even for the neutral scholar,

Fig. 2.2. Fatima, "Little Egypt."

groups such as the Mormons and the Oneida Community and physicians from Christian cultures present real problems of classification.

This chapter takes a broad and inclusive approach to "Christianity," arguing that the years between 1650 and 1900 saw several movements that unified the Christian world with regard to sex. Most importantly throughout the period, conquerors who were accompanied by Christian clergy inflicted sexual servitude, enforced by slavery and colonial domination, on large populations in the Americas, Africa, and Asia. The men who led these empires simultaneously deprived women in their home nations of property, legal rights, and cultural influence. In reaction, women saw the parallels between themselves and slaves and gained much ground in the nineteenth century, but the most successful leaders of women adapted to the new, imperial world.

Fig. 2.3. Frances Willard. © Bettmann/CORBIS.

CONTROLLING SEX

Within global empires of faith, Christian clergy, lay leaders, and doctors made successive efforts to control sex. For example, in 1680, Roman Catholic priests removed women from their parents' homes to prevent forced marriages both in Spain and in New Mexico; twenty years earlier, a Maryland civil court had arranged for a woman to live in the home of a neutral family while a suitor disliked by her family visited her; and in the course of the 1600s, every English colony in North America passed laws attempting to forbid secret marriages. All Christian cultures of the sixteenth and seventeenth centuries were becoming more intrusive about regulating marriage and punishing irregular sex. Another universal trend emerged in the nineteenth century when an evangelical doctor from Kentucky named J. Marion Sims practiced operations on the vaginas of twelve slaves, invented the speculum, and eventually worked at the royal courts of Paris and Moscow. Most Christians of the nineteenth century accepted medical doctors as the leading experts on sex, and most doctors saw a religious dimension in their work on sex.

A geographical shift accompanied the modernization of sex in Christendom. From Columbus through the eighteenth century, the Americas served as a setting where European Christians worked out their sexual fantasies, fears, and hopes. By the middle of the nineteenth century, the direction of influence had become reversed, and the drive of Christians from the United States to lead the way to a promised land of sexual justice was already being felt throughout the world. English advocates of birth control went to jail in 1877 for reprinting *Fruits of Philosophy, or The Private Companion of Adult People*, which was first published by a Boston doctor, Charles Knowlton, in 1831. American radicals such as the Shakers (who practiced communal celibacy), the Mormons (who practiced polygamy), the Oneida Community (who maintained a complex marriage among two hundred people), and the feminists of Seneca Falls became known around the world for their visions of a new sexual dispensation.

Meanwhile, more specific transformations also took place during the centuries since 1600. Several forms of sexual behavior, ranging from bestiality to masturbation to the frequency of marital sex to female orgasm to male homosexuality, were targeted in turn for control. By 1900, the elements of the sexual revolutions of the 1920s and 1960s were in place. The rule makers of the seventeenth century, the slave owners and libertines of the eighteenth, and the reformers of the Victorian age had made sex so central to Christianity that battles over the direction of the Christian world came to focus on sex in the way that such struggles for power had once concerned the roles of popes and emperors, the uses of art in worship, or the nature of grace and the sacraments.

Some facts about sexual behavior correspond to the three transformations in Christian thinking about sex. A dramatic fall in European birth rates through the nineteenth century has long been established and attributed both to the dissemination of contraceptive knowledge (douching and condoms) and to Victorian repression of sexual activity in marriage. By 1850, France no longer had a birth rate adequate to reproduce its population. Even in the United States, where abundant land and industrial expansion encouraged fertility, white women living to menopause averaged 7.04 children in 1800, 5.21 children in 1860, and 3.56 in 1900, and the downward trend continued through the 1930s. Reliable measures of illicit sexual behavior are elusive, but statistics for births, marriages, sexual crimes, and lawsuits indicate that the Christian world—or at least the middle classes—between 1650 and 1900 experienced a falling, rising, falling, and once again rising rate of heterosexual intercourse outside marriage, with low points around 1650 and 1850 (the latter particularly in the Anglo-American empire) and long bulges of increased nonmarital sex starting in the 1700s and 1850s, especially in Britain and North America. Repression appears to have taken hold first among the middle class of the United States in the early 1800s but gradually spread among the middle classes of England and Europe as the nineteenth century progressed. The Berlin of Frederick the Great, a city of 150,000, had about eight thousand registered prostitutes living in a hundred brothels in 1780; by 1844, when the government closed the brothels, only twenty-six houses and 240 prostitutes remained. Then in the last half of the nineteenth century, prostitution rose dramatically, along with cases of syphilis and gonorrhea. Higher rates of illegitimacy relative to the total number of births are reported for the 1880s in Scotland, England, and France, probably reflecting neglect of marriage by poor people who ceased to affiliate with churches.[2]

The curve of illicit sexual activity corresponds to the divisions of this chapter. Beginning with the expanding empires and authoritative systems of the Renaissance and Reformation, the narrative moves through the alterations of those systems in the eighteenth century and concludes with the triumphs of evangelicals, women, and doctors. Behind all three stories, the pervasive influences of slavery and colonialism should never be forgotten.

Conflict and convulsion over sex, marked and perhaps caused by authoritative systems attempting tight control, filled the seventeenth century. A spectacular outbreak of sexual possession in a convent at Loudun, France, ended in 1634 with the burning of a priest at the stake; a firestorm of demonic possessions of women in France, Italy, England, and North America, called a "witch craze" by historians, burned out after Salem in 1692. Puritans in England and America campaigned against prostitution and made sexual sins into crimes, punished by the civil courts. Spanish conquerors had by the 1600s obliterated most of the native sex practices, including male trans-sexualism, that appeared in civilizations from New Mexico through South America. At first amazed by the free movements of women in the Caribbean and Mexico, and especially by their swimming in light clothing, the Spanish excused themselves for taking the conqueror's usual privilege of rape; but in this case, rape became an effective weapon of conquest. Between the devastations of disease and the passing of immunity to mixed offspring, the conquistadors transformed whole populations into *mestizos* in a few generations. In the North, a handful of French explorers were paid a bounty to marry Native American women until 1684, when such marriages were forbidden; those who did marry did not make the natives French but founded the small, mixed cultures of the Metis along the Great Lakes and the Creole in Louisiana. Slaves from Africa brought their own religions, with their own sexual themes, to the Caribbean islands and to North and South America, while slavery put African men and women, Christian masters and their wives into a new sexual context.[3] Although both slavery and African religions would undermine the control of Christian clergy over sex, the first consequence of slavery for the clergy was their perception of a need to set forth new rules for control. Priests in the Spanish territories often protested sexual exploitation by the conquerors. During the witch trials at Salem, the slave woman Tituba, an Indian from South America who had learned African practices in Barbados, was first to be named a witch by the accusing girls.

In Roman Catholic theology, the age of rule making transformed books of penances inherited from the Middle Ages and intended primarily for monks into volumes of precise instructions for confessors of laypeople that were published during the late sixteenth and early seventeenth centuries. The church moved from an era when cardinals and popes competed to employ flamboyantly gay men such as Michelangelo and Leonardo into a time when Paul VI ordered that all the nudes Michelangelo had painted in *The Last Judgment* on the wall of the Sistine Chapel, from Christ to the damned in hell, be covered at least by a strategic piece of cloth. A special Vatican court, called the Roman Penitentiary, for hearing questions that arose in the confessional was created by Pius V in 1569. By the mid-1600s, textbooks for confessors had become battlegrounds in a war between "laxists," who held that no sin could be mortal (deserving of hell) unless it was done with a conscious intention to defy God, and "rigorists," who found mortal sin in many acts. The Jesuit general Aquaviva in 1612 instructed his entire order, under pain of excommunication, never to teach that any sexual sin could be less than mortal because it lacked "gravity of matter"; in other words, a small lie or theft could be sinful without entailing damnation, but the slightest consent to sexual pleasure outside of marital intercourse would bring a soul to hell unless repentance and absolution intervened. This doctrine continued to terrorize young Catholics well into the twentieth century. Even in marriage, according to a 1679 ruling of the Inquisition under Pope Innocent XI, sex acts were sinful if they were done solely for an individual's pleasure, without regard for other goods (such as fulfilling one's duty to a spouse, attempting to procreate, or avoiding temptation to sin). Pope John Paul II surprised many when he reaffirmed this teaching in his letter to families of 1994.

On the level of practice, the Roman Catholic Church of the 1600s tried to increase its control over marriage—for example, teaching that priests who thought that young women were being forced to marry had the right to take the women from their families and place them temporarily in convents or rectories. Enforced by Franciscans in Spanish New Mexico, this clerical attempt to intervene in the lives of unmarried women—coupled with the usual cases of sexual coercion by governors and priests—probably contributed to the Pueblo Revolt of 1680, in which Hopi, Zuni, and other Indians of the pueblos killed dozens of priests, burned villages of Christian converts, and drove the Spaniards from their territory for twelve years. More peacefully,

Catholic insistence that slaves and Indians had the right to sacramental marriage made a permanent difference in racial attitudes, not obliterating but softening race distinctions in the Catholic lands of the Americas. Denial of marriage to slaves made race into a more and more absolute category in the Protestant areas of North America and the Caribbean, despite the sex that continued to produce children across racial lines.

Although Catholic theology emphasized sexual sin, broad routes to liberalization remained with regard to intention. Saint Alphonsus Liguori (d. 1787) settled the dispute between laxists and rigorists with the principle of "equiprobabilism," under which the moral status of any act was determined by weighing authorities and reasons on both sides of a dispute. Sometimes Liguori came down on the side of the laxists: for example, he advised confessors not to tell men who confessed sex with prostitutes that their sin was serious, because the belief of the men that their sin was venial made it so, and instruction would not change their behavior but only the degree of their guilt. Similarly, Liguori concluded that oral sex in marriage could be exempted from sin, even if an accidental orgasm occurred, if it was undertaken as preparation for genital intercourse, and that spouses could licitly stimulate each other making use of the anus if the *affectus* or feeling of sodomy was not indulged. On the other hand, Liguori's emphasis on intention meant that one orgasm in masturbation might involve many mortal sins, one for each act of consent to sexual pleasure outside marriage.

The balance of Catholic theology between 1748, when Liguori's moral theology first appeared in print, and 1831, when the Roman Penitentiary declared that confessors could follow his conclusions in all things, suited a world of dalliance in operas and formal gowns that left one breast exposed. According to the Italian saint, attendance even at "notably shameful" plays was not sinful if it was done simply out of curiosity rather than

---

The Mechanics of Copulation

"If the man retracts himself after semination, but before the semination of the woman, may she immediately excite herself by touches to seminate?"

Liguori answered yes, "because the semination of the woman pertains to the completion of the conjugal act, which consists in the semination of both spouses; whence, if the wife can by touches prepare herself for copulation, thus she can also perfect the act of copulation.... And because, as several feel, the semination of the woman is necessary, or at least bears much upon generation: for nothing vain is done by nature."

—Alphonsus Marie de Liguori, Theologia Moralis (1748; Graz, 1954), book 6, par. 919.

from a desire for illicit pleasure.[4] By the eighteenth century, French and Irish rigorists were tainted with the heresy of Jansenism, a Catholic version of Calvinism that popes condemned several times in the 1600s. Conquest by rape declined as the Spanish conquistadors and their Franciscan or Dominican priests relaxed in their victory and blended Catholicism into the cultures of the Americas. Though the plots and costumes of European theater and dance grew less explicit as the eighteenth century turned into the nineteenth, the presence of Catholic priests in theater audiences still shocked Protestants, and Liguori's conclusions on sex remained in print to shock them even more.

The Anglo-American and northern European branches of Christendom witnessed an attempt to enforce stricter control in the seventeenth century that paralleled the witch trials and central authorities of Catholic lands. In Scotland, Presbyterians developed a system of kirk sessions, or courts composed of a minister and elders, that met in each of nine hundred parishes and coordinated their decisions under supervision by more than sixty presbyteries, dozens of synods, and a national General Assembly. The church courts of Scotland used penalties such as excommunication and imprisonment to reduce the rate of births out of wedlock from almost 10 to less than 5 percent after 1660 and to maintain that very low level throughout the eighteenth century, holding firm against trends that increased illegitimacy to 30 percent in other Protestant countries.

Meanwhile, in England, Puritans tried to eliminate prostitution and shut down the theaters of London from 1642 to 1660, while New England colonists hanged six men for bestiality and one for sodomy. A spectacular case occurred in 1662, when William Potter, an elder of sixty years who was one of the original settlers of New Haven, Connecticut, was caught by his teenaged son with one of his sows. Before Potter was hanged, he pointed out every animal he had treated in this way, which resulted in the executions of one cow, two heifers, three sheep, and two sows; this fulfilled the sentence prescribed by Leviticus 20:15, which was also the criminal law of New Haven. Until the Salem witch panic of 1692, accusations of men for bestiality in New England approximated the number of accusations of women for witchcraft, and both crimes seemed to play a similar role in defining the ultimate outsider. A far more serious hunt for offenders occurred under the aegis of civil courts in Lutheran Sweden, where about eight hundred males, mostly teenaged boys, were hanged between 1680 and 1810 for bestiality.[5]

Homosexuality, on the other hand, resulted in a roughly equal number of trials as bestiality but only one execution in New England colonial court records, even though the Bible pronounces the same death sentence on males who have sex with each other as on those who commit bestiality or witchcraft. From the diaries of Michael Wigglesworth, the Puritan poet, we know that seventeenth-century Puritans were capable of feeling and expressing deep sexual desire in homoerotic terms, but we do not find many of them acting upon these desires in public or prosecuting homosexual acts in court. In the same era, two great Anglican poets, John Donne and George Herbert, consistently addressed God and some of their friends in homoerotic terms without anyone taking it amiss. Definition and control of homosexuality would not become a major issue until the late nineteenth century.

The seventeenth-century Puritan Revolution, with pietist extensions in Sweden and Germany, sought to establish patriarchal Protestantism and what were seen as biblical standards of behavior. Prostitution, though forbidden in the Hebrew Scriptures, had long been tolerated by Catholics. Augustine and Thomas Aquinas likened brothels to sewers, without which society would fill with worse crimes, and justified the church in collecting rent from them. After the Reformation, Catholic attitudes grew slightly less tolerant; but Puritans tried to eliminate prostitution along with the theater, with which it was associated. Puritans exalted marriage to the point that John Milton, the greatest of Puritan poets, wrote movingly in 1643 for the necessity of divorce if the souls of the married did not agree. Prosecutions for adultery were moved from ecclesiastical to civil courts, which also took up cases of fornication, and both crimes were punished more severely and more effectively than before. In New England, citizens were fined not only for fornication itself but for failing to report known offenders to the magistrate.

The most lasting sexual heritage of Puritanism in England and America was the loss of legal power and status by women. Women's rights to share property with their husbands, to consent to marriage, and to be considered as plaintiffs in trials for rape had all been better protected by ecclesiastical and equity law than by the Bible or the common law of England, which now became the standards. English common law gave married women no property rights, refused to hear cases of rape if pregnancy had resulted, and set the age when a female could legally consent to sexual intercourse at ten.

INDULGING IN SEX

When the Puritan Revolution failed in England and monarchy was restored in 1660, the London theaters reopened, now featuring few tragedies but many bedroom farces. Scotland and Sweden maintained their Protestant strictness, but in England and even in New England, the churches lost control of sex. The new mood was exemplified by Charles II himself, who had more than one notable concubine, and by writers such as Daniel Defoe and businessmen such as Samuel Pepys, who recorded sexual adventures in his famous diaries. By the early 1700s, 30 to 40 percent of marriages in New England resulted in childbirth within eight months. Abortion by homemade medicines was well known in Connecticut under the title of "taking the trade."[6] Accusations of witchcraft were ridiculed, and men no longer were brought to court for bestiality, whatever they might have been doing in the barns and the fields. Perhaps the growing number of women and their increasing willingness to engage in premarital sex made recourse to animals less attractive.

Among the factors making for more hedonistic attitudes was slavery, which greatly increased opportunities for sex among slave-holding men. The diary of a Jamaican slaveholder, kept between 1750 and 1786, recorded 1,774 sexual acts with slaves over one fourteen-year period, an average of 126.7 per year, with 7.8 different women each year. Besides that period of intense sexual activity as an overseer, the Englishman in question maintained a continuous relationship with one slave woman for thirty-two years. He even died owing her money, which she collected in the form of a cow from his estate. He fathered children by slaves, and these children remained in slavery but increased the status and wealth of their mothers. The situation in Jamaica was extreme: male Africans were constantly brought for sugar harvesting and quickly worked to death, while both English and African women were in short supply. Still, recent revelations about the genetic likelihood that many black Americans can claim descent from Thomas Jefferson, and the public emergence of the African American daughter of segregationist Senator Strom Thurmond, have underscored the lasting effects of slavery on sexual behavior. White women of Anglo-American slave societies sometimes also had sex with slaves and bore children with African males. Such pregnancies, at least before the crises of the 1840s and the Reconstruction era, could result in the divorce of the women by their white husbands but not in the lynching of black men who came to be associated with such activity later.[7]

Across the world in the Dutch colony of Batavia (modern Jakarta, Indonesia), poor funds administered by the Reformed Church were supporting thousands of mixed-race single mothers, the descendants of slaves bought in India and taken as concubines or used as prostitutes by Dutch men, by 1700. In the Danish West Indies, Governor General Peter von Sholten lived openly with a black woman named Anna Heegard for twenty years, despite having a wife and children in Denmark; Governor General Adrian Bentzon and Henritta Franciska, another black woman, had two children out of wedlock, and Franciska had another with the American consul, Joseph Ridway, while Bentzon was in Denmark. Few Danish men moved to the Danish West Indies, where Irish and Scots often served as slave masters, but all men there found laws that made the rape of slaves impossible to punish and customs so rigidly opposed to interracial marriage that a Moravian minister who performed such a wedding in 1738 lost his ordination after a government investigation instigated by a Danish Reformed pastor. The interracial couple was then separated and punished for cohabitation without marriage, the white man sent to a penal colony for life, and the black woman sold, with the proceeds benefiting the hospital at St. Croix.[8]

While slavery provided a global field for eighteenth-century libertinage and sexual exploitation, libertines also flourished at home in Europe, as the memoirs of the Marquis de Sade and the novels of

Richardson, Fielding, and Voltaire testify. Catholics responded with the flexible theology of Liguori, and Protestants adapted to the loss of public control over sex by emphasizing interior exercises of piety and personal holiness, in the fashion of Anglican William Law and the Methodist and German evangelical pietists. Practical advice to Protestants came from such divines as John Witherspoon, a Presbyterian who also served as president of Princeton, and Timothy Dwight, a Congregationalist who became president of Yale, both of whom feared that marriage was endangered by the spirit of their age and praised it as the foundation of the church. The sexual sentimentality that prevailed among Protestants of the Victorian era was prefigured by Emmanuel Swedenborg (1688–1772), the mystic and amateur theologian whose visits to heaven began a tradition of asserting that earthly marriages were crucial to spiritual growth and continued in the afterlife. In his *Catechism of Reason for Noble Ladies* (1798), Friedrich Schleiermacher (1768–1834) urged women to seek sexual fulfillment and to lose their inhibitions about discussing sex; Søren Kierkegaard (1813–1855) devoted much of his thinking and writing to his own broken engagement, the analysis of marriage, and the life of the libertine.

John Wesley (1703–1791), the founder of Methodism, gave the world a doctrine with potential both to attack social tolerance for libertines and to infuse Christian sexual practice with a positive ideal of ecstasy: the doctrine of sanctification, or perfect love. Unlike Luther and Calvin and the Anglican Thirty-nine Articles, all of which taught that Christians would remain sinful until they died, even if their sins were forgiven, Wesley preached that complete sanctification—a state in which the Christian felt no hatred or lust, but only love—was possible through the power of the Holy Spirit, indwelling as a second blessing after the grace of Christ in salvation. Wesley never claimed to have received this blessing himself, but he wrote about others who had. For decades after his death, the doctrine was nearly forgotten, except among the more severe Methodists such as those who rejected slavery and nurtured Elizabeth Cady Stanton. Then, in the 1830s, the second blessing entered the mainstream with the work of Phoebe Palmer (1807–1874), whose book *The Way of Holiness* remained in print through the 1980s. Palmer taught that people could gain in an instant what Wesley expected them to seek for years. Over the last half of the nineteenth century, Holiness churches (including the Salvation Army in England, and in America the Church of the Nazarene) emerged to lead millions to perfect love. People seeking holiness began the traditions of summer camping on Martha's Vineyard and the New Jersey shore, among many other locations in the United States. Though the unmarried, deeply pious John Wesley seemed outside the mainstream in the secular and hedonistic eighteenth century, Wesley's doctrine of sanctification gave Methodists, women, and members of the new Holiness churches a path that led beyond the acceptance of sin in society and beyond the association of sex and sin in personal life.

As Methodists preached to African slaves in North America, they opened yet another, related path of development for Christianity and sex. At revival meetings that extended from the eighteenth to the twentieth century, the message of a second blessing by the Holy Spirit mixed with rituals of possession from West African religions and helped give birth to Pentecostal Christianity. The characteristic Pentecostal practices of falling down (being slain in the Spirit) and speaking in tongues had analogies both in Yoruba religion and in Sufi Muslim devotions that were widespread in the African lands where most slaves were taken. People responding to Christian preaching and singing fell to the ground, spoke in tongues, danced, and laughed involuntarily at racially integrated revivals in many places, but most notably at Cane Ridge, Kentucky, in 1801; Topeka, Kansas, in 1901; and Azusa Street, Los Angeles, in 1906. Wesleyan evangelicals and Pentecostals, some of whom absorbed practices from African religions, had taught Protestants that people could be completely free of sin and that the fulfillment of life could be found in a moment of ecstasy. Later Pentecostals included sexually compromised preachers such as Aimee Semple McPherson and Jimmy Swaggart, as well as such undeniably sexual and occasionally religious figures as novelist James Baldwin and singers Jerry Lee Lewis, Little Richard, and Elvis Presley.

Direct influence of Wesleyan tradition on sex worked through the life of Margaret Sanger (1879–1966), the founder of Planned Parenthood and inventor of the phrase "birth control," who was raised in a Roman Catholic family but educated at the Methodist Claverack College, where she studied for three years beginning in 1895. Surrounded by professors and students who were noted in the school newspaper for having received "the baptism of fire," Sanger gave her first speech for women's rights in the Claverack chapel. The president of Claverack, the Reverend Arthur H. Flack, used textbooks such as Francis Wayland's *Elements of Moral Science*, which held that pleasure in sex was the will of God; Flack also argued in class that emotions and passions could be completely sanctified. By the 1920s, Flack's student Margaret Sanger was often arrested for obscenity as she gave public speeches on birth control, in which she claimed that "the right understanding of our sexual power and of its creative energy . . . gives us spiritual illumination."[9]

With regard to the details of sex, Protestant theologians wrote nothing comparable to Catholic textbooks for confessors. One English book attained great popularity on both sides of the Atlantic: a compilation called *Aristotle's Master-Piece*, representing itself as a translation from ancient sources, which first appeared in London in 1684 and went through thirty-two printings in America before 1831. The text stressed sexual desire in women, saying that at puberty such a surplus of blood arises in them that "their desire of venereal embraces becomes . . . almost unsupportable." It ascribed a vital role to the clitoris, asserting that without it women neither desire sex nor conceive children, and that "according to the greatness or smallness of this part, they are more or less fond of men's embraces." With regard to theology, "Aristotle" taught that God intended sex to be pleasurable and that Eden "could scarcely have been paradise without it." Reflecting the change of mood since the Church of England adopted its Thirty-nine Articles in 1563, the *Master-Piece* mentioned no corruption of sexual desire into lust, or "concupiscence," by original sin. Benjamin Franklin printed an edition of *Aristotle's Master-Piece* in Philadelphia, and he probably found its perspective congenial. In Franklin's famous list of thirteen virtues, which he practiced every week in the effort to attain perfection, the description of what it meant to follow chastity struck a rational, practical, and far from Puritan tone: "Rarely use venery except for health or offspring, and never to the damage of your own or another's reputation."[10]

MAKING SEX MEDICAL

Franklin's notion that moderate use of "venery" might be necessary or useful for maintaining health testifies to an old wisdom that would soon pass from the scene as Christian thinking about sex became influenced by modern medicine. While doctors of the Renaissance and the early eighteenth century sought to balance the vital fluids or "humors" of the body and favored systemic approaches to disease, the progress of experimental science led to a search for more specific empirical causes and cures. In 1760, a Swiss physician and friend of Rousseau's named Simon Tissot encouraged the empirical shift in sexual medicine with his book *Onanism*, a warning against masturbation that presented semen and vaginal secretions as humors, but understood them not in terms of balance but in terms of conservation. According to Tissot, the loss of one ounce of semen took a toll on the body equal to losing forty ounces (more than a quart) of blood, and vaginal secretions were even more precious. By exhausting their bodies, male and female masturbators risked debility, blindness, insanity, and death. Doctors in England, France, and America believed Tissot, and the masturbation phobia that began with him extended, in various forms, through the era of psychoanalysis and Freud's concern for the resolution of infantile masturbation. Female masturbation retained its negative connotation until the 1970s, when Shere Hite finally called it "a cause for celebration" because it was the most reliable source of orgasm for women,[11] and sex therapists integrated it into their repertoire. For males, masturbation has never been entirely cleared of the suspicion of harm.

Simply to call masturbation "onanism" gave it a biblical context, because the name came from Onan the second husband of Tamar, who was slain by God for withdrawing from her and spilling his seed on the ground in Genesis 38. The fact that the biblical Onan was not masturbating but protecting his own share of the family property by refusing to do his duty of impregnating his dead brother's wife made no difference; the fate of Onan demonstrated God's disapproval of the waste of seed. Tissot himself made no religious points in his argument against masturbation, but he was a man of the eighteenth century, a doctor committed to Enlightenment rationalism. While Foucault has argued for a transition from clerical to medical control over sex, in which religion became increasingly irrelevant to the discourse, a close reading of many nineteenth-century doctors reveals that they saw themselves as evangelists, working for the redemption of the race. Meanwhile, nineteenth-century preachers and theologians took up the new findings of the doctors and incorporated them into Christian messages. This combination of medicine and Christianity was integrated into numerous schemes for reform and social movements during the nineteenth century. Enough of the doctors were women, and so many of the male doctors were especially concerned with women, that the modern women's movement can be counted among the offspring of the alliance between Christianity and Victorian medicine.

The medical transformation of Christianity took place in the context of global forces of nature and science. Though the thesis is still controversial, it seems likely that syphilis spread from the Americas to Europe in the wake of the rape and intermarriage that accompanied Spanish and French and English exploration, while Europeans brought gonorrhea to the Americas. Both diseases ravaged Christendom to a point at which it was estimated that, in the Berlin and Hamburg of 1900, 37 percent of males contracted syphilis between ages fifteen and fifty, while the average male contracted at least one case of gonorrhea.[12] The nineteenth century would witness the discovery, in 1879, of the gonococcus that caused gonorrhea and the development, in 1884, of a way to prevent blindness in children born of gonorrheal mothers by cleansing the eyes of the newborn with silver nitrate. The spirochete that causes syphilis was not discovered until 1905. Treatments for both diseases existed in 1900, but really effective treatment awaited the applications of salvarsan in the 1920s and penicillin after 1941.

Scientific knowledge of conception before the 1600s generally followed Aristotle in thinking that the father alone begat the child, with the mother providing material and nutrition; such reasoning resulted in male masturbation being considered a form of homicide in Catholic penitentials of the Middle Ages. Dissenting experts followed Galen, an ancient Roman physician who thought that women released a seed in orgasm, or the English scientist William Harvey, discoverer of the circulation of blood, who theorized in 1651 that all life came from the egg or ovum, which the male only stimulated to develop. In 1678, Antonius van Leeuwenhoek presented the English Royal Society with proof that seminal fluid contains microscopic animalcula, with round bodies and long tails, that swim independently. His evidence seemed to support Aristotle, but the defenders of the egg and of female semination did not give up. Catholic moral theology continued to link ovulation to female orgasm, with the intriguing result that all Catholic manuals of the nineteenth century taught that a married woman could licitly bring herself to orgasm by hand after coitus, because her orgasm pertained to the completion of the act and probably contributed at least to the perfection of any child conceived. In 1877, two hundred years after Leeuwenhoek saw sperm, the Swiss biologist H. Fiol observed a sperm cell entering the ovum of a starfish. Only in the 1920s would the process of ovulation in humans and its relation to conception be correctly understood, but both sperm and egg were securely identified by 1900.

Within the broadening spheres of disease and discovery, the Christian and medical discourses on sex proliferated and flowed together. Foucault long ago pointed out that the nineteenth century, far from being repressive of sex, actually invented "sexuality" as a separate subject, investigating it and presenting it as the great secret of life. But Foucault inherited Freud's tragic view of civilization, and so he missed the optimism that accompanied the discovery of sexuality. By studying sex, nineteenth-century experts hoped to banish many diseases, to manage heredity, to overcome original sin, and even to obtain world domination without war, through what the American theologian and pastor Horace Bushnell called "the out-populating power of the Christian stock." According to Elizabeth Blackwell, a pioneer among the seven thousand women who practiced medicine in the United States by 1900, "the regulation of sexual intercourse in the best interests of womanhood" was the "unrecognized truth of Christianity" that would soon yield "a fresh spring of vigour . . . for the human race."[13]

Americans led the way in developing the physical side of sexual medicine, though not in psychology. Building on the work of Dr. Sims, the inventor of the speculum, the United States had the first national society of gynecologists and eleven regional associations, more than in all of Europe and Russia, by 1880. Before Dr. John Harvey Kellogg invented the cornflake (itself intended as part of a diet that would restore sexual health), he studied at the Paris laboratory of Dr. Charcot, the same place where Freud first sought the secrets of hysteria. Unlike Freud, Kellogg continued to believe that physical (especially sexual) trauma caused nervous disease and that physical treatments beginning with diet could cure it. Kellogg set up his first sanitarium at Battle Creek, Michigan, under the auspices of the Seventh-day Adventist Church, which had paid his way to medical school; among the patients who sampled his cereals was C. W. Post, who founded General Foods. Both Kellogg and Post followed the path of Sylvester Graham, a former candidate for the Presbyterian ministry who pushed the country toward whole-wheat flour and invented the graham cracker, again as part of an effort to control sex. If sex were rightly ordered, Graham promised freedom from disease throughout life and death without pain.

Of course, most Christian health experts of the nineteenth century warned against overindulgence in sex. They spread the masturbation phobia, sometimes repeating Tissot's fear of the loss of fluids but more often focusing on the nervous shock of orgasm. Although marital sex was seen as less dangerous than masturbation, Graham recommended limiting it to once a month for healthy young people; by the end of the century, many experts, such as Kellogg and Dr. Mary Wood-Allen, who led the Purity Department of the W.C.T.U., set a standard of sex for procreation only.

But not everyone went so far, and even purity crusaders sometimes praised sexual pleasure. As Dr. Elizabeth Blackwell wrote in 1894, "In healthy loving women, uninjured by the too frequent lesions which result from childbirth, increasing physical satisfaction attaches to the ultimate physical expression of love." Blackwell praised the "repose and general well-being" arising from "natural occasional intercourse" and warned that "total deprivation" leads to "irritability." In an early expression of the distinction between vaginal and clitoral orgasm that would plague sexual medicine and psychology until Masters and Johnson in the 1960s, Blackwell criticized the "crude fallacy" of those who compared the penis with "such a vestige as the clitoris," while directing attention to the "vast amount of erectile tissue, mostly internal, in the female, which is the direct seat of special sexual spasm." Blackwell claimed that "the feeling of sex . . . is even stronger in women than in men," but she insisted that this referred only to sex "in its highest sense," as a "mental as well as physical phenomenon."

In regard to the cultivation of these higher feelings, Christian civilization was superior to all others. Parallels to Blackwell's fervently Christian language and hope could be drawn from virtually all of the many doctors who wrote on sex in the late nineteenth century. Even Dr. Horatio Bigelow, an advocate of regulated prostitution, compared Jesus Christ to the steam engine "as a practicable and available force" to overcome "sin and iniquity."[14]

Though Victorian doctors produced many warnings against excesses of passion and many prescriptions for limiting the frequency of sex, they also developed a consensus favoring mutuality in pleasure between husbands and wives. Dr. Russell Thacher Trall hoped for a time when the knowledge of ovulation would enable acts of intercourse to be limited to the number of desired offspring, yet believed that heredity improved if "as much at-one-ment as possible" prevailed between the spouses and that making sex "as pleasurable as possible to both parties" would prevent illicit lust. This consensus on mutual pleasure linked those who differed on other points. For example, Dr. Horatio Bigelow defended regulated prostitution as an application of the Christian view that humanity is "essentially bad," but urged husbands to love their wives with "all the necessary ardor" to help them "have the full genesic spasm." Dr. Alice Bunker Stockham, who practiced medicine in Kansas and Indiana from 1854 through 1887, then combined physical medicine with Christian

Science, Sexual Purity, and the Spirit of Christ

If we compare the mental and moral status of women, in a Mohammedan country, with the corresponding class of women in our own country, we perceive the effect which generations of simply sensual unions have produced. . . . In the savage state, in semi-barbarous countries, and in the slums of all great towns, both men and women are grossly unchaste. . . . To us medical women, the special guardians of human life, has been opened the path of scientific medical knowledge. . . . In that path, guided by our God-given womanly conscience . . . in the everlasting spirit of THE CHRIST . . . [we] will take part in that mighty work of regeneration, which from our present small beginnings will, I fully believe, grow and transfigure the twentieth century.

—Elizabeth Blackwell, Counsel to Parents on the Moral Evaluation of their Children (1879; New York: Brentano Brothers, 1883), 37; Elizabeth Blackwell, "The Human Element in Sex" and "Medical Responsibility in Relation to the Contagious Diseases Act," in Essays in Medical Sociology, (1902; New York: Arno Press, 1972), 1:104, 2:103–4.

Science and New Thought healing techniques until her death in 1912, wrote in 1883 that couples should have sex rarely but "take time for the act" and "have it entirely mutual from first to last." Count Leo Tolstoy was so impressed with Stockham's *Tokology: A Book for Every Woman* that he had it translated into Russian and wrote a preface saying that it dealt with "what nobody talks about and everybody needs to know." By 1896, when Stockham wrote *Karezza: Ethics of Marriage* to promote intercourse without orgasm as a way to enhance marital love, she had become an international celebrity, a visitor to Europe, Russia, India, China, and Japan who was praised by the W.C.T.U. and by British socialists.[15]

Doctors such as J. Marion Sims and John Harvey Kellogg, and pioneer women doctors such as Elizabeth Blackwell and Alice Bunker Stockham, all came from the United States and became world leaders in sexual medicine. With regard to sexual theory, Americans produced no accomplishments to rival Richard von Krafft-Ebing's classification of sexual behaviors (see below) or Freud's diagnosis of sexual development; American strength lay in practical science, as Alexis de Tocqueville had predicted. With regard to religion, European sexual medicine became more and more secular, even hostile, while American doctors maintained their ties with Christianity. Meanwhile, Protestant theologians in the United States began to sound like doctors. The greatest of antebellum revivalists, Charles Grandison Finney, warned in his *Systematic Theology* that those who "indulge themselves in a stimulating diet" turn their bodies into sources of "powerful and incessant temptation to evil tempers and vile affections." Horace Bushnell's *Christian Nurture* claimed that "the wrong feeding of children . . . puts them under the body," so that the "vice of impurity is taught . . . at the mother's table."[16]

From the 1840s to the present, Roman Catholic theology with regard to sex has been dealing with issues raised in the United States. The first American Catholic writer in moral theology, Archbishop Francis Kenrick of Philadelphia, whose *Theologiae Moralis* appeared in 1843, was also the first Roman Catholic theologian to list "to foster love" among the reasons why a husband might be obligated to offer his wife sex. Twenty-six years later, the French moralist Jean-Paul Gury produced the first text of moral theology by a European that added love to procreation, fulfillment of the marital contract, and avoidance of sin as an acceptable reason for married people to have sex. But even then, Europeans wrote nothing comparable to the general obligation that Archbishop Kenrick placed on men to love their wives. "The man sins gravely," said Kenrick, "when he makes his wife feel she is loved less, in order to make her unhappy, or expresses jealousy without good reason, or finds fault with her and treats her harshly because he wearies of her company." A husband "who frequents taverns, theaters, and other places . . . and does not return home until the night is already advanced; and who, not having known his wife," goes to sleep apart from her, fails "gravely" (and here Kenrick used an adverb that usually indicated mortal sin) with regard to "that affection with which a wife ought to be pursued."[17] Such a comprehensive and positive vision of marital sex and love would not become the mainstream of Catholic thought until personalism triumphed in the documents of Vatican II and the writings of Karol Wojtyla (later Pope John Paul II).

PURIFYING SEX

Archbishop Kenrick's focus on a wife's right to be loved connected with the women's movement, which was another part of the history of sex that emerged with special strength among Christians in the United States. As Dr. Elizabeth Blackwell noted in an address in London, the United States in 1889 had three thousand women practicing medicine, while England had only a handful; by 1900, the number of female physicians in America had reached 7,387.[18] Unlike in England and Europe, where the most prominent advocates of women's rights were humanists such as Mary Wollstonecraft and John Stuart Mill, in America most aspects of the women's movement were Christian. Oberlin College was led by evangelist Charles Grandison Finney in the 1830s, when it became the first American institution to grant degrees to women; the Seneca Falls Convention of 1848 took place in a Wesleyan Holiness church that belonged to the same tradition that had nurtured its leader, Elizabeth Cady Stanton; and women attained their first positions of political leadership in movements to abolish slavery and to prohibit alcohol that grew directly from Christian perfectionism. Women in America first wore pants in the Oneida Community, a group of about two hundred Christians practicing "complex marriage" and sex without male orgasm that lasted from the 1840s until the 1870s.

Though standard histories of feminism do not spend much time discussing convents of nuns and the Virgin Mary, nineteenth-century women had an enormous impact on the world and on the Christian settlement of sexual values through these vehicles. Communities of celibate women began in Christianity with the "widows" mentioned by Paul and continued through the desert hermits to whom Saint Jerome wrote letters and the formal orders of the Middle Ages, but until the nineteenth century, nuns were always much less numerous and significant than monks. With less need for large families and a growing middle class among industrial nations, the proportion of females to males in Catholic religious life suddenly reversed itself, so that by the twentieth century, Catholics had many more nuns than monks or priests. Between 1790 and 1920, 119 new orders for women were founded in Europe and 38 new orders in the United States. The number of nuns in the United States grew from about 200 in 1820 to 88,773 in 1920. Whole genres of literature, including pretended exposés such as Maria Monk's *Awful Disclosures of the Hotel Dieu Nunnery* (1835), in which nuns made pregnant by priests murdered their infants and destroyed the bodies in a lye pit, and pious novels by Catholic writers, presented the lives of nuns to the public. Meanwhile, appearances of the Virgin Mary, which had sometimes been reported by middle-aged men such as Saint Bernard of Clairvaux in the Middle Ages and by a Mexican male at Guadalupe in 1531, began to be described by young women, beginning with the twenty-year-old novice nun Catherine Laboure in Paris in 1830. That appearance gave rise to the Miraculous Medal, which bears the inscription "Mary, conceived without sin, pray for us." Decades before the Roman Catholic Church declared that Mary, alone among all human beings except for Jesus, had been conceived without original sin, the novice nun announced that doctrine, which implied that sex did not always pass original sin to children. In 1858, an even younger girl, the fourteen-year-old Bernadette Soubirous, drew tens of thousands to watch her pass into an ecstatic trance as she prayed to a woman who called herself "the Immaculate Conception." The Virgin became such a power that even a Protestant such as Henry Adams, a great historian of the Middle Ages who was descended from two very Puritan presidents and Lincoln's ambassador to Britain, made it the central task of his life to explain her history, though Adams did not notice that her cult still lived and grew around him in the nineteenth and twentieth centuries. Through the nuns and the Virgin, Catholic women represented the ideas that women could have religious lives apart from men; that women could lead men, even teaching new doctrine to the whole church; and that women could find transcendence in ecstasies that left them with no need for sex.[19]

The women of all Christendom had a great deal of ground to make up in the nineteenth century with regard to what most feminists saw as sexual purity and justice. Prostitution, already prevalent in the colonies, had exploded throughout the Western world as the Industrial Revolution called populations from traditional villages to new centers of production. By 1887, Wisconsin and Michigan had at least sixty camps housing 577 prostitutes, licensed by towns and inspected by doctors, near logging camps; locally licensed prostitutes worked not only in the wild Western cities of San Francisco and St. Louis but also in Boston and Newark. Nineteenth-century estimates of the numbers of prostitutes in Paris ranged from 30,000 officially registered with police to a total of 120,000; the London Society for the Suppression of Vice claimed that 80,000 prostitutes worked there, and Vienna was believed to have one prostitute for every seven adult males, though many were said to work primarily with tourists.[20] In 1886, no state in the United States set the age for a girl to consent to sex any higher than twelve; most had enacted the English common-law standard of ten, and the law of Maryland made girls of seven legally available for sex.

Despite more than forty years of feminism since Seneca Falls, despite alliances with evangelical churches and doctors, the crusade for "social purity" that Frances Willard represented at the Columbian Exposition of 1893 faced an uphill battle. During the Spanish-American War of 1898, the federal government established legal prostitution near army camps in Nashville, Tennessee, in Havana, and in the Philippines. This policy was reversed when Theodore Roosevelt, a friend of the purity movement, succeeded William McKinley as president, but it would still be decades before women could vote and even longer before the double standard for males and females underwent substantial change. Late in the 1940s, Kinsey found that two-thirds of American men had some experience of sex with prostitutes.

The conjunction of Fatima the veil dancer and Frances Willard revealed tension and contradiction, but also the potential for synthesis. Willard and the W.C.T.U. tried to ban all dancers in tights, including ballerinas, but here the reformers found themselves working against the tides of history. Most Christians of the late nineteenth and early twentieth centuries rejected the sexual ethic that saw sex as holy and exalted romantic love. They limited intercourse to procreation and sought to reduce sexual stimulus; instead, they tried to learn to dance. In an ethic I have called "innocent ecstasy," they came to agreement on a moral imperative that sex should be enjoyed to the limits of physical capacity without consciousness of guilt. Though disagreement persists about what behaviors should entail guilt, this overall standard remains. Real sensuality has lagged behind intellectual approval of sex, however, and suspicion of the body has both psychological and social effects. Modern versions of Fatima's theater still reveal one of the legacies of slavery and colonialism: the predominance of white Christian men in the audience and people of color, women, and non-Christians among the performers.

EXPLORING SEX

Perhaps the most enduring example of mutual influence between Christianity and sex in 1900 was the appearance and acceptance of Sigmund Freud and psychoanalysis. Though Freud was an atheist of Jewish descent, his system proved appealing to Christians from Carl Jung (the son of six generations of Swiss Reformed pastors) to G. Stanley Hall (a former candidate for the Congregational ministry who invited Freud and Jung to Clark University in 1909), and for good reason. Freud inherited and supported all of the restrictions of sex that Christian theologians and doctors had developed, from the masturbation phobia to the desirability of sublimation to the limitation of sex to genital acts between adult males and females (with all other acts condemned as perversion). Just as much as Sylvester Graham or John Harvey Kellogg, Freud saw sexual energy as a limited quantity that must be directed into healthy and productive channels. But even more importantly, he gave the Christian concept of original sin, which after Darwin was under attack but which had in some ways been rescued by relating it to sex, a place in the lives of individuals by means of the conflict of parent and child that he saw at the heart of both psychology and religion. For Freud, the old stories of Abraham nearly killing his son Isaac and God actually sacrificing Jesus reflected the feelings of all fathers and sons. The gospel message that sinners could be forgiven by admitting their desire to kill God and accepting that Jesus, who made himself equal to the Father, had been punished for this sin, made perfect sense to Freud. Even Christian anti-Semitism, which drove Freud from Vienna to London just before his death, seemed explicable to him as the natural resentment that Christians would feel toward those who had also killed God but who refused to admit their guilt as Christians did. In a sense, Freud derived his entire picture of sexual development from the Bible, or at least imposed biblical history (his own, distant father had been a Talmudist) on the histories of his patients. Whatever clinical successes his method obtained may have also derived from the background of his patients in a culture saturated in the biblical story. It seems unlikely that the South Sea Islanders, West African villagers, Indian swamis, and Japanese Buddhist leaders who attended the Columbian Exposition of 1893 would have found psychoanalysis as well suited to their personalities as did the Jews of Vienna or the children of Protestants in Switzerland, England, and America.

In a paper on the cause of hysteria that Freud delivered to the Viennese Society for Psychiatry and Neurology in 1896, Freud provided an image of the self, and of religion within the self, that corresponds to the image of Frances Willard and Fatima, the White City and the Midway, at the Columbian Exposition.

The phallic columns revealed the temple; perhaps the design of the temple also revealed what must be done. In the audience for this talk was Richard von Krafft-Ebing, the doctor who three years earlier, in his *Psychopathia Sexualis* (1893), had coined the word "hetero-sexual."

Krafft-Ebing did not believe Freud's hypothesis (which Freud later abandoned) that all hysterics suffered from sexual abuse as infants, but he surely sympathized with the judgments on certain types of sexual behavior that Freud expressed. According to Freud, sex acts that expressed and caused neurosis were "very repellent to the feelings of a sexually normal individual." The father of psychoanalysis referred specifically to acts in which "the buccal cavity [the mouth] and the rectum are misused for sexual purposes."[21] Before this, Western civilization had considered the morality of oral and anal sex only in the allowances for these acts within marriage that appeared in Catholic textbooks for confessors after 1743. With Freud and Krafft-Ebing, medical morality proved less permissive than Catholic readings of the Bible and natural law.

For Freud and the other pansexualist doctors and leaders of reform movements who were shaping the future of Christian civilization in 1900, sex had become religion, the secret of religion lay in sex, and the way of progress was a way of purification. The liberal sides of issues such as birth control, the legal status of homosexuality, premarital sex, easier divorce, and gay marriage would find Christian friends among the heirs of Victorian pansexualists who were constantly seeking perfect love. The extent to which Christians should tolerate cultures with different attitudes toward sex—especially Muslim cultures, but also Hindu and Buddhist, Japanese, Chinese, and African—would still come into question at times because the other cultures seemed too sensual, but more often because they offered too little freedom, whether for women or for sexual pleasure. Yet the heirs of Fatima have continued to do more dancing than their former colonial mistresses and masters, and the heirs of Frances Willard have continued to exhort.

Psychoanalysts explored pleasure and pain with metaphors drawn from archeology of the colonial age.

Imagine that an explorer arrives in a little-known region where his interest is aroused by an expanse of ruins . . . He may content himself with inspecting what lies exposed to view, with questioning the inhabitants—perhaps semi-barbaric people—who live in the vicinity, about what tradition tells them . . . and he may then proceed on his journey. But he may act differently. He may have brought picks, shovels and spades with him, and he may set the inhabitants to work with these implements. . . . If his work is crowned with success, the discoveries are self-explanatory: the ruined walls are part of the ramparts of a palace or a treasure-house; the fragments of columns can be filled out into a temple.
—Sigmund Freud, "The Aetiology of Hysteria" (1896), trans. James Strachey in The Freud Reader, ed. Peter Gay (New York: Norton, 1989), 97–98.

FOR FURTHER READING

Bloch, Ruth. *Gender and Morality in Anglo-American Culture, 1650–1800.* Berkeley: University of California Press, 2003.

Gardella, Peter. *Innocent Ecstasy: How Christianity Gave America an Ethic of Sexual Pleasure.* New York: Oxford University Press, 1985.

Kennedy, Kathleen, and Sharon Ullman. *Sexual Borderlands: Constructing an American Sexual Past.* Columbus: Ohio State University Press, 2003.

Noonan, John. *Contraception: A History of Its Treatment by the Catholic Theologians and Canonists.* 1965. Enlarged ed. Cambridge: Harvard University Press, 1986.

ECONOMIC CHANGE AND EMOTIONAL LIFE

JOHN CORRIGAN

CHAPTER THREE

CULTURES OF EMOTION

The historiography of Christianity in recent years has begun to explore the ways in which the religious lives of persons are shaped by socially embedded emotional codes. Such codes, which govern the performance and concealment of emotion in collective settings, and which condition behaviors privately enacted as well, are rarely explicit. Interwoven in culture with ideology about gender, race, class, sexuality, and other aspects of human life, sets of culturally grounded rules of feeling develop and are altered as social settings change. As historian William A. Christian Jr. has written in analyzing ritualized religious weeping in early modern Spain, the "relative frequency and intensity of emotions and their public expression varies from culture to culture and within cultures over time. This variation has a certain logic that we ought to be able to study and understand."[1] For medievalist Catherine Peyroux, one cannot appreciate Christian devotionalism without understanding the role of feeling. Peyroux warns that "when we write histories of the past in which feeling is omitted, we implicitly disregard fundamental aspects of the terms on which people act and interact, and we thus deprive ourselves of important evidence" for appreciating how "our subjects conducted the business of their lives."[2] Attention to emotion in the study of Christianity leads to engagement with unfamiliar data that complicate interpretation and inspire new perspectives about motivation, action, and collective meaning. Such an undertaking is potentially valuable, especially to a "people's history" focused on religious life that flourishes alongside the thought systems and institutions of official religion.

Although the current renaissance in emotions research is only beginning to make inroads to the history of Christianity, study of the historical relation of Christianity to capitalism is well established. The most familiar voice in this regard is that of Max Weber, who proposed the relation of Puritan inner-worldly asceticism to the emergence of capitalism. But Weber, too, noticed the emotional component of that linkage. His research ultimately took him in other directions, but not before he declared famously that the descendants of the Puritans were "specialists without spirit, sensualists without heart."[3] Karl Marx, who, like Weber, did not in the end systematically pursue the topic of emotion, also remarked on its relevance to the history of Christianity and to capitalism, complaining, somewhat uncharacteristically, for example, that the bourgeoisie had "drowned the most heavenly ecstasies of religious fervor . . . in the icy water of egotistical calculation."[4] Such statements, while sweeping, nevertheless provoke consideration of the possibilities for scholarly survey of the history of Christianity. Religion, emotion, and capitalism are intertwined, and it is through examination of their interrelationship that we can establish pathways into understanding religious experience, moral systems, authority, and community.

In this chapter I refer to collective emotion, and especially to emotional climates, which, as Joseph de Rivera has written, are "dependent on political, religious, economic and educational factors and may change within the course of a single generation." For Rivera, an emotional climate "may be labeled by using names for emotions, such as joy and fear," as well as by using terms that "directly refer to the emotional relationships that are involved, such as hostility or solidarity."[5] I organize this brief historical overview of emotion, capitalism, and Christianity with respect to three emotional climates, which I have designated (1) self-deception, (2) self-assurance, and (3) self-control. Each of these climates highlights a certain cluster of emotions. In the case of a climate of self-deception, fear and guilt are primary. Historical instancing of self-assurance references hope and joy. Discussion of climates of self-control corrals a wide range of emotions, including fear and hope, but with regard to certain patterns of affiliation among those various emotions. In each case, specific features of social orga-

nization as conditioned by the development of capitalism are represented in the emotional aspect of religious life.

The blind advance of capitalism has been accompanied by social
upheaval. To wade into debate about the precise ways in which societies have been created and destroyed by capitalism is to engage the
term in its most perilously freighted form and to risk stumbling under
its weight. I offer, then, with that qualification proffered, a few abbre-
viated claims about how capitalism has been involved in social change
and a few experimental definitions of capitalism that are of potential
use in thinking about religion and Christianity since 1650.

One cannot speak of capitalism without referring to commodities
and markets, and the mechanisms of trade that determined the relationship between them. In the seventeenth century, an increase in the
number and availability of commodities created a threshold of economic activity that made possible the explosive debut of capitalism
as an economic system in the eighteenth century. The consequence of
this event was the triumph of commodity, what historian of capitalism Michel Beaud has called "the reign of commodity." That reign is
evident in the "submission to market forces of all aspects of mankind's
life, and all aspects of society's functioning. . . . In a word: the commodification of man, society, and earth."[6] The reign of commodity
has been accompanied by the development of a culture of negotiation. Trade of commodities is made possible through agreement on
processes that determine the values of commodities and that structure
the exchanges that constitute trade. Transactions are negotiated. In
short, again, everything is a commodity, everything is negotiable, and
negotiation becomes cultural practice relevant to every aspect of life,
including religion.

Capitalism also has brought with it profound changes in the experience of social relations. Most importantly for our purposes, the
development of capitalism after 1650 coincided with the demise of
equitable relations among persons in society. This is not to say that
relations between aristocrat and peasant were equitable, but rather to
focus on the relationships among peasants themselves. Jane Schneider,
in extending the insights of anthropologists into interpretation of
European social history, has argued that we ought to see the social
world of the peasantry in early modern Europe largely in terms of

relationships guided by a strong sense of equity. That is, it was in the interest of members of the social group to avoid the appearance of inequities, to mask them, so as not to upset the fragile distribution of power in society. Such an environment was not well suited to the development of capitalism. As Schneider writes, "Capitalists could never have cultivated their self-confident 'spirit of capitalism' had their ethics kept them shackled to equitable exchanges with . . . the fellow members" of society. Only through the development of inequities, through the normatization of asymmetrical relationships of wealth and power, could the accumulation of property necessary for capitalism take place.[7]

The Reformation fostered emotions favorable to the development of capitalism by refining Christian theology in ways that focused on the struggle for individual salvation and separated that salvation from social custom. Some of the new forms of Christianity that had begun to establish themselves in the late Middle Ages and took definitive form in the sixteenth century were characterized by a theology that in several important ways distanced God from humanity. For Calvinists and those influenced by them, as well as for some other Reformation groups, God was less knowable, even unpredictable. God, unlike the spirit of an ancestor or a local spirit (such as a saint), was supremely powerful, potent far beyond the capability of humans to understand, and did not transact business with humans through equitable exchanges. God was, therefore, not inclined to negotiate with humans. Followers of Calvin, for example, learned that God predestined persons to heaven and to hell. The Counter-Reformation, in some of its incarnations, embraced Christianity as the icy judgment of a remote God. These movements within Christianity demanded that their adherents embrace an idea of relationship to God radically different from the relationship with the supernatural represented in the traditional pagan-inflected religiosity practiced by medieval peasants alongside their Christian devotions. Sometimes religion thus led the way in reshaping society, and economy followed. At other times, the growth of capitalism proved the impetus to theological rethinking. In many instances the two collaborated in reciprocal fashion, cutting a zigzag path through history by their give-and-take.

SELF-DECEPTION

The march of religious ideology that hastened the detachment of God from the everyday lives of persons frequently spurred on and reinforced the deterioration of equity in social relations that accompanied the rise of capitalism. The consequences of this dynamic process were significant. Loss of social equity and the specter of a God removed from negotiation threatened familiar patterns of feeling. Where equity set the predominant tone for relations with other persons—and with supernatural personages—individuals could engage in ritual activities of sharing and sacrifice that reinforced confidence in a fair system of exchange, in predictability, and in the possibility of systematically righting wrongs. But with God at a distance from the world, with communication all but ruined by unapproachability, there was little way of knowing whether one's words or behavior, were in fact "right." This led to doubt and to an assortment of emotional orientations we might gather together under the rubric of "self-deception" because they represent the self as "discovered" in its fraud, caught out on lies that it had embraced as the real.

It is impossible to read Puritan diaries without being struck by the ubiquity of guilt and fear. Operating under the terms of a theology that insisted on the inability of humans to influence their situation in the afterlife, Puritans worried constantly about whether they were "saved," that is, one of the godly, or whether their souls were permanently corrupt and destined for eternal punishment. As has often been pointed out, Puritans responded to this perceived impotence by imagining themselves in a covenantal relationship with God, a relationship that, while not explicitly acknowledged as such, offered a glimpse of a relationship with God that was rationalized according to terms incumbent on each party, God and the individual. But for the most part, Puritans who liked to think of themselves as among the elect at the same time fretted that they were only deceiving themselves. The diary of the English Puritan Samuel Ward illustrates how a concern with self-deception, and a fear of what might happen as a result, dominated his thinking in the early seventeenth century. Writing constantly about his "great fear" while at the same time declaiming, "Blessed is the man that feareth always," Ward prayed to God,

---

**Puritan Anticipation
of Final Judgment**

Now it comes in, and every sin
　　unto men's charge doth lay;
It judgeth them and doth condemn,
　　though all the world say nay.
It so stingeth and tortureth,
　　it worketh such distress,
That each man's self against himself,
　　is forcèd to confess. . . .

All filthy facts and secret acts,
　　however closely done
And long concealed, are there
　　revealed
　　before the mid-day sun.
Deeds of the night, shunning the light,
　　which darkest corners sought,
To fearful blame and endless shame
　　are there most justly brought.

And as all facts and grosser acts,
　　so every word and thought,
Erroneous notions and lustful motion,
　　are unto judgment brought.
No sin so small and trivial
　　but hither it must come,
Nor so long past, but now at last
　　it must receive a doom.
　　　　　—Michael Wigglesworth,
　　"The Day of Doom" (1662), in The
　　American Puritans: Their Prose and
　　Poetry, ed. Perry Miller (New York:
　　　　　Anchor Books, 1956), 288–89.

"Lett me not be convicted of dishonesty." Ward complained repeatedly that God seemed distant and inaccessible. His daily habit of writing was to confess guilt for his multitude of sins, which he listed. Totaling as many as several dozen in a day, they ranged from "my immoderate laughter" to "my slacknes in going to prayer" to "my over-much quipping" to "my ill dream." His most emotional confessions focused on how he sometimes fraudulently, and audaciously, believed himself to be spiritually upright, a defect that in his more clearheaded moments he often identified as his sin of "pride," by which he meant imagining himself more than he was, thus deceiving himself.[8] Weber wrote at length about these Puritans and the rise of capitalism, but we must understand especially that the Puritan God was distant and acted always from a position of vastly superior power. That God represented for Puritans an inequitable cosmos, a world in which persons did not take care to negotiate as equals. So, too, the social world of Puritanism eventually gave way to inequity as capitalism flourished. As long as God remained distant and inscrutable, Puritans remained guilty and afraid. These conditions, however, were favorable to the rise of capitalism.

The cluster of self-deception, fear, guilt, and the sense of a remote but judgmental God was especially visible in Salem, Massachusetts, in the 1690s, at a time when the advance of capitalism via the transatlantic trade was reshaping Puritan New England in dramatic fashion. In a colonial context marked by the obvious deterioration of equity, as represented by the new mansions on the waterfront, the fancy clothes, and the expensive furnishings, some Puritans experienced an episode of extreme social disorientation, imagining themselves under attack by demons who had slipped into the community, unchallenged by a far-off God. The language in the records of the Salem witch trials reveals the extent to which the emotions of fear and guilt came to the forefront of village life, framed always by charges of deception of self and others. The Salem examiners wanted to know of Sarah Good, "Hath the devil ever deceived you?" a common concern among the Puritan witch hunters in the village. They warned Rebecca Nurse to realize her self-deceptions with the entreaty, "If you be guilty pray God discover you," because, at bottom, "you do know whither you are guilty." Sarah Wilson relented to the court, professing that they knew her better than she knew herself and declaring that she "was in the dark as to the matter of her being a witch. And being asked how she was in the dark, she replied, that the afflicted persons crying out of her as afflicting them made her fearful of herself." Martha Tyler, under pressure to confess her witchcraft, finally admitted that she was "guilty of a great sin in belying of herself," and so emotionally that, said the court recorder, "it exceeds any pen to describe." Mary Taylor, likewise goaded to confess, turned the tables on her accuser and warned the woman that even "her God would deceive her."[9] The distance between humanity and the Calvinist God, a God pushed even farther from the community by the local spike of capitalist activity and the sudden deterioration of equitable relations among persons, is represented repeatedly at Salem in the guilt, fear, and anxiety about self-deception among the local population.

The rapid growth of capitalism in Spain in the late nineteenth and early twentieth centuries—a development historically linked to the social change and political polarization that precipitated the Spanish Civil War—likewise brought with it theological recalibration. Changed by their experience of the new social order of capitalism, many persons, especially migrating Spanish males, found the Roman Catholic experience of an accessible and generally benevolent God altered as well. The men who returned to their villages in the Piedramilla region, in northern Spain, after a time spent in social worlds restructured by capitalism, brought back with them a sense of their distance from God and a concomitant sense of guilt about that relationship. Observing the miraculous animation of sacred statuary—in this case the movement of the figure of Jesus on the cross of the local church—they were struck with fear, fainting in terror having glimpsed the head of Jesus turned suddenly toward them, the open eyes gazing blankly at them. As the local priest wrote to his bishop, "There are some men and boys from the village who almost always see it; and some are so scared that now they do not dare to go and look at it." Women and children, who had not been to other places in Spain where the social order was being transformed by capitalism, also saw the crucifixes move. In their case, however, the Jesus figure smiled sweetly and happily. If they fainted, it was not from fear bordering on terror but from a sense of being flooded with love.[10]

In colonial Africa we see another instance of the religious culture of self-deception. Traders and entrepreneurs from Holland, "the capitalist nation *par excellence*" in the words of Karl Marx, were in the African Cape by the middle of the seventeenth century. There the Reformed Church, with its Calvinist theology that discouraged negotiation with God by emphasizing the predestined fates of persons, played a key role in shaping the colonial culture. Framed by religion, capitalism and racism converged in an aggressive Boer (or Afrikaner) colonial culture—the cultural practice of colonizing generally expressing capitalist sensibilities after 1650—that fixed the distance between itself and native Africans in a series of confrontations beginning with the Xhosa military engagements with Trek Boers in the late eighteenth century. As part of their developing colonialist mentality, Afrikaners took African natives to be radically different, inferior as producers of wealth, and religiously deficient. As the Afrikaner economy advanced, and especially with the success of mining in the nineteenth century, they became confirmed in their view of themselves as the part of the social body preferred by God. While one might imagine that Afrikaner piety accordingly would be characterized by assurance and a sense of security, in fact that was not the case. The diaries of Afrikaans women kept during this period reveal their authors' piety to be characterized above all by guilt and by such a sense of self-deception that they invented rituals of self-humiliation and self-hate, in the form of prolonged and excessive confession of sins, as the means by which to represent their attempt to discover wrong in themselves.[11]

SELF-ASSURANCE

Religious cultures of self-assurance are more likely to be associated with social situations in which relations between persons are conducted more equitably than is the case with cultures of self-deception. Where power is more evenly distributed in society, and where theology situates God more clearly as a partner in transactions with humans, religious expression is more likely to represent emotions of hope, wonder, acceptance, and comfort. Instances in which these elements converged are numerous in the period 1600–1900. The maturing of the Industrial Revolution, the refinement of banking and finance infrastructures, and the advance of communication and travel technologies complicated nineteenth-century religious cultures of emotion. In settings where power was to some extent shared and where capitalism developed slowly, however, the mood sometimes was one of assurance. Religious ideology in such cases made God a divine neighbor. The several legacies of the Enlightenment—including the promotion of reason and self-reliance, among other things—played a role in reinforcing cultures of self-assurance. They also frequently recast the religious sensibilities of those cultures, however, and to such an extent that it is difficult to compare, for example, the self-assured Unitarian culture of late nineteenth-century America with the similarly self-assured religious culture of rural French Catholicism of the same period. Feelings of assurance were present in different ways in Christian communities as modernity gathered momentum in its reshaping of social relations.

In seventeenth-century Germany, under the theological umbrella of Lutheranism, we find some instances of the religious culture of self-assurance. As the German historian Peter Blickel has pointed out, a number of regions in Germany (especially in parts of the south and in the southwest) that embraced emergent Lutheranism were characterized by strong experiences of communal solidarity, or *Gemeinde*. These close-knit communities, many of which were in southern Germany, retained traditions of equitable relations between community members well into the seventeenth- and eighteenth-century development of capitalist economics. Lutheranism played a role in that retention by offering theological arguments for the support of the "common man" and the "common good," even in places farther north.[12] With its emphasis on salvation through faith, and an orientation toward the world represented by the motto "Sin boldly," Lutheran Christianity offered its followers the vision of a God who was close enough to humanity to forgive trespasses, yet distant enough so as not to be swayed by earnest "good works." God knew the heart of the sinner and the sinner's desire for forgiveness. As in cases of customary social relations between persons in places where there was strong *Gemeinde*, more formal means of religious transaction, such as the infamous purchase of Catholic indulgences, were unnecessary for these Christians.

The classic work of Christian devotion, *Pia Desideria*, published in 1675 by Philipp Jakob Spener, a Lutheran pastor in Frankfurt, reveals much of the same religious self-assurance. Overflowing with appeals to "heart religion," the book likened the relationship of a person to God as a matter of family, or community, love. It modeled Christian piety as a matter of hope and joy and pictured the Christian promise of salvation as assurance given by a friend, rather than the outcome of uncertain negotiations with a distant and mysterious divine personage. Moreover, it placed lay religious endeavor on an equal footing with activities involving clergy. This message was most impressively embodied in the early eighteenth-century community of Moravian Brethren who found refuge at Herrnhut, a village built for them by Spener's godson Count Zinzendorf on his estate in Saxony. Like Spener, Zinzendorf conceived of the three members of the Trinity joined with believers as a family, sometimes referring to the Holy Spirit as "mother." His sense of equity was manifest, in one way, in his encouraging women to preach and his support for their ordination. He professed the certainty of knowing God by feeling God. At Herrnhut, in an environment standing apart and protected from social dislocations arising from the German development of market capitalism, the Moravians built community founded on trust between neighbors and in God.

In various places in France during the eighteenth and nineteenth centuries, other Christians likewise shaped a religious culture characterized by trust and assurance and, in some instances, through direct engagement with emergent capitalism. French Catholicism varied widely in its style from region to region. In the Midi, the southern region, extending from the Pyrenees in the southwest to the Alps in the northeast, which was not fully joined to France (politically) until 1860, Catholics favored a baroque piety that included frequent church attendance along with festivals, processions, and other spectacular public performances. Unlike the more sober and orthodox Catholicism of the Vendee, and certainly distinct from the unenthusiastic Catholicism of Paris, piety in the Midi was neither intellectual nor mystical.

Catholicism bore a long theological tradition focused on transactions with God—through prayer, the sacraments, good works, and perhaps most famously, indulgences. Such a notion rested on trust that God was near, listening, and prepared to engage in exchange. At times, it is true, persons came to despair over their spiritual state when, under the expectation of engaging in friendly conversation with God, they experienced no answer to prayer, nor comfort for their worries about their salvation. The medieval religious anguish of Albigenses or Cathari penitents in procession offer the most striking image of guilt and fear, and as historian Ralph Gibson has argued, the "religion of fear" prevailed in France until the nineteenth century. But God for the most part was not remote, and peasant communities in both the South and the Midi remained rooted in traditions of equity. When capitalism did come to those regions, Catholics understood it in relation to familiar religious practices of transaction with God and within the context of equitable community order. Accordingly, it did not reinforce theological and social ideas of inequity and distance. Rather, read as a code of negotiation, capitalism tipped the religious style of these regions toward positive emotional orientations. As Gibson has observed, "What is crucial about the history of Catholicism in France in the nineteenth century, however, is that this fear-laden religion was gradually replaced by one of reciprocal love between God and man."[13] This was above all true for the Midi.

Such was the way in which capitalism, absorbed into social life against a specific local background, contributed to self-assurance

> ## A Religion of Trust
> Hope, cross in hand, walks before us on the path to life. . . . The spiritual world, shining with the emblems of eternal union, is but the radiance of Christ living among men to satisfy their hunger for truth and love.
>
> —Abbé Gerbet, the eventual bishop of Perpignan, in 1829, quoted in Ralph Gibson, A Social History of French Catholicism 1789–1914 (New York: Routledge, 1989), 252.

rather than to self-deception. Over a century and a half later, community life in parts of the Midi, such as Languedoc, was still distinguished by a social praxis in which, as Winnie Lem has shown, the "parameters of the market, ironically, guided participants in their reckoning of equivalence, potentially setting limits on the exploitative tendencies inherent" in exchanges.[14] This was assurance, whether it be in reckoning one's relationship to human trading partners or to God.

We see again how religion, emergent capitalism, and an emotions culture characterized by assurance came together in Russia in the latter part of the nineteenth century. There, with the completion of a network of railways, agricultural products came to play a key role in the development of the market economy. Russia became the world's largest exporter of grain, and Russian business cycles followed European business cycles as the Russian economy was integrated into the world economy. "Normal" market principles increasingly set the terms for prices and costs. However, the social world of the Russian peasantry, embedded especially in the traditions of the agricultural commune, changed little and gave the appearance of being an economic world apart from the developing market economies elsewhere in Russia. For Russian Orthodox peasants, social life remained largely a communal experience reinforced by a Christian theology that deemphasized hierarchies of authority (such as were characteristic of Roman Catholicism) and envisioned the church as an organic whole, each member joined to another in a great spiritual union. Suffering and struggle loom large in the pages of Dostoevsky's nineteenth-century novels, but that should not obscure the fact that for the Orthodox Russian there was little separation between the human and the divine. And it should not prevent us from appreciating Dostoevsky's deeply felt assurance that salvation is a matter of solidarity with others as well as trust in God.[15]

The convergence of Orthodoxy, peasant society, and market economies in late Tsarist Russia, somewhat like the process of change that

> ### Salvation in Community
>
> Love a man even in his sin, for that is the semblance of Divine Love and the highest love on earth. Love all God's creation, the whole and every grain of sand in it. Love every leaf, every ray of God's light. . . . My friends, pray to God for gladness. Be glad as children, as the birds of heaven. . . . There is only one means of salvation, then take yourself and make yourself responsible for all men's sins.
>
> —Father Zosima in Fyodor Dostoevsky's The Brothers Karamazov (1880), trans. Constance Garnett, ed. Ralph E. Matlaw (New York: Norton, 1976), 298–99.

we have observed in the nineteenth-century Midi and in Lutheran towns, took place within an environment that was partially insulated from more aggressive capitalist enterprise on its margins. In a different example of emotional assurance, English Quakers succeeded as entrepreneurs in major business enterprises during the initial period of English industrialization in the eighteenth and nineteenth centuries in ways that dovetailed with their feelings of closeness to God. The extent of Quaker involvement is a matter of record. Quakers were exceptionally active as entrepreneurs and investors, prospering in an international business environment in which risk was high and corruption was rampant. George Fox, the founder of the Society of Friends, spoke especially clearly to the latter problem, complaining about the "deceitful merchandise and cheating and cozening" that plagued commerce in his day. As far as Fox was concerned, Quaker piety was completely inconsistent with that kind of behavior. Quakers emphasized the experience of the Inner Light, which represented a strong confidence in the nearness of God; the "quakings" of persons in prayer typically were interpreted as indications of contact with the divine. The Society, moreover, valued equality among members and, in fact, was renowned for its leadership in abolitionist crusades, its refusal to stratify its community by gender, and its promotion of trust between individuals as the bedrock of ethical practice. Quakers, following Fox, believed that they "knew God experimentally," that is, through experience. Accordingly, they trusted that God heard their prayers and responded to them lovingly, and they described their religious life as a rich spirituality of hope and joy. William Penn, a convert to the Society of Friends, expressed such a view of Quaker religiosity when he wrote of Fox: "Thus he lived and sojourned among us, and as he lived so he died, feeling the same eternal power that had raised and preserved him in his last moments. So full of assurance was he that he triumphed over death."[16]

Quaker entrepreneurial activity developed within a matrix of business contacts with other "family" members. The meetinghouse served as a business clearinghouse in the sense that it provided both a footing for commercial success—providing stability and sharing risk— and a refuge from the world. English Quakers, who were among the principal shareholders in several English railway ventures in the

Fig. 3.1. Popular perception of the combination of business skill and a steady, positive emotional disposition in Quakers made the Oats logo a success. "Quaker Oats Man," registered ® logo, Quaker Oats image created by Haddon Sundblom, 1957. The Quaker® logo is a trademark of Quaker, a unit of Pepsico Beverages & Foods.

early nineteenth century, operated like other investors in searching out profitable enterprises and negotiating their involvement in them. At the same time, they remained deeply conscious of their difference from non-Quaker partners and passed over investment opportunities in cases in which the business did not appear honest and forthright. Feeling assured of their closeness to God, and trusting that God would guide their commercial undertakings, they chose not to involve themselves in projects that did not conform to standards set by the code of conduct clearly set forth in the London Yearly Meetings. In this way they launched strikingly successful business initiatives within the broader culture of English commerce while at the same time maintaining some measure of adherence to a social ideology that rested famously on the equality of the members. All of this flourished under an emotional umbrella of hope and trust in God, a felt nearness to God that Quakers joyously confessed in prayer, to each other, and to non-Quakers.

EMOTIONAL CONTROL

The gradual but decisive turn toward emotional control in modernity has been the focus of a wide range of scholarship, from Norbert Elias's early twentieth-century investigations of the coalescence of social conventions to Peter Stearn's recent studies of anger and jealousy. Social change arising from shifting demographic patterns, migration, adoption of technology, communications improvements, the implementation of democratic forms of government, and, not least of all, the maturation of capitalism as an economic system has resulted in a strengthening of ideals of emotional control. This process has taken place most obviously in places where Christianity is the predominant religion, including the nations of Western Europe as well as in many of their far-flung colonies that have become sovereign nations.

The tendency in modernity toward emotional control has developed alongside the disintegration of the "peasant community" and the corresponding acceptance of both mobility and inequities in the structuring of society. As we have seen, a key part of the transition to capitalist economy was the willingness of populations to accept that new opportunities for wealth, mobility, and status would coincide with differences in property ownership among people who, in previous generations, shared a common lot. If capitalism were to succeed, persons had to be willing to accept such differences and the "rightness" of social asymmetry in communities previously committed to maintaining at least the appearance of even distribution of wealth and power.

At the same time, however, that traditional notions of community were decaying, persons found ways to order social relations that deflected some of the consequences of the loss of *Gemeinde*. Nationalism, especially as it coalesced under the umbrella of a civil religion, grew more fervent. The development and enrichment of social institutions in the areas of education, government, commerce, and the military likewise offered a certain kind of alternative to traditional community (stable but not personal). Kinship networks, though weakened by migration, still provided a point of reference for collective identities. And religious community, taking many different forms, served as a social standpoint for persons as they hashed out available meanings of belonging, status, authority, and power.

The God of modernity, of that part of the population that was most affected by these social changes and that embraced most fully these alternatives, was a God who was both distant and close. The God associated with a religious culture of self-deception was far off and inscrutable, acting and judging according to a set of principles and standards that were simply unavailable to humanity. The religious culture of self-assurance, on the other hand, was grounded in trust that God was always near at hand, listened to and understood prayer, shared with humanity a clear set of understandings about good and evil and agency and outcomes, and could be relied upon to act predictably and generally benevolently. The religious culture of self-control was associated with a theological position that combined elements of the other two in ways that encouraged equanimity in the face of unpredictable change. God's will was sometimes obvious and at other times obscure. God was available to humanity in prayer and worship, but sometimes God did not respond to prayer nor to collective performances of devotion in institutional settings. God was sometimes high in the heavens and at other times walking side by side with the faithful on earth. Moreover, there was a substantial amount of theological volatility in the religious culture of self-control. God might seem impossibly alien one day, and the next like a member of the family. Prayer might bring joy and assurance for months on end, then suddenly be answered only with doubt, guilt, and forlornness. The movement between these emotional states and the determination of persons to control that movement formed the core of the religious culture of self-control. Belief in God was a good bet, and the emotional rewards of investing oneself in pursuit of contact with God were great. At the same time, the potential tragedy of seeking God and not finding him, or of believing that God would act in one way only to discover that God had a completely different purpose in mind, was a risk that believers had to take.

The religious culture of self-control, then, was a middle ground characterized by volatility and therefore framed through consideration of the merits of self-control. One ventured boldly into a faithful reliance upon God, but not so boldly as to burn one's bridges to self-reliance. As for the capitalist investor, a certain amount of risk was good for the system, but immoderate risk, the overinvestment in a certain commodity, was dangerous. The regulation of investment, the assumption of reasonable risk, was the key to successful capitalist venture just as it was the key to religious life. Control of emotion—not the stifling of emotional life but the regulation of it—likewise was the key principle governing the emotional orientation of persons in this kind of religious culture. Persons felt hope and joy, experienced trust in God, and engaged in dramatic performances of emotion involving weeping, howling, and other behaviors. Persons also sometimes felt distant from God, separated by a gulf of doubt and fear, and they poured out their sense of guilt about that experience in public and private displays. Most importantly, persons recognized that a certain amount of emotional expression, representing their faith in God, was good for the soul, while at the same time they were careful not to invest so deeply in that faith that they could not rebound emotionally when their hopes did not pan out. In practice, this style of religiosity frequently took shape as a movement back and forth between active, creative emotional expression and a more careful and limited approach.

Some of the complexities redolent in a religious culture of emotional control can be observed in the case of the Businessman's Revival of 1858. This American Protestant revival, which spread quickly throughout the nation—fanned by newspaper reports of extraordinary happenings at prayer meetings—followed directly on the heels of the economic crash of 1857. The crash, which came about initially through the failure of railroad construction ventures and which spread from there to other sectors of the economy, paralyzed the nation's trade, choked currency circulation down to a trickle, and resulted in mass unemployment as well as the suicides of many unsuccessful investors. In analyzing the reasons for the crash, investigators subsequently came to the conclusion that the market had become "overheated." While making clear that entrepreneurial capitalism could advance only if persons were willing to take a certain amount of risk with their capital, reports on the crash stated equally clearly that there should be limits to investment. Various academic societies and government leaders called for regulatory codes that insured against wildly speculative investment. Experts declared that the market worked best when it was "excited" short of the point of "frenzy." When speculation became "frenzied," when managers departed from sound standards of regulation of investment, the market in a burst of activity overheated, burning itself out and collapsing. The trick accordingly was in determining just how far to excite the market, how much capital to feed it, so that it attained peak performance without tumbling out of control.

The Protestant Christianity that framed the revival was undergoing significant change in the 1850s. The doctrine of predestination, which had shaped American Congregationalism (as well as several other denominational theologies), was becoming a thing of the past. The remote God of Calvinism was by degrees giving way to the more approachable, more responsive God of nineteenth-century evangelicalism, particularly through the influence of an assortment of innovative theologians, from Charles Grandison Finney to Horace Bushnell. Protestant prayer manuals popular in the 1850s assumed that Christians trusted God to respond directly to their petitions. Manuals, in fact, warned readers that unless one asked for something in prayer, one's faith was weak, and that the more specific and ambitious the

THIS IS NOT THE NEW YORK STOCK EXCHANGE, IT IS THE PATRONAGE EXCHANGE, CALLED U. S. SENATE.

Fig. 3.2. "This Is Not the New York Stock Exchange, It Is the Patronage Exchange, Called the U.S. Senate" (1881) by J. A. Wales. For *Puck*'s readers, frenzied commercial activity on the floor of the New York Stock exchange was of a cloth with certain kinds of political enthusiasm.

prayerful request, the better it expressed trust in God to deliver. Prayer increasingly became the centerpiece of Protestant devotions, so that by 1858 religious gatherings purely for the purpose of prayer were common in congregations in most cities. The Businessman's Revival, which took its name from the unusually large number of businessmen who attended the noon-hour prayer meetings, was a mass exercise in petitionary prayer. Persons typically wrote their requests on pieces of paper as they entered the meeting room, and then, during the course of the hour, slips were pulled from the box one by one and collective prayer offered for everything from the cure of an alcoholic spouse to the recovery of a sick child to a better job to a woodpile to last the winter. The God of the revival was a God with whom persons could negotiate in prayer. Christians, in fact, offered their "hearts" to God, treating them as commodities, in exchange for those favors that they believed God could grant them. Like the capitalist world of commodities that were exchanged according to certain rules, and with an eye to certain values, Protestants valued their "heart" (that is, the emotional self) above all and offered it to God in the expectation of receiving

something in return. What made the transaction particularly engaging and exciting was the chance that God would not respond, that a person could not know for certain that the transaction would be completed. Petitioners risked experiencing profound anxiety and despondency in such cases. Such risk kept the relations between Christians and their God from becoming simple, fully calculable, mean transactions. It made petitionary prayer an adventure, and the payoff to prayer more dearly appreciated than in a system in which returns were entirely predictable and unenchanted.

Fig. 3.3. The performative connection to religion, as in this strikingly similar nineteenth-century depiction of the Salem witch trials, likewise was obvious. The Trial of George Jacobs, August 5, 1692 by T. H. Matteson, 1855. Photo: The New York Public Library/Art Resource, N.Y.

Weeping was typical in the prayer meetings. Various other kinds of emotional expression, including shouts of joy, were encouraged. But the revival was not like earlier revivals, in which persons fainted, rolled on the floor, barked, and enacted other dramatic performances of emotion, setting a more "frenzied" tone for the gathering. Rather, the Businessman's Revival in most places unfolded in a more controlled fashion, with certain limitations expressly stated (for instance, no more than three minutes per prayer from anyone in the congregation) and assumed (shaking, wild shouting, jumping, barking, and other revival exercises were rare). Businessmen, after all, had to return to work that afternoon and thus could not afford to drift too far from the civility of the streets and office. The preeminence of the noon-hour meeting is in fact understandable precisely for its place in the middle of the day, when worshipers could not afford to engage in a "frenzy" that would make it impossible for them to put in a productive afternoon in commerce.

The Businessman's Revival, then, exemplifies the manner in which several cultural streams flowed together in a religious event: (1) the American experience of capitalism as an economic system that required a certain amount of excitement but not so much as to become over-heated; (2) the God close by with whom one could negotiate in prayer but whose will could not always be known; and (3) the combination of encouragement of emotional expression and limitations placed upon it in prayer meetings. These three streams together constituted the religious culture of self-control in mid-nineteenth-century American Protestantism.[17]

Religious cultures of self-control similar to that of the Businessman's Revival were present in other places during the period 1650–1900, although in almost all instances they were nineteenth-century phenomena. The maturation of capitalism, though a rapid process once begun, contributed to a religious culture of self-control only after it intersected with a religious ideology that joined images of God as both near and distant. That did not happen until the early nineteenth century, when, on the heels of the Enlightenment, Christianity began a century-long process of selective absorption of empirical and ratio-nalistic philosophies and sought to come to terms with science, tech-nology, the dramatization of racial and gender inequalities, and other potentially liberalizing cultural events.

The emergence of religious cultures of self-control against the background of nineteenth-century transitions can be observed in some other contexts, such as in France, where it took shape in con-nection with a new devotion. That devotion, centered on the Sacred Heart of Jesus, reached its peak in the campaign to build the Sacré Coeur in Montmartre in Paris. The image of the heart of Jesus, which had played a growing role in French Catholicism since the seven-teenth century, became a popular emblem of conservative Cathol-icism in the nineteenth century. Catholics in the western parts of

France, including the Vendee and surrounding areas, developed an especially strong connection with the Sacred Heart. During this time, industrialization and the development of capitalism were proceeding rapidly in many parts of France, including in the western port city of Nantes, on the Loire River. The economy of Nantes changed rapidly in the nineteenth century as the city became a major shipbuilding site as well as a leader in sugar refining and preserved foods. By the 1880s, there were at least four financial journals in that city that steered persons to banks and brokerage houses that offered investment opportunities. The social bonds of the peasant economy in the area of Nantes were reshaped, with the consequence that the peasant "community of equity" gave up much ground to a new social order in which differences of wealth and status developed. The older system did not entirely collapse, however. Many features were retained, with the result that social bonding itself remained relatively strong throughout the century.[18]

Unlike Catholicism elsewhere in France in the nineteenth century, the religion of persons in the region remained strongly orthodox. In contrast to the Midi, which had always been to an extent experimental in its piety, the western part of the nation, with some exceptions here and there over a few hundred years, embraced the notion of a God who reigned from heaven on high and who did not hesitate to bring down violent judgment on the people. Nantes itself, though more supportive of the French Revolution in the 1790s than some other towns in the region, by the late nineteenth century boasted one of the highest church attendance rates of any city in France, exceeding 90 percent for men and 97 percent for women.[19] That ultra-Montanist orthodoxy translated into, among other things, periodic bouts of anxiety, especially guilt arising from perceived drift from the religion of Rome. Nevertheless, this region of France, like others, was at the same time moving away from a religion of fear toward one characterized by a notion of reciprocal relationship with a loving God. Nantes was one of the most important places in France for the development of devotion to the Sacred Heart, a piety drenched in images of tenderness, refuge, love, and care. In places like Nantes, however, love did not simply replace fear, and a sense of reciprocity did not entirely replace consciousness of God's judgment. Rather, the assurance of God's love and protection developed alongside the more established perception of God as judge and avenger with whom one did not negotiate. The delicate balance between expectations for social equity rooted in peasant community and the experience of stratification and inequity made more visible by the growth of capitalism was religiously represented in the blending of vengeance and love in the figure of God.

The intermingling of doubt and assurance in the practice of Catholics in Nantes is evident in the words of Monsignor Felíx Fournier, who delivered a sermon following the German defeat of the French in 1870. Fournier previously had pictured God as a parent outraged by the behavior of a child, explaining that the defeat in war "can only be because we are guilty: sin attracts the terrible blows of divine justice." In his sermon, he placed this aspect of God alongside God's other, loving aspect, which was symbolized by God's presence in the Sacred Heart of Jesus.[20]

In a city that was poised between traditional social order and a new experience of status and wealth distinctions that came with the development of capitalism, Christianity took shape as a balance of fear and hope, of trust and doubt. Most importantly, this balance was tenuous and required constant vigilance so as not to topple one way or another. People had to control their feelings of loving union with God enough to remember that God was punishing them for not keeping to the narrow road of Catholic orthodoxy. At the same time, people were to remember that in the midst of their anguish and guilt over their sinfulness, they had refuge available in the Sacred Heart.

This kind of monitoring of the self, while not precisely the same as that practiced by participants in the Businessman's Revival, nevertheless represents a form of the religious culture of self-control as it emerged in local form in a nineteenth-century Christian context.

The Interplay of Fear and Assurance

[J]ustice is passing over France like a tempest. . . . In your anguish you will ask me if there is no refuge against this tempest of divine anger. . . . There is one. . . . [The Sacred Heart] will receive us with gentleness and tenderness, and when we are hidden in his sweet and mysterious recesses, we will have nothing more to fear, neither from the world nor from the inferno.

—Monsignor Felíx Fournier, Bishop of Nantes (1870), quoted in Raymond A. Jonas, "Anxiety, Identity, and the Displacement of Violence during the Annee Terrible: The Sacred Heart and the Diocese of Nantes, 1870–1871," French Historical Studies 21 (1998): 62–64.

FEELINGS AND ECONOMIC ORDER

The practice of Christianity has developed over centuries and continues to develop in social settings where people enact their feelings. Performances of emotion in Christianity accordingly ought to be seen in connection with the social environments in which they flourish. Because every social environment is different, and because changes in the communities that make up these environments result from a myriad of influences, generalizations about the character of social order are most useful when engaged as scaffolding that helps organize the details of historical understanding. The interpretation of the relationship between religion, emotions, and capitalism proposed in this chapter, then, is more suggestive than definitive and rests on a view of social order as leaning more or less toward equity. That is, in some settings, people are committed to at least giving the appearance that negotiations about commodities (from the sale of fish to the marrying of a daughter) take place on a relatively equal ground. In other places and times, social experience is one of inequity, of asymmetrical power relations and lack of any attempt to pretend otherwise. In this chapter, various kinds of Christian outlooks as well as emotional styles have been charted alongside different kinds of social order. There is much flexibility in the definitions offered here of three kinds of emotional cultures—self-deception, self-assurance, and self-control—as distinctive blendings of those outlooks and styles. At the same time, taking a lead from Max Weber and his analyses of religion, economy, and social order, these three types of religious cultures of emotion are "ideal types" that ought to serve as clearly distinct categories of emotional performance.

The emotions named in this chapter do not constitute a complete list of what we find in the three religious cultures of emotion between 1650 and 1900. Alongside love and fear, there were jealousy and wonder. Besides feeling guilty or hopeful, religious persons felt angry and sad. Individuals and groups regularly enacted terror. Many wept with joy. Emotions such as these, which played central roles in the religious lives of people, sometimes register in a pattern of feeling that one finds in the three cultures outlined above. Sometimes they do not. It is the fact of those cases in which some emotions or clusters of emotion do not seem at home in the categories offered here that provokes thought about ways to complicate our understanding of the intersection of the history of Christianity with the history of feeling. In the twenty-first century, a globalism driven by capitalist ideology has profoundly affected the ways in which we experience and think about community. It likewise has challenged the ways we imagine ourselves as feeling creatures. Christianity as a global religion, and as a repository of different kinds of "feeling rules" and "feeling rituals" that have served culture in the past, has continued to play a role in the process of human adaptation. For many persons, indeed, it remains a primary reference point, a model, for how to feel.

FOR FURTHER READING

Beaud, Michel. *A History of Capitalism 1500–2000.* Translated by Tom Dickman and Anny Lefebvre. New York: Monthly Review Press, 2001.

Corrigan, John. *Business of the Heart: Religion and Emotion in the Nineteenth Century.* Berkeley: University of California Press, 2002.

Corrigan, John, Eric Crump, and John Kloos. *Emotion and Religion: A Critical Assessment and Annotated Bibliography.* Greenwood, Conn.: Greenwood, 2000.

Gibson, Ralph. *A Social History of French Catholicism 1789–1914.* New York: Routledge, 1989.

Stearns, Peter N., and Carol Z. Stearns. "Emotionology: Clarifying the History of Emotions and Emotional Standards." *American Historical Review* 90 (1985): 813–36.

Weber, Max. *The Protestant Ethic and the Spirit of Capitalism.* Translated by Talcott Parsons. New York: Scribner's, 1958.

VULGAR SCIENCE

RONALD L. NUMBERS

CHAPTER FOUR

The founders of modern science often treated the common people with contempt. The great German astronomer Johannes Kepler, in dedicating his *Mysterium Cosmographicum* (1596) to his noble patron, insisted that he wrote "for philosophers, not for pettifoggers, for kings, not shepherds." He dismissed "the majority of men" as too stupid and ignorant to appreciate his work. The English natural philosopher Isaac Newton reportedly told an acquaintance that "he designedly made his *Principia* abstruse" in order to "avoid being baited by smatterers in Mathematicks." A spokesman for the newly founded Royal Society in England celebrated the fellows' lack of "ambition to be cry'd up by the common Herd." Given the lack of interest that most people showed in the arcane worlds of natural philosophy and natural history, it may have been prudent of Kepler, Newton, and the founders of the Royal Society not to seek public approval. However, there is no excuse for historians of science and religion to adopt a similarly condescending attitude toward the common people. Thanks to recent research on the history of popular science and popular Christianity, we are now in a good position to sketch out a new, populist narrative, one that features the views and attitudes of the common folk, commonly called the vulgar.

THE SACRED AND THE NATURAL

In his classic study *The Origins of Modern Science*, Herbert Butterfield famously claimed that "since the rise of Christianity . . . no landmark in history" has rivaled the scientific revolution in importance. But

for whom was the alleged revolution so important? Most Europeans could not read, and of those who could, only the most learned
were fluent in Latin, the language of choice for natural philosophy.
Even readers fluent in Latin could not always follow the reasoning of
some of the leading philosophers of nature. When Francis Bacon sent
King James I of England a copy of his *Novum Organum* (1620), now
regarded as one of the founding documents of modern science, the
uncomprehending king likened it to "the peace of God, that passeth
all understanding." Another acquaintance of Bacon's caustically noted
that "a fool could not have written such a work, and a wise man would
not." An editor of an early scientific journal complained that "every
hard word," to say nothing of mathematical symbols, served as a bar-
rier to reaching a broad reading public.

What, then, did the "vulgar"—the farmers and merchants, the
homemakers and artisans—think about the revolutionary scientific
changes taking place around them? Unfortunately for us, they left
little evidence of their thoughts, and much of what we have is filtered through the writings of those who observed them. The scant
information we have suggests that the new astronomy, the traditional
centerpiece of the scientific revolution, attracted little notice and even
less assent. Despite all of the subsequent attention heaped on Nicholas Copernicus for dislodging the earth from the center of the solar
system and setting it in motion around the sun, he won few converts
in the period between the publication of his *De Revolutionibus* (1543)
and the end of the sixteenth century. A leading Copernican scholar
has found only *ten*, though he may have missed one or two. Even the
intellectual elite of Europe virtually ignored the debate between geo-
centrists and heliocentrists before about 1615, the date Galileo Galilei
used to mark "the beginning of the uproar against Copernicus." The
first popular exposition of Copernicanism did not appear until 1629.
For Bible believers, the notion of the earth whirling around a fixed sun
seemed to contradict passages in the Psalms that had the sun moving
"out of his chamber" (19:4-5) and the earth abiding in its established
place (119:90). Most astronomers and theologians seemed to have
reached agreement by the beginning of the eighteenth century, but
large numbers of laypersons remained unpersuaded that they were
whipping around the sun at a ridiculously high speed. "Although we

live in a very enlightened century, wherein all arts and sciences have been elevated nearly to their summit," wrote a Dutch Copernican in 1772, "one still finds many, even wise and prudent people, who cannot believe the motion of the earth. . . . They feel that it is contrary to Scripture."

Even the notorious 1633 trial and condemnation of Galileo for teaching Copernicanism initially failed to arouse much popular interest. Although the Roman Inquisition took the unusual step of publicizing its condemnation of Galileo, and the papal nuncio to Cologne printed posters to notify the public, there was no popular outcry. After visiting Galileo in Italy in the late 1630s, the English poet John Milton drew the attention of polite society to Galileo's so-called imprisonment (actu-

Fig. 4.1. A natural philosopher explains the plurality of worlds and the Copernican system to an inquisitive French noblewoman. Frontispeice from Bernard le Bovier de Fontenelle, Entretiens sur la pluralite des mondes (Conversations on the Plurality of Worlds), first published in Paris in 1686.

ally house arrest in his Tuscan villa) in the *Areopagitica* (1644). This, says Maurice A. Finocchiaro, "immortalized Galileo's image as a symbol of the struggle between individual freedom and institutional authority." But it was not until the middle of the nineteenth century that Galileo's trial became a *cause célèbre* in Western Europe and North America.

Nevertheless, even away from the centers of urban culture, on remote farms and plantations, the new cosmology slowly transformed the ways in which many ordinary people viewed the world around them. They may have continued to talk about the sun's rising and setting, but they rarely resisted the growing conviction that, scientifically if not experientially, the sun stood at the center of the solar system. "Astronomy, like the Christian religion," noted the Philadelphia astronomer David Rittenhouse in 1775, "has a much greater influence on our knowledge in general, and perhaps on our manners too, than is commonly imagined. Though but few men are its particular votaries, yet the light it affords is universally diffused amongst us; and it is difficult for us to divest ourselves of its influence so far, as to frame any competent idea of which would be our situation without it."

Although the vast majority of common people, lacking leisure and literacy, ignored the cosmological revolution—and remained indifferent to their alleged loss of status in the cosmos—we do know from Carlo Ginsburg's *The Cheese and the Worms* that at least one Italian villager read widely and thought deeply about the nature of the cosmos. The trial records of a late sixteenth-century miller known as Menocchio reveal that his shameless "preaching and dogmatizing" aroused the ire of the Inquisition and led to his arrest. Under oath, Menocchio shared his homespun cosmogony: "I have said that, in my opinion, all was chaos, that is, earth, air, water, and fire were mixed together; and out of that bulk a mass formed—just as cheese is made out of milk—and worms appeared in it, and these were the angels. The most holy majesty decreed that these should be God and the angels, and among that number of angels, there was also God, *he too having been created out of that mass at the same time.*" Not surprisingly, the Inquisition, unimpressed by Menocchio's creativity, found him guilty of heresy.

Spinning cosmogonies may have excited few peasants and artisans, but considerable evidence shows widespread concern with astronomical phenomena seen by the naked eye: eclipses, meteors, and comets. No less than their socially superior neighbors, the common folk agonized over the meaning of such portents. Might the appearance of a heavenly messenger, they wondered, herald the onset of plague, famine, earthquake, or even the end of the world? Priests and pastors encouraged such questioning, hoping thereby to smite the hearts of their sinful parishioners. "For the eclipses, comets, and evil appearances of the outer planets bode ill," warned one Lutheran minister; "we should not ignore these signs as heathens might, but rather with that much more ardour call to God and pray that He may reduce the meaning of nature's omens, forgo punishment, or at least show some mercy."

In contrast to such clergy, who fostered the view of comets as supernatural signs of God's wrath, astronomers increasingly stressed their natural periodicity. As almanacs, tracts, and news-sheets flooded the market, they carried the scientific discussion of the meaning of astronomical anomalies to the masses. For those in the marketplace too busy (or too uneducated) to read for themselves, there would sometimes be public readings. In seventeenth-century England, a team of pamphleteers promised that their chapbooks on comets came devoid of "any Cramp words or Quaint Language, but [appeared] in a homely and plain Stile." Ballads about current and foreboding events, writes Sara Schechner, "were sung on the commons and in the alehouses where they papered the walls." According to one contemporary account, the balladeer's "frequent'st Workes goe out in single sheets, and are chanted from market to market, to a vile tune, and a worse throat; whilst the poore Country wench melts like her butter to heare them. And these are the Stories of some men of Tyburne, or a strange Monster

Fig. 4.2. Illustration of Halley's Comet seen in the city. Drawing by Fodestrum. Photo: © Bettmann/CORBIS.

out of Germany: or . . . Gods Judgements." In contrast to Copernicanism, which left popular opinion unruffled, assurances of the periodicity of comets, suggests Schechner, may well have "depreciated their value as portents" and calmed worried minds.

Popular interest in comets was not far removed from enthusiasm for astrology, which helped the bewildered cope with the vicissitudes of life by relieving them of personal responsibility—or scared them witless by predicting dire events. Despite frequent condemnations by religious leaders, the practice of casting horoscopes thrived, engaging even Kepler and Galileo. "This wicked art is everywhere practiced and run after by most men and women, but especially of some who would needs be taken to be professors of the Gospel of the Lord Christ," fretted one Anglican critic in the mid-seventeenth century. Christian astrologers, for the most part, remained impervious to such reprimands. As Keith Thomas has noted, "All claimed that their art was compatible with their religion, and that the heavenly bodies were merely instruments of God's will." Even pious physicians and their patients frequently found it helpful to account for bodily humors in terms of celestial influences.

Alchemy, especially its medicinal applications, also thrived in the shadow of ecclesiastical suspicion. Because alchemists, in their effort to transmute metals, tampered with the divine creation, some religious authorities accused them of being "nothing but irreligious impostors who assume the power of God and wage war on nature." Nonetheless, "respect for alchemical medicine was diffused through all ranks of society," claims Charles Webster. "Its devotees extended from the monarchs of England and Scotland, through court circles, the aristocracy, gentry, scholars, churchmen and religious nonconformists, to lawyers . . . surgeons, apothecaries, and distillers." Tracts addressed to "house fathers" and "house mothers" carried the religio-chemical gospel into the homes of all classes. The high priest of alchemical medicine was a wildly eccentric sixteenth-century Swiss physician-prophet named Theophrastus von Hohenheim, better known as Paracelsus, whose vernacular writings attracted a large following. Poor practitioners and their patients seemed particularly fond of metallic and mineral remedies. As Neil Kamil has emphasized, the language of chemical medicine, the talk of distillation and fermentation, "was very familiar to rustic artisans, farmers, herdsmen, and midwives, mostly from practical experience, or just intuitive understanding of the process of transformation from the same basic set of sources."

As the popularity of Paracelsian medicine suggests, religion and healing, the sacred and the natural, remained tightly intertwined in early modern Europe. During times of epidemics, physicians might prescribe natural remedies and order quarantines while the clergy encouraged the sick to gather together for fasting and prayer. In the words of one English cleric, "In the time of Pestilence, Penitencie and Confession are to be preferred before all other medicaments." When Catholic priests in Italy ordered public processions in order to seek divine relief from the plague, they occasionally clashed with public health authorities. When the plague struck the small Italian town of Monte Lupo in 1631, for example, the local priest defied the quarantine imposed by the public health magistracy and led his parishioners in a risky procession through the streets. Galileo's daughter, a nun, reported that on occasion the commissioners of health paid for intercessory prayers as well, as they did at her monastery in 1633: "For a period of 40 days we must, two nuns at a time, pray continuously day and night beseeching His Divine Majesty for freedom from this scourge."

Whether out of morbid curiosity or a desire to acquire useful knowledge, the public did take advantage of opportunities to learn about human anatomy. In recycling some of Andreas Vesalius's famous drawings of the human body, a popular science writer in Germany invited readers to "come along and look at the Lord's work, for the Lord is wonderful and his work unfathomable." As he explained in one tract on healing, he intended his work for the "common man": "As I don't want to carry water to the Rhein, I do not write this little book for the educated people, for they already know this art. Nor do I write for those ignorant blockheads whose brains you could make into pig's troughs. I write only for the simple, respectable, and devout little people who have until now, through God, asked for my advice and help."

Even human dissections, sometimes performed in churches to accommodate the ticket-buying public, directed attention to God's handiwork and, when done on the bodies of hanged criminals, demonstrated the wages of sin. Persons who crowded into the anatomy theater in Amsterdam could scarcely avoid the dire message that appeared prominently on the wall:

Evildoers who harm while still alive,
Prove of use after their demise.
Medicine seeks advantage, even from death.
The carcass teaches without a breath.

At the University of Leiden, the medical faculty invited the public to visit its anatomy theater, which, explains Lissa Roberts, functioned "as a museum of divinely sanctioned natural history and morality." Although people from all walks of life visited the exhibits, one medical student cheerfully noted that they appealed especially to country girls.

The microscope, though invented about 1610, attracted little popular attention before the 1660s, when interest in examining objects invisible to the naked eye boomed among Europeans and Americans wealthy enough to purchase an instrument or fortunate enough to know someone who owned one. By the end of the century, the English microscopist Robert Hooke was complaining that this valuable scientific instrument was being used mainly for "diversion and pastime." Among the religious, the complexity of the observed objects, from tiny insects to human sperm, gave striking evidence of God's designing power. Before long, allusions to microscopic wonders had become a staple in the literature of natural theology.

The early modern years in Europe also gave rise to what Katharine Park and Lorraine J. Daston have called a "culture of monsters and prodigies," embraced by "erudite humanist scholars . . . literate urban merchants and artisans . . . and by peasants, laborers, and others without direct access to the written word." From their examination of woodcuts, ballads, broadsides, and "prodigy books," Park and Daston have demonstrated a widespread fascination with the meaning of such marvels as grossly deformed humans, hermaphrodites, and conjoined twins, which raised a host of pressing theological questions. Did human monsters possess souls? Should *both* heads of Siamese twins be baptized? Were these marvels signs of divine wrath or "wonders of nature"? By the eighteenth century, leading naturalists and theologians had largely lost interest in such questions, but among the unlettered they lingered for generations to come.

The dissemination of scientific information exploded in the seventeenth century. Already in 1600, William Gilbert, author of a seminal work on magnetism, was complaining about the "ocean of books" inundating London, causing "the common herd and fellows without a spark of talent [to be] made intoxicated, crazy, puffed-up." The passage of time did nothing to stem the flood. But despite the growing interest in natural knowledge, the common people largely ignored the mechanical universe being constructed by René Descartes and Isaac Newton. In fact, the gap between natural philosophers and the public may have been widening. "It is, because Philosophy has been spun out, to so fine a thread, that it could be known but only to those, who would throw away all their whole Lives upon it," explained an early historian of the Royal Society. "It was made too subtle, for the common, and gross conceptions of men of business." Even Newton's magisterial *Philosophiae naturalis principia mathematica* (1687), which unified the physical laws of the heavens and earth, failed to attract more than an estimated hundred readers. One of Newton's colleagues claimed not to have "met one Man that puts an extraordinary value upon his Book."

THE VULGAR ENLIGHTENMENT

The tide carrying Newton's ideas to the masses began to rise even during his lifetime, as men of science avidly sought public support for their ideas and activities. One of the earliest efforts to publicize Newton's achievement was a series of sermons funded by the pious chemist Robert Boyle to demonstrate the truth of Christianity "against notorious Infidels, *viz.* Atheists, Theists, Pagans, Jews, and Mahometans." Begun in 1691, these lectures aimed at demonstrating that "the same God who created all things by the Word of his Power, and upholds and preserves them by his continual Concourse, does also by his All-wise Providence perpetually govern and direct the issues and events of things." As Larry Stewart has surmised, many parishioners no doubt "dozed in the middle of yet another denunciation of deism," but at least they had an opportunity to learn about the new science in non-technical language they could understand. Sometimes, however, the Boyle lectures produced an unintended effect. When a fifteen-year-old printer's apprentice in the town of Boston, Benjamin Franklin, read one of these sermons, he found that "quite contrary to what was intended by them . . . the Arguments of the Deists, which were quoted to be refuted, appeared . . . much stronger than the Refutations." He promptly became a "thorough Deist."

Newton's renown in France awaited the return in 1729 of the Anglophile *philosophe* Voltaire from England, where he had been exiled a few years earlier and where he had become enamored of Newtonianism. His popularizations in the 1730s brought Newton's philosophy "within everybody's reach" and turned the now-deceased Englishman into an international celebrity. "Voltaire finally appeared," exclaimed one hyperbolic reviewer, "and at once Newton is understood or is in the process of being understood; all Paris resounds with Newton, all Paris stammers Newton, all Paris studies and learns Newton." By the second half of the eighteenth century, even children were learning about the immortal Newton and his divinely ordered universe. In one book for juvenile readers, *The Newtonian System of Philosophy, Adapted to the Capacities of Young Gentlemen and Ladies* (1761), the hero, Tom Telescope, helped children see "the Wonders of God in the Works of the Creation." During the eighteenth century, claims Stewart, "popular lectures and cheap pamphlets smashed the boundaries of public education." This occurred in rural as well as in urban areas. In France, for example, colporteurs hawked the inexpensive *Bibliothèque bleue* to country folk, while coffeehouses catered to the denizens of the rapidly expanding cities. On the continent as well as in the colonies, newspapers and broadsides carried news of celestial novelties and terrestrial rumblings, of epidemics and fossils. They paid little attention, however, to the breakthroughs in celestial mechanics or to other scientific landmarks of the century. "Notwithstanding the great advances in learning and knowledge which have been made within the last two centuries," mourned the Anglican author of *The Inanity and Mischief of Vulgar Superstitions* (1795), "lamentable experience but too clearly proves how extremely deep these notions are still engraven upon the minds of thousands."

While natural philosophers and learned parsons debated the possible physical causes of the horrendous earthquakes that struck repeatedly during the eighteenth century, the common people followed their hearts—and consciences. A notable quake in New England in 1727 prompted some women to lay "aside their Hoop Petticoats" in an act of repentance. In the wake of the earthquake, New England ministers reported bumper crops of conversions and rebaptisms. Similarly, Benjamin Franklin's instructions for erecting iron rods to protect buildings from lightning, announced in *Poor Richard's Almanack* for 1753, fostered discussions about understanding God's will. Because churches, with their high steeples, typically proved most vulnerable to lightning strikes, some clergy eagerly welcomed this innovative protection against the violence of nature. One French abbé, however, reflecting what Franklin described as "the superstitious prejudices of the populace," denounced the devices for presuming to guard "against the *Thunders of Heaven!*" Some of Franklin's friends in Philadelphia decried the "Superstition" that caused "the Ignorant . . . [to] imagine that it is the immediate Voice of the Almighty and the Streaming Lightening [*sic*] are Bolts launched from his Right Hand and commissioned to execute his Vengeance."

Although eighteenth-century natural philosophers and their allies generally sought to still the fears of the public, on one subject they aroused widespread anxiety: masturbation. Before the early eighteenth century, neither men of science nor men of the cloth had paid much attention to this common, if private, practice. That changed dramatically "in or around 1712" with the appearance of an anonymous tract titled *Onania, or The Heinous Sin of Self Pollution, and All Its Frightful Consequences, in Both SEXES Considered, with Spiritual and Physical Advice to Those Who Have Already Injured Themselves by This Abominable Practice*. The enterprising author, probably an English surgeon who peddled "Prolific Powder" and "Strengthening Tincture" on the side, tied "willful self-abuse" to the crime of the biblical Onan, who spilled his seed on the ground instead of inseminating his dead brother's widow. *Onania*, described by Thomas W. Laqueur as "one of the first books to be extensively advertised in the nascent country press," enjoyed immense popularity. The rise of masturbation "to prominence," writes Laqueur, "constitutes one of the most spectacular episodes of intellectual upward mobility in literary annals: in just over fifty years, it moved from Grub Street to the *Encyclopédie*, the greatest compendium of learning produced by the high Enlightenment." This newfound respectability derived less from *Onania* than from a book by the famous Swiss Calvinist physician S. A. D. Tissot, *L'Onanisme, ou Dissertation physique sur les maladies produites par la masturbation (Onanism, or A Treatise upon the Disorders Produced by Masturbation,* 1760), which became "an instant literary sensation throughout Europe." Tissot, a sworn enemy of "superstition," also authored a popular health manual, addressed primarily to country teachers and ministers but also to "the yeomen, several of whom, full of sense, judgment, and good will, shall read with pleasure this book and eagerly spread its maxims."

In the English-speaking world, one of the most successful eighteenth-century popularizers of science and medicine was the founder of Methodism, John Wesley, who wrote on subjects ranging from masturbation to electricity and natural history. Before departing for America in 1735, he spent several months studying medicine in hopes of being "of some service to those who had no regular physician among them." After a disappointing two years in Georgia, he returned to England, where he continued to take a special interest in the problems of the ill. Assisted by an apothecary and a surgeon, he opened his own dispensary in 1746. The next year he published a hugely successful medical guide, *Primitive Physick*, designed to provide the layperson with "a plain and easy way of curing most diseases." It recommended, as an adjunct to pills and potions, "that old-fashioned medicine—*prayer*." Such recommendations, as well as Wesley's well-known belief in witchcraft and satanic possession, prompted some Anglican clerics to charge him with fostering "superstition." As one of them complained in 1795, "The belief of these extravagances was indeed gradually yielding to the powerful progress of science, but of late it has again been nourished and revivified, in no inconsiderable degree, by the many extraordinary relations, which the late venerable MR. WESLEY inserted in his *Arminian Magazine*."

Many eighteenth-century clerics, like Wesley, combined physical healing and preaching in what the Puritan divine Cotton Mather quaintly called the "Angelical Conjunction." In midcentury the Swedish physician-naturalist Carolus Linnaeus met a country priest who had made "a considerable reputation for himself as a doctor amongst his parishioners." The encounter apparently inspired Linnaeus to propose giving every theology student an eight-day crash course in the fundamentals of medicine: "The poor peasant shuns the pharmacy, where life is often sold at a high price, he dreads physicians and surgeons which he does not know how to choose. He puts his greatest trust in his own priest and likes to ask his advice in an emergency.

It would be of very great benefit to the state if most rural clergymen would understand how to cure the most common diseases, which destroy so many thousands of country folk every year."

Although Linnaeus's proposal produced no immediate action, the Swedish diet in 1810, over the protests of some clergy, voted to provide fifty scholarships for students at the Universities of Uppsala and Lund who wished to become priest-physicians. In both Europe and North America, clergy often led efforts to immunize the public against smallpox. Indeed, the Puritan theologian Jonathan Edwards died from the disease after subjecting his entire family to inoculation.

POPULAR SCIENCE AND RELIGION

The first half of the nineteenth century witnessed major developments in one scientific discipline after another: from geology and chemistry to physics and pathology. These achievements coincided with a continuing revolution in publishing that, by the 1830s, was bringing scientific news to a huge readership. As the Unitarian clergyman William Ellery Channing observed: "Science has now left her retreats . . . her selected company of votaries, and with familiar tone begun the work of instructing the race. . . . Through the press, discoveries and theories, once the monopoly of philosophers, have become the property of the multitudes. . . . Science, once the greatest of distinctions, is becoming popular."

Indeed, it was. The *Penny Magazine*, published by the British Society for the Diffusion of Useful Knowledge, was by this time reaching a million readers, by far the highest circulation of any periodical. The literary eruption continued into the second half of the century, which saw the appearance of science journalists, who translated the writings of scientists into popular language. "Never before," exclaimed one such popularizer, "was there such a profusion of books describing the various forms of life inhabiting the different countries of the globe, or the rivers, lakes and seas that diversify its scenery."

By midcentury some members of the clergy were beginning to worry that the press threatened to drown out their messages from the pulpit. "Millions who listen, week after week, to the living voice of the preacher, are daily fed by the press; and millions more are only accessible by its instrumentality, and to them it is the great teacher," observed one concerned Scottish preacher. Inexpensive books, he noted, were democratizing both reading and infidelity. "Speculations, decidedly hostile to true religion and to man's best interests, are no longer confined to the upper and more refined classes of society; but they have descended through the many channels opened up by the prolific press to the reading millions of the present time."

The spread of "infidel" science in the middle third of the nineteenth century—facilitated not only by cheap books and magazines but also by itinerant lecturers, traveling exhibits, and museums—provoked a religious backlash, characterized by a torrent of popular literature on "science and religion," a novel phrase that began appearing with frequency after about 1830. In the 1840s and 1850s in Britain, the evangelical Religious Tract Society launched an extensive publishing program of inexpensive books and articles on science and religion, hoping thereby to teach the middle and working classes how the study of nature revealed the wisdom and goodness of God. In foreign fields, missionaries drew on these works to help win "heathen" souls. One of the society's most successful authors, the disgraced minister turned schoolmaster and lecturer Thomas Dick, became widely known as "the Christian philosopher." A prolific writer, Dick aimed "particularly [at] the middle and lower ranks of the community." Espousing what was rapidly becoming an obsolete view, he insisted that science, "from whatever motives it may be prosecuted, is in effect and in reality, *an inquiry after God*. It is the study of angels and other superior intelligences." An American educator reported to Dick that his books "are read, Sir, daily, by thousands and tens of thousands in these United States. They are in all our schools, and libraries, and private families. Select Readings have been collated from them, and *Stereotyped* as a Class-book for our Primary Schools."

Popular works on science and religion typically highlighted natural theology. Early in the century, for example, the English *Methodist Magazine* began running a section called "Physico- or Natural Theology," which provided readers with an "account of the gracious provisions of Providence, of the wisdom and design of the Creator." Dominating the discourse of design was the Anglican archdeacon

William Paley, whose canonical *Natural Theology* (1802) featured "evidences of the existence and attributes of the Deity, collected from the appearances of nature." Arguably the most widely read and admired cleric in the English-speaking world of the early nineteenth century, Paley and his watchmaker God became synonymous with natural theology for decades to come. But despite its ubiquity in popular science writing, natural theology never rivaled revealed revelation in theological significance. As Aileen Fyfe has recently observed, it "was always considered a devotional exercise, something that would illustrate and deepen . . . faith rather than provide a foundation for it." It might comfort, but it rarely converted.

Three decades after the appearance of Paley's book, the frequently reprinted set of *Bridgewater Treatises* (1833–1836) drew attention to "the Power, Wisdom and Goodness of God as Manifested in the Creation." Written mostly by well-known men of science, these testimonies, according to Jonathan Topham, ranked "among the scientific best-sellers of the early nineteenth century" and "attracted extraordinary contemporary interest and 'celebrity.'" A staple of the shelves of mechanics' institute libraries, they were, suggests Topham, read more for their "safe science" than for their pious thoughts.

The two mainline sciences that generated the most popular enthusiasm in the first half of the century were geology and astronomy. By the mid-1830s, geology, with its stunning revelations of the history of life on earth, had become "the fashionable science of the day." The *American Journal of Science*, edited by the devout Benjamin Silliman, reported in 1841 that "lectures upon geology are demanded and given in all our larger towns; and the wonders of this science form the theme of discussion in the drawing-rooms of taste and fashion." The construction of the so-called geological column, based on the discovery of distinctive assemblages of fossils, prompted reinterpretations of the first chapter of Genesis that accommodated these findings. The Scottish divine Thomas Chalmers led the way with his proposal that a vast, indefinite period of time elapsed between an initial creation "in the beginning" and the relatively recent six-day creation associated with the Garden of Eden. During this gap in the biblical record, the earth experienced the series of catastrophes and creations revealed in the rocks. Another view, popularized in the early 1830s by Silliman and later by the Scot Hugh Miller, met the geological challenge to Genesis by interpreting the "days" of the first chapter as vast geological ages.

We'll never know how many people wrestled with the implications of geology for understanding the Bible, though one Pennsylvania mill owner recorded his experience:

> The yet not fully understood science of geology may interfere with the literal sense of the first chapter of Genesis, but can never overthrow the Christian theory; and it is satisfactory to find eminent geologists—those who have adopted the opinion that the world has existed many thousand ages—fully and unequivocally believing in the truths of revelation. . . . Thus it was with me when geologists assumed the position that the world, instead of being the Almighty's work in six of our days, was clearly many thousands or millions of years in becoming what it now is. I felt confounded, but further reflection makes me think differently; and if geologists establish their position, and agree among themselves—which as yet they are far from doing—I shall find no difficulty in adopting the theory, without its interfering in the least with my religious sentiments.

In the early 1840s, Silliman declared that "multitudes" had reached the same conclusion. A decade later, another American estimated that only "half of the Christian public" remained wedded to the idea that the history of life on earth could be squeezed into a mere six thousand years.

"Astronomy," proclaimed Silliman, "is, not without reason, regarded, by mankind, as the sublimest of the sciences," simultaneously inspiring awe and humility. The public devoured it. The Cincinnati astronomer Ormsby MacKnight Mitchel, one of the most popular lecturers in antebellum America, drew thousands of listeners a night to theaters and halls across the county, where he demonstrated the words of the psalmist: "The heavens declare the glory of God." After listening enthralled as Mitchel described the wonders of the skies, one awestruck woman concluded that he was "doing more good by these lectures to draw men's minds toward God than many missionaries of the Gospel." Even Mitchel's espousal of the controversial nebular hypothesis did not dampen his hearers' enthusiasm—or tarnish his reputation as a man of God. In 1796, the French mathematical astronomer Pierre Simon Laplace had proposed a way in which the solar system could have developed naturally from the rapidly spinning atmosphere of the primitive sun, later identified as a nebula. Despite Laplace's notorious (and perhaps apocryphal) quip about not needing God as an explanation—"I have no need of that hypothesis"—his nebular theory gained a strong following among Christians, especially in America. Contemporaries marveled at its popularity. The nebular hypothesis "had scarcely been formed," observed one academic, "before it was seized as the Biblical cosmogony or doctrine of creation."

No astronomical topic garnered more popular attention than the possibility of extraterrestrial life or what was called "the plurality of worlds." Curiosity about this subject dated back to the seventeenth century, when telescopic revelations of the topography of nearby heavenly bodies raised questions about their possible habitability. Had God populated these remote regions of the universe with life-forms similar to those on earth? Had he located hell on a comet? The first to popularize these issues and explore their theological implications was Bernard le Bovier de Fontenelle, whose *Entretiens sur la pluralité des mondes* (*Conversations on the Plurality of Worlds*, 1686) attracted such a wide readership that years later Voltaire complained that the book had "spoiled" the young women of his generation for more serious topics.

In 1815, Thomas Chalmers (the Genesis exegete) attracted throngs in Glasgow with his sermons on "the relation of Christianity to extraterrestrial life," which described the planets as "mansions of life and of intelligence." As one of his listeners later recalled, "He had to wait nearly four hours before he could gain admission as one of a crowd in which he was nearly crushed to death. It was with no little effort that the great preacher could find his way to the pulpit. As soon as his fervid eloquence began to stream from it, the intense enthusiasm of the auditory became almost irrestrainable [*sic*]; and in that enthusiasm the writer, young as he was, fully participated. He has never since witnessed anything equal to the scene."

When Chalmers brought out his lectures in book form a couple of years later, it became an instant best seller, running, in the words of one astonished contemporary, "like wild-fire through the country." Speculation about extraterrestrial life—the scientific evidence, the theological implications—remained a hot topic of debate through the remainder of the century, often engaging the scientific elite as well as backyard philosophers. The theologically trained Richard A. Proctor, arguably the leading popularizer of science in the late nineteenth century, launched his career with *Other Worlds than Ours* (1870). And down to the present, discussions of unidentified flying objects (UFOs) remain suffused with religious overtones.

Although widespread, discussions of the possibility of life on other worlds caused far less public commotion during the first half of the nineteenth century than phrenology, the "science of mind" developed by two Germans, the anatomist Franz Joseph Gall, a Deist, and his student Johann Spurzheim, who had abandoned theology for medicine. According to phrenological theory, the human brain comprised a number of distinct "organs"—some counted thirty-seven—each corresponding to an exotically named mental "faculty," such as amativeness (love of sex), acquisitiveness (love of money), or philoprogenitiveness (love of children). Since the relative strength of any propensity could be determined by measuring the size of its matching organ, it was not difficult for the initiated to "read" a person's character by carefully examining the skull. Plaster-of-paris models of the skull, identifying each faculty, became ubiquitous in urban shops. Almost from the beginning, the phrenologists encountered opposition from some theologians and clerics, who found such a naturalistic rendering of the human mind incompatible with the notion of free will and the sanctity of the soul. According to the American Unitarian Theodore Parker, phrenology weakened "the power of the old supernaturalism" by demonstrating "that man himself could be brought within the purview of science and that mental phenomena could be studied objectively and explained by natural causes."

The great apostle of phrenology in Great Britain and North America was an apostate Calvinist from Scotland, George Combe, whose *Constitution of Man* (1828) during the middle third of the century probably outsold all other books, excepting only the Bible, *Pilgrim's*

Progress, and *Robinson Crusoe*. By the time of the Civil War, Americans alone had purchased some 200,000 copies, eager to learn how to live longer, healthier, and happier lives. The "laws of nature," advised Combe, dictated how to live: what to eat and drink, where to live, when to marry. Violations would produce "formidable and appalling" results. According to one favorably impressed British writer, "If in a manufacturing district you meet with an artisan whose sagacious conversation and tidy appearance convince you that he is one of the more favourable specimens of his class, enter his house, and it is ten to one but you find Combe's *Constitution of Man* lying there." A London paper claimed in 1858 that

> no book published within the memory of man, in the English or any other language, has effected so great a revolution in the previously received opinions of society [as *Constitution of Man*]. . . . The influence of that unpretending treatise has extended to hundreds of thousands of minds which know not whence they derived the new light that has broken in upon them, and percolated into thousands of circles that are scarcely conscious of knowing more about Mr. Combe than his name, and the fact that he was a phrenologist.

Despite Combe's assurance that phrenology did not "directly embrace the interests of eternity" and that Christians had nothing to fear from phenology, the materialistic implications of phrenology troubled many clerics and at least some lay readers. One schoolteacher recorded her torment that followed her reading of Combe's book:

> My mind was painfully exercised while I read, again and again, the 9th chapter, "On the Relation between Science and Scripture." Many of the views *seemed* to be at variance with Revelation. I could not disbelieve the evidence of my senses on the one hand, or relinquish my hold of scripture truth on the other. To recede appeared to be folly; to advance, madness. . . . "Perish the knowledge of the science," I thought, "if it can only be obtained by the abandonment of my hopes for eternity!" . . . But, after all, Mr. Combe's work had given me more light and assistance than I had

obtained from any other source, and, after I had laid it aside, I found myself constantly acting upon the ideas I had received from its perusal.

During the 1830s, both Spurzheim and Combe visited the United States, electrifying large audiences up and down the East Coast. "When Spurzheim was in America," wrote one English observer, "the great mass of society became phrenologists in a day, wherever he appeared." In New Haven the venerable Professor Silliman served as his host. Over the next two decades, their most fervent American converts, Orson Squire Fowler and his bother Lorenzo, fomented a national craze. From their headquarters at Clinton Hall in New York City, the Fowler brothers created a phrenological empire that reached into every segment of American society. Orson alone claimed to have examined "a *quarter of a million* [heads], of all ages and of both sexes." Each month twenty thousand families pored over the *American Phrenological Journal*, one of the nation's most successful magazines, while thousands of others went out and purchased the multitude of guides and manuals the Fowlers annually published on all aspects of mental and physical health. As part of their effort to improve the human race, they rapidly branched out from phrenology to embrace the whole gamut of health reforms then in vogue. Their "one great obstacle," they complained, was the conservative clergy. Thus in works titled *The Christian Phrenologist* (1843) and *Religion, Natural and Revealed* (1844), Orson Fowler sought to reassure doubters, with only partial success, about the compatibility of "the religion of phrenology with the religion of the Bible."

In 1844, an anonymous British author, later identified as the Edinburgh publisher Robert Chambers, wove together threads from the nebular hypothesis, historical geology, Lamarckian evolution, and phrenology into a sensational little book called *Vestiges of the Natural History of Creation*. As one contemporary journalist noted, it carried the debate over evolution "beyond the bounds of the study and lecture-room into the drawing-room and the public street." The historian James Secord credits *Vestiges* with bringing "an evolutionary vision of the universe into the heart of everyday life." For some time after its publication, recalled one Victorian reader, "the name of the book was in every mouth, and one would be accosted by facetious friends, 'Well, son of a cabbage, whither art thou progressing?'" Even decades after the appearance of Charles Darwin's monumental *Origin of Species*, *Vestiges* was outselling it. Chambers denied dispensing with the Creator, but critics thought otherwise. The teaching of *Vestiges*, fumed one irate Christian, was nothing but "atheism—blank atheism, cold, cheerless, heartless, atheism." An accused murderer blamed *Vestiges* and Voltaire for turning him into an infidel; the jury found him not guilty by reason of insanity. Though *Vestiges* circulated widely and sparked much debate, it failed, as Daniel Thurs has pointed out, to "inspire many itinerant lecturers or evolutionary societies," as phrenology had done.

The heralded discovery of such invisible yet powerful forces as gravity, electricity, and magnetism led to much speculation about the material and spiritual implications of this unseen world. The reading public eagerly consumed news of "extraordinary experiments" and creative conjectures about the electrical nature of life. But it found most fascinating the notion of animal magnetism, an invisible fluid that coursed through the human body, discovered in the 1770s by Franz Anton Mesmer. According to the Jesuit-trained German doctor, obstructions to the free flow of this imponderable fluid caused disease, which could be cured by the magnetic emanations from another person's hands or eyes. Such treatment often put the subject in a deep trance, with unpredictable and sometimes entertaining results. When Mesmer moved to France in 1778, he touched off an "epidemic" of mesmeric enthusiasm. Despite the verdict of a royal commission that attributed the phenomena associated with mesmerism to imagination rather than magnetism, mesmeric healing flourished throughout late eighteenth-century Europe, where, despite Mesmer's own denial, it was often attributed to supernatural forces—or, alternatively, to satanic delusions. Mesmer's novel therapy attracted little American interest until 1836, when a French medical school dropout named Charles Poyen landed in Portland, Maine, and began lecturing, with striking success, on the topic. By the early 1840s, itinerant mesmerists were traveling throughout New England, and Boston alone claimed "two or three hundred skilful [*sic*] magnetizers." One successful practitioner, who hailed mesmerism as "a religious engine of great power," reportedly filled a Boston chapel with "more than two thousand for six nights running." Within a few years, mesmerism had spread throughout the United States, enticing followers from all walks of life. One of Poyen's erstwhile disciples, Phineas P. Quimby, treated or taught an estimated twelve thousand people during a seven-year period in Portland; and one of Quimby's patients, Mary Baker Eddy, went on to even greater heights as a healer. In the end Quimby rejected traditional mesmerism for a modified version he called the "Science of Health." This "introduction of religion based on science," he announced optimistically, "is the commencement of the new world."

During mesmeric trances, hypnotized subjects (as we now call them) often gave and received messages they regarded as divinely inspired. Such supernatural communications closely paralleled those associated with spiritualism, which blossomed in midcentury America and, shortly thereafter, in Europe. Widely seen as a spiritual analog of the telegraph, it became so popular for a time that the skeptical Theodore Parker predicted the likelihood of spiritualism's becoming

Fig. 4.3. A handbill announcing lectures in mesmerism and phrenology, delivered in 1847 by the Rev. Dr. Eden in Banbury, England. Courtesy of Alison Winter.

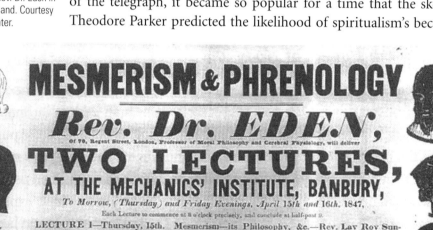

"the religion of America." Because spiritualists, like scientists, placed so much stress on empirical evidence— hearing, seeing, and feeling— they laid claim to the mantle of science. One British believer argued that spiritualism stood "mid-way between the opposing schools" of faith and science; thus "it gives to the one a scientific basis for the divine things of old, whilst it restores to the other the much-needed evidence of its expressed faith in the duality and continuity of life."

On occasion, mesmerism and spiritualism fused with phrenology, which in turn spawned interest in anatomy, physiology, and hygiene. Sporadic attempts at educating the American public in how to live gave way in the 1830s to a full-blown health crusade led by the egotistical and controversial Sylvester Graham, a sometime Presbyterian evangelist and temperance reformer, who sought to reform the eating, drinking, bathing, sleeping, and love-making habits of Americans. In 1839, he published his oft-repeated *Lectures on the Science of Human Life*. Graham and his fellow health reformers routinely linked physical and spiritual health. One Grahamite, Larkin B. Coles, whose books sold so well that a medical editor joked that it seemed "as though the friends of reform not only read, but eat the books," insisted that "it is as truly a sin against Heaven, to violate a law of life, as to break one of the ten commandments." A few years later Ellen G. White, founding prophet of the Seventh-day Adventists, adopted this slogan verbatim. During one of her own mesmeric-like "visions," God stamped his imprimatur on her call for a vegetarian diet, dress reform, sexual purity, drugless medicine, and abstinence from stimulants.

The quest for reliable information about the human frame led medical educators in the early nineteenth century to engage in what one disgustedly called "a traffic of dead bodies." To stem the illegal activities of grave-robbing "resurrectionists" and to provide medical schools with needed cadavers, a number of state legislatures introduced bills to legalize the practice. This prompted one New York state legislator to remind his fellow lawmakers that "Holy Writ" declared that "God made man in is own image." "We may pass a bill to permit the immolation of this sacred image upon the altar of science," he argued, "yet . . . a higher law . . . will hold us responsible for granting so questionably a license to a class of men . . . who laugh at the jest and top off the bowl, while before them quivers the flesh of inanimate humanity." In response to some Christians' concerns about reassembling body parts at the time when Christ would resurrect the righteous, the British surgeon Thomas Wakley replied with ridicule, "What an idea of omnipotence is conveyed in [the] supposition, that the miracle of the resurrection could be frustrated, or affected by the misdemeanour of a body-snatcher!" Public suspicion and hostility led to riots on both sides of the Atlantic. In Aberdeen, Scotland, an angry mob set the medical school on fire, "amid the loud and continued cheers of not less than 20,000 individuals." As the demand for bodies grew to thousands a year, probably nothing brought "science to the poor man's door," as one critic memorably phrased it, more immediately than having his deceased loved ones serve as anatomical objects.

In the medical sphere, epidemics continued to provoke the most intense public discussions of divine will, though as soon as diseases could be assigned to specific natural causes, religious explanations tended to give way to physical ones. Just as theological interpretations of smallpox had declined in the eighteenth century with the advent of inoculation, so, too, did religious explanations of cholera fade with the knowledge of its etiology. Charles E. Rosenberg has shown that as long as the origin of cholera remained a mystery, religious persons felt free to regard it as a miracle, "a *scourge*, a *rod* in the hand of God." As a result of midcentury epidemiological investigations that traced the cause of cholera to contaminated water supplies, public health authorities learned how to keep the disease from spreading. Thus when cholera threatened to strike the United States in 1866, community leaders (especially in New York City) tended to devote their energies to improving sanitation rather than to discussing the theological meaning of the event. "Whereas ministers in 1832 urged morality upon their congregations as a guarantor of health," writes Rosenberg, "their forward-looking counterparts in 1866 endorsed sanitary reform as a necessary prerequisite to moral improvement." The extent to which parishioners absorbed this message from the pulpit remains unknown (and perhaps unknowable); but with the demise of cholera, other medical mysteries, especially ones associated with sexually transmitted diseases, became the focus of religio-medical speculation.

OF MONKEYS AND MEN

Before the publication of Charles Darwin's landmark book *On the Origin of Species* (1859), which substituted a natural explanation for a miraculous one, the issues that captured the people's imagination had seldom dovetailed with the breakthroughs dominating the triumphalist history of science. Although it would be years before Darwin's volume would outsell *Vestiges*, it immediately acquired a notoriety unprecedented in the annals of mainstream science. As early as 1860, Darwin's disciple Thomas H. Huxley hyperbolically described the phenomenon:

> Overflowing the narrow bounds of purely scientific circles, the "species question" divides with Italy and the Volunteers the attention of general society. Everybody has read Mr. Darwin's book, or, at least, has given an opinion on its merits or demerits; pietists, whether lay or ecclesiastic, decry it with the mild railing which sounds so charitable; bigots denounce it with ignorant invective; old ladies, of both sexes, consider it a decidedly dangerous book, and even savans [*sic*], who have no better mud to throw, quote antiquated writers to show that its author is no better than an ape himself; while every philosophical thinker hails it as a veritable Whitworth gun in the armoury of liberalism, and all competent naturalists and physiologists, whatever their opinion as to the ultimate fate of the doctrines put forth, acknowledge that the work . . . is a solid contribution to knowledge which inaugurates a new epoch in natural history.

A year later, an American Methodist proclaimed that "perhaps no scientific work has ever been at once so extensively read, not only by the scientific few, but by the reading masses generally; and certainly no one has ever produced such commotion." Darwin did not identify apes as the ancestors of humans until he published *The Descent of Man* (1871), but from the beginning the biggest buzz was about ape ancestors, not about natural selection or speciation. "The Darwinian theory would lose half its interest with the public," speculated one religious writer, "if it did not culminate in a doctrine on the origin of the human species." When *The Descent of Man* finally appeared, describing "man" as the descendent of "a hairy quadruped, furnished with a tail and pointed ears," it sealed the link between Darwinism and ape ancestors. "In the drawing-room it is competing with the last new novel," wrote a contributor to the *Edinburgh Review*, "and in the study it is troubling alike the man of science, the moralist, and the theologian."

The disclosure of this pedigree did not sit well with many Christians. In contrast to the Bible, which "places a crown of honor and dominion on the brow of our common humanity," fumed one critic, "Darwinism casts us all down from this elevated platform, and herds us all with four-footed beasts and creeping things. It tears the crown from our heads; it treats us as bastards and not sons, and reveals the degrading fact that man in his best estate—even Mr. Darwin—is but a civilized, dressed up, educated monkey, who has lost his tail." Some Christian apologists adopted a more conciliatory position. Of these, perhaps the most influential was Henry Drummond, a Scottish associate of the American evangelist Dwight L. Moody and the operator of an urban mission for the working classes of Glasgow. A charismatic speaker, he would on occasion draw an audience of twenty thousand to his center. Convinced that evolution followed a divine plan, he shared his insight in a book titled *Natural Law in the Spiritual World* (1883), which enjoyed phenomenal sales for decades. The intellectual elite never embraced Drummond, but "all the religious world," noted an admiring Matthew Arnold, "have accepted the book as a godsend, and are saying to themselves that here at last is safety and scientific shelter for the orthodox supernaturalism which seemed menaced with total defeat."

As long as discussions of biological development remained confined mostly to scholarly circles, Christians who objected to evolution on biblical grounds saw little reason to rise up. As the debate spilled over into the public arena during the 1880s and 1890s, however, so-called creationists grew increasingly alarmed. "When these vague speculations, scattered to the four winds by the million-tongued press, are caught up by ignorant and untrained men," warned one alarmed premillennialist in 1889, "it is time for earnest Christian men to call a halt."

In early twentieth-century America, sporadic protests turned into an organized campaign against evolution, which culminated in the 1920s in the passage of several state laws banning the teaching of human evolution. The populist politician William Jennings Bryan, resentful of the undemocratic attempt of a "scientific soviet" to dictate to "the forty million American Christians" what should be taught in their tax-supported schools, appealed directly to the people. "Commit your case to the people," he advised creationists. "Forget, if need be, the highbrows both in the political and college world, and carry this cause to the people. They are the final and efficiently corrective power." Ironically, at that very same time in Soviet Russia, the Communist Party's Central Committee was indoctrinating workers, peasants, and soldiers in biological evolution to wean them from relying on the Bible. Occasionally, this effort led to *real* conflict between science and religion when communist agitators beat up protesting priests.

The infamous Scopes trial in 1925 in Dayton, Tennessee, in which a young high school teacher was convicted of violating the recently enacted law banning the teaching of human evolution, pitted Bryan (for the prosecution) against the agnostic lawyer Clarence Darrow. According to one Tennessee newspaper, "In Constantinople and far Japan, in Paris and London and Budapest, here and there and everywhere, at home and abroad, in pagan and in Christian lands, where controversialists gather, or men discuss their faith, to speak the name of Dayton is to drop a bomb, to hurl a hand grenade, to blow the air of peace to flinders." An American scholar calculated that the trial was discussed by "some 2310 daily newspapers in this country, some 13,267 weeklies, about 3613 monthlies, no less than 392 quarterlies, with perhaps another five hundred including bi-monthlies and semi-monthlies, tri-weeklies and odd types." His search had turned up "no periodical of any sort, agricultural or trade as well, which has ignored the subject." For the first time in history, radio transmitted a science-and-religion debate to the people. A new day in the popularization of science and religion had commenced.

The headline-grabbing controversies over evolution may have eclipsed other popular debates over science and religion, but they did not exhaust the public's range of religiously inspired responses to scientific developments. The increasing use of animals for physiological and pharmacological investigations led to an ongoing battle over vivisection, which turned especially virulent in Protestant Great Britain and North America (but provoked little reaction in Roman Catholic countries). The germ theory of disease evoked a wide range of religious sentiment, from debates over government-sponsored campaigns to contain the syphilis germ (heatedly opposed by Catholics) to soul-searching over the hygienic nature of the common communion cup. Despite its name, Christian Science repudiated the very principles of scientific medicine—including the existence of germs—in favor of mesmeric-inspired mental healing. Christian Science, in turn, inspired various mind-healing alternatives, from the Episcopalian-sponsored Emmanuel Movement to the imitative Jewish Science.

At the very time that scientific medicine was proving its worth in longer and healthier lives, growing numbers of Christians professed their faith in the healing power of prayer. Roman Catholics had never forsaken religious healing, but leading Protestants since the days of Martin Luther and John Calvin had adopted a skeptical attitude toward reports of modern healing miracles. In the late nineteenth and early twentieth centuries, however, the holiness revival that swept through Methodism spawned numerous independent ministries and Pentecostal sects, which embraced the healing power of prayer. During the twentieth century, these groups captured the devotion of hundreds of millions of Christians around the world. Scientific tests of the efficacy of intercessory prayer for healing, denounced in the late nineteenth century as sacrilegious, came to be hailed a century later as compelling testimony to the power of God.

The turn-of-the-century rediscovery of the genetic basis of heredity handed biologists the intellectual tools they needed to guide evolution, for humans as well as corn and cows. The effort to breed better humans, called eugenics, found Catholics overwhelmingly opposed and Protestants divided. The same was true for science-based sex education. Christian ministers introduced many a parishioner to the principles and techniques of modern psychology, but both liberals and conservatives resisted the reductionist implications of Freudianism (which dismissed God as an illusion) and behaviorism (which viewed God as a scientifically irrelevant metaphor).

CONCLUSION

Our "vulgar" history of science and Christianity has taken us far beyond the typical confines of the subject. It has shown that a focus on Copernicus, Galileo, Newton, Darwin, and Einstein barely touches the issues troubling the greatest number of believers, most of whom remained oblivious to the alleged theological implications of elite science. In many instances the public reacted to popularized versions of science and theology, which trickled down from professional circles. In other cases—Christian Science, creation science, and Native American science come readily to mind—various publics constructed their own alternative "science." While intellectuals wrestled with the theological ramifications of heliocentrism and the mechanical philosophy; the nature of force and matter; the manifestations of vitalism; the meaning of thermodynamics, relativity theory, and quantum physics; and the implications of positivism and scientific naturalism, the common people, to the extent that they paid any attention to science at all, concerned themselves largely with developments that impinged on their daily lives and self-understanding: diseases, disasters, and descent from apes.

FOR FURTHER READING

Finocchiaro, Maurice A. *The Galileo Affair: A Documentary History.* Berkeley: University of California Press, 1989.

Fyfe, Aileen. *Science and Salvation: Evangelical Popular Science Publishing in Victorian Britain.* Chicago: University of Chicago Press, 2004.

Park, Katharine, and Lorraine Daston. *Wonders and the Order of Nature, 1150–1750.* Rev. ed. Brooklyn: Zone Books, 2001.

Rosenberg, Charles E. *No Other Gods: On Science and American Social Thought.* 2nd ed. Baltimore: Johns Hopkins University Press, 1997.

Thomas, Keith. *Religion and the Decline of Magic.* New York: Scribner's, 1971.

REGIONAL VARIANTS

Part 2

TROPICAL CHRISTIANITY IN BRAZIL

H. B. CAVALCANTI

CHAPTER FIVE

The first Europeans ever to step on Brazilian soil were puzzled and inquisitive about the new world they accidentally "discovered." Searching for a quicker route to the Indies, they had not counted on finding an entire continent along the way. They thought the place was an island, calling it—in good Catholic fashion—the Island of the True Cross. Imagine how it was:

It is Easter Sunday, April 26, 1500, and the Portuguese sailors are about to celebrate their first mass on the new land. On a coral reef bank, by the shore, a rustic cross is erected to serve as an altar. Friar Henrique de Coimbra, a Franciscan brother, elevates the host and brings forth the sacramental presence of Christ, aided by the five other Franciscans who are part of Captain Cabral's expedition. Soldiers, officers, and natives gather around the scene. A new stage in the religious history of the new world is unfolding.

As the Latin words come forth and the elaborate rituals of pre-Trent worship are enacted, the natives watch closely. Hunters and gatherers, they have never seen such a sight. Strangely dressed men—some clad in long robes, others in iron and rich cloth— engage in a ritual performance that requires standing, kneeling, raising one's arms to the heavens. The natives follow along, not quite sure what to make of it. The Portuguese interpret this willingness to participate as a sign of the natives' religious receptivity, a promise of an open field of neophytes ready for proselytizing. European power has come ashore. Christianity is symbolically central to that arrival on that Easter Sunday.

Imagining this moment (depicted in plate A), we see how the fragmentation of Western Christianity in the 1500s had pushed European nations to reach beyond their borders, with the search for new converts paralleling the desire to expand colonial rule. Iberian nations were first to carry the banner of Catholicism to the shores of South America. In time, the English, Dutch, and French would bring Protestantism as well. For the next two centuries, European colonies would be established all along the continent, bearing their own brands of Catholicism or Protestantism. Political power, economic prowess, and conquest were all part of the mix, as Christianity played its role in mediating European efforts to extend their societies in the new world.

The first wave of Catholic expansion in South America could be seen simply as a function of Europe's colonial interest or increased trade, but from a religious viewpoint, it carried the urgency of a besieged faith. The Catholic-Protestant European conflicts in the 1500s had been preceded by European wars on Muslim lands in the previous century. The Roman Catholic Church found itself fighting the external enemy Islam, only to have that followed by an internal schism within Western Christianity. By the mid-1400s, the Pope was calling on Catholic nations (*Romanus Pontifex*, papal bull of 1454) to sail across the ocean to recruit Indian Christians that could aid in the battle against "the Saracens." Forty years later, Pope Alexander VI (in the papal bull who led to the Treaty of Tordesilhas) would divide the new world between Spain and Portugal, charging them to use their new lands to strengthen the position of the Catholic faith. (See plate A in gallery.)

Such expansion of a besieged Catholic faith was fraught with unexamined zeal and unexpected consequences. Ultimately, it changed the culture of Catholicism as well as the native cultures encountered by Iberian Catholics. This chapter looks at Brazil as a case study of Christian expansion in the South Atlantic tropics, focusing on two waves of missionary enterprise: the first European contact in the early sixteenth century and the following Protestant wave three centuries later.

The First Mass in Brazil, April 1500

And when the mass was finished and we sat down for the sermon, many of them stood up and blew a horn or trumpet and began to leap and dance for a while. . . . And at the elevation of the Host, when we knelt, they placed themselves as we were with hands uplifted, and so quietly that I assure your Highness that they gave us much edification.

—Pero Vaz de Caminha, "Letter to the King of Portugal," in The Brazil Reader: History, Culture, Politics, ed. Robert M. Levine and John J. Crocitti (Durham: Duke University Press, 1999), 21.

Plate A. *First Mass in Brazil* (A Primeira Missa no Brasil), April 26, 1500, by Victor Meirelles, 1860. Museu Nacional de Belas Artes (National Museum of Fine Arts) in Rio de Janeiro, Brazil.

Plate B. Feast Day of San Estevan, patron saint of the Pueblo of Acoma c. 1904. Seventeenth-century Franciscan missionaries introduced Catholic worship to the Acoma, who incorporated it into their religious life.

Plate C. Born in West Hartford, Connecticut, but raised as an indentured servant in Granville, Lemuel Haynes joined Timothy Mather Cooley's church in 1785 and briefly served as pastor of the town's middle parish. Haynes later moved to Rutland, Vermont, where he developed a national reputation for his powerful preaching and controversial abolitionist publications. Courtesy of the Museum of Art, Rhode Island School of Design.

Plate D. *A Plantation Burial* by John Antrobus, 1860. Reprinted by permission from The New Orleans Collection.

Plate E. Last look at a loved one in Muncie, Indiana. Coffin lid is opened outside family home so that photographer has enough light for this wet plate memento, nineteenth century. Image:© Bettmann/CORBIS.

Plate F. A church reader explains to Russian peasants the picture of the Last Judgment, 1868, by V. V. Pukirev. Photo: State Museum of the History of Religion, inv. no. A-346-IV.

Plate G. *Vendor of Images*, 1862, by N. A. Koshelev. The Russian Museum, St. Peterburg, inv. no. Zh-1340.

Plate H. Icon Procession, 1893, by I. M. Prianishnikov. The Russian Museum, St. Petersburg, inv. no. Zh-4166.

SOCIOLOGICAL DIMENSIONS OF MISSION WORK

In theory, the goal of missionary expansion is straightforward: to reproduce the beliefs, practices, community structures, and social relations of the missionaries' own faith in a different social setting. Missionaries go to great lengths to recreate their own religious ethos abroad, organizing religious work in line with congregational styles, denominational structures, and religious teachings and practices found back home.

In practice, however, missionary expansion is not so straightforward. Local factors—cultural differences, political pressures, economic demands, and the presence of other religions—interact with the transplanted faith, affecting the ultimate outcome of mission work. Scholars describe the process as the "naturalization" or "acculturation" of the faith. Transplanted churches respond to local challenges by taking on some of the cultural characteristics and the social relations found in the host country. The irony is that these churches change as they maximize their outreach. Prospering among local residents means adopting aspects of the local way of life. The end result is the gradual creation of hybrid religious forms.

Many factors influence the adaptation of a new religion. There is the larger historical context to consider, including economic and political forces that shape the encounter with a new religion, along with the host country's openness to innovation. On both sides of this encounter, religious beliefs and practices explain reality, guide behavior, and represent the strength of a people and their linkage to the past. These sacred traditions provide stability and are not easily overthrown. At the same time, they often mediate social change and facilitate the social process through which different groups work out their relationships with one another.

Missionary expansion always involves human agency. Missionaries have personal styles, with ethnic, class, and gender backgrounds that color the way their faith is transmitted. The people whom missionaries encounter also have personal styles, with ethnic, class, and gender backgrounds that affect the way the message broadcast by missionaries is interpreted and received. Insofar as the transmission succeeds, the locals, in time, will bring the most resilient elements of their cultural backgrounds to the new faith, making it their own. As they gain the upper hand in the nascent church, the faith becomes more reflective of the local culture.

For native peoples, accepting a new religion is akin to pouring new wine in old wineskins. European and American missionaries who brought Christianity to Brazil carried powerful new ideas that deeply affected local inhabitants. In the short run, Christianity threatened the local order of things. In the long run, it provided local converts with the intellectual and organizational tools for decoding and reshaping their own culture.

FOR GOD AND KING

For the Iberian Americans in Brazil, church and nation were part of the same imperial dominion. In the sixteenth, seventeenth, and eighteenth centuries, Brazil was a Portuguese colony and Roman Catholicism was its official religion. The Treaty of Tordesilhas (1494) gave the Portuguese religious sanction to settle the South American Atlantic coast, but Brazil's "discovery" was really a by-product of the Portuguese search for a sea route around Africa. The original intent was to attack Islamic countries in the Middle East by going around the usual Mediterranean route. The explicit goal was the conversion of Muslims to Christianity. The ultimate payoff, however, was the takeover of the profitable Islamic trade. In that search, Portugal created trading posts (called factories) and forts all along the African and Asian coasts, and eventually along the Brazilian coast as well. Faith and profit went hand in hand as the imperial rulers of Portugal expanded their political and religious power through the extraction of natural resources and the establishment of lucrative trade routes.

Both Portuguese and Spanish powers relied on the Roman Catholic Church as an important means of implanting their rule in South America and did not tolerate or acknowledge the legitimacy of any other religion. The church that arrived in Brazil was a highly stratified organization with a relatively cohesive sense of purpose and a disciplined corps of workers. These advantages did not necessarily translate into victory, however. The church's limited resources in Brazil during the sixteenth and seventeenth centuries meant that at any point in time, only a few hundred priests were available to minister to hundreds of thousands (if not millions) of natives and thousands of European settlers in a country of continental proportions. The number of Christian churches, convents, schools, and hospitals built during this period were but a handful, dwarfed by Brazil's vastness. Support for religious work was often a low priority for colonial governors. Despite the hard work of dedicated individual missionaries, such as the Jesuit fathers José Manoel da Nóbrega and José de Anchieta, who established missionary villages for natives, codified indigenous languages, created schools for the children of European settlers, and extended some health care to natives and Africans, transplanting Christianity to Brazil did not proceed as quickly or as straightforwardly as missionaries hoped.

Unlike the Spaniards, whose colonial expansion in the Americas aimed at possession of the entire continent, the Portuguese were more concerned with establishing coastal trade routes. Their first century of rule in Brazil was limited mostly to Brazilian shores. Nevertheless, trade required the taming of Brazil's indigenous population for

Fig. 5.1. Pelourinho, Salvador, Bahia—colonial downtown—showing the church of Nosso Senhor Do Rosario Dos Pretos, the "Slaves Church," built over a hundred-year period by slaves. Photo: © Jeremy Horner/CORBIS.

Subjugating Heathens to Christ and King

Since I have been in this land, to which I came with Your Majesty, two desires will torment me always. . . : one was to seek a bishop, such as Your Majesty and I portrayed for reforming the Christians; and another, to see the heathens subjugated and thrown under the yoke of obedience to the Christians, so that there can be impressed in them all that we might want because the heathen is of a nature that, once subdued, the faith of Christ will be written very well in his understandings and desires, as was done in Peru and the Antilles, since the heathen appears in a similar condition as them; and we now are starting to see by the eye of experience, as below I will tell, if they leave him in his liberty and free will, as he is a brutal heathen, nothing will be done with him; as by experience we saw that during this whole time we expended much work on him, but without reaping more fruit from it than a few innocent souls that we sent to heaven.

—Friar Manoel da Nóbrega, "Letter to Governor Tomé de Sousa," [the colony's first governor] (1549), in The Brazil Reader: History, Culture, Politics, ed. Robert M. Levine and John J. Crocitti (Durham: Duke University Press, 1999), 37–38.

the sake of creating a regimented and compliant colonial labor force. Religion's role in that effort was twofold: it supported the establishment of the European way of life in the colony, and it reached and "pacified" natives (and eventually Africans) to render them more predisposed to the demands of the new political order.

For its first century of operations, Catholic mission in Brazil leaned heavily on religious orders. Portugal's population was too small to provide the colony with a steady supply of secular priests. The Society of Jesus, an international order of missionary priests, was appointed by the crown as its official agent in the pacification of natives. God and king were united in this effort: the first six Jesuits to reach Brazil were part of the official cortege of Brazil's first governor general (1549). By the end of the sixteenth century, they would number between 128 and 170 and be spread throughout different regions of the colony.

Missionaries from a variety of religious orders arrived after 1580, determined to set up convents, chapels, and schools alongside the country's main colonial settlements. The Benedictines founded their first convent in Salvador, Brazil's brand-new capital, in 1581. Other convents followed to the south in Rio de Janeiro (1586) and São Paulo (1598), and to the north in Olinda (1590). The Carmelites settled in the Pernambuco province in 1583, building their first convent in Olinda and setting up other convents in Salvador (1586) and Rio (1590). The Franciscans founded their first convent in Olinda in 1584, following it with convents in Vitória (1585) and Salvador (1587).

During its first hundred years of operation, the Roman Catholic Church in Brazil was centralized in a single diocese. With the Vatican's blessing, the crown established Brazil's first diocese in Salvador (1551) only two years after centralizing the country's rule under a Portuguese governor. The Salvador diocese, with its canonical courts, seminary, and other activities related to an official Catholic See, operated for more than a century as the ecclesiastical center of Catholic life in the colony. New dioceses were created in 1676, one in Pernambuco, another in Rio. A fourth diocese was established in the Amazon region in 1677.

MISSIONS AMONG EUROPEANS

Not surprisingly, Christian expansion in sixteenth- and seventeenth-century Brazil was most successful among European settlers. It was for them, first and foremost, that Portugal established a network of religious institutions in the new world. For these European transplants and many of their offspring, Catholicism was the religious expression of Portuguese life in the colony. Even as they were changed by the conditions found in Brazil, the church and Euro-Brazilian adherents strove to maintain their European contours. The church supported the European way of life in the colony by providing Portuguese settlers with sanctuaries, schools, and hospitals located in the most important colonial towns. Regular masses, confession, observance of the religious calendar, and parochial education were aimed, first of all, at sustaining a European religious community in the tropics.

Religious orders of Spanish and Portuguese laypeople (that is, "third orders") helped to create tight networks for the elites, serving as microcosms where they would "forge familial ties and informal and formal allegiances."[1] Although the religious orders drew their membership from most social classes in the colony, some members became powerful figures in colonial life: one could count among them governors, regional political leaders, high-ranking civil servants, crown judges, and landed aristocracy. Distinguished individuals held elected offices within religious orders, lending the religious enterprise time, money, and personal influence.

The lay orders were a key component of civil society in tropical America. Catholics came together in those associations to respond to the religious and charitable needs of the colony. They also supported regular worship, upheld the Catholic calendar and sponsored feasts of patron saints, built sumptuous sanctuaries that dotted the downtown areas of colonial settlements, and furbished sanctuaries with religious objects for the upkeep of the faith. In many respects, they strove to preserve the framework of European Catholicism in tropical America.

Nevertheless, the lay orders found themselves changing over time as they operated on Brazilian soil. At first they tried to duplicate in the colony their Portuguese standards. Rigid membership requirements included demonstrable financial resources, the respect of one's peers, good moral standing, and, more important, "pure blood." No applicants with parents or grandparents of "Jewish, Moorish, mulatto ancestry, or any other infected people" were to be accepted.[2]

Growing numbers of people of mixed birth constantly challenged those standards of exclusivity. By 1751, Brazilian canonical courts were issuing waivers that exempted some applicants to religious orders from the "purity of blood" requirement. A 1773 law abolished the distinction between "Old" and "New" Christians, forcing the orders to further relax the "pure blood" requirement. Finally, as many important members married spouses with "suspect" lineage, the orders were pushed to create even more lenient admission standards. Slowly, the religious orders in Brazil began to reflect the faces of the people.

EARLY JESUIT MISSIONS TO NATIVES

By some estimates there were anywhere from 500,000 to two million natives in Brazil (some estimate as many as eight million) at the time of the Portuguese arrival. Tribes were divided into more than one hundred separate language groups. As hunters and gatherers, some beginning to transition into a horticultural economy, Brazilian natives lacked the political centralization of the Andean and Mesoamerica peoples and also their ability to resist the invaders.

Brazilian tribal groups also lacked integrated religious systems that could unify them into broader coalitions. Native religions were local, based on animistic "spirits of the forest" represented by animals, plants, and other natural phenomena. Local shamans, or *pajés*, played important roles in determining how particular groups negotiated their social and natural environments. *Pajés* established contact with particular spirits who represented group identity and fostered group solidarity.

Called by the Portuguese crown to pacify the natives of Brazil, the Jesuits strove to convert these hunter-gatherers with Stone Age technologies into acculturated agricultural laborers like those in Europe, while also protecting them from slave raiders and wars waged on them by the colonists and attempting to manage the consequences of colonial rule. Portuguese action in setting up colonial structures directly contributed to a steep decline in the indigenous population. The newcomers brought smallpox, measles, and other infectious diseases that killed natives by the thousands. They waged war on Brazil's indigenous peoples as the excuse to enslave them into backbreaking labor on sugar plantations. All of this was justified by religious sanction, since the Catholic Church gave Portugal permission to use weapons, warfare, and slavery as tools of missionary expansion.

Fig. 5.2. Ruins of the Jesuit Mission Church of San Miguel, Brazil. Photo: © Bojan Brecelj/CORBIS.

Furthermore, the colony's demands on food production contributed to widespread famine among natives. Native Brazilians had a subsistence economy that was not prepared to sustain newcomers in addition to their own populations. The long-term result of disease, war, slavery, and famine was the decimation of entire indigenous nations and the displacement of other native peoples into the hinterlands of the colony. Some thirty years after the arrival of Brazil's first governor, the Portuguese were already importing more than two thousand African slaves a year to replace native Brazilians in their plantation economy.

Unlike the enslaving Portuguese planters, Jesuits worked toward the "Europeanization" of Brazilian natives. Their goal for Brazilian natives was to turn them into an organized and compliant peasantry. To that end, the Jesuits employed detribalization and acculturation, removing natives from their original settlements and reorganizing them into mixed-nation mission villages. In these *aldeias*, Jesuits taught Christianity, European morality, work habits, and artisan trades, including farming techniques and other useful means of employment. Unlike the Jesuit work in India where missionaries presented Christian thought in relation to Hindu scriptures, or in China where Jesuits accommodated Christianity to Taoist and Confucian philosophies, Jesuits in Brazil attempted to eradicate indigenous lifeways.

The historian H. B. Johnson divided the Jesuit's *aldeia* system into stages. In the period of initial exploration from 1550 to 1553, Jesuits focused on understanding native languages. The next four years represented an interlude of missionary work without results. Then from 1557 to 1561, the *aldeia* system began to take hold, representing the peak of Jesuit success. During the next two years, colonial war waged by the new governor general on the Caeté nation brought disease, famine, and death to thousands of natives. In the decade following the end of that war in 1564, the *aldeia* system disappeared.[3] While the experiment lasted, native responses ranged from curiosity to partial acceptance to desertion, evasion, and hostility.

Despite its failures, the Jesuits had some success in broadcasting Christian ideas. In twenty-five years, the Jesuits established twelve *aldeias* in the Bahia province alone (one of four Jesuit stations in the country), with a total population of about forty thousand natives. That number was greatly reduced by epidemic and slave raids. But by 1630 there were still some seventy thousand converts under Jesuit care, this time from multiple Brazilian regions, drawing from tribes as diverse as the Raris and Cariris in Rio de Janeiro, the Miramoninis in São Paulo, the Paraíbas and Potiguars in Pernambuco, and the Aimorés and Tapuias in the upper Amazon.

From a cultural viewpoint, the *aldeia* system imposed a heavy burden on converts. Their removal from precolonial communities and resettlement in missionary villages greatly contributed to their loss of tribal identity and cultural integrity without providing them the benefit of full integration into the European world of the colony. The language used in the *aldeias* was *Tupi*, a hybrid language codified by the Jesuits from different native sources. This new lingua franca distanced natives from their particular linguistic roots and the distinctive cultures associated with them. European norms intruded in native ways of dressing, residential patterns (with villages divided by clans and by certain age and sex groups), regulation of kinship ties and family forms, tribal social rankings, and multiple aspects and practices of everyday life.

The colonists' deeply held negative attitude toward the indigenous population also had a direct impact on the Jesuit mission's success. Even if the Jesuit order had managed to "civilize" fully the peoples of Brazil through its *aldeia* system, plantation owners and other European settlers would still treat natives as subhuman, denying them the rights or opportunities to become fully integrated into colonial society. Enslavement through raids was far more profitable to planters than the semifeudalistic peasant system proposed by the Jesuits. In fairness, the *aldeia* system held the promise of gradual social stability and peaceful coexistence between European and native peoples, but only over a very long period of time—time the Jesuits did not have.

If life in the *aldeias* imposed a cultural burden, it also offered natives some immediate material advantages. Converts benefited from temporary protection from raids, housing for extended families, and land grants that supported larger communities. The farming programs run by Jesuits provided some degree of economic stability. Mission villages sponsored plenty of community feasts and celebrations as well, including dances, games, and plays. But in the end, disease, warfare, enslavement, and famine limited Jesuit success in transforming the lives of native peoples. Those converts who survived inhabited a kind of limbo between their original cultures and the Catholic Christian world of the Portuguese.

MISSIONS AMONG AFRICAN SLAVES

The transition from indigenous to African slave labor took place gradually during the second half of the sixteenth century. From 1570 to 1587, estimates of the number of African slaves in Brazil increased from two thousand to fourteen thousand, and the slave trade became well established in Brazil during this time. Unlike Brazilian natives, most African slaves came from pastoral and farming backgrounds, which made them better prepared for plantation work than natives. At first used for skilled labor positions, they eventually replaced the indigenous population as the main engine of the plantation economy. By one estimate, Brazil received more African slaves (some 3.65 million) than any other region of the continent.[4]

In theory, the church was responsible for the spiritual care of these new inhabitants, but planters discouraged and curtailed mission work to newly arrived slaves. Jesuits did try to reach out to the African population, but slave owners restricted clerical access to the workers and resisted the church's insistent pleas for the better treatment of the slave population. In practice, spiritual care was negligible. Few plantations had resident priests. At most, clerical visits took place once a year for the purposes of baptizing individuals and legalizing marital unions.

The persistence of African religions affected the spread of Christianity among the slaves. In rural areas African religious practices were forbidden but still practiced in clandestine ways either in the forest or under the guise of weekly entertainment allowed by slave owners to boost morale. In urban areas, those practices were not repressed. Some colonists encouraged the practice of African religions as a means of "dividing and conquering," separating slave populations by tribal affiliation and fostering diversity within the slave class.[5]

Christianity took hold slowly among Africans in Brazil. Despite their limited exposure to official Catholic teaching and practice,

Christianity fared better among them than among the native population. Beginning in the sixteenth century, African slaves adopted the European faith on their own terms, using the pantheon of Christian saints as representatives of African deities. In the seventeenth century, the creation of black confraternities provided institutional structures for free blacks that grew alongside religious institutions for the European Catholic community. Black confraternities aimed to alleviate the suffering and respond to the needs of the Afro-Brazilian community. Early on, these black associations sought help from the Vatican for recognition of the rights of free blacks and for support of slaves who sought manumission in the colony.

For African slaves, Christianity was both the religion of the oppressor and the means to hold on to their own religious ethos. The Catholic Church was the church of slave owners, men and women who traded in human beings. But it also provided a religious context in which Africans preserved and grounded African life in the new world. Blacks realized early on that their African religions could be maintained in Brazil only if practiced under the guise of Christianity. Later on, Afro-Brazilian leaders took advantage of black confraternities to structure their own society along the lines of Catholic piety and communal representation.

THE INDIGENIZATION OF CATHOLICISM AND THE EMERGENCE OF NEW RELIGIOUS MOVEMENTS

Over the course of centuries, Catholic Christianity eventually became an indigenous religion in Brazil. In its popular expression, Catholicism became eclectic, heterogeneous, and decentralized in ways that reflected the informal, pantheistic, mystical, and decentralized living of natives and Afro-Brazilians. In their assimilation of Catholic beliefs and practices, the people of Brazil altered many of the beliefs and practices of European Christianity, undermining the strict certainties of moral and social order that European missionaries wanted to inculcate and making Catholicism more Brazilian—more spontaneous, more magical, and more permeating in its pantheistic understanding of all aspects of everyday life.

From native Brazilians, Catholicism inherited a stronger attachment to local spiritual forces in the form of patron saints. It also inherited a large variety of local religious practices. In many cases, local religious leaders gained ascendance to saintly status upon their death, contributing to the development of local cultic traditions in different regions of the country. Brazilian Catholics also inherited a more magical relationship to their faith—certain sanctuaries or shrines had special magic powers that could be employed to solve personal problems or medical conditions. People also used sacred objects to protect themselves from evil, in the same way that certain amulets protected natives going into battle.

From African religions, Catholicism inherited a whole new cosmology, one that paralleled the sacred Catholic parameters brought from Europe, but with added spiritual qualities. Similar to the religious traditions of native Brazilians, African religions had an animistic approach to the world. But African religious cosmologies were strengthened by their merger with Catholicism to a degree that native cosmologies were not. Afro-Brazilian cosmology involved a vast spiritual patronage system, one that in many ways resembled the Portuguese and Roman Catholic pantheons of saints. But African traditions added an even larger web of connections for the believer with the natural world. In Afro-Brazilian cosmology, the numinous and the natural world formed a continuum, populated by spirits with great supernatural power. Those spirits were organized into an extensive spiritual hierarchy, with the least powerful interceding with the power holders on behalf of human beings.

The religion known in Bahia as Candomblé exemplifies the fusion of African and Catholic elements in the Brazilian context. An African word for a dance honoring spirits, Candomblé combines easily with local traditions and is known by other names elsewhere in Brazil—Macumba in Rio, Babassuê in the Amazon, Xangô in Pernambuco, Tambor in Maranhão. In Candomblé, Orishas are the spiritual forces of nature. According to historian Sheila Walker, because Orishas "are associated with specific leaves, animals, foods, minerals, colors, and human activities, social principles, and interactions, people can be constantly in rapport with their spiritual energies via the intermediaries of any of these elements."[6]

Afro-Brazilians superimposed the spiritual hierarchy of Orishas on the Catholic pantheon. Olorun or Olodumare was the creative principle who made the heaven and earth, the sun, the moon, the stars, and all plant and animal life on earth. Olorun's wife, Oba, gave him a son, Aganyu, and a daughter, Yemanja, who was the goddess of the water and one of the symbols of motherhood and fertility. Some of the gods begotten by Yemanja included Chango, the god of fire, thunder, and lightning; Oshun, the goddess of fresh water and maternity; Oshossi, the god of hunters, birds, and wild animals; and Oggun, the god of war and iron. Other Orishas included Omolu, the god of disease and pestilence, and Eshu, a mischievous Yoruba deity who was in charge of all communications. Afro-Brazilians worshiped hundreds of Orishas—some with very local cultic appeal and others whose devotion spread throughout the African diaspora in the Americas.

Following the principle that Orishas were responsible for particular areas of life and acted as intermediaries on behalf of human beings, African slaves adapted their cosmology to the Catholic faith. The Christian God represented Olorun. Jesus Christ became associated with Oshala, the creator of human life and the father of humankind. Different manifestations of the Virgin Mary were equated with Yemanja and other goddesses associated with water (Oba and Oshun). Saint Anthony was represented by Oggun. Saint George, in his dragon-slaying depiction, was comparable to Oshossi. Omolu represented Saint Lazarus, the leper. Even the Christian devil had a counterpart in Eshu.[7]

This layer of extra meaning still permeates Catholic worship to this day. The Orishas are venerated in their forms as Catholic saints following the church's calendar of feast days of the saints. Most Afro-religious leaders, priestesses, and priests are baptized Catholics who insist that their followers be members in good standing of the Roman Catholic Church. Afro-Brazilian religion practitioners attend mass in churches devoted to their particular saint/Orisha. For instance, Oshala initiates are asked to attend mass at the Church of Our Lord of Bomfim in Bahia on the Friday following their initiation, since that is the day of the week sacred to Oshala. On August 16, while Catholic mass is taking place at the Church of Saint Lazarus, Omolu initiates enter trance states in front of the church.[8]

The Catholic God and saints in Brazil have become part of a dense web of spiritual connections for the believers who go beyond their usual attributions in European Catholicism. As the number of syncretic Afro-Brazilian religions multiplied—some with greater indigenous influence in the Amazon area, others with greater "orthodoxy" in northeastern cities with greater concentrations of the Afro-Brazilian population, and still others with more spiritualist syncretic forms in southern Brazil—a huge array of amulets, particular cloths or colors, foods, and rituals have been developed in devotion to saints/Orishas. Faithful Catholics attend mass but also frequent the *terreiros*, the religious settings for Afro-Brazilian services. They often claim devotion to a particular Orisha, one who guides their spiritual life and spiritual development.

SEPARATING CHURCH AND STATE: THE PROTESTANT MOVEMENT

Representatives of numerous Protestant churches arrived in Brazil during the nineteenth century. Lutherans were the first to arrive in 1824, only two years after Brazil's independence. Methodists followed in 1836. Presbyterians, Episcopalians, and Congregationalists arrived in midcentury at the peak of the rule of Brazil's second emperor (1840–1889). Southern Baptists arrived late, in 1881, eight years prior to the advent of the Republic. Imagine this new wave of Christian influence:

It is Sunday morning, another Easter Sunday, this time in the mid-1860s. A small group gathers in a living room somewhere in Brazil's capital, this time for Presbyterian worship. Gone is the pomp of Cabral's first expedition, the ironclad worshipers replaced by men in suits and ties and women in modest dresses. Americans file in, accompanied by a few British expatriates and local Brazilians. The room is devoid of icons, crosses, or candles. The stark emptiness of the religious space bespeaks the faith's Scottish beginnings. Portuguese is the language of worship, but the accents are mostly American. The small community sings American and

British hymns, hurriedly translated, and offers prayers to the God of the Reformation. The simple service emphasizes the importance of the Bible and its usefulness as a guide for daily living. Bible readings occupy a prominent place in the service, along with a sermon that explains the meaning of those readings for the lives of the individuals and their families in the room.

The Protestant wave comes mostly from North America; Protestant missions are a part of the Western capitalist expansion that takes place during the nineteenth century, in a period marked by increased world trade. In the hustle and bustle of Rio de Janeiro's fast-growing urban life, European immigrants and Brazilian middle-class citizens mingle, working on the creation of a new era of Brazilian history. As industry develops, American businessmen and government consultants offer a new paradigm to the Brazilian population, one based on the promises of rationalism and the modern world. American missionaries are but a sign of things to come. They herald a new economic system along with their religious vision, in a country steeped in Catholic imperialism and its interplay with native and African religious feeling.

This wave of Protestant influence differed from the earlier wave of Catholic influence, which was based on an imperial, established church. Catholicism was part of a larger social order being exported; it was the religious expression of the colonizing power. Catholic missionaries used the colonial infrastructure, including law enforcement and land grants as well as transportation and communication systems, to expand their work in more or less monopolistic ways.

Nineteenth-century Protestant Christianity followed the "market" model of open religious competition, in which churches came into being as "sects" or "denominations" that vied with each other for local adepts, without support from the state. The American constitutional separation of church and state led Protestant churches to develop as autonomous religious organizations, without governmental sanction or support. At home in an industrial economy, they competed openly in the American religious market for "shares" of the country's faithful. Through their world mission programs, these churches reproduced similar religious strategies abroad.

The main difference between the colonial and industrial mission models is the greater amount of cultural support the first received as a result of its official establishment. As part of Brazil's cultural and national tradition, the established church existed within a mutually reinforcing social order in which government, economy, education, and health care all contributed to affirm the legitimacy of religious work. In this sense, the overall social order provided the church with a larger frame of cultural authority.

In the industrial mission model, religious missions operated more as cultural novelties, with less support from other social institutions. Missionaries benefited from the commercial ties between their countries and the countries they served but did not receive the kind of moral and economic support that Catholic missions received from the state. In many cases local arrangements only increased the costs of Protestant missionary work. Given the voluntary nature of their operation and the absence of government sanction, Protestants in the nineteenth century had to develop consumer-oriented programs of recruitment in order to grow.

The growth of Protestant Christianity in Brazil occurred in the context of cultural disparity between the oligarchic, Iberian system of social relations present in the country, and the practices brought by modern Americans and Europeans. To a certain degree, American missionaries were exporting a jingoistic faith, one that unquestioningly accepted the United States as the beacon of progress. American exceptionalism was a strong, driving force behind nineteenth-century Protestant mission work; Americans in Brazil commonly attributed the success of the United States to its Protestantism, often explaining that Protestant faith was the moral foundation of America's political liberties, voluntary associations, and civic service.

Not surprisingly, American Protestant missionaries perceived Latin American nations as backward and unenlightened. As their correspondence reveals, these missionaries felt burdened with the daunting task of "civilizing" local societies and driven to instill in their Latin American converts the same faith and values that had made their country great. They blamed the imperial Catholic heritage of Latin America for the region's lack of development. Catholicism's "failure" only increased their sense of urgency. Mission work required nothing less than the complete religious reinvention of Latin American countries. In some ways, their approach was not unlike that of the Jesuits who sought to eradicate the native cosmology they found.

These missionaries of the industrial age arrived as part of a larger invasion of bankers, financiers, exporters, and shipping clerks drawn to Latin America by dreams of capitalist expansion. As cultural entrepreneurs, their presence had a destabilizing effect in the local "religious market." They sold an alternative "product" that threatened the status quo and denigrated Brazil's religious heritage. When early Protestant missionaries in Brazil succeeded, they exacted a heavy toll on people, asking converts to renounce their Catholic identity and culture and, in many cases, their relatives, friends, and associates as well. Those willing to convert tended to be poor and marginalized people with the most to gain from the promises of a foreign culture.

THE BRAZILIAN CONTEXT

Three factors facilitated the expansion of Protestantism to the tropics: Brazil's first wave of modernization, a weak Catholic religious monopoly, and the surge in European and North American immigration to the country. Emperor Don Pedro II facilitated the first wave of modernization with the adoption of pro-business legislation (the 1846 permission to import machinery duty-free), the creation of new financial institutions (the 1849 law of commercial incorporation, the 1850 commercial code, and the formation of the Bank of Brazil in 1851), and the levying of higher import taxes (the 1844 Alves Branco tariff law).

This modernization of Brazil's infrastructure made it easier for Protestant missionaries to evangelize. The transportation system jumped from eight hundred miles of railway tracks in 1874 to six thousand miles in 1889, connecting fourteen of the country's twenty provinces. Communications grew exponentially: the Brazilian Post Office went from handling fifty million letters in 1880 to more than two hundred million in 1890. The country was connected to Europe by transoceanic cable in 1874. Six months later all southern provinces were linked by telegraph. By 1896, telegraph lines reached as far north as the Amazon and as far west as Mato Grosso. From 10 stations in 1861 with 40 miles of lines transmitting 233 messages, Brazil grew to having 171 stations in 1896 with 6,560 miles of lines processing over 600,000 messages. Phone services became available in São Paulo, Campinas, Rio de Janeiro, and Salvador during the 1880s. Brazil's industrial park grew from 175 factories in 1875 to more than 600 in 1890. By 1875, there were more than 50,000 registered industrial workers in the country.[9]

Modernization also transformed ports and coastal cities, providing urban dwellers with improved water, sewage, and gas services, paved streets, and the streetcar. People moving to the fast-growing urban centers faced problems and opportunities unknown to previous generations. "Journals and newspapers, artistic and cultural associations, inns, theatres, cafés and shops mushroomed, and the big cities acquired a more cosmopolitan atmosphere."[10] These developments provided missionaries with a rising pool of converts among the urban middle classes.

As prosperity spread, consumers turned to Europe and North America for information, lifestyle tips, and political ideas. European ideologies (the Enlightenment, Darwinism, and Positivism) grabbed hold of Brazilian urban circles, inspiring new middle classes into activism and social reform. Intellectuals, professionals, military officers, and other urban groups created voluntary associations to promote liberal causes, such as abolitionism, European immigration, federalism, the separation of church and state, campaign reform, and the republican form of government.

The arrival of American Protestant missionaries coincided with an era of new openness to innovation and receptivity to ideas from the Northern Hemisphere. Along with the newly developed infrastructure, which made traveling and communications easier, the growing industrial centers were filled with an educated and rising middle class, one that presented missionaries with an ideal mission field. Cordial relations between the United States and Brazil enabled a steady flow of secular and religious resources from the United States. Although receptivity to religious innovation lagged behind receptivity to other forms of modernization, it increased as the century unfolded, as a comparison of Presbyterian and Southern Baptist missions will show. Arriving at midcentury, Presbyterians had a much harder time preaching the promises of modernity than Southern Baptists did twenty-two years later.

THE PRESBYTERIAN EXPERIENCE

Ideologically, Presbyterian missionaries aligned with the broad values of nineteenth-century American culture. They prized religious freedom, capitalism, education, and scientific progress. Their ethics emphasized a modicum of orthodoxy and asceticism: the faithful were expected to follow the right doctrines, live righteous and humble lives, and combat sin in themselves and the world. Presbyterians emphasized the importance of honoring parents, marital fidelity, honesty in all business dealings, and hard work as a sign of character and decency.

Presbyterian mission work began in Rio de Janeiro, with the arrival of the Reverend Ashbel Green Simonton in 1859 and the founding of the first Brazilian congregation four years later on May 15, 1863. The northern and southern branches of American Presbyterianism cooperated in mission work in Brazil, but growth came slowly. Some twenty years separated the creation of the first presbytery in Rio de Janeiro (1865) by northern missionaries from the presbyteries of Campinas and Minas (1886), organized by southern missionaries. Both groups contributed to the organization of the fourth presbytery in Recife in 1888, this time with the help of local Presbyterian clergy.

The Brazilian Presbyterian Church (Igreja Presbiteriana do Brasil—IPB) reached national status with the creation of its first synod in 1888. At that meeting, the church reorganized the Rio de Janeiro Presbytery (São Paulo gained its own jurisdiction) and created the first national seminary for Brazilian clergy. By 1890, thirty-one years after Simonton's arrival, the mission had twenty missionaries in the field, twelve ordained Brazilian ministers, and fifty-nine congregations across the national territory. Membership consisted of 3,199 adult members and 1,461 children.

It is easy to see why the doctrine-driven Presbyterians, with their intellectual defense of modernity, would attract mostly well-educated Brazilians from the middle and upper classes. Among the early IPB members, one finds a marquis, a baron, a few relatives of the Portuguese imperial family, the families of two leading industrialists, an engineer, and two leading Brazilian politicians. Presbyterians also attracted military officers, middle-class businessmen, and a variety of professionals including attorneys, doctors, professors, teachers, and writers. Southern Baptists, on the other hand, found greater receptivity among urban working classes.

Reproducing the Presbyterian faith in Brazil was somewhat problematic. By the time of the church's first synod, the denomination was already in the throes of internal dissension. The first crisis came in 1879, when the missionary faith clashed with Brazilian mysticism. The missionaries defined Presbyterian faith along the lines of an ascetic, pragmatic, and rational religious program. Brazilian converts, on the other hand, longed for a more immediate and emotional experience of the sacred. That longing led a group headed by Dr. Miguel Vieira Ferreira to leave the IPB on September 11 and create the Evangelical Church of Brazil (Igreja Evangélica Brasileira).

The second crisis came over control of the church. At the 1903 synod, local clergy closed ranks in pushing for nationalization of the church. The 1880 proclamation of republican government boosted Brazilian nationalism, and the fervor spilled into the Protestant community. During the synod meeting, Brazilian clergy defended the excommunication of Free Masons (most missionaries were Free Masons) and voted for more Brazilian control of church affairs (including the Rio de Janeiro seminary and the national network of Presbyterian schools). The end result was another splinter with the creation of the Independent Presbyterian Church of Brazil (Igreja Presbiteriana Independente).

Heightened nationalism also brought external pressures to bear upon missionaries and converts. There were broad suspicions of disloyalty, which seriously limited Presbyterian work. Presbyterians were forbidden to bury their dead in local cemeteries, their weddings were not legally valid, their sanctuaries could not resemble Catholic churches, and their converts were detained by police for attending non-Catholic services. In some places, local mobs stoned Protestant converts who attempted to meet for services.

Internal divisions and the external pressures stunted Presbyterian growth and contributed to a pattern of organizational instability that lasted for much of the church's history. Throughout the twentieth century, the IPB lost leadership, congregations, presbyteries, and even a whole synod to internal dissension. As dissenters left, the remnant became more entrenched, defensive, and dogmatic, until the democratic and representative Presbyterian system transplanted from the United States was reduced to a highly centralized, dictatorial, and theologically isolated body of believers.

The mission's timing of arrival did not help things much. Presbyterian missionaries brought a Reformed version of Christianity to Brazil at a time when Brazilians were still struggling with their emerging identity as an independent nation. The search for a national identity reinforced Catholicism's monopoly over the culture, along with the primacy of Iberian customs.

THE SOUTHERN BAPTIST EXPERIENCE

Southern Baptists arrived as the Catholic Church reached its lowest point of religious monopoly. The authority of the Catholic Church eroded during the nineteenth century as a result of the cumbersome nature of state patronage of religious work and the emperor's lack of enthusiasm for the church. As the defender of the faith, Pedro II enjoyed much the same control over religion in his realm as his Portuguese predecessors had in colonial days. Dependence on the king for the appointment and training of the clergy and for the maintenance of parish work seriously limited Roman Catholic growth. Given Pedro II's lukewarm approach to Catholicism, it is no surprise that by the end of the century, the church was quite depleted: understaffed, with inadequate clergy, overseeing a limited number of parishes, and engaged in weak catechetical work.

The timing of the Baptists' arrival proved advantageous. The Catholic Church was in much poorer shape to oppose Baptist evangelicalism than it had been at midcentury, when it was better able to fend off Presbyterian evangelism. Furthermore, Southern Baptist missionaries were more aggressive in attacking Roman Catholicism. From the pulpit and in the printed media, Baptist missionaries deplored the Roman clergy's moral and intellectual mediocrity and the superstitious, quasi-pagan practices of its laity. Brazilians, they argued, were

Protestants Equate Catholicism with Heathenism

There is as true idolatry in Brazil as in China or India. Romanism is only heathenism with Christian names for its gods. . . .

Superstition is gross and heathenish. The minds of the masses are filled with superstitious terrors. Charms are worn by men, women, and children. All kinds of figures are used for this purpose: measures of the "saints," pads filled with powder, pictures of the saints, crosses, hands, images, little stones, and "marine horses" of various substances. Crosses and horns are placed on fruit-stands, or hung up by the doorway to keep away witches and evil spirits. Figures of arms and hands and legs, or other members diseased or disabled, are made and placed in shrines in order to effect cures.

Immorality is universal. The priests, the religious leaders of the people, are grossly licentious. Almost all of them are living in open concubinage. It is a common thing to hear people speak of the priest's "family." Many of these men have, I am reliably informed, two or three mistresses. Can people with such spiritual guides be moral? The facts are sad enough. Thousands are living in shameless concubinage. Marriage among the lower classes seems to be the exception rather than the rule. The priests, in their eager desire for gain, charge dearly for their services in performing marriage ceremonies, and as civil marriage is not lawful, the masses go unmarried.

Other sins are dark and numerous. There is no Christian Sunday. The Lord's Day is made a season of revelry and sin, or of toil or idleness. Some spend the day as any other of the week—with shops open, carts running, shouts and confusion; others spend the day in dancing and other recreations; others spend it in drunkenness and brawls. Few, if any, think of spending the day in devotion or religious rest. Lying is thought to be a sin of little moment.

Romanism is responsible for these things. The converted Brazilian leaves these sins and shows his faith by good fruit, and a moral life—just as the Anglo-Saxon does.

—W. B. Bagby, "Brazil," Foreign Mission Journal 15, no. 9 (April 1884): 3.

Catholic by heritage, not by true conviction.

To make matters worse, the Catholic Church's political conservatism became a handicap as the monarchy came to an end. In 1870, the church's theological battle with Pedro II drained it of much-needed political resources. Opposition to liberal trade policies and its continuous support of the monarchical system left the church open to attacks by pro-republican forces. Those groups were convinced that only modern institutions could push Brazil forward, and perceived the church as part of Brazil's outmoded past. No one was surprised when the republican regime decreed the separation of church and state in 1889. Even the Vatican hailed the decree, since it gave the Catholic Church in Brazil greater autonomy.

The erosion of the Catholic faith for much of the second half of the century created room for Protestantism in Brazil. Protestant missionaries found a growing audience amid disaffected middle and working classes who were already looking for religious alternatives. Urban sprawl provided missionaries with new places for congregations, places untouched by Catholic service. Once given leadership positions in the mission churches, converts became aggressive proselytizers, fiercely attacking their Roman Catholic roots.

Baptist mission work in Brazil began in 1881, with the arrival in São Paulo of William Buck Bagby and Ann Luther from Texas. The Bagbys were sent by the Southern Baptist Convention to work with American immigrants in southern Brazil. A year later they were joined by Zachary and Kate Taylor. Despite being sent to work among American expatriates, both couples arrived in Brazil with plans to reach out to Brazilians, which is one of the reasons they moved the mission headquarters from São Paulo to Bahia.

The immigration of American and European workers to Brazil in the last quarter of the nineteenth century helped fuel the spread of the Protestant faith. Abolition of slavery in 1888 and the continued growth in the coffee trade required skilled labor. The Brazilian government hired recruiting agents in Europe and North America to attract immigrants, paying the settlers' travel expenses and providing quick naturalization once they arrived. Between 1875 and 1910, about 4.5 to 5 million Europeans and Americans migrated to Brazil, the majority settling in the southern provinces of the country. While most were Catholic, there was a Protestant minority among them including a significant number of Americans who left the American South during Reconstruction.

Northern Hemisphere immigration contributed to the spread of Protestantism in two ways. First, immigrants brought new technologies to Brazil, which gave them a positive image in the eyes of Brazilians. Technology furthered the impression that all things immigrant were more developed, perhaps faith included. American settlers were credited with introducing the first trollies, plows, and wagons into Brazilian agriculture. They also brought other modern amenities such as brick houses, stoves, kitchen utensils, the coffee pounder, the kerosene lamp, the sewing machine, the buckboard, new land-surveying techniques, and four new crops: upland cotton, rattlesnake watermelons, grapes, and pecans.

Second, Protestant settlers pushed for greater religious freedom. With the emperor's blessing, they sent for missionaries back home.

As the Brazilian government relaxed control over non-Catholic practices, it became easier to spread the Protestant faith. Here again, coming late proved advantageous to the Southern Baptists. Earlier in the century, Presbyterian missionaries had to learn the language and culture mostly by themselves, amid a very small international community in Rio de Janeiro and São Paulo. Southern Baptists, on the other hand, started mission work among compatriots who had already made a favorable impression in the local population. They even learned Portuguese in a language school set up by Presbyterian missionaries in Campinas!

Facilitating their evangelical efforts, Baptists brought a strong congregational model of American Christianity to Brazil: a coalition of free, autonomous local congregations, united by a common theology of individual salvation. Baptists believed that individuals experienced a saving encounter with God (being "born again") and were called to live out their salvation by congregating with like-minded peers. Since individual responsibility was the cornerstone of Baptist faith prior to the emergence of fundamentalism in the twentieth century, individuals were responsible for searching the Bible to make their own religious choices. They were also collectively responsible for congregational choices. The denomination could not dictate religion; each congregation was responsible for its own life.

To promote cooperative work, local congregations organized themselves into local, state, and national associations. At the end of the nineteenth century, Baptist associations had no hierarchical oversight over the supporting congregations. They existed to undertake large-scale endeavors such as missions, education, theological training, or religious publishing. The overarching national association (or convention) was a coordinating rather

---

Protestantism Equated with Progress

The causes which led to the change to republican form of government in 1889 were various. The proximity of the United States of America, with our wonderful material prosperity, was a pervasive and constant influence which affected the minds of the Brazilians in favor of our form of government. Then, too, thousands in Brazil were weary of priestly and churchly dominations, and insufferable obstacles to progress which this domination continually interposed. The ignorance and superstition and indolence, fostered by the Romish faith, were in the way of Brazil's progress, and her more discerning sons discovered this fact. No doubt ambition, selfish and personal, entered into the motives of many of the leaders who overthrew the former government, but nevertheless the change in Brazil's form of government was a distinct advance in the line of modern civilization and progress.

—E. Y. Mullins, "Views of Brazil," The Foreign Mission Journal 47, no. 2 (June 1896): 60.

than a governing body and did not enforce doctrinal policy or speak on behalf of local churches. The convention existed for the purpose of expediting the agendas of local churches.

From the beginning, Baptists focused on converting individuals and organizing congregations. Unlike Presbyterians, who struggled for four years to organize their first congregation, Southern Baptists had their first church organized in Salvador, Bahia, only a year after their arrival (October 15, 1882). The first converts were common folk—a former priest and his wife, the missionaries' house servants, and a tin-worker. A year later the congregation had twenty converts and six "preaching points" (public spaces for revival meetings). The work in Bahia was hard and often unrewarding, given the region's heavy Catholic nature. But the Baptist faith seemed easier to spread since Baptist converts could be ordained without theological education. Local converts soon found themselves in charge of their own congregations.

Fig. 5.3. Igreja Batista da Capunga in Recife, which is an example of U.S. Southern architecture in Recife.

Their simpler theological approach made it possible for Baptists to adapt more easily to the needs of the local population, especially the working-class world of their new adepts. Simpler, basic evangelical doctrines offered less possibility for disagreement and dissent. By contrast, even the Presbyterian laity was expected to be fully versed in Calvin's treatises and obscure points of systematic theology before they could serve in appointed offices. Rigorous training for potential Presbyterian ministers took a minimum of five years and required knowledge of church history, theology, and the original languages of the Bible.

Much like Presbyterians, Southern Baptists faced a lot of resistance from the Catholic Church. But they were more aggressive in fighting back. They constantly pointed to Catholic doctrinal "errors" in their preaching and publications to justify the need for their proselytizing in a country considered "Christian" among European and American circles.

They saw Brazilian Catholicism as nothing more than folk religion, built on superstition, religious syncretism, and medieval practices. It lacked the spiritual power to lead Brazilians to progress. Those sentiments only grew as missionaries extended their tenure in Brazil.

Southern Baptist missionaries were convinced that only Protestantism (more specifically the Baptist faith) could promote democracy, individual liberty, equality, and intellectual freedom in Brazil. Catholicism fostered anti-democratic practices that deprived individuals from thinking for themselves and making their own choices. Such lack of freedom was evident in Catholic schools and in catechetical work. Without a freethinking and educated citizenry, they reasoned, democracy and true religion could not flourish. With this rationale, Baptists created a network of schools throughout the country.

In 1884, the mission set up a second base of operations in Rio de Janeiro. The move to the national capital proved critical for the church's national expansion. Rio provided missionaries with an educated, cosmopolitan, rising middle-class population from which they could recruit qualified converts to send out throughout the country. In fact, eight years after the founding of their first congregation, Baptists had three national newspapers, eight churches in six different regions of Brazil, two native ministers, and 312 Brazilian members.

Unlike Presbyterians, Southern Baptists did not face deep internal divisions. With a decentralized system of church governance and simpler faith, they were able to keep conflicts at the congregational level. Divisions, when they existed, centered more on personality clashes than doctrinal differences. Even then, the disaffected were free to leave the local congregation and start a new Baptist community down the road.

Historian Antônio Mendonça argues that Baptist work differed from other Protestant work in four critical ways: Baptists were aggressive proselytizers and strongly anti-Catholic in their approach (others were more accommodating); they

Fig. 5.4. Another example of American architecture in Brazil: the temple of the First Baptist Church in Rio de Janeiro. Photo: Marcos Decotelli. © Primeira Igreja Batista do Rio de Janeiro. Used by permission.

employed a vigorous method of direct recruiting while others relied on education and medical work to reach converts; they had a simpler church-planting strategy, in which leadership was learned "on the job"; and Baptist ethics required higher levels of commitment. Converts who failed to live up to standards were expelled. That increased the cost of deviance and strengthened church loyalty.[11]

The Baptists had fewer problems with internal dissension than Presbyterians. Presbyterians lost precious market share every time they splintered. Losing trained leadership was costly because they spent a greater amount of time training leaders. Southern Baptists, on the other hand, kept dissension localized. Theological complexity may be partly to blame for the Presbyterian internal clashes. The more straightforward Southern Baptist message and the faith's autonomous church format proved more pragmatic, more geared to faster expansion, and more attractive to middle- and working-class Brazilians. From a market-share perspective, the Baptist organizational advantages were critical for their greater success.

Mission work grew faster after the 1889 separation of church and state decree. First, regional associations were formed, and then they came together to create the Brazilian Baptist Convention. The first regional association was formed in 1894 by six Rio de Janeiro congregations. Six years later, in 1900, the second association was created in northeast Brazil by nine congregations. In 1904, seven congregations organized the São Paulo association, and in 1906, seven congregations formed the Amazonian association. Finally, in 1907, the Brazilian Baptist Convention was established, twenty-five years after the Bagbys' arrival.

In 1900, Baptists had 21 missionaries, 35 churches, and 1,932 members. Seven years later, by the time the national convention was formed, there were 83 churches in 20 states with 4,276 adult converts. In comparison, twenty-one years after their arrival in Brazil, Presbyterians had 32 churches and 1,729 members. The results indicate that in the Brazilian case, a late arrival, a decentralized form of church governance, and a simpler faith made all the difference.

Measured in terms of conversions, Protestants were only modestly successful. By the end of the century, most of the 17.3 million Brazilians were still Catholic (albeit nominally). The total sum of

Baptists and Presbyterians in the country did not add up to eight thousand converts altogether. Yet both missions established foundations during the nineteenth century for a Presbyterian and Southern Baptist presence that has lasted to this day. No less important, the missions helped to facilitate a process of modernization that affected the whole country.

CHRISTIANITY IN BRAZIL

Both Catholicism and Protestantism in Brazil originated with missionaries. Although neither faith penetrated the entire population, by 1800, the Roman Catholic Church was firmly established in Brazil and Catholic beliefs and practices had intermixed with native and African traditions. In the nineteenth century, the Protestant faith gained adherents among the rising middle and working classes, faring better among individuals who had the most to gain from a shift in religious allegiance.

While early Catholics spread the European influence slowly in a country with little infrastructure to support their work, Protestants arrived at a time when Brazil had a network of rails and ports, along with state capitals teeming with growing urban populations. Protestants did not encounter a multitude of indigenous people unacquainted with Christianity or European civilization, so they were not burdened with the steep clash of cultures that Catholics had faced three hundred years earlier. Protestants also did not depend on governmental aid to support their work. The funding of Protestant missions was completely detached from the government of Brazil, allowing missionaries to enjoy considerable freedom in implementing the faith.

From their outset, Protestant missions emphasized the importance of creating a trained Brazilian clergy. While Catholicism relied on imported clergy from European orders to do most of its work, Protestants established national centers of theological training in different regions of the country, training Brazilians to represent churches and extend denominational outreach. Presbyterians had seminaries in Rio de Janeiro, Vitória, and Recife; Baptists operated seminaries in Rio, Recife, and Belém.

The erosion of the Catholic religious monopoly and the influx of European and American immigrants facilitated the transplantation of Protestant faith, as did the modernization of Brazil's society and infrastructure. New means of mass communication proved especially useful to Protestants, who imported printing presses to propagate their message and bypassed the local media, which in many cases favored the Catholic monopoly. Protestant newspapers, pamphlets, tracts, doctrinal books, hymnbooks, and educational materials quickly reached the country's educated population. Printed material also allowed the missionaries to reach unclaimed regions of the country. In 1900 alone, Southern Baptists printed 300,000 tracts and leaflets to propagate their faith.

Protestant-sponsored education had enormous impact in nineteenth-century Brazil. Given their advanced pedagogical methods, Protestant schools were highly successful in recruiting Brazilian children, even though they did not generate the conversions the missionaries expected; some Brazilian parents appreciated the modern education but forbade their children to convert. In its long-term result, Protestant education contributed to the formation of modern society in Brazil and also to tolerance of Protestant influence in the country.

In its Protestant as well as Catholic forms, Christianity gradually became "Brazilianized." The rational nature of Presbyterian and Baptist liturgies seemed insufficient to many Brazilians eager for the immanence of the divine and for the powerful emotional in-taking that is so real in native Brazilian and Afro-Brazilian religions. Just as the practice of Catholicism evolved to incorporate the colors, sounds, and mysticism of native

Brazil Is Still a Catholic Country

Another fact that militates greatly against the native colporter and his work is the contempt in which converts from Romanism are held by the masses generally. Many think it is all right for the foreigner who was born and brought up in the Protestant faith to follow that way and even engage in the active work of propagating his religion. But for a native Brazilian, who was brought up a Roman Catholic, to apostatize and become a Protestant is intolerable; such are held in great disdain, and by some are considered unworthy of respect. It is difficult for the foreigner to realize fully the position in which the native convert is placed when he abandons the religion of his country and of his ancestors. Rome's assumption of the claim to be the only true Church with an infallible head, a regular and uninterrupted transmission of ministerial authority through bishops and priests, and an elaborate form of ceremonial worship has through the centuries maintained a firm hold upon the minds of the masses. Many religious rites and ceremonies have become social customs, inseparable from the real social life of the people. For one to abandon these is in a great measure to ostracise himself from his people.

—Hugh C. Tucker,
The Bible in Brazil (New York:
Revell, 1902), 263–64.

and Afro-Brazilians, becoming different things to different segments of the Brazilian population, the practice of Protestant Christianity also evolved to incorporate Brazilian forms. Presbyterianism lost its strong Scottish format and became less rationalistic and doctrinaire as it grew to embrace the mysticism and emotionalism of Brazilian culture. Baptists found fertile soil in Brazilian cities, where they managed to maintain their American appearance in worship and church structure but also gained a Brazilian flavor influenced by working-class families and their ethnic traditions of fellowship and respect for religious feeling. As in other parts of the Americas, Christianity became deeply intermixed with native and African traditions, despite efforts on the part of both Catholic and Protestant missionaries to keep them separate. The explosion of charismatic Protestantism that took place in Brazil during the twentieth century can be understood in these terms, as a wedding of the biblical rationalism characteristic of Protestantism with the emotionalism and mysticism of native and Afro-Brazilian traditions.

In many ways Brazil is still a Catholic country; and in that sense the Protestant practice in Brazil often overlaps with popular aspects of Catholic spirituality in its practice. Nevertheless, the old European religious division caused by the Reformation found a new home in Brazil during the nineteenth century. In Brazil, as in other parts of the world, Protestants helped mediate the process of modernization. They also contributed to the diversification of Christianity, similar to the diversification of Christianity in North America, yet uniquely Brazilian in the praxis of its faith.

FOR FURTHER READING

Alves, Rubem. *Protestantism and Repression: A Brazilian Case Study.* Maryknoll, N.Y.: Orbis Books, 1984.

Camps, Arnulf, Libertus A. Hoedemaker, Marc R. Spindler, and Frans J. Verstraelen, eds. *Missiology: An Ecumenical Introduction.* Grand Rapids: Eerdmans, 1995.

Crabtree, A. R. *Baptists in Brazil.* Rio de Janeiro: Baptist Publishing House, 1953.

Dawsey, Cyrus, and James Dawsey. *The Confederados: Old South Immigrants in Brazil.* Tuscaloosa: University of Alabama Press, 1998.

Pierson, Paul Everett. *A Younger Church in Search of Maturity: Presbyterianism in Brazil from 1910 to 1959.* San Antonio: Trinity University Press, 1974.

Russell-Wood, A. J. R. *Fidalgos and Philanthropists: The Santa Casa da Misericórdia of Bahia, 1550–1755*. Berkeley: University of California Press, 1968.

Schmidlin, Joseph. *Catholic Mission History*. Techny, Ill.: Mission Press, 1933.

Schwartz, Stuart B. *Sovereignty and Society in Colonial Brazil*. Berkeley: University of California Press, 1975.

Willems, Emilio. *Followers of the New Faith*. Nashville: Vanderbilt University Press, 1967.

ICONIC PIETY
IN RUSSIA

VERA SHEVZOV

CHAPTER SIX

A people's history of Orthodox Christianity in Russia—the home of the largest Orthodox culture of modern times—is best told by means of icons. Of all the ways of relating to God, Christ, and the saints, icon veneration was the most preferred and ingrained among Orthodox believers. Russia's Orthodox laymen and laywomen may have attended church irregularly, and most would have partaken of the Eucharist only annually; believers among the peasantry may not have memorized many prayers. A different picture emerges, however, when the people's Christianity is examined in the light of icons and their veneration. Believers from all social classes and walks of life were engaged with matters of faith by means of icons. As one foreigner traveling to Russia in the seventeenth century noted, icons signified dogma, church history, and even liturgy in believers' lives. Struck by the ubiquity of icons in Russia, another seventeenth-century traveler was under the impression that it was forbidden to pray in Russia without one.[1]

Despite its steadfast place in the Orthodox believer's world, the icon did not remain insulated from new ways of thinking or from attitudes that have since been associated with the term "modern." Philosophical trends born from the Reformation and the Enlightenment, Western cultural influences, and growth in the market economy ushered in ways of thinking and seeing that the icon could not escape. This chapter examines two aspects of Russia's iconic culture that were brought into particular relief during the period 1600–1900: attachment to particular iconographic styles and the special veneration of icons. While debates about iconographic style and special veneration often took place among the clergy and intelligentsia, this chapter explores how ordinary men and women shaped the discourse of those debates through their practices.

"WORTHY OF THE CHRISTIAN GAZE"

Icons in modern Russia were not simply confined to the hallowed spaces of churches and icon corners in homes. People could also see them in roadside chapels, in makeshift shrines in fields, on barns and stables, and in government offices, retail shops, and trains. Icons guided believers' imaginations regarding the celebration of events in the life of Christ, Mary, and the saints. They also inspired commemoration of noteworthy events in their communities such as alleviation from droughts and famines. And they accompanied believers through the major events in their personal and familial life cycles—birth, marriage, childbearing, illness, and death.

The icon was in many ways a resting place, a visual "home" for the Orthodox Christian, and figured into Orthodox identity formation. Given the pervasive presence of icons within believers' public and private lives, it is not surprising that from the seventeenth century through to the Bolshevik Revolution in 1917, many of Russia's educated Orthodox Christians voiced concerns over what people saw when they prayed before an icon. Linking visual experience with spiritual knowledge, insight, and healing power, they would have wholeheartedly agreed with a 1669 statement by Tsar Alexei Mikhailovich, who maintained that pious gaze at an icon caused believers "to be led to a contrite heart, to tears of repentance, to a love of God and His saints, to imitation of their God-pleasing lives, and to be able to imagine themselves standing in the heavens before the faces of the prototypes."[2] In accordance with this view, the tsar issued a directive forbidding "unskillful iconographic art" that would deter from the awe and reverence that an icon was meant to inspire.

Such high standards might suggest that iconography was a carefully regulated vocation and a defined craft in modern Russia. Indeed, throughout the modern period, concern for proper iconographic style led to periodic efforts by church and state officials to direct the production of icons and thereby to influence what believers saw when they stood before their sacred images. For instance, in the early eighteenth century, Emperor Peter the Great established a short-lived office dedicated to overseeing iconographic activity, an effort that was subsequently also taken up by the highest administrative body in the Russian Orthodox Church, the Holy Synod. Another example occurred in 1722, when several peasants arrived in St. Petersburg from the Vladimir Diocese, a historically important region for icon production in Russia, prepared to sell the more than eight hundred icons that they had brought with them. Submitting these works for review to church officials as demanded by the current rulings, the peasants soon learned that only 26 of these icons were considered of average quality. The review committee had deemed 311 more to be of average to low quality, 484 of lower quality, and 13 as simply prohibitive. As an act of compromise, the committee allowed the peasants to sell the 337 icons from the first two categories.[3]

In their attempts to institutionalize "good" iconography, many church and state officials were guided by an aesthetic outlook that often saw little or no opposition between the Western-styled art of the academically trained secular artist and the traditional Orthodox icon. A directive issued by the Holy Synod in 1880 illustrates the paradox. "In order for church painting to adhere strictly to church tradition while at the same time to correspond to the needs of art," the directive encouraged enlisting members of the Imperial Academy of Art as mediators between those who commissioned iconographic work for their churches and the iconographers. With this cooperation, the directive maintained, works of church art could influence the development of "good taste" among the people. Throughout the eighteenth and nineteenth centuries, church directives further instructed priests to remove unseemly, "strange," or "seductive" icons from churches and even from private homes of parishioners.

Such efforts to supervise Russia's iconographic enterprise, however, had little lasting value in large part because Orthodox Christians in Russia seemed unable to agree upon what constituted an icon "worthy of a Christian gaze." Although church directives concerning iconography repeatedly referred to the need for "correct" and "skillfully" painted icons, there was no clearly defined standard enabling believers to understand these terms uniformly. Iconic styles ranged from those that resembled salon paintings in the Italian or "Frankish" style to those of the darker, more austere "Greek" style. In between were the so-called *friazhskie* icons, which attempted to fuse the modern with the traditional by combining the Western "freedom of artistic painting" with the "sanctity of the Greek style." Although a council in 1551 had maintained that the iconographic standard in Russia should be the work of Andrei Rublev, the fact that Western reproductions of Michelangelo and Leonardo da Vinci were found even in Russia's rural, predominantly peasant iconographic workshops indicates that the ancient standards were being modified or at least combined with or joined by others.[4]

Church officials were more articulate about what they did not like, identifying impropriety on two fronts—"foreign" and "native." Foreign influence, especially the "admixture of Latinism," some churchmen believed, could be distracting and even harmful for the soul of the Orthodox believer. In the seventeenth century, for instance, two clergymen who were otherwise bitter antagonists—the archpriest Avvakum Petrovich and Patriarch Nikon (Minin)—agreed when it came to the evaluation of icons that were written "in the manner of Franks and Poles." In a treatise devoted to the subject of icon writing, for instance, the archpriest Avvakum rebuffed the style that portrayed Christ with a "plump face," "corpulent hands," and "puffy fingers." As a product of "fleshly thoughts" and human lusts, such a style, he maintained, was foreign to Russia insofar as it was focused on "earthly things." Patriarch Nikon responded even more vehemently, not only threatening to anathematize those who continued to write icons in the "Frankish" manner or to keep them in their homes, but also publicly destroying such images.

The nineteenth century witnessed similar criticism. In 1827, the bishop from Saratov complained about the alluring nature of some of the images written according to "Italian taste" that were hanging in the churches of his region. He maintained that some laypeople found it sinful to gaze at these images and consequently often opted to bring their own icons to church to pray before them. In the second half of the nineteenth century, joining strong populist currents in Russian intellectual circles at large, many emerging Russian icon specialists reacted no less negatively to what they felt was an oppressive impression left by those icons that had been heavily influenced by Western artistic realism. Commenting in 1892, the icon specialist P. Pankratiev alluded to the colonizing effects of post-Renaissance influences on Russian iconography when he compared these artistic influences to the superimposition of a foreign language on the people's native tongue.

Churchmen tried to protect the Orthodox believer from other types of "foreign-looking" religious images as well. For instance, in 1722, the Holy Synod issued a directive against the use of carved images in churches, a directive that was reiterated again in the first half of the nineteenth century. Making an exception for well-carved crucifixes, the directive maintained that carved images were not found in other Orthodox countries and that these images had appeared in Russian churches by way of "Roman" influences. Similarly, the synod maintained that no depictions of the coronation of Mary should be present in churches since the subject did not correspond "with the spirit and teaching" of the Orthodox Church.[5]

While some Orthodox believers looked critically at icons produced in light of Western influences, others directed their criticism at the more "native" icons produced by peasants in rural areas. Beginning in the seventeenth century, monastic sway over the iconographic enterprise in Russia ceased and icon production passed to the hands of skilled peasant masters, many of whom identified with the Old Belief, a term used to refer to those believers who ceased to identify with the state-supported Orthodox Church between the years 1654 and 1666. While peasant iconographers could be found throughout Russia, a cluster of villages in the Vladimir and Suzdal regions southeast of Moscow in particular emerged as a center of icon production. Sometimes referred to as "folk iconographers" (*narodnye ikonopistsy*), the work of this region's peasant craftsmen was distributed by peddlers throughout Russia as well as in other parts of the Orthodox East, including Serbia and Bulgaria. In addition, many of the iconographers from this region were commissioned to work on churches throughout the empire, thereby spreading their renown. By the end of the nineteenth century, some of them had established studios in major urban centers, including Moscow, St. Petersburg, and Kiev.

Icon production in villages such as Kholui, Palekh, and Mstera was often a collective endeavor involving entire families in which technical knowledge was passed from father to son. As the population of Russia grew, so did the demand for icons. By the nineteenth century, village workers produced millions of icons every year. Locally painted icons varied widely in quality and style; they ranged from costly and subtly detailed images in the Byzantine, Stroganov, and Novgorodian styles that were written for private orders to inexpensive, mass-produced images that were sold in urban and rural marketplaces.

While the quality and skill of the costly images might have "wrapped in wonder" those who beheld them, the mass-produced images challenged what some educated Russians perceived as ancient iconic practices. As demands grew, some iconographers developed an assembly-line approach to icon production, with one person specializing in clothing, another in the background, and so forth. In order to economize time and meet the high demand for icons, less qualified iconographers as well as ones in training often painted only the face and hands and then covered the partial image with a metal or foil setting that exposed just these parts. Moreover, market demand encouraged the production of icons on paper instead of wood. These trends resulted in churchmen criticizing believers for subjecting their iconic judgment to the purse strings. Orthodox Christians, in the view of one seventeenth-century iconographer, would be better off praying to God by means of no icon than by means of one that was poorly written. Churchmen also criticized Russia's peasant iconographers for being driven in their work by a spirit of capitalism more than by the inspiration of the Holy Spirit. In doing so, churchmen maintained, they produced images that became objects of ridicule for those who did not identify with the Orthodox faith.

Whereas some churchmen feared that believers would become "contaminated" by Western influences, they expressed no less concern for the potentially negative effects of poorly produced peasant iconography. Some clergy maintained that the "crude" and "unsightly" style in which these icons were written reflected a low educational level and threatened to cool the religious sensibilities of all those who prayed before them—charges that many peasant iconographers found insulting and largely ignored. Perceptions from Russia's capitals, Moscow and

St. Petersburg, often echoed what one early nineteenth-century priest from the Kostroma Diocese maintained, namely, that on the local level Russia had few iconographers who were formally trained artists, and consequently many of the images produced "startled one's gaze." In 1829, the merchant P. V. Lukinchikov wrote to Emperor Nicholas I complaining that the icons produced in Russia's rural icon centers were often so poorly written and displayed so many errors that they drove knowledgeable peasants to turn away from the church. Educated believers nicknamed local craftsmen who produced inexpensive and unskillfully rendered images as "god-daubers" (*bogomazy*) and raised concerns not only about the potential negative spiritual influences of such images but about the potential ridicule such images might draw from their Western Christian counterparts.[6]

While in the eighteenth century many of Russia's lay educated elite disregarded Russia's "native" iconographic style, seeing it as inferior to the images inspired by Western artistic styles and produced by academically trained artists, by the mid-nineteenth century, such evaluations were shifting in favor of the native Russian icon. In large part, the shift toward the native icon was part of a general renewed appreciation within Russian educated society for its own indigenous ways and a romantic view of Russia's pre-Petrine past that followed Russia's victory over Napoleon in 1812. Renewed interest in things "Russian," however, often grew more out of national and academic sentiments than out of Orthodox theological or devotional awareness per se, thereby giving a nuanced meaning to academic claims that the Russian people had preserved genuine Orthodox iconography.

THE IMPACT OF PRINT CULTURE

Prior to 1900, innovations in technology and print culture changed the production and character of icons. Beginning in the second half of the seventeenth century, Orthodox believers found their sacred visual worlds augmented by the introduction of popular graphic paper prints (woodcuts, lithographs, and eventually chromolithographs) known as the "people's pictures" (*narodnye kartinki*) or *lubki*. Initially inspired by Western woodcuts and Piscator's German Bible, these prints were produced both by urban and rural artisans and by monastic communities. In the late seventeenth and early eighteenth centuries, believers from all social ranks, including the aristocracy and clergy, purchased such images. By the nineteenth century, however, because they were so affordable, paper religious prints were increasingly found in homes of peasants and townspeople. Demand for them grew among the poorer population to such an extent that by the end of the nineteenth century, the production of such prints constituted a highly lucrative business venture, in which not only Russia's monasteries but also Russian and foreign entrepreneurs participated. Already in the late 1870s, production of folk prints in Russia's monasteries and by well-known private Russian firms such as I. D. Sytin and E. I. Fesenko were being challenged by Polish and German firms, whose technology was superior and could produce brighter, more colorful images.

At the time of their introduction in the mid-seventeenth century, religious prints were modeled on well-known icons. The festive, bright colors of the earliest prints, including the religious ones, would have reminded people of candy wrappers. These prints embellished interior spaces and, although not confused with secular art, were nonetheless more decorative and pedagogical in their function than they were meant for prayer. "Looking at them [these prints] in the light of the [hut's] flame during the idle winter evenings," wrote one nineteenth-century researcher of Russia's popular religious prints, "peasants like to listen to the literate neighbor read and offer commentary on the descriptions that often accompany these images."[7] (See plate F in gallery.)

Among the images most favored by rural lay believers and townsmen were the colorful, illustrated versions of well-known prayers, such as the Lord's Prayer. These prayer sheets visually associated potentially abstract words and ideas with well-known biblical scenes and scenes from believers' everyday lives. For instance, one pictorial representation of the Lord's Prayer included scenes of the last judgment to illustrate the phrase "Thy kingdom come," Christ in Gethsemane to accompany the phrase "Thy will be done," and Adam and Eve in the Garden of Eden to portray the notion of not leading one into temptation. The phrases "Give us this day our daily bread" and "Forgive us our trespasses" were depicted with illustrations of an annual blessing of the harvest and of the sacrament of confession respectively, both of which would have been very familiar to the viewer (fig. 6.1).

Another favorite print, that of the last judgment graphically illustrated what many believers considered the most important event of life—namely, death and the eventual judgment that believers trusted they would face (fig. 6.2). Combining two scenes—the second coming of Christ with the last judgment—woodcuts and later machine-produced prints of this popular scene were based on ancient models adopted in medieval Russia from Byzantium. Inspired in part by the literary work of Saint Ephrem of Syria, depictions of the last judgment guided believers' imagination and helped to sustain age-old Orthodox understandings of death and the end times. The description of events that were widely anticipated to mark the last judgment (Matt. 25:31-46) often accompanied the handmade and machine-made prints. The prints urged viewers to meditate on the time-limited nature of hope with respect to the afterlife, on the expectation that humans would be judged for sins that they did not recognize they had committed, and on the urgent need to mend one's ways during his or her lifetime. Because of their broad appeal and

Fig. 6.1. The Lord's Prayer. Prints Collection, Russian National Library, St. Petersburg.

pedagogical use, religious prints found their way into missionary hand-bags and parish school classrooms as useful tools in teaching about the Orthodox faith.

Although their pedagogical function continued, the boundary between religious prints and icons eventually blurred. Market forces influenced believers' understanding of what constituted an icon. Since mass-produced paper images were among the most affordable religious images available, Russia's poorer rural and urban believers attempted to transform these paper images into icons. They purchased such images, had them blessed by their parish priest, mounted them on boards or thick cardboard, and framed and hung them in the spaces in their homes that were reserved for icons. Late nineteenth-century ethnographic reports from Russia's rural areas frequently noted the inexpensive prints of Christ, Mary, and the saints that decorated the walls of peasant homes, usually in or near the sacred space of an icon corner.

Curiously, not only images of Christ and officially canonized saints found their way onto popular prints and subsequently into icon corners, but also images of individuals who, though not official saints, enjoyed

Fig. 6.2. A picture of the last judgment of God. Prints Collection, Russian National Library, St. Petersburg.

widespread public recognition as holy men and women. One example is that of Ksenia of St. Petersburg, an eighteenth-century woman who by the nineteenth century was widely known as a "holy fool" for having given away her possessions, having donned the clothes of her deceased husband, and having prayed in the fields outside the capital at night, while during the day roaming the streets of St. Petersburg collecting alms for the poor (fig. 6.3).[8] While simultaneously reflecting and informing people's understanding of Orthodoxy, mass-produced prints contributed to the makings of modern Orthodox saints by helping to keep their memory alive and, when hung near an icon corner, by visually situating them among the blessed. Positioned somewhere between the witness of a photograph or portrait and the testimony of an icon, prints of holy people satisfied believers' yearning for visual authentication of oral stories since seeing made believing easier. By incorporating these paper prints into their home shrines, even if only at the periph-

Fig. 6.3. The Servant of God, Ksenia, the Fool for Christ. Prints Collection, Russian National Library, St. Petersburg.

ery, believers testified to their acceptance of both the paper and the person depicted on it into the purview of their sacred worlds.

Educated Russians were mixed in their evaluations of the religious *lubki*. Similar to evaluations of peasant-written icons, estimations of religious folk prints depended to a large extent on any given believer's sentiments toward "the people." Those who tended to view "the people" as "dark masses" often dismissed woodcut and etched prints as crude and primitive. Others who considered "the people" more positively—as bearers of Orthodoxy and cultivators of the native Russian spirit—looked to the prints as cultural expressions of the inner life of the Russian people.

The topic of paper icons and religious prints also surfaced in a broader discourse concerning the preservation and dignity of the icon in a consumer age. Already in the second half of the seventeenth century, the patriarch of Russia, Joachim (1674–1690), issued an encyclical in which he criticized the extensive sale of printed paper images, claiming that they were not fit for veneration. Some church-men considered paper more transitory than wood and therefore less worthy to bear an image of Christ or the saints. Moreover, because of a paper icon's more transitory nature, a believer might approach it with less reverence than one depicted on wood.

Concerns escalated even more when production of paper images passed out of human hands to machines. In 1899, peasants represent-ing more than eight thousand men and women involved in the local iconographic cottage industry in the Vladimir Diocese petitioned the Holy Synod to prevent the sale of inexpensive, machine-made icons produced by the Moscow-based French firms Jacquot and Bonnaker. The mass production of these inexpensive images threatened not only the economic viability of entire communities, argued critics, but also the integrity of the Orthodox faith. Machine production threatened to compromise the authenticity of an icon. No longer associated with direct divine inspiration or with the spiritual disposition of the Ortho-dox iconographer, the machine-produced image could not help but be a qualitatively different product. Critics of machine-produced images, however, stopped one step short of evaluating believers' prayers before a machine-produced icon. Given these concerns, it is not surprising that at the beginning of the twentieth century, educated laymen were discussing ways in which the manufacturing of machine-produced icons might be limited or at least directly overseen and monitored by Russia's main monastic communities.

Orthodox concerns about the proper viewing of icons extended beyond the formal act of icon veneration and the immediate devo-tional context framed by prayer. A believer's disposition toward an icon involved almost every aspect of approaching and touching an icon, including the manner of its purchase and sale (see plate G in gallery). As late as the end of the nineteenth century, peasant believers resisted using the word "purchase" with respect to icons; instead, they preferred the word "exchange," even though that exchange was often for money. As one observer writing from the provincial regions of Russia noted at the end of the nineteenth century, God and the mar-ket are not easily combined in the thought-worlds of many peasant believers. Despite these verbal precautions to safeguard the sanctity of icons in the face of potential commodification, the seventeenth through the nineteenth centuries saw widespread complaints about the treatment of icons in the marketplace.

Critics partly blamed traveling salesmen for the poor quality of inexpensive icons, claiming that for the salesmen, a raw desire for profit surpassed any spiritual concerns regarding the images they were selling. Critics also maintained that the context in which icons were purchased and sold directly influenced how believers beheld them. As one seventeenth-century critic noted, traveling peddlers bartered icons as if they were children's toys. Nineteenth-century churchmen voiced similar complaints about the sale of icons as simple goods that were bought and sold indiscriminately at haberdasheries and transported to bazaars "like logs" in carts. Seeing the icon in that manner, in their estimation, directly threatened people's sensibilities regarding the sacred. Consequently, in 1900, the Holy Synod directed priests to oversee the sale of icons in their localities in order to ensure that the marketing of icons did not pose any "temptations" to believers.

Despite multileveled attempts to monitor, direct, and preserve believers' iconic gaze, the continued variety of iconographic styles and competing forms of icon production in Russia up to the 1917 revolutions testify that neither Russian iconographers nor the faithful at large uniformly shared official criteria for a "good" image. Traveling in Russia in the mid-seventeenth century, Paul of Aleppo observed that in their "great attachment to and love of icons," Muscovites took into account neither the beauty of the image nor the mastership of the painter. For them, "all icons, beautiful or not, are the same."[9]

Although this and similar observations throughout the eighteenth and nineteenth centuries did not give due justice to the nuances of lay believers' judgment with regard to icons, such comments nevertheless indicate that believers often evaluated the quality or authenticity of an icon by standards other than aesthetic ones. Other factors were clearly at work when, for instance, in the seventeenth century lay believers were openly critical of Patriarch Nikon's destruction of icons painted under European artistic influences. Believers reportedly "judged that he had sinned greatly" and pronounced him "an open enemy" with respect to icons. Similarly, believers apparently saw nothing un-Orthodox in carved images of Saint Nicholas and of "Christ in the

Dungeon" that could be found throughout Russian parishes even at the beginning of the twentieth century (fig. 6.4). In 1899, the bishop of Tver, Dmitrii (Sambikin), complained that some of the faithful in his diocese purchased Roman Catholic images not only for their homes but for churches as well.[10]

Fig. 6.4. Miracle-working icon of Our Savior in the Dungeon. Library of Congress, Prokudin-Gorskii Collection.

OLD BELIEF

Indeed, Orthodox believers took numerous considerations into account in evaluating the quality or authenticity of an icon. In part, a person's appreciation of a particular icon depended on whether he or she identified with the form of Orthodox Christianity supported by the state or with the Old Belief. While ostensibly associated with a series of church reforms, the rise of dissenters during this period was

provoked as much by the manner in which these reforms were instituted as they were by the actual content of the reforms themselves.

Believers who identified with the Old Belief, or who were at least
sympathetic toward it, favored older, darker icons painted in the
"Greek" style. Darkness suggested age, and age indicated a production date prior to the mid-seventeenth-century schism. Sensitive to
the needs of Old Believers, nineteenth-century Russian iconographers made darker, Byzantine-style icons to meet their demands. Old
Believers also evaluated an icon's authenticity in terms of particular
features depicted in the image—the way in which Christ held his hand
in blessing and the spelling of the name of Jesus, for instance—since
these issues had figured into debates about ritual and reform in the
seventeenth century. Given that in some rural areas the confessional
lines between Old Believers and the faithful who were officially registered as Orthodox Christians was often blurred, iconic preferences
were often shared by those of both groups.

For Old Believers, ancient icons (or those made to resemble the
ancient style) served as symbolic, visual links to the pre-Petrine era
and bore testimony to what Old Believers understood as a more
authentic form of Orthodoxy. Old Believers did not enjoy brightly colored icons or those that depicted Christ and the saints in naturalistic
forms, as did some of their non–Old Believer Orthodox counterparts.
For Old Believers, Western-styled icons pointed to the degenerative
path onto which the state church had embarked. Old Believers joined
their Orthodox counterparts in questioning the iconicity of printed
instead of hand-painted images, especially when the prints came to
be produced by machines. Already in 1722, a peasant from the Iaroslavl Diocese with leanings toward the Old Belief, Matvei Grigoriev,
found himself under investigation for having thrown an icon that had
been hanging in a choir loft to the floor. Grigoriev maintained he was
driven to do so by the fact that the icon was printed on paper and by
the sentiment that it was "not proper" to venerate images found on
paper. Although according to Russia's laws in the eighteenth century
an act of iconoclasm warranted the death penalty, state officials chose
to spare Grigoriev's life on account of the recent peace treaty signed
with Sweden and because of his illiteracy and "simple-mindedness."[11]

Because icons containing overtly pre-Nikonian features reinforced the division between Old Believers and the state-sponsored

Russian Orthodox Church, possession of such icons could be and sometimes was perceived by church and state officials as expressive of political resistance or subversion. Consequently, such icons were periodically confiscated from the homes of Old Believers. Nevertheless, as the eighteenth and nineteenth centuries progressed and church and state officials became more amicable toward Old Believers, they also became more sensitive to their attitudes toward icons. A synodal ruling in 1888, for instance, directed priests in localities with large populations of Old Believers to be aware of Old Believer aversion to the "Italian style" and to make sure that their churches contained icons written in the Greek style.

Generally, in their evaluation of icons, Orthodox laymen and laywomen tended to emphasize the prayerful use of an icon and the role it played in their lives. With the exception of Old Believers for whom certain aspects of iconic depictions were nonnegotiable, many Orthodox Christians favored familial icons, icons associated with poignant life events, or icons before which they felt an especially prayerful connection, however questionable its visual qualities. The gaze of faith often challenged modern aesthetic and confessional sensibilities.

MIRACLES, MEMORY, AND MODERNITY

In a homily composed in 1901, the bishop of Kostroma, Vissarion (Nechaev), addressed some of the challenges that Russia's "new-style" icons posed for the Orthodox Christian. Agreeing with those who argued that icons written under the influence of Western art satisfied the demands of secular aesthetic taste above all else, he also maintained that Orthodox principles regarding icon veneration allowed believers to pray before these images just as they did before those written in the Greek style. If the honor shown to the image passes to the prototype—to Christ and the saints—as Orthodox teachings maintained, then "it is understandable why we must honor with equal zeal ancient icons and those written according to the rules of new art." Bishop Vissarion supported his view with one of the conventional arguments that Orthodox believers had used for centuries to justify their use of icons in general—namely, that the miracles attributed to prayer before icons demonstrated that icon veneration was pleasing to God. Accordingly, reasoned the bishop, since miracles had been attributed to icons written in the new style, then these images were not displeasing to God. Bishop Vissarion's homily presupposed that from a believer's perspective, icon veneration engaged various types of seeing—not only "bodily" sight but also spiritual sight by which believers hoped and often claimed to discern the workings of God's grace.[12]

Believers did not equally value each icon they encountered in the course of their lives. They held in higher esteem, for instance, those icons that had been in the family for generations and that had been associated with momentous events in the lives of their ancestors. Believers from all social classes had icons that they associated with episodes in their family's history and in their own lives. These icons provided believers with a sense of continuity among generations, a means by which family history was preserved for posterity, a stimulus for remembering God, and a focal point within their lives. These icons typically enjoyed a place of honor in the home—wealthier families sometimes had an entire room devoted to prayer in which they kept their most revered icons; less wealthy believers placed their icons in special icon corners. Believers marked an icon that held special meaning by placing a burning candle or lampada before it, decorating it with flowers or with a silver setting.

Icons also became specially revered by entire communities locally, regionally, and even nationally. Nationally revered icons enjoyed tremendous popularity and served as prototypes for numerous copies made of them. Housed in urban cathedrals or monastery churches, these icons enjoyed a prominent place in the church's interior space and would have been immediately identifiable even to an outsider. The miracle-working Smolensk icon of the Mother of God, for instance, was celebrated annually on July 28 throughout the Russian Empire (fig. 6.5). Named after a well-known Byzantine iconic type—the Mother of God called Hodegetria—the story of the Smolensk icon included themes that were shared with other nationally revered images of the Mother of God: an association with the evangelist Luke and the ancient story of his having painted images of Mary; an association between Russia and the former center of Orthodoxy—Byzantium; Mary's election and protection of Russia in the face of the medieval challenges of Islam from the East and the more modern challenges of

Fig. 6.5. Miracle-working icon of the Mother of God-Hodegetria in the Assumption Cathedral, Smolensk.

the West; and the grounding of these national narratives in continued reports of healings and "signs" among laypeople at large.

Between specially revered familial icons within homes and those that were known and commemorated empirewide, believers also honored locally revered icons associated with stories of healing, comfort, and aid. Many locally revered images originated as familial icons that were later donated to parish churches because believers outside of the family network expressed a desire to venerate them. As was the case with their nationally known counterparts, the veneration of locally revered icons was a phenomenon that crossed gender, socioeconomic, and sometimes even confessional lines.

Historically, both clergy and lay believers contributed to the advancement of locally revered icons by orally recounting episodes from the icon's life and by incorporating the icon into liturgical celebrations. In the second half of the nineteenth century, icon-related stories began appearing in print on a wide scale in diocesan newspapers, devotional pamphlets, local parish histories, and ethnographic accounts. The expansion of print culture fueled the special veneration of particular icons and confounded boundaries between popular and official, local and national Orthodox cultures. What were once stories that belonged predominantly to the domain of local, oral culture now became formally available in texts on which clergy and laymen and laywomen could draw for inspirational and pedagogical purposes.

The Diocese of Tambov, located some three hundred miles southeast of Moscow, was one of several dioceses in the late nineteenth century that published a brief description of its locally specially revered icons, the overwhelming majority of which, as in other dioceses across the land, were of Mary, the Mother of God. (In the mid-seventeenth century, Paul of Aleppo noted that he had never seen a Russian church without an icon of the Mother of God.) Thirteen different types of images appeared among the twenty specially revered icons of Mary in the Tambov Diocese. Tambov's list of locally revered icons also included images of Saint Nicholas of Myra, the Old Testament Trinity, and Saint Panteleimon. Significantly, the Tambov list did not include any locally revered images of Christ depicted alone. (The icons of Mary depicted her with the infant Christ child). This pattern typified what could be found in other dioceses as well, with images of Christ and the saints being much less prevalent than images of Mary.

More than half of the foundational narratives of Tambov's honored icons recounted the experiences of laypeople who were from different social classes. Although the foundational narratives that characterized Tambov's list of icons included no experiences of believers from the peasantry, this was atypical. The nineteenth century in general in Russia saw a marked increase in reports of specially revered icons whose foundational narratives often involved peasant believers. Because the second half of the nineteenth century continued to see the "births" of such icons, many iconic narratives were still in the making and consequently did not yet register in formal, published lists. Given the relatively minimal role that laypeople played in the institutional structures of the church, and given that the one domain of church life where insights into lay experiences might have been expected—the officially recognized roster of saints—was instead heavily dominated by male monastics, narratives associated with specially revered icons offered a unique record of lay testimony to the perceived workings of God in their midst.

In the nineteenth century, a growing number of laity reported self-renewing images—icons that had darkened through time but had inexplicably lightened. Other signs included seeing an icon in a dream and finding an icon that had been discarded or forgotten or that lay in an unusual locality, such as under a tree, in a field, or on a riverbank (fig. 6.6). Believers often constructed chapels and occasionally even churches on the site where an icon had been found. Many of the more than 23,000 chapels counted in Russia in 1914 were constructed on such sites.

Fig. 6.6. Chapel commemorating the appearance of an icon of St. Nicholas the Wonderworker, Shadrinsk.

The story of a specially revered icon of Saint Panteleimon in the Tambov Diocese reportedly began in the mid-nineteenth century. Aleksander Koltynianskii, a landowner and military man, returned to his home village for retirement. As an elderly invalid, he ceased being able to attend church regularly. In 1869, he became critically ill and, having exhausted his medical options, prayed for relief. One night, he heard a voice from the icon stating that here was his healer. Moved by this experience, he ordered an icon of Saint Panteleimon from the well-known Russian monastic community of Saint Panteleimon in the Eastern Orthodox monastic center of Mount Athos. Koltynianskii was reportedly healed by prayer before this image once it arrived.[13]

Believers frequently spoke of experiences involving icons as signs of God's grace. Icons revered by individuals and families became part of collective religious life when others heard about the icon and began gathering to pray before it. Koltynianskii's icon of Saint Panteleimon emerged in public light after his death, when the estate he had willed to the church was transformed into a monastic community and a neighboring landowner was reportedly healed from prayer to Saint Panteleimon before this icon. Believers traveled from neighboring towns and villages to venerate this icon on the feast of Saint Panteleimon, and soon believers from other localities requested that the icon visit them.

Among the twenty-six reported locally revered icons in the Tambov Diocese, the foundational narratives of nine were associated with women. Believers related these nine icons to such experiences as a woman's anguish over a wrongfully imprisoned spouse, a mother's despair over a daughter's repeated stillbirths, an unexpected healing of a pregnant woman scheduled for an abortion, and a woman's abduction. Not unusual among nineteenth-century foundational iconic narratives were those that involved peasant women with abusive husbands whose main emotional support often seemed to come from members of their faith communities, often including the local parish priest.

An example of the processes by which these stories became part of believers' religious worlds can be seen in the case of the Kazan icon of the Mother of God from the Vyshenskii Dormition women's monastic community in the Tambov Diocese. In 1812, at the time of

Napoleon's invasion of Russia, the nun Mironia decided to leave her monastic community in Moscow for a more remote, secure community. Taking a few possessions, including an icon of the Mother of God that she kept in her cell, she left for the Tambov Diocese. On the way, her driver decided to rob and kill her. Mironia later attributed her deliverance from bodily harm to fervent prayer to the Mother of God. Some fifty years later, after Mironia had died, believers constructed a chapel in honor of this icon in Tambov's central marketplace in commemoration of alleviation from a cholera epidemic in 1871. Within this chapel, they placed a copy of Mironia's icon, which they had the iconographer frame with depictions of episodes from Mironia's life that involved the icon. Mironia's story, therefore, became intertwined with the local history of a community and enshrined for posterity in an iconic depiction of the Mother of God.

RITUAL PRACTICE

As an icon's renown grew within a community, believers included it in many rituals (see plate H in gallery). In addition to bowing before it and kissing or decorating it as they would any other icon, believers would hang particularly valued or symbolic items on a specially revered icon in honor of the icon's role in critical life-events. Such items included personal baptismal crosses, gold and silver strands, flax and linen, candles, oil for the lampada that burned before the icon, and, in some regions, similar to Roman Catholic practices in the West, votives such as miniature hands, legs, or eyes that represented the body part that believers claimed were healed on account of prayer before the icon. Continuing a practice that had become more common in Russia beginning in the mid-sixteenth century, believers who had fulfilled vows expressed their gratitude to God by providing specially revered icons with metal coverings or settings, usually made of silver. Each gift before an icon signified an often dramatic life-story and was left by the believer as an offering to God, Christ, and often a saint as a fulfillment of a vow or in simple recognition of the power of God's grace in their lives. While periodically criticized as "dead capital" that only distracted believers from prayer, these settings also found defenders who argued that they encouraged prayer since they were expressions of people's love of God. Ironically, these same metal or silver settings that believers donated as offerings were criticized by late nineteenth- and early twentieth-century academic icon experts, revealing competing approaches to the understanding of icons. Writing in 1916, the well-known Russian philosopher Prince Evgenii Trubetskoi spoke of these settings as hiding and "imprisoning" the icon. In his estimation, they were "a product of that pious bad taste that went along with the decline in religious feeling."[14]

The desire to see and venerate specially revered icons resulted in the development of an involved, often dramatic ritual—the icon visitation. By the end of the nineteenth century, approximately eight hundred specially revered icons were taken annually from their "homes" in parish churches, monasteries, or cathedrals in order to visit local and distant rural and urban communities. Lay believers initiated most visitations. Representatives of town councils, village assemblies, or parish communities contacted the monastery, parish church, or cathedral where the icon was housed to make necessary arrangements, which could sometimes be elaborate and occasionally included the input not only of the direct parties involved but also of the offices of the diocesan bishop, the provincial government, and even the Ministry of Internal Affairs and Chancellery of the Holy Synod.

For instance, in 1846, a landowner from the Saratov Diocese requested an annual visitation of an icon of the Kazan Mother of God from the Nizhelomov monastery in the neighboring Diocese of Penza. The landowner nostalgically recalled frequent family visits to this monastery as a boy and now desired that the same icon visit the villages that comprised his estate. He agreed to arrange the trip of the two hieromonks and two novices who would accompany the icon on its 165-mile journey. Along the way, church officials expected the icon to be greeted by the clergy in every village with banners and bell ringing. In 1879, members from the town of Aleksandrov Posad in the Pskov Diocese offered to send thirty members of their community and six horse-drawn carts annually in order to bring two specially revered icons from the well-known Pskovo-Pechera monastery.[15]

Even though diocesan officials did not honor all requests, an icon's itinerary could still be quite extensive. The visitation schedule for the well-known icons were composed annually and publicly posted. While visitation schedules for most icons were modest, the itineraries for Russia's best-known icons typically became more involved with time and by the end of the nineteenth century could last many months. Given the high demand for visits by some of the best-known icons, towns and villages prepared ceremoniously to greet the icon at any time of day or night.

Visitations usually included a personal and a communal component. They were associated with a town's or a village's local history as well as with the lives of individual believers since believers routinely requested that the "guest" bless their homes with a visit as well. A large number of Russia's villages and urban areas sponsored annual icon visitations to commemorate such events as droughts, epidemics, floods, and fires. Occasionally, a request for an icon visitation would come from a particular subgroup of a local community. In 1860, for instance, the head of the merchants' group in the Chernigov province requested an annual visitation of a specially revered icon of the Mother of God in order to mark the opening of the city's trade fair. The presence of the icon, he maintained, would act as a "visible sign" of God's blessing of their trading activities.

Faith and doubt regarding these icons stemmed in large part from an understanding of the miraculous and of what constituted proper discernment. These issues might have periodically tested the Orthodox practice of the veneration of icons since Byzantine times but resurfaced anew in light of modern cultural change. Modernity brought ways of seeing that challenged even the sincerest believers in their evaluation of an icon's place in their lives.

Although proper and orderly icon veneration was a subject of concern to Orthodox Church officials prior to the eighteenth century, the reign of Peter the Great (1682–1725) inaugurated a new level of awareness, especially as this veneration applied to specially revered icons. Prompted by a European-inspired desire for rational order that drove his numerous other reforms, Peter's church reforms were aimed at organizing matters of faith and establishing church legislation that would enable everything to be done "properly and according to Christian law," as he and his advisers envisioned it. One of the results of his efforts was the institution in 1721 of the so-called *Spiritual Regulation* which remained the foundational legislation governing the institution of the Orthodox Church in Russia until the Bolshevik Revolution of 1917.

Among the terms that appeared in the *Regulation* to refer to certain aspects of church life that were amiss was "superstition." Though having first appeared in ecclesiastical legislation in the mid-sixteenth century, the term at that time had referred mostly to charms, spells, and other activities associated with black magic or to beliefs and customs attributed to Russia's pagan past. In the *Spiritual Regulation*, however, superstition also referred to certain church-related rituals and behaviors defined as "superfluous, not essential for salvation, and beguiling the simple." In this context it addressed the activities of clergy even more than those of laity. Concerned that some of the activity around specially revered images could be interpreted by foreigners as superstition, the Holy Synod in the early eighteenth century attempted to divest icons of outward features that marked them as "uncommon" or "special" by controlling how an icon was placed in a church, what was done with it, and how it was handled outside of church.

Although they never indicated the standard by which they judged such matters, church officials also attempted to manage the ornamentation of icons, ensuring there be nothing "excessive or uncharacteristic" about it that would compromise the sacredness of church space. In the early eighteenth century, limiting ornamentation meant putting the wealth accruing to icons to practical use. A short-lived church ruling (1720–1725) called for clergy to remove all gold and silver strands that believers brought as testimony and to use the proceeds from their sale to purchase needed liturgical goods, such as vestments or flour for the baking of bread. This type of ornamentation, claimed the directive, "brings disgrace to the image and reproach from foreigners."

Church officials also tried to make sure that icons did not lose their ecclesial orientation. They attempted to prohibit believers from lighting candles before icons that were situated outside of churches, on church walls or in roadside shrines. Such a practice, an eighteenth-century church directive maintained, was unhealthy and in "disagreement with the word of God" since it drew believers away from corporate prayer in church and to "vain prayers" at crossroads and in marketplaces. At the same time, they also prohibited believers from keeping their personal and familial icons in churches. These icons, too, misdirected a believer's gaze; instead of participating in a collective gaze encouraged by corporate prayer, believers spent much of the Divine Liturgy concentrating on their own icons. In fact, as the bishop of Moscow, Sergii, reminded believers in 1895, state regulations prohibited believers from venerating icons during liturgical services because the act distracted believers from the ritual at hand.[16]

In 1722, the Holy Synod also forbade icons to be taken from parish and monastery churches to private homes. If believers needed to venerate the icon, the directive argued, they should go to the icon and not request the icon to come to them. Otherwise, these visitations would breed "superfluous devotion." Although the Holy Synod rescinded this ruling in 1744 by somewhat surprisingly citing ancient church testimony to the efficacy of prayer before icons in terms of healing the sick, the sentiments behind it periodically resurfaced in the nineteenth century when hierarchs attempted to limit the practice of icon visitations. Frequent visitations, along with an icon's long absence from its home base, reasoned certain clergymen, threatened it with overexposure to the elements and to the public. Recurring public displays bred familiarity with the sacred, and familiarity, in turn, could breed contempt. For similar reasons, periodic church rulings emphasized proper public treatment of icons: believers could not talk during processions and they had to transport icons in a becoming manner—either by hand or in a carriage.

THE REGULATION OF MIRACLES

Neither Peter the Great nor the *Spiritual Regulation* denied the reality of miracles or of miracle-working icons; church officials did not question the veracity of stories associated with already established, ancient, or well-known miracle-working images that were liturgically commemorated annually. In this sense, the *Regulation* cannot be compared to criticisms of images leveled by certain Protestant reformers against Roman Catholic piety or to the treatises of rational Enlightenment thinkers who categorically dismissed perceived miracles as fabrications, misperceptions, or simply that which humans cannot yet explain. Instead, the legislation was preoccupied primarily with "false miracles" and with the fraud and profiteering that often lay behind them. In many ways, these concerns paralleled the concerns of Catholic churchmen during the Council of Trent who, as one historian has noted, sought "to prevent their flock from crying miracle too easily."[17]

The concern with false miracles introduced tension between the notions of superstition and miracle that carried over into church legislation that had lasting impact throughout the nineteenth and early twentieth centuries. According to a 1722 law, which was never officially rescinded before 1917 and which church officials periodically continued to implement, any newly surfaced, reportedly miracle-working icon was to be taken from private homes (or parish churches) and placed in a monastery church or in the provincial cathedral for safekeeping while the stories associated with the icon were officially investigated.

When enforced, the 1722 ruling subjected believers' religious experiences to modern investigative practices carried out by appointed clergy, civil officials, and physicians, who were assigned to "examine everything completely." The proclamation of false miracles was a civil offense that subjected laypeople to strict punishment, which in the eighteenth century sometimes included corporal punishment and imprisonment. Clearly men and women who willfully reported their experiences did not believe their reports to be false. By the second half of the nineteenth century, civil courts had become reluctant to consider these cases, claiming that these were matters for the church to decide. When cases involved primarily clergy and monastic men and women who were found guilty of spreading unsubstantiated rumors of miracles or who were suspected of profiteering through their encouragement of public devotion to a particular icon, church officials responded swiftly. They suspended such people from their responsibilities, subjected them to fines, or sent them to monasteries for a period of several months for "edification." In some cases parish priests who were found guilty of exploiting the people by perpetuating "false miracles" were defrocked.

While aimed to protect the integrity of the Orthodox faith by staving off crude, money-making hoaxes, keeping the "dark masses" from spiritual predators, and refining believers' devotional gaze in light of modern sensibilities, the 1722 law instead often sparked tensions between local communities and central church officials, and between laity and clergy. For many Orthodox believers—clergy and laity—a specially revered icon was not to be equated with common church property to which governing churchmen could lay claim. Accordingly, laymen and laywomen in whose families or parishes these icons often originated usually remained firm in their claims to an icon, often going to extremes to protect what they believed was lawfully theirs.

Believers generally regarded a specially revered icon as a distinct, divinely established focal point of spiritual and even ecclesial life, basing their view on the principle that since God had revealed his goodwill, mercy, and divine blessing by means of an icon in a particular locality, the icon should remain there, despite the will of any single member of the community or the desires of institutional representatives. Believers viewed the veneration of these icons as a means of "communion," broadly conceived, that did not technically require the administration of a bishop or clergyman. Sermons and devotional literature often supported such a view. Icons, maintained one priest in 1917, were a means by which people could enter into communion with God. For that reason, people should look at the face of the Savior and "imbibe him by one's gaze." Not surprisingly, faced with the removal of their icon, a group of parishioners from the Vladikavkaz Diocese in 1900 responded, "The bishop is subordinate to the icon and not the icon to him."[18] In this sense the specially revered icon raised broader issues concerning ecclesial ordering and the proper locus of ecclesial gatherings. Church officials often responded negatively to gatherings of believers around these icons when these gatherings were not under direct clerical supervision. At least for some of them, such gatherings seemed to provide a ripe environment for "self-willed" or "sectarian" activities that could threaten the integrity of hierarchically ordered church life. Laymen and laywomen, on the other hand, by and large viewed the icon as a supplemental focus of ecclesial affiliation, with the actual spatial setting—home, chapel, field, or church—taking on secondary importance.

Miracle-working icons also prompted reconsideration of the use of the term "superstition" as it applied to perceived miracles. While use of the term in the *Spiritual Regulation* served the purpose of making Orthodoxy "presentable" in an eighteenth-century European world, its use by certain clergy often frustrated believers. In 1821, for instance, a group of parishioners from the Kostroma Diocese petitioned Tsar Nicholas I to intervene on their behalf before the Holy Synod in order to secure the safe return of an icon that had been taken from their parish church. They heatedly protested the charge of superstitious behavior, maintaining that they did nothing that ran counter to the rules of the holy fathers. Instead of "tempting" the faithful in some negative way, they argued, the icon in question had only exerted a positive influence on parish life by drawing increasing numbers of people to communal worship.[19]

Believers who protested against the use of the term "superstition" to describe their special veneration of an icon sometimes pointed out that their veneration of a newly surfaced, specially revered icon in a small rural parish differed little from the veneration of icons in urban cathedrals. Insinuations of conflicting standards in ecclesial life were even more apparent in the second half of the nineteenth century when Orthodox attempts at systematic reflections on miracles in general and miracle-working icons in particular appeared with more frequency. Arising as a response to challenges posed by the "spirit of the times," which in the estimation of one Orthodox apologist began in Paris as a product of the French Revolution, this literature defended the notion of the miracle in the modern age. According to nineteenth-century Russian Orthodox treatises on the subject, miracles were the "activity of the Spirit of God," which was experienced differently by different people at different times. As a "manifestation of the mercy of God," miracles could not be proven but were said to lead to edification and to repentance while also eliciting a deep sense of joy. Icons, according to this literature, were a means by which God allowed signs and miracles in order to help establish believers in his church; they were a means by which God showed forth his grace. Consequently, apologists spoke of miracles in terms of enlightenment and salvation. In 1887, the bishop of Mogilev, Sergii, maintained that those who denied miracles through icons were guilty of no less than blasphemy against the Holy Spirit (Matt. 12:31). Taking a less confessional stand, graduate of Moscow Theological Academy and seminary professor Sergei Glagolev maintained that faith in miracles was a general human faith, innate to all, even to those who voiced disbelief in such. Rooted in hope, this faith in miracles, he wrote, should serve as the "regulatory principle of our world understanding."[20]

Icons in modern Russia were linked to the notions of spiritual discernment and the role of the Holy Spirit in history, especially as manifested in perceived miracles. Influenced by modern European intellectual thought and a negative view of "the people," some of Russia's churchmen throughout the eighteenth and nineteenth centuries regarded the signs and miracles that laypeople ascribed to the Holy Spirit as evidence of the people's backwardness and superstition. Yet, ironically, the persistence of laymen and laywomen in their defense of God's signs and miracles in their lives might also be interpreted as a manifestation of "modernizing" trends within the Orthodox Church. Perceiving miracles engaged believers as active agents in the Orthodox Church, whose institutional structures made little practical room for the unordained or nontonsured. Insofar as laypeople associated particular icons with the direction of their personal lives, the history of their communities, and even the history of the Russian nation, they acted as active witnesses to a personal God and to God's perceived workings in their midst. When pressed in this role by their hierarchical superiors or by modern philosophical standards, believers often questioned the judgment and the ascendancy of these various authorities in matters of faith. Directly tying personal and communal religious experiences to particular images, icons enabled believers to weave their histories into the history of the broader ecclesial community. By doing so, icons empowered Orthodox believers in the modern world to uphold what one nineteenth-century Russian Orthodox bishop referred to as the "inviolability of the freedom of Christian sensibilities" that have their own rights.[21]

FOR FURTHER READING

Bushkovitch, Paul. *Religion and Society in Russia: The Sixteenth and Seventeenth Centuries*. New York: Oxford University Press, 1992.

Freeze, Gregory L. "Institutionalizing Piety: The Church and Popular Religion, 1750–1850." Pages 210–49 in *Imperial Russia: New Histories for the Empire*. Edited by Jane Burbank and David L. Ransel. Bloomington: Indiana University Press, 1998.

Jenks, Andrew L. *Russia in a Box: Art and Identity in an Age of Revolution*. Dekalb: Northern Illinois University Press, 2005.

Nichols, Robert L. "The Icon and the Machine in Russia's Religious Renaissance, 1900–1909." Pages 131–44 in *Christianity and the Arts in Russia*. Edited by William C. Brumfield and Milos M. Velimirovic. New York: Cambridge University Press, 1991.

Ouspensky, Leonid. *Theology of the Icon*. Vol. 2. Translated by Anthony Gythiel. Crestwood, N.Y.: St. Vladimir's Seminary Press, 1992.

Shevzov, Vera. *Russian Orthodoxy on the Eve of Revolution*. New York: Oxford University Press, 2004.

Sytova, Alla. *The Lubok: Russian Folk Pictures Seventeenth to Nineteenth Century*. Leningrad: Aurora Art Publishers, 1984.

Tarasov, Oleg. *Icon and Devotion: Sacred Spaces in Imperial Russia*. Translated and edited Robin Milner-Gulland. London: Reaktion Books, 2002.

RELIGIOUS EXPERIENCES IN NEW ENGLAND

DOUGLAS L. WINIARSKI

CHAPTER SEVEN

Timothy Mather Cooley knew well the challenges that he faced when, in 1796, he accepted a call to serve as the third pastor of the Congregational Church of Granville, Massachusetts. Founded during the tumultuous religious decade of the 1740s—a period of intense revival activity known as the "Great Awakening"—Granville had struggled to maintain a settled ministry over the next two decades. Competing factions of parishioners had wrangled over religious doctrine and fought to control key church offices; seemingly petty squabbles among neighbors had erupted into disputes that lasted for decades. In fact, Granville had been without an ordained pastor since the dismissal of the controversial Jedidiah Smith in the mid-1770s.

The task of restoring discipline to what in previous decades would have been Granville's sole established, tax-supported religious institution began with an inventory of the extant church records. Smith had failed to keep a formal record book. Instead, Cooley inherited a chaotic collection of manuscripts, and organizing them into an orderly system required concerted effort. Carefully sorting the loose papers into neatly folded dockets, the young Yale graduate proceeded to label each with a brief notation regarding its subject matter. He would follow this procedure meticulously over the course of his six-decade pastorate, and by the time of his death in 1859, the Granville clergyman had assembled one of the largest and most detailed collections of church papers in antebellum New England. There were letters of recommendation from neighboring churches, depositions and confessions relating to cases of church discipline, minutes of church meetings, correspondence with colleagues, sermon notes, and most important, brief autobiographical narratives submitted by candidates for full church membership.

Cooley's endorsements on this last group warrant careful scrutiny. During the eighteenth century, parishioners seeking access to the sacraments of baptism and the Lord's Supper in New England's Congregational churches were required to compose a brief written statement in which they described their personal beliefs and religious experiences. Jedidiah Smith initially had referred to the short narratives as "Relations"; but four decades later, Cooley wrote the word "Experiences" beneath his predecessor's original notations. What was the significance of the changing terminology? The question becomes even knottier when we stop to consider that during the seventeenth century, Puritan clergymen called these same church-admission testimonies "confessions." Adding to the confusion, modern historians have classified this distinctive genre of New England religious literature as "conversion narratives," but even a cursory examination of their theological arguments, autobiographical content, and physical appearance suggests that their meaning and significance changed dramatically over the two centuries in which they were employed as a formal test to gauge the spiritual fitness of prospective church members.

This chapter examines the shifting language of conversion in New England Congregationalism—the bastion of Puritan culture in North America—from the period of settlement in the 1630s to the eve of the Civil War. Evidence is drawn from a database of more than a thousand church-admission narratives from nearly three dozen communities scattered across Massachusetts, Connecticut, and New Hampshire.[1] Throughout this period, most Congregational ministers remained committed to a Calvinist theology that emphasized innate human depravity, unconditional election, limited atonement, and irresistible grace. Yet the importance of conversion—the sacred calculus through which God winnowed saints

Fig. 7.1. Timothy Mather Cooley served as pastor of Granville's First Congregational Church for sixty years. By 1845, he had admitted more than 330 people to full communion. Courtesy of Denison University.

from sinners—waxed and waned through the centuries, and New Englanders affiliated with local churches for a variety of reasons, including, but not always limited to, their hopes for eternal salvation. By the mid-1800s, recurrent waves of religious revivalism had recast the extended Puritan "morphology of conversion" into a discrete and often instantaneous temporal experience of being "born again" in the Holy Spirit—the hallmark of American evangelicalism. In tracking the generic conventions of New England church-admission narratives over two centuries, we can begin to appreciate the important role that early American evangelicalism played in mediating larger processes of cultural change and modernization. (See plate C in gallery.)

PURITAN CONFESSIONS

The Granville church-admission narratives were part of a unique genre of American Protestant devotional literature with deep roots in the history of New England Congregationalism. The peculiar practice of relating experiences of divine grace emerged slowly from the shadowy world of the English Reformation. By 1600, a few independent churches required candidates for full membership to assent verbally to the doctrines defined in the church covenant. Radical reformers—particularly English separatists living in exile on the continent—extended this practice one step further by urging their members to explain their personal beliefs "in their own words and way." In addition, many early Reformed churches demanded a formal confession of sin before admitting members to the Lord's Supper. During this second, autobiographical oral performance, prospective communicants lamented their innate sinfulness and expressed their desire to repent of past misdeeds, employing events drawn from personal experience to convey the depth of their sorrow.

By 1640, New England Puritans had knit these disparate strands of English dissenting practice into a vigorous church-admission standard through which they sought to differentiate God's predestined saints from the mixed multitude of unregenerate sinners. From their inception, Puritan communities recognized a distinction between "congregation" and "church." The former was a geographical term referring to the collective body of settlers who, by law, were required to attend Sabbath meetings. The more restrictive notion of a church, by contrast, denoted an inner circle of "visible saints" who voted on ecclesiastical issues, placed themselves under the holy watch of their neighbors, and enjoyed privileged access to the sacraments of baptism and the Lord's Supper. According to the first systematic exposition of New England ecclesiology, *A Platform of Church Discipline* (1649)— commonly known as the Cambridge Platform—those seeking access to the "*doors* of the Churches of Christ upon earth" were expected to make their "calling" as members of the elect visible to the community by reciting a "personall & publick *confession*" in which they declared "Gods manner of working upon the soul."[2]

The daunting public-speaking performance capped a lengthy period of preparation. Prospective communicants first appeared before the ruling elders in a private meeting several weeks in advance, where they articulated their desire to join the church and responded to a series of "probatory questions." Successful applicants were then "propounded" for a period that usually lasted a fortnight but occasionally stretched over several months. In the intervening weeks, candidates labored to resolve existing disputes with other members of the community or acknowledged scandalous behavior in a formal confession of sin. On the appointed Sabbath, men and women stood before the congregation, recited their spiritual experiences aloud, and answered questions. In some churches, friends, neighbors, and family members offered testimonies endorsing the sincerity of the candidates' narratives. Finally, the elder called for a "handy" vote, asked the applicant to assent to the church covenant, and extended the "right hand of fellowship" to the newly admitted church member.

New England church-membership testimonies conformed to a narrative pattern that drew upon the works of notable English theologians in the late sixteenth and early seventeenth centuries. Eminent scholars such as William Perkins argued that the experience of regeneration unfolded through a series of discrete stages. This "morphology of conversion" typically began with an awakening incident that wrenched sleepers from their spiritual security and initiated a period of intensive introspection. Convicted of sin and languishing under legal fears of impending divine wrath, the penitent faithful consulted with friends and family members and sought the advice of local pastors. Devotional routines such as Bible study, meditation, secret prayer, journal writing, and private rituals of covenant renewal, in turn, provided brief sanctuary from the anxieties of living in bondage to sin, as broken sinners learned to rely on Christ alone for divine grace and salvation. They labored incessantly to recreate and routinize these spiritually refreshing moments. In Perkins's morphology, conversion was characterized by a distinct narrative plot involving a gradual progression from one stage to the next. Despite occasional periods of backsliding and persistent anxieties that slowed them down, true saints would "grow in grace" over time and exhibit their transformed souls through sanctified behavior.

Parishioners in Cambridge, Massachusetts, displayed a familiarity with the stages of Perkins's developmental theory of conversion in their church-admission testimonies. Town minister Thomas Shepard recorded more than seventy such "confessions" in a pair of small notebooks during the 1630s and 1640s, and these narratives were saturated in the Calvinist language of human depravity. Candidates often associated "worldly" misfortunes and "afflictions"—illnesses, deaths, or failed business enterprises—with the preliminary legal stages of conviction. Although they frequently resorted to various devotional routines to assuage their fearful consciences, many of these first-generation New England emigrants equally feared the danger of "resting" in "duties" and the empty forms of religious practice. Like many zealous English Protestants, Shepard's congregants began their narratives by recalling their growing attraction toward the Puritan movement. Some admitted to living in "popery" or "ignorance" for years before encountering "godly" laypeople or ministers who convinced them of the need to separate themselves from the "mixed ordinances" of the Church of England and the necessity of conversion.

Inspired preaching guided the faithful through the stages of conversion. Cambridge parishioners cited an astonishing array of biblical texts—more than eleven per testimony—nearly half of which were related to sermons. Repeated references to "hearing" the Word suggest that the Puritans listened carefully and labored to apply what they heard each Sabbath to their individual spiritual situations. Laymen and laywomen envisioned sermons as a medium of divine communication, as Abram Arrington explained when he stated in his confession that "the Lord spake" through Shepard's weekly performances. The power of the Holy Spirit, "opened" through the preached Word, roused secure sinners to their dangerous condition, "stayed" the despondent, "answered" the questioning, and "cheered" the hopeful. If any of the Cambridge confessors had become "gainer[s] in a spiritual way" and managed to glean evidence of their divine election, it was the result of the preached Word.

Church-membership candidates such as Harvard student Comfort Starr knew that God redeemed his saints "from wrath by certain stages and degrees," yet few laypeople claimed to have followed Perkins's path to its final destination. Instead, the New England confessions deviated in striking ways from their transatlantic counterparts. In the flush days of the English Commonwealth, zealous Protestant dissenters on both sides of the Atlantic spoke of intensive inner struggles to gain assurance of salvation. They spiritualized the political turmoil of the era and sought out the fervent preaching of Calvinist clergymen. Yet English Puritans who had suffered under an oppressive Anglican regime expressed greater confidence in their hopes of being counted among God's elect, and they willingly testified to miraculous encounters with the sacred in dreams, visions, and other ecstatic forms of spiritual rapture. Parishioners in John Rogers's transplanted Puritan congregation in Dublin, for example, frequently concluded their testimonies on a high note, claiming that they were "*fully satisfied*" and had received "*full assurance*" of "*Gods love* to me in *Christ*."[3]

In contrast to the confidence of these English confessions, early New England testimonies were often narratives of failure, as speakers lingered on the initial halting steps in the conversion process rather than its culmination. Dozens of prospective communicants in the Cambridge and Wenham churches offered vivid descriptions of their efforts "to enjoy the presence of the Lord in the liberty and purity of his ordinances," yet they often experienced disillusionment and alienation following their arrival in the New World. Many spoke of falling into "trials" and "discontent"; they were buffeted by worldly temptations and languished through "unprofitable" periods of carnal security—despite living under the "means" of grace. "I found my heart dead and sluggy," admitted Elizabeth Dunster, sister of the first president of Harvard College. Deacon Gregory Stone's daughter concurred, asserting that the promise of religious liberty in New England had led only to complacency. "I was sure of water," she explained in a particularly evocative statement, "dry, though not thirsty, [in a] state of sin" and yet "not troubled for particular sins." "Since I came hither," Nathaniel Eaton summarized, "I have not found my heart to walk so closely with God as I should." Still committed to the developmental model of Puritan conversion described by writers such as William Perkins, few church-membership candidates in New England during the 1640s claimed to have reached the final stages of assurance, election, and union with the divine.

The somber tone of the New England confessions—indeed, the very impulse to regulate the narration of religious experience through a formal ritual—developed in the context of an unusually acrimonious ecclesiastical dispute known as the Antinomian Controversy (1636–1638). Just two years after his arrival, Shepard participated in the prosecution of the charismatic Boston church member, healer, and midwife Anne Hutchinson. During her trial, Hutchinson voiced a short experiential narrative that bore a family resemblance to the testimonies that Shepard would record in the Cambridge meeting-house a few years later. Like many of her neighbors, she chronicled her struggles to conform to the Church of England, and she framed her decision to immigrate to New England as a religious quest to rejoin her former minister, Boston's prominent theologian John Cotton. But where the Cambridge confessors hedged their accounts with stories of spiritual backsliding, Hutchinson brazenly claimed to have received definitive answers to her deepest spiritual concerns in the form of "immediate revelations"—biblical passages that were "opened" to her alone through the inner illumination of the Holy Spirit. And to make matters worse, she channeled her unusual supernatural communications into a blistering critique of Shepard and his more conservative Puritan colleagues in a series of weekly conventicles during which she debated the sermons of local ministers in the mixed company of men and women.[4]

In the wake of the protracted ecclesiastical dispute that banished Hutchinson and her supporters to Rhode Island, Shepard and his

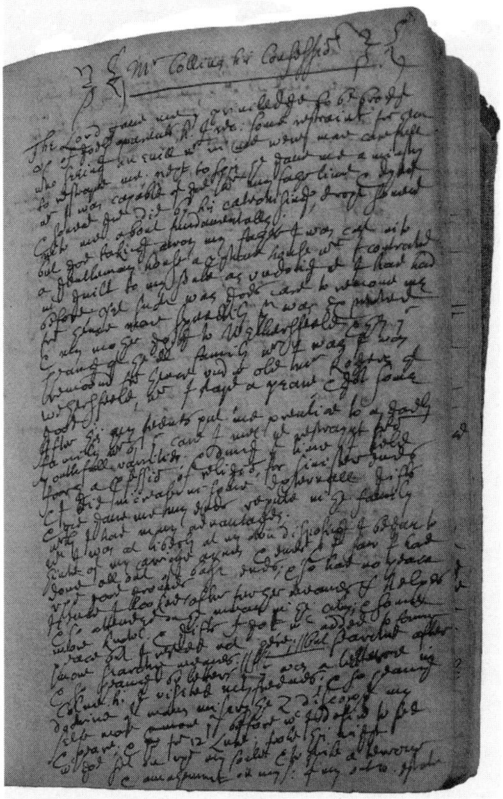

Fig. 7.2. The crabbed handwriting of Cambridge minister Thomas Shepard is typical of seventeenth-century orthography, yet his ca. 1640 transcription of Edward Collins's "Confession" also appears to have been written hastily—perhaps as his parishioner spoke the words himself. Courtesy of the New England Historic Genealogical Society, Boston, Mass.

ministerial colleagues instituted the practice of reciting confessions as a prerequisite for church membership. The word "Confession" fronting the narratives that Shepard inscribed in his church-admission notebooks reinforced his growing concern that fallible human beings could or even should hope to gain full knowledge of their eternal estates in this sinful world. Increasingly, he retreated into a theological model of conversion that emphasized "preparation" for salvation through a lifetime spent in diligent introspection and dogged devotional practices, and he expected that the confessions of his parishioners would conform to this pattern. In an extended sermon series on the *parable of the foolish virgins* that he preached during the late 1630s, the Cambridge minister inveighed against the "wearisome," "uncomely," and "odd confessions" of the Hutchinsonians. Members of his congregation cited this sermon series repeatedly in their church-admission narratives, and the overall pattern of these texts conformed closely to his conservative model of conversion.

Bold expressions of individual inspiration would eventually take hold in New England, but in the 1630s, ministers succeeded in keeping them down. In swift reaction against the inspirations that Hutchinson and her followers claimed, Shepard and his New England colleagues reinforced the boundaries of appropriate religious expression and seldom tired of preaching on limits of assurance. The dominant trope of their new preparationist paradigm was the "weary pilgrim," an image made famous in both the haunting poetry of Anne Bradstreet and John Bunyan's classic allegory, *The Pilgrim's Progress* (1678). Shepard, too, described conversion as an earthly pilgrimage toward a heavenly destination in his poetic masterpiece, *The Sound Beleever* (1645). Drawing on Hebrews 11, he likened the saints to "strangers" who "have no abiding city" in this world, but rather "live alone as Pelicans in the wildernesse," patiently awaiting the final resolution of their spiritual yearnings at the day of atonement.[5] Similar metaphors of spiritual asceticism and ceaseless striving colored the confessions of the Puritan laity. When Wenham goodwife Tryphean Geere hinted that her "broken heart" was perhaps a sign of her saintly status, an unnamed church member challenged her to explain the difference between "a legal and a[n] evangelical breaking." "Ice, if broken by a breath may congeal again," he explained. Only when the sun rose high enough in the sky would the thaw be lasting. The message was clear. True Christians in this world should not expect to bask endlessly in the glorious sunshine of divine grace like the confident saints of Rogers's Dublin congregation. Nor should they expect to receive immediate revelations like Anne Hutchinson. Not even the solemn ritual of church affiliation would relieve the faithful from what Shepard called "winter seasons," for, in his words, "very few living Christians have any settled comfortable evidence of God's eternal love to them in his Son."[6]

> ## Puritan Conversion as Solemn Preparation for Salvation
>
> I confess it is not fit that so holy and solemn an Assembly as a Church is, should be held long with Relations of this odd thing and tother, nor hear of Revelations and groundless joyes, nor father together the heap, wherein they have got any good; nor Scriptures and Sermons, but such as may be of special use unto the people of God, such things as tend to shew, Thus I was humbled, then thus I was called, then thus I have walked, though with many weaknesses since, and such special providences of God I have seen, temptations gone through, and thus the Lord hath delivered me, blessed be his Name &c.
>
> —Thomas Shepard, *The Parable of the Ten Virgins* (London, 1660), in *The Works of Thomas Shepard*, ed. John Albro (Boston, 1853) 2:200.

PROVINCIAL RELATIONS (1690–1740)

From the outset, a vocal minority of ministers and laypersons balked at New England's restrictive, anxiety-inducing church-membership standards. The practice of reciting confessions in public provoked bitter criticism from moderate reformers and earnest laypeople on both sides of the Atlantic, who questioned its scriptural foundation and accused their zealous Puritan brethren of excessively narrowing the gates of the church. In response to the host of problems that emerged from the new membership "tryall," the Cambridge Platform encouraged church members to exercise a "judgment of charity" in the examination of prospective candidates and accept new communicants on the basis of the "weakest *measure* of faith." In addition, the results of the Platform included a provision allowing unusually fearful candidates to narrate their religious experiences in private meetings with the minister and elders.[7] Over the next fifty years, churches throughout New England adjusted their admission criteria. By 1700, written "relations"—formal statements drafted by or on behalf of candidates by their ministers—had supplanted the oral performances of the founding generation. Increasingly, these paper instruments assumed a contractual form whose rigid structure, theological content, and narrative organization rapidly overshadowed the Puritan morphology of conversion.

The clergy's role in regulating the admission process expanded in direct proportion to the extent that oral confessions receded from public view. A new professional class of Harvard-trained clergymen took command of the task of interviewing candidates for full membership in the privacy of their studies and drafting relations on their behalf. Nearly two-thirds of the 235 extant church-admission narratives from the Essex County town of Haverhill—the single largest collection of eighteenth-century relations—were composed in the steady hand of minister John Brown. These brief documents were laced with terse biblical citations, frequent abbreviations, and shorthand symbols. The Haverhill pastor composed each relation separately on small, uniform pieces of paper measuring four by six inches. On the reverse side, he identified each candidate, numbered the relation, and noted the dates on which the applicant was propounded and admitted to the church. In cases where parishioners

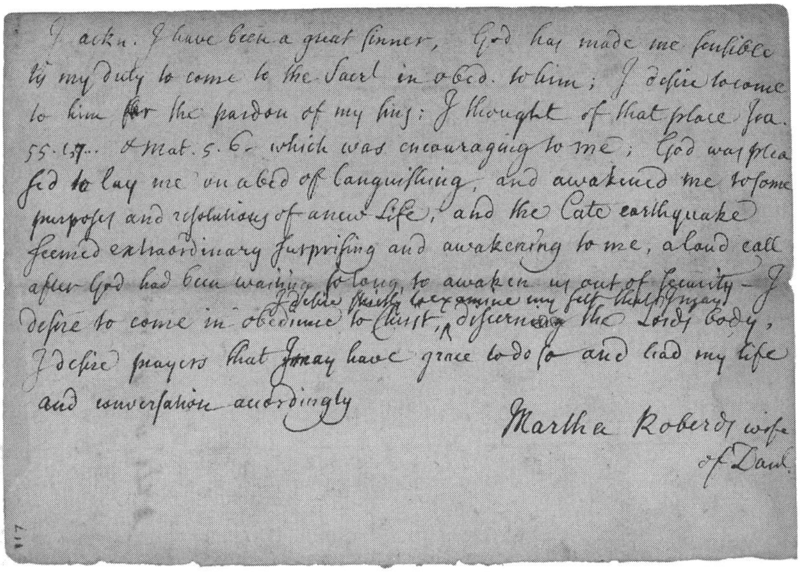
I ackn. I have been a great sinner, God has made me sensible of my duty to come to the Sacr^l in obed. to him; I desire to come to him for the pardon of my sins: I thought of that place Isa. 55.1,7.. & Mat. 5. 6. which was encouraging to me; God was pleased to lay me on a bed of languishing, and awakened me to some purposes and resolutions of a new Life, and the Late earthquake seemed extraordinary surprising and awakening to me, a loud call after God had been waiting so long, to awaken us out of security — I desire to come in obedience to Christ, I desire strictly to examine my self that I may discerning the Lords body, I desire prayers that I may have grace to do so and lead my life and conversation accordingly

Martha Roberds wife of Danl.

Fig. 7.3. John Brown's system for recording the written relations of parishioners is evident in Martha Roberds's 1727 narrative. Courtesy of Haverhill Public Library, Haverhill, Mass.

drafted their relations independently, Brown occasionally altered the content, marking grammatical errors, substituting words, striking phrases, and in a few cases, introducing entirely new material. Ministerial gatekeepers like Brown, in short, created a genre of devotional literature that was characterized by rigid formalism in physical appearance as well as uniformity in rhetorical style and narrative content.

References to the lively stirrings of grace declined as church-admission standards became more regulated. Most early eighteenth-century written relations bore little resemblance to the descriptions of conversion outlined in the works of Perkins, Shepard, and other Puritan divines. Instead, they frequently consisted of basic Reformed doctrines strung together in a series of creedal affirmations. Church-membership "professors," as the candidates were often called, typically asserted that the Bible was the "word of God and a perfect rule of faith and practice." In addition, a number of Haverhill candidates described the trinitarian essence of the divinity and God's role in creating heaven and earth in seven days. References to original sin, the authority of Scripture, and other basic Calvinist tenets also appeared with regularity. Eighteenth-century candidates continued to express their desire for "growth in Grace," yet few of their professions mentioned seasons of hope and despair, awakening sermons heard, or rapturous experiences of ecstatic release. Indeed, there was little to differentiate many of these documents from the formal church covenants that local clergymen inscribed at the beginning of their parish record books.

Statements of belief rarely appeared in church-admission narratives before 1720, but within a decade relations containing doctrinal professions outnumbered purely autobiographical narratives by a margin of two to one. Demands by local clergymen that candidates display a mastery of basic Reformed doctrines, in turn, gradually transformed the meaning of church affiliation from a signifier of visible sainthood into a mandatory obligation incumbent on all believers regardless of their eternal estate. In the massive Haverhill collection, for example, the word "duty" appeared over two hundred times, and candidates occasionally resorted to contractual language to describe the meaning of church fellowship. "I hope I am desirous & willing to Embrace Jesus Christ on his own Terms," wrote the prominent surveyor Richard Hazzen, and "to Yield Sincere Obedience to all his

Commands." Terms, obligations, contracts, commands, duties—the intensely legalistic language of early eighteenth-century relations heralded the dawn of a new era in which the formal performance of outward devotional practices eclipsed the introspective conversionist piety of the founding generation.

Among the Christian duties mentioned in surviving relations, none was more important than the observance of the public ordinance of the Lord's Supper. Scores of books on the subject poured from New England presses between 1690 and 1740. Widely distributed and eagerly consumed by the laity, these works included sermons, informal dialogues, and devotional handbooks that were designed to help prospective communicants prepare to receive Christ's body and blood. Statements regarding the significance of the sacraments in the lives of the faithful—absent in seventeenth-century narratives—occupied an increasingly prominent position in later written testimonies. One in five Haverhill candidates cited Christ's command to commemorate his death by consuming his body and blood (Luke 22:19) as the primary reason for joining the church, while prospective communicants in Lynnfield, Medfield, Westborough, and Boston claimed to have read sacramental handbooks in preparation for admission or glossed the theological significance of the Lord's Supper in their doctrinal professions.

At the same time, the late-seventeenth-century renaissance in Puritan sacramental theology generated a new type of anxiety for the laity. Ministers repeatedly exhorted their congregants to fulfill their commanded duties through church affiliation; yet they also issued stern warnings urging prospective communicants to examine their hearts before approaching the Lord's Table, lest they, in the words of 1 Corinthians 11:29, "eateth and drinketh" their own "damnation" by receiving the elements unworthily. No other biblical verse was cited more often by church membership applicants in the central Massachusetts village of Westborough, and it ranked among the top five most frequently quoted passages in all towns for which relations survive in the period from 1690 to 1740. "I have had many thoughts of Joining to the Church of Christ in this place, and to draw near to God in special ordinances," explained George Barber of Dedham, "but was discouraged" by Paul's stern warning to the Corinthians. "I thought in the consideration [of this text] that if I should come unworthily to the Lords Table it would be far worse for me in the day of Judgment than if I had never come." Puritan sacramentalism thus created a hopeless dilemma for many would-be saints, and no one exposed the conundrum better than Haverhill's Mary Sanders, who lamented that "I sin in Coming unworthily & I sin in staying away unworthily."

It was for this reason that scrupulous laymen and laywomen in the early eighteenth century approached the communion table with great reluctance, if at all. Although they were knowledgeable in doctrine and sensible of their sacramental obligations, even deeply pious women such as Haverhill's famed Indian captive Hannah Duston elected to defer their decision to close with the church until the "Eleventh hour." "Many Years ago I had a Desire to join with the Church," explained one of Duston's neighbors, "but I tho't twas time eno' for me Yet." Others proceeded cautiously, electing "to Live a Litle Longer In the neglect" of the ordinances, or to "stay [away] till I was better prepared." Potential church-membership candidates thus hung suspended between fear and duty, and only a dangerous period of affliction or a major change in family status could tip the scales in favor of affiliation.

By the early decades of the 1700s, admission rituals marked an important life-course transition that signified both temporal and spiritual maturation. On rare occasions, candidates echoed the private sentiments of Boston magistrate Samuel Sewall, who noted in his diary that his decision to apply for the privileges of church membership was motivated by a desire to secure the right to baptize his children.[8] Demographic studies have shown that these family strategies were never far from the candidates' minds. Three out of four men and women were married at the time they joined the church. Spouses often covenanted on the same Sabbath, and during the 1730s, this practice gave rise to the creation of joint relations drafted on behalf of husband and wife. In some parishes, upwards of 75 percent of all new communicants presented a child for baptism within a month of joining the church.[9]

The period of family formation also exposed men and women to emotional stress and physical danger—perhaps for the first time in their lives. Marriage, of course, brought children, a third of whom would sicken and die before their tenth birthdays. New brides spent the next two decades of their lives in a relentless and often frightening reproductive cycle that brought dangerous periods of childbirth "travail" every twenty months. It was during these years, too, that men inherited or purchased farms, adopted trades, and entered the military. The emotional anxieties of family life, when coupled with an increased risk of accident, illness, or sudden death, drove many to close with the church. Mary Rocket of Medfield offered a powerful reflection on the relationship between life-course transitions and church membership in her 1697 relation. She began by lamenting that she had delayed her "repentance time after time." Only after entering "into a married estate" did she finally consider performing her duties at the Lord's Table, for she had "met with many sorrows, troubles, and afflictions" following her marriage, and these misfortunes "did something awaken" her. Benjamin Phinney of Barnstable echoed these sentiments two decades later, writing that he "met with new duties & new difficulties" in the years since God had been "pleased . . . to bring me into a married State."

Temporal afflictions, especially the death of a parent, sibling, spouse, child, neighbor, or favorite minister, also stirred reluctant parishioners to embrace their sacramental obligations. Meditating on the "passages of Providence" in her life, Lynnfield's Mehitable Osgood recalled the "heavy Stroke" of her father's recent passing. "This moved me to Resolve to give up my Self to God in an everlasting Covenant"— a "resolution" that she "put . . . in practice" when she joined the church in 1728. A few years later, Margaret McHard watched with growing alarm as a diphtheria epidemic claimed the lives of thousands of children along the northern New England frontier. Among the more than forty new communicants who swelled the ranks of the Haverhill church in a brief two-year period in 1736 and 1737, she noted in her relation that she had "been awakened to my duty by sundry Instances of sudden Death of late which are loud calls to me to prepare." Overall, nearly half of all candidates in Medfield and one-fifth of the applicants in Haverhill cited the death of a family member or neighbor as an awakening event that impelled them to join the church.

In times when God's afflictive hand gripped entire communities—as was the case with droughts, Indian raids, or epidemics—

dramatic surges in church membership often followed. One of the largest religious revivals in New England history was triggered by a powerful earthquake that rattled buildings and toppled fences throughout the Merrimack Valley on October 29, 1727. In the ensuing weeks, Haverhill town minister John Brown reported that he was "fully employ'd in discoursing" with distressed parishioners "about their souls . . . by night & day," "*rain* or *shine*," and "some Days from Morning till 8 a clock at Night, without so much as time to take any bodily refreshment." More

Fig. 7.4. Eighteenth-century laypeople associated earthquakes with the voice of God, calling loudly for repentance and moral reformation. The 1727 shocks triggered powerful religious awakenings in churches throughout northern New England. © New York Public Library / Art Resource, N.Y.

than two hundred people joined Brown's church in the next year, and at least one-quarter of these candidates described the "Great Earthquake" as a "loud call" from the "awfull & Dredfull voice" of God that "quickened" the rhythms of their devotional lives and banished all fears of spiritual unworthiness.[10]

Provincial New Englanders fully recognized that their heightened devotional activities could never merit salvation for them, yet prospective church members persisted in the belief that fulfilling ritual obligations might lift the heavy hand of divine affliction from their families and villages. Consequently, eighteenth-century relations were filled with solemn vows in which candidates agreed to perform their sacramental duties in exchange for divine protection or restored health. "It Pleased God . . . to lay me on a bed of sickness, for a Considerable time," explained Medfield's Joanna Kingsbury in what was a typical case. She prayed to God to spare her life "a Little Longer that so I might make my Peace with him." Fearing that he would bleed to death after receiving a "bad wound" in combat, James Stewart of Rowley "beged the Lord to spare my life," promising in return that "I would not sin against him as I had [previously] done." In all, thirteen of the fifty-seven extant Medfield relations composed between 1697 and 1740 mentioned accidents or personal illness, and more than half of these testimonies incorporated an explicit promise to join the church if raised to health again. Smaller percentages of healing vows appear in surviving collections from Haverhill, Rowley, East Windsor, Connecticut, and Boston's First Church.

Previous generations of New England divines like Thomas Shepard undoubtedly would have found these seemingly self-serving narratives deficient, for unlike their oral predecessors, written relations seldom reflected experiences beyond the preliminary stage of legal terror in the morphology of conversion. But in the irenic and cosmopolitan culture of provincial New England, early eighteenth-century relations also spoke to practical issues; for many, assurance of salvation was a secondary concern. Consider the testimony submitted by Elizabeth Dwight of Medfield in the winter of 1715. Previously, she had been awakened to her sacramental duties by the sermons of local ministers and the sudden death of an infant. Yet through it all, she had never experienced conversion, and she frankly admitted as much in her testimony: "Allthough I cannot find the clear manifestation of the Love of god to my soul which I do desier . . . yet have I some comforttable hopes which arises from the burden of sin." For Dwight, closing with Christ "on his own terms" was the "most reasonable" thing to do. In one sentence the Medfield goodwife encapsulated the dramatic transformation in popular piety that had taken place during the early eighteenth century. Church affiliation had become a carefully measured, voluntary decision that was influenced by a variety of factors, not all of which involved the eternal disposition of one's immortal soul.

NEW LIGHT CONVERSION NARRATIVES (1740–1790)

The arrival of the famed British revivalist George Whitefield in Newport, Rhode Island, on September 14, 1740, marked the emergence of a new vocabulary of religious experience in the lexicon of New England church-admission narratives that enabled many Christians to find relief from the oppressive weight of religious guilt and anxiety. Over the course of his six-week sojourn, the "Grand Itinerant" traveled the length and breadth of the Puritan colonies and performed an estimated 175 well-publicized and aggressively marketed sermons to eager audiences numbering in the tens of thousands. A masterful orator, Whitefield eschewed written notes in favor of a direct, flamboyant, and emotionally engaging rhetorical style that capitalized on English theater techniques. Doctrinally, his sermons revolved around a cluster of traditional Reformed doctrines—the authority of the Bible, original sin, the necessity of divine grace, justification by faith, and sanctified moral behavior—repackaged in a concentrated description of what he called the "new birth."[11]

The impact of Whitefield's 1740 preaching tour on New England's Congregational churches was unprecedented. Local clergymen such as Harvard tutor Daniel Rogers adopted his artful rhetorical tactics and began itinerating in parishes from downeast Maine to southern Connecticut. Churches organized protracted meetings that lasted for days on end and included late-night singing and prayer exercises, as well as sermons delivered by visiting ministers. Many of these dramatic preaching performances included lurid images of hellfire and damnation, and the expressive power of the new sermon style made a powerful impression on audiences. In the two years following Whitefield's electrifying preaching tour, towns across the region experienced an extraordinary surge in church membership. In striking contrast to prevailing patterns of religious affiliation, most of the new communicants were unmarried young people in their teens and early twenties. And in some cases, the euphoria of the revivals temporarily overturned existing hierarchies as inspired women, children, and African slaves arrogated to themselves the authority to preach and exhort their unconverted neighbors. Collectively, the revivals of the early 1740s generated bitter divisions among the ranks of Congregational clergyman. When Whitefield returned to New England several years later, he encountered a landscape rife with acrimonious infighting between Old Light revival opposers and New Light advocates.

Early observers of Whitefield's unique ministry claimed that he preached "much like that of the old English Puritans," yet it is clear that his theology of the new birth represented a significant departure from the Puritan morphology of conversion.[12] To be sure, the Anglican evangelist was rightly credited with restoring the concept of the new birth to theological preeminence over and against the prevailing concern for

Evangelical Conversion as Experience of New Birth

Upon the road [to Middleborough] I felt a Burden heavy on my Heart beyound what I had ever Experienced before preaching, which lead my Thots to Matthew 11:28. This oppression went off before I began. I was enlarg'd to speak upon the Subject. I hope God made It a word in season to weary Souls. A number of Awakened sinners cry'd out the greatest part of the Time. The rest of the Assembly gave great Attention. I felt much of the Presence of God in my soul [and] heard afterwards that 30 persons were Awakned with this sermon. Blessed be God who makes his Word quick and powerfull.

—Diary of itinerant preacher Daniel Rogers, October 31, 1741.

formulaic professions of belief. In fact, he and his itinerating New England colleagues roundly castigated church-membership candidates for what they considered to be their excessive preoccupation with doctrinal orthodoxy and the outward performance of empty religious duties. They disparaged doctrinal knowledge, sacramental duties, devotional practices, healing vows, and family concerns as the sandy foundations of faith. But while the Anglican evangelist shared many of the Calvinist sentiments of his seventeenth-century predecessors, he telescoped the Puritan notion of conversion as a lifelong pilgrimage into a single transformative event: the descent of God's Holy Spirit into the bodies of the regenerate faithful.

Whitefield's truncated model of conversion dramatically reshaped the theological content of the relation genre. Ardent New Lights believed that the saints could identify the specific time and place of their conversions, and church-membership candidates after 1740 incorporated a keen sense of temporal events into their testimonies. Freetown parishioner Irene Shaw, for example, claimed to have received "Comfortable Satisfaction" that she had "become a new Creature in Christ Jesus" after hearing a sermon preached by her local minister on April 15, 1753; Lucia Thomas of Middleborough obtained a "Clearer Sence" of her original sinfulness "Last Summer"; while fellow parishioner Nathan Eddy labored under conviction for "2 years & ½." Others dated their moments of spiritual illumination to "last winter," "about four years ago," "the 7th of May last," or at "the Lecture where Dr. Turners Child was Baptized." Relief from the terrors of conviction, in other words, arrived at precise, datable moments that, in the words of one Middleborough parishioner, the candidate would "never forget."

In addition, virtually every spiritual autobiography penned during the 1740s contained allusions to passages from Scripture that leapt to mind with "sweet power" in a moment of blackest despair to dispel the author's spiritual darkness. These "impulses" or "impressions," as revival critics derisively labeled them, appeared with regularity in now-classic spiritual autobiographies by Isaac Backus, David Brainerd, Nathan Cole, Hannah Heaton, and Sarah Osborne. Nor was this emerging New Light exegetical trope a peculiarly American phenomenon, for "darting" Scriptures were ubiquitous among the narratives that William McCulloch recorded during the famed Scottish revivals at Cambuslang in 1742. As one minister summarized in *The Christian History*, one of several magazines that broadcast revival intelligence to a transatlantic audience, conversion "Discoveries" generally were triggered by "some Texts of Scripture: Or if they had no Text of Scripture as they remember at first, there immediately came many flowing in upon their Minds."[13]

These darting biblical texts were more than just examples of the Puritan tradition of *sola scriptura*. Often, they dominated Awakening-era church-admission narratives, and the metaphors that laymen and laywomen used to describe their unusual encounters with Scripture were equally provocative and instructive. Bible verses "rained" down from the heavens and "dropped" into the converts' heads unexpectedly, without conscious thought or preparatory meditations. They came with "thunder" or "uncommon power"—and most often in moments of darkest spiritual despair. Sinners wallowing in conviction spoke of being "pierced," "touched," or "struck down" by the Word and miraculously transformed, often in the blink of an eye. Others described biblical texts that "ran in my mind for sum time" or "followed me & kept sounding in my mind" as they went about their daily routines.[14]

Church-membership relations composed during the revival years and in the decades that followed registered the growing popular fascination with this radical new form of supernatural communication. Statistically, references to biblical impulses and impressions reveal a significant break with the literary conventions of the past. Prior to

---

New Light Sermons Convey Religious Power

I desire to Bless God that I was born in a land of light and that my parents took Care to have me Babtised in my minority and that I was Instructed to Read Gods word. But notwithstanding of all these pr[e]cious privileges I Remained a stranger to the power of Godliness till it pleased God to send his servant mr Daniel Rogers who preached in our meeting house upon these words in mathew the 11 and 28 . . . under which sermon it pleased God to Convince me of my danger in living a stranger to Jesus Christ under which Distress . . . I Continued not many days. Then it pleased God to Reve[a]l Christ to my soul as a suficient saviour with aplication to my own soul.

—Relation of Priscilla Booth, Middleborough, Mass., August 16, 1747.

the revivals of the 1740s, church-membership professors throughout New England typically spoke of the Bible as a "rule" of Christian faith and practice, and they scoured the Scriptures for "encouraging" texts that validated their decisions to conform to Christ-mandated duties. Yet the overall universe of cited passages was quite limited. In the pre-Awakening Haverhill relations, for example, the top quartile of frequently quoted texts accounted for almost 85 percent of all biblical references. In fervent pro-revival parishes such as Middleborough and Granville, by contrast, that same figure dropped to 29.4 and 20.0 percent respectively during the decades prior to the American Revolution. New Lights, in other words, engaged the Scriptures in highly personal, selective, and idiosyncratic ways.

In addition, men and women claiming to have experienced the new birth cited chapter and verse not to confirm their measured decisions to apply for full membership, but as the trigger mechanism of their nearly instantaneous conversions. More than 40 percent of all biblical texts cited by Middleborough candidates had been "impressed" on their hearts or "came with power" to their minds in a flash of supernatural illumination. "God has I think opened to me some of his precious promises & perticularly set home on my [heart] that word in Isaiah 55:3," reported Middleborough's Elkanah Shaw in what was a typical reference. Deborah Billington heard the distressing words of Isaiah 50:11 "sound in mine ears," and the experience instantly convicted her of sin; but she was speedily delivered by Matthew 11:28, which "came into my mind." Among the New Light faithful, such supernatural biblical impressions were not abstract "promises"; rather, they signaled the indwelling presence of the Holy Spirit "speaking" to the converted saints, "opening" and "enlightening" their hearts, and allowing them to "see" their glorious future estate.

The result was empowering. Conversion was, in the language of the day, an "enlarging" experience. For Shepard's seventeenth-century Cambridge congregants who doggedly plied the means of grace through countless seasons of hope and despair, complete assurance of salvation always lay around the next corner; they spoke with an accent of constant uncertainty. Coming of age in the heady decades following the Great Awakening, eighteenth-century evangelicals were far more confident of their future estates, and they narrated their experiences in an assertive idiom. John Leach's testimony is a classic example. The Middleborough layman could find "no effectual relief" from sin until "one Morning after I awoke from sleep, when a New Sense, & I think, Divine Light Shone into my mind. My [heart] felt Changed, it now seemed easy to turn to god. I asked myself, if I chose Christ for my only Portion? My [heart] answered yes."

Occasionally, these seemingly mystical infusions of divine grace were accompanied by palpable sensations of what one woman called "unspeakable Joy." A few New Light converts described feelings of being physically "overcome" and "ravished" by divine love. More often, however, early evangelicals described their conversion experience as a "great Change." Revival participants in Medfield, for example, claimed to have seen the entire world in a new light after receiving converting texts of Scripture that spoke directly to their spiritual conditions. "I think I can plainly see Things look quite otherwise than they used to do," admitted Keziah Bullen after two passages from Isaiah leapt to mind and convinced her of the vanity of earthly desires. Likewise, a Middleborough woman was converted by a series of biblical impulses, whereupon she "Imediately felt a Change in my heart. I found Submission to the will of God." "I felt my soul go out after [Christ]," explained one of her neighbors the following year; "I felt as if I was in a new world."

For a small contingent of radicals, the Holy Spirit was manifest through dreams, trances, and visions. During the peak months of the Great Awakening in New England, dozens of young men and women fell to the ground and languished in cataleptic trances that lasted for hours and even days at a time. When revived, the visionists reported to astonished onlookers that they had traveled to heaven in spirit form and seen their names written the Book of Life as described in Revelation. Despite the fact that such events were universally branded as delusive "enthusiasm" by revival proponents and critics alike, they appeared with increasing regularity in the diaries of radical New Lights, Congregational separatists, and separate Baptists over the next two decades.[15] Dreams and visions occasionally intruded into church-membership relations as well. Harvard student Samuel Fayerweather, for example, hinted in his narrative that he had seen the devil in the likeness of a bear during the college revival in the winter of 1741. Two decades later, Ichabod Billington of Middleborough reported a series of miraculous encounters with God that culminated in a dramatic nighttime vision in which he saw the door to heaven standing wide open before him. Likewise, Granville parishioner Timothy Robinson described an unusual event in which "all Nater semd to vanish" and he beheld a vision of Jesus and Satan vying for his soul. For some, these unusually vivid and controversial images appeared only to the "eyes of faith," although laymen and laywomen like Robinson often struggled to determine whether or not they were simply conjured by their "Emagination."

In the wake of Whitefield's 1740 tour of New England, Congregational laypeople began to harness their church membership testimonies to a distinctive narrative form that championed conversion as a discrete event. An early example of this transformation appears in the diary of a Boston merchant who visited York, Maine, during the peak months of the Great Awakening in the fall of 1741 and listened to the "affecting Relations of 10 young Persons admited into the Church." Unlike those of their parents and grandparents, the testimonies of the youthful candidates eschewed the standard litany of doctrinal knowledge and healing vows. Instead, the anonymous diarist noted that they "Declar'd there Exp[e]riance of the Grace of God, upon there souls" during the recent remarkable work of the Holy Spirit in town. "Most of them" claimed to have been "awakened" by the "Powerfull Preaching" of nearly a dozen traveling preachers who visited the town in a brief two-month period. As nineteen-year-old Abigail Brewer of Boston's prestigious Old South Church explained earlier that spring, "God has of his great mercy ben pleased by the powerful preaching of his servants which of late has ben sent among us to convince me of my wretched estate both by nature and by practis."[16] Evangelicalism had taken root in the stony soil of Puritan New England.

EVANGELICAL EXPERIENCES (1790–1840s)

By the time Timothy Mather Cooley began reclassifying the Granville church-admission narratives as "Experiences," a dramatic shift had taken place in the physical appearance, theological content, and emotional tenor of the genre. Of course, New Englanders had been experiencing religion all along—even in the early eighteenth century when the Puritan morphology of conversion had fallen into acute decline—but the revival innovations of the Great Awakening reshaped the very idea of what constituted an authentic religious experience. To talk about religious "experiences" now meant speaking of conversion as a discrete event, one that usually unfolded during an intensive period of religious revitalization.

The religious landscape of New England had changed as well, as the young nation lurched into the modern era. The centripetal forces of the early national period—industrial development, the transportation revolution, a burgeoning but volatile national market economy, and frontier migration—conspired to uproot the once-stable Puritan communities of the colonial era. Religious disestablishment further transformed the region into a competitive religious marketplace in which Congregationalists vied for souls with upstart denominations and sects, including the Baptists, Methodists, Shakers, and Universalists. For most of these groups, revivals had become a routine part of church life, as evangelicals during America's Second Great Awakening adopted the "new measures" of Charles Grandison Finney—Whitefield's nineteenth-century successor—and mastered the art of engineering periodic harvests of eager young converts.[17]

No longer the dominant religious institution in Jacksonian New England, Congregational churches now catered to the tastes of the individual, and church-admission narratives followed suit. Granville parishioners, for example, delivered their testimonies to Cooley in the form of a personal letter, a stylistic device that underscored the growing distance between individual experience and ministerial control. Revival innovations found their way into the Granville experiences as well. Laymen and laywomen frequently dated their conversions according to revival seasons, and they referenced a greater variety of revival venues as well. Cooley's parishioners attended "anxious meetings," "young Peoples" meetings, "school House" meetings, "protracted" meetings, and a host of informal private meetings. And, of course, there were those like the people of Granville's Abijah Church who "loved to see those trembling Christians" at revival meetings. It was during these church gatherings that many people claimed to have "gotten" religion—an emerging evangelical catchphrase that signaled just how far New England "Yankees" had drifted from their Puritan roots.

By 1850, few Congregationalists continued to speak the language of sacramental duties, healing vows, or family pedigrees as their ancestors had done a century before; nor were they content to trudge toward an unknown eternal destination as the Puritan founders had done in the seventeenth century. Instead, antebellum evangelicals experienced conversion as an instantaneous moment of transformation. They learned to compartmentalize and commodify their spiritual lives, as they spoke of "getting religion" through the newly bureaucratized revivals that periodically swept through the region. And in direct contrast to anxious seventeenth-century Puritans, nineteenth-century church-membership candidates rarely experienced protracted seasons of terror before resting "Safe in the hands of a Sovereign God." In short, they mastered the tropes of the conversion narrative—the revival contexts, the brief period of conviction, the despair of failed devotional routines, the precise moment of supernatural release, the world transformed—and adapted those conventions to suit the needs of an increasingly mobile, fragmented, competitive, individualistic society.

FOR FURTHER READING

Caldwell, Patricia. *The Puritan Conversion Narrative: The Beginnings of American Expression.* New York: Cambridge University Press, 1983.

Cohen, Charles Lloyd. *God's Caress: The Psychology of Puritan Religious Experience.* New York: Oxford University Press, 1986.

Greven, Philip. *The Protestant Temperament: Patterns of Child-Rearing, Religious Experience, and the Self in Early America.* Chicago: University of Chicago Press, 1977.

Juster, Susan. *Disorderly Women: Sexual Politics and Evangelicalism in Revolutionary New England.* Ithaca, N.Y.: Cornell University Press, 1994.

Morgan, Edmund S. *Visible Saints: The History of a Puritan Idea.* Ithaca, N.Y.: Cornell University Press, 1965.

Payne, Rodger M. *The Self and the Sacred: Conversion and Autobiography in Early American Protestantism.* Knoxville: University of Tennessee Press, 1998.

Shea, Daniel B., Jr. *Spiritual Autobiography in Early America.* Princeton: Princeton University Press, 1968.

DOMESTIC PIETY
IN NEW ENGLAND

AVA CHAMBERLAIN

CHAPTER EIGHT

In March 1758, Jonathan Edwards, who had arrived at Princeton in January to assume the presidency of the College of New Jersey, lay on his deathbed. Complications had developed from a recently administered smallpox inoculation, and colonial America's greatest theologian knew it was time to set his affairs in order. Because his wife, Sarah, had remained at the Stockbridge mission—where Edwards had served as a missionary to the local Indian population after his dismissal from his Northampton pastorate—to ready their large family for the move, he could not convey his final thoughts to her directly. Instead, he asked his daughter Lucy, who was attending her father in his final illness, to "give my kindest love to my dear wife, and tell her, that the uncommon union, which has so long subsisted between us, has been of such a nature, as I trust is spiritual, and therefore will continue forever: and I hope she will be supported under so great a trial, and submit cheerfully to the will of God." He also addressed a few words of encouragement to his children, who "are now like to be left fatherless," that this sad condition "will be an inducement to you all to seek a Father, who will never fail you."[1]

Edwards's final resignation to God's will is testimony to the persistence well into the eighteenth century of Puritan devotional practice, which counseled all persons to live each moment of their lives in preparation for death. In both his private meditations and his public ministry, Edwards had emphasized the glories of heaven and the raptures of union with Christ that the saint would experience in the next life. Now that the long-anticipated moment was before him, he faced it with calm assurance of his salvation. He likewise expected his family to endure this trial as befitted devout Christians. In hoping his children would find their loss a source of spiritual gain, he repeated to them the counsel he had frequently given to members of his Northampton congregation at the sudden death of a loved one. And Sarah's lifetime of submission both to God and to her husband well prepared her to enter widowhood with the proper humility.

> ## Spiritual Experience through Marriage
>
> [G]ive my kindest love to my dear wife, and tell her, that the uncommon union, which has so long subsisted between us, has been of such a nature, as I trust is spiritual, and therefore will continue forever.
>
> —Jonathan Edwards to his wife, Sarah, March 22, 1758 (enclosed in a letter from William Shippen to Sarah Edwards, March 22, 1758), Trask Library, Andover Newton Theological Seminary.

In his last moments, Edwards also offered his wife a few words of comfort. He reassured her of his love for her and of his satisfaction with their thirty-year marriage. But by the poignant phrase "uncommon union," he referenced more than the exceptional nature of their domestic partnership. In his theological writings, Edwards had regularly used the term "common" as a synonym for "natural" and to describe a quality lacking the redemptive influences of spiritual and supernatural grace. His uncommon union with Sarah, then, was one formed by more than the natural love between husband and wife; because this love was through divine grace subordinate to the love of God, their marriage was also spiritual, a true image of that union between the heavenly bridegroom and his earthly spouse formed by the marriage of Christ to his church. As he lay dying, Edwards undoubtedly contemplated the consummation of this heavenly union with Christ, which he hoped soon to experience. This was the union that he, not wanting to assume the certainty only God could possess, "trust[ed]" would "last forever" and that Sarah would share with him once she too was glorified by Christ in heaven.

PIETY NURTURED IN FAMILY LIFE

This touching deathbed scene reflects the popular piety that linked marriage and family life with the multifaceted devotional practice defining the Puritan movement. Charles Hambrick-Stowe notes that "popular piety infused the experience of nearly everyone in New England society, though obviously in varying degrees."[2] In his life and writings, Edwards attempted to exemplify the ideal of disciplined devotion to God, but it was a popular ideal open to all who aspired to it. Puritanism, like Protestantism generally, eliminated the sacramental division between clergy and laity, emphasizing instead that although pastors performed a distinct function in the church, their piety was not qualitatively different from that available to ordinary folk. Because celibacy was no longer a prerequisite for clerical sanctity, marriage became the proper context for all persons to live the religious life. God's judgment of Adam in his solitary state, that "it is not good that the man should be alone" (Gen. 2:18) applied to everyone, clergy and laity alike. Consequently, the status of the family in society increased, as did the position of women in the family, and family life acquired a religious significance it had previously lacked. English Puritans ensured that the family would be the foundational institution of the new society they would form in Massachusetts Bay by immigrating to New England in intact family groups. And in the "holy common-wealth," both church and state closely regulated domestic relations to promote the formation of well-ordered families.

Colonial law dictated that all persons had to live in households. Lone individuals could not either by definition or by law constitute a household but were required to join another person's family as servants or boarders. The colonial family consisted of a series of three hierarchically ordered relationships: husband-wife, parent-child, and master-servant. A household did not need to contain all three, but in Massachusetts Bay many did, with the demand for additional labor being supplied initially by indentured servants and subsequently by African slaves. It was, then, as members of families that husbands and wives, children and servants, joined the larger social networks that knit together their communities and towns and participated in other social institutions, such as the church and the government. Not until the eighteenth century did the concept of an individual defined by inherent rights rather than reciprocal relations begin to challenge the essentially communitarian organization of colonial society.

Men and women began their lives as children in their parents' households and at marriage moved out to form their own, having perhaps spent some time as servants in their masters' homes. Puritans considered marriage a civil union, not a sacrament, which required the free consent of both parties. Although a wedding was often celebrated with lavish festivities, the ceremony itself was a modest affair generally performed by a justice of the peace. As God made for Adam "an help meet for him" (Gen. 2:18 KJV), a man wanted for his wife a woman who was his economic partner in the running of the household, his sexual partner in the conception of children, and his spiritual partner on the journey to salvation. This pious helpmeet was obliged by law to submit to her husband's authority as head of the household, but as Laurel Thatcher Ulrich notes, she also frequently acted as "deputy husband," assuming the man's role "as long as it furthered the good of her family and was acceptable to her husband."[3] Woman's civil inequality was also mitigated by her spiritual equality. Puritan piety was not gendered; women were by nature neither more prone to sin nor more capable of virtue than men. Both men and women were expected to live lives of disciplined devotion to God, and since devotional practice began in the home, piety was a prerequisite for the capable housewife.

Certainly, Sarah Edwards's own religious achievements were as responsible as those of her husband for their "uncommon union." From the earliest days of their acquaintance, Edwards was attracted to her in large part for her piety. When they were courting, he wrote a lyrical description of the "young lady . . . who is beloved of that almighty Being, who made and rules the world," which he apparently copied onto the flyleaf of a book that he presented to her as a gift. Although Sarah was only thirteen at the time of this composition, he portrays her as an exemplar of the Puritan religious ideal. In "certain seasons," he writes, God "comes to her and fills her mind with exceeding sweet delight." Unconcerned with earthly pleasures, she looks forward to the time when she will "be raised out of the world and caught up into heaven," where she will "dwell with" Christ and "be ravished with his love, favor and delight, forever."[4] Moreover, Sarah's ecstasies and her husband's admiration of them continued throughout their marriage. In his 1742 treatise defending the evangelical revival then sweeping New England, Edwards included an extended description of his wife's religious experiences. Without revealing Sarah's identity in the text, he observes that the Holy Spirit gave this paradigm of heartfelt religion "a clear and lively view or sense of the infinite beauty and amiableness of Christ's person" that continued "for five or six hours together, without any interruption." Her "extraordinary views of divine things" were "attended with very great effects on the body," such as a "fainting with the love of Christ," "an unavoidable leaping for joy," and "an increase of a spirit of humility and meekness." If such experiences are "the fruits of a distempered brain," he exclaims, "let my brain be evermore possessed of that happy distemper!" (*WJE* 4:332, 333, 335, 341).

Religious activity in the Puritan household was, however, generally occupied with things more mundane than the happy distempers of Sarah Edwards. The "familie is a little Church," wrote William Gouge in his 1622 treatise *Of Domestical Duties*, and consequently each family member had distinct religious responsibilities. Each was expected to foster his or her own spiritual growth through a daily regimen of prayer, Bible reading, and self-examination, but even these "secret devotions" occurred within the context of the family. Puritans, especially in the seventeenth century, had little concept of personal privacy; they did, however, respect the need to withdraw regularly from the daily round of activities in the household. At times, family members even constructed a small devotional room to fulfill Jesus' command to "enter into thy closet" in times of prayer (Matt. 6:6 KJV). For example, when he was a boy, Jonathan Edwards "built a booth in a swamp, in a very secret and retired place, for a place a prayer" (*WJE* 16:791). But if it were not literally possible to "shut thy door" and "pray to thy Father which is in secret," spiritual solitude was sought in woods or fields or in a quiet corner of the house. These private devotions, Hambrick-Stowe observes, "lay at the very heart of New England spirituality."[5]

> **Family Life as the Building Block of Puritan Society**
>
> [A] familie is a little Church, and a little commonwealth, at least a lively representation thereof, whereby . . . men are fitted to greater matters in Church or comonwealth.
>
> —William Gouge, Of Domestical Duties (1622), 18.

Passing this spiritual practice on to the next generation also began in the family. Although other institutions participated in this process, training children in godly habits was primarily the parents' responsibility. The father's position as head of the family shaped his

Fig. 8.1. Title page of Lewis Bayly's The Practice of Piety (London, 1620). Photo © Folger Shakespeare Library, Washington, DC.

religious role in the household. As the pastor of this "little church," he regularly catechized the children, offered prayers of thanksgiving before meals, and conducted the twice-daily family devotions. These devotions were short, but they contained all of the elements of a formal worship service, including prayer and confession of sin, psalm singing, and Scripture reading. Families commonly used one of the popular devotional manuals, such as Lewis Bayly's *The Practice of Piety*, to guide their daily worship, and they generally took turns reading aloud chapters from the Bible, which the father improved by a brief application of the text. The mother, being her husband's spiritual equal, had an equally important, although complementary, religious role in the household. "Mothers," Laurel Thatcher Ulrich observes, "represented the affectionate mode in an essentially authoritarian system of child-rearing."[6] A woman, then, fostered her children's piety as an expression of her mother love. She taught more by example and small daily acts of religious nurture than by formal instruction, which was the father's duty. And frequently she exemplified the Puritan religious ideal more completely than her husband, for by the late seventeenth century, women comprised the majority of church members in all New England congregations, a distinction they maintained for the remainder of the colonial period.

Although employing different means, both mother and father shared the same aim, to guide their children through the crucial early years of the spiritual pilgrimage that, for the Puritans, ended only at death. This journey began with baptism. Parents knew their children were born in sin, for they had heard ministers such as Jonathan Edwards frequently condemn their progeny as "young vipers" (*WJE* 4:394). To ensure their children's access to the sacrament of baptism, which cleansed an infant of its natural depravity, new couples—especially the bride—often became church members or renewed their church covenants just prior to marriage when they first faced the prospect of becoming parents. But even with baptism, children continued to live in sin and at risk of damnation until the Holy Spirit transformed their hearts in the conversion moment. And youth was the time for conversion. As Edwards notes, "The younger persons are, the fairer they stand for regeneration," for in youth the habit of sinfulness was not yet deeply entrenched (*WJE* 20:76). Sarah Edwards, for example, displayed her spiritual precocity by being converted "when a little child of about five or six years of age," and all godly parents encouraged the ideal of early piety (*WJE* 4:335). They prepared their children to reach this first goal of the religious life by teaching them to read. Puritans embraced the Reformation principle that all Christians should be able to read and interpret the Bible for themselves. Mothers first instructed their children in the home, using a primer and the Bible. Boys who aspired to a profession would continue their education at a "dame" or grammar school, but fundamentally reading was part of children's religious education, for it allowed them to practice the secret devotional exercises and participate in the daily family worship, which the Holy Spirit used as a means of converting grace.

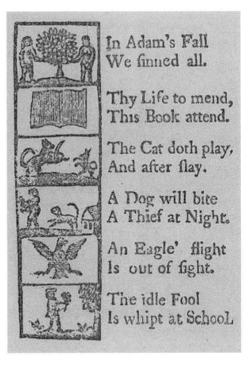

Fig. 8.2. First alphabet page of The New England Primer (Boston, 1727).

FAMILIES AT CHURCH

Parents also ensured that the members of their household regularly attended the pubic preaching of the Word, the second means of grace. Although Sabbath observance was mandated by law, church attendance was the family's responsibility. Beginning with private and family devotions after sundown Saturday, the Sabbath was marked by public worship that lasted all day Sunday, with morning and afternoon services each about three hours long. During these services, the minister preached for at least an hour, using a plain style to ensure his congregation followed his exposition and application of the chosen Scripture text. The major prayer followed the sermon and equaled it in length. Using an extemporaneous style, the minister pleaded with God to assist a parishioner who was ill or laboring under convictions, to revive the town's piety or reduce its contention, and to aid the colony in a time of warfare or spiritual declension. In addition, worship included Scripture readings, psalm singing, and the celebration of the Lord's Supper at regular monthly or bimonthly intervals. Although all colonists were required to attend Sunday services, only church members participated in the Lord's Supper. Some congregations, such as Jonathan Edwards's in Northampton, began relaxing membership requirements in the late seventeenth century, but most asked applicants to demonstrate their visible sainthood by means of a conversion narrative related to the pastor and congregation. Private striving for conversion was thereby incomplete without the public acknowledgment by the church, while the church's evangelistic mission failed without family support.

The church's seating arrangements reflected its complex interrelation with the family. In the eighteenth century, family pew boxes began to appear in New England churches; prior to this time, men, women, and children sat separately during the Sabbath services. Children and servants were relegated to the gallery, while men—ranked according to social standing in the community—sat on the benches to the left of the pulpit and women on the corresponding benches to the right. This arrangement erased family units and enhanced ministerial authority, leaving each person to face God alone. It also affirmed the essential role of women in the church, who embraced church membership as the only public distinction available to them in this patriarchal society, and who, although permitted neither to vote in church affairs nor to hold church office, provided a crucial base of support for the local pastor.

Baptismal practices revealed, however, that churches were composed fundamentally of families, not individuals. Initially, ministers only baptized the children of full church members, but even when the so-called Halfway Covenant expanded the reach of this sacrament to the children of baptized but not full (i.e., halfway) church members, it reaffirmed the view "that grace descended within families." Godly parents were a double blessing to their children. Through family worship they raised their offspring in the habit of piety, and through baptism they, as David D. Hall observes, "enclosed" them in the protective "shelter of religion." The most direct means of salvation, then, was to be born into a godly family. This coincidence between grace and blood created, according to Edmund S. Morgan, "a defensive, tribal attitude" that turned the church "into an exclusive society for the saints and their children." Although Puritans never abandoned efforts to convert the unregenerate, this tribalism displayed the insular side of domestic piety.[7]

Puritan theologians reinforced the family's integral role in the cultivation and perpetuation of piety by using domestic images to depict the relation between Christ and the church. Although paternal and even maternal metaphors were common, spousal imagery was considered the most comprehensive. As Morgan notes, "Marriage, which the Puritans regarded as the highest relationship between mortals, was generally accepted as the closest comparison to the believer's union with God."[8] This imagery had biblical roots in the erotic love poetry of Canticles and other Scripture texts, but unlike the medieval tradition, which interpreted the relation between the heavenly bridegroom and his earthly spouse in the context of sexual chastity, Protestants experienced this spiritual marriage not as a substitute for ordinary domestic relations but as an affirmation of them. Puritan husbands and wives considered their marital union to be, in Edwards's words, a "type of the union between Christ and the church." Because it reflected a higher spiritual reality, marriage was, he notes, citing Ephesians 5:32, "a great mystery" (*WJE* 11:53, 54). This typological relation elevated the religious significance of marriage, making it the primary referent for the Puritan experience of grace.

MARRIAGE AS A SYMBOL OF SPIRITUAL FULFILLMENT

Edwards frequently compared the religious life to a godly marriage; however, one of his most thorough explorations of this type is found in his sermon on Matthew 25:1, the introduction to a nineteen-unit sermon series on the parable of the wise and foolish virgins (Matt. 25:1-12), which he preached in the winter of 1737–1738.[9] In this

Fig. 8.3. Francis Quarles, *Emblems* (1635), book 5, emblem 2, illustrating the passage "My beloved is mine, and I am his: He feedeth among the lillies" (Cant. 2:16). Reproduced with the permission of Rare Books and Manuscripts, Special Collections Library, the Pennsylvania State University Libraries.

discourse Edwards draws from his text the doctrine "The church is espoused to the Lord Jesus Christ," and he develops this doctrine with frequent reference to the social norms regulating both betrothal and marriage in eighteenth-century New England. In every particular Christ is a most excellent match. He is, first, a most attractive suitor. In comparison with him, all other lovers "are base and vile in their nature." These rivals have a "seeming beauty and loveliness," but it is only "a mask that they put on." Christ is also a most "profitable" suitor. "This glorious person that seeks your love and invites you to a spiritual espousal to him," Edwards notes, "is one that is of unsearchable riches." He has a substantial estate from his Father, who "is the great possessor of heaven and earth, and if you will yield to his suit and your soul becomes his spouse, his riches shall be yours." Consequently, he has the "wherewithal to feed you" and will "feast you and satisfy your soul." He has "wherewithal to cloth you"; if you marry him, he will adorn you in "glorious robes." His rivals, however, will leave you "in rags and nakedness as you are."

Once by faith and through grace the divine match is made, the union between Christ and his betrothed spouse is the perfect likeness of the Puritan marital ideal. As Amanda Porterfield observes, "Puritans expected marriage to be simultaneously hierarchical and affectionate." Edwards likewise characterizes spiritual marriage as a relation not simply of willing subjection but of mutual companionship. "The love of Christ to his church is that which transcends all the love of earthly lovers," Edwards writes. He "promises forever to cleave to her" and to "take care of her and be her everlasting friend and portion." Their union is one of "mutual communion, cohabitation and enjoyment as friends and companions," but it is not the love of equals. Christ is united to the church, Edwards explains, "as her friend and companion, yet she is subject to him as Lord." Christ condescends to accept "a little feeble poor insect to be his bride," and she responds by depending upon him "for guidance, protection, and provision." This simultaneously hier-archical and affectionate union also has the erotic dimension, which, according to Porterfield, "lent a primitive kind of sexual excitement to desires for grace."[10] Although full consummation comes only after death, on that wedding day "a truly believing soul" will "be received into the arm of Christ as his bride, to go home to him to dwell with him in his house." And there the "King shall bring her into his cham-ber," writes Edwards, paraphrasing Canticles, "to behold his glory and to enjoy his love forever and to enjoy the most free and intimate converse with [him]." As a result of this heavenly intercourse, Christ's spouse "travails in birth with souls," which she conceives "through the seed of divine grace." Christ, therefore, is an attractive, wealthy, loving, wise, strong, and fertile suitor. Edwards warns his congregation, as if he were a parent admonishing a reluctant daughter, that to "reject so honorable a match . . . will end in everlasting disgrace and contempt."

Espousal theology, like that used by Edwards in this sermon, permeated Puritan understand-ing of both marriage and the religious life. The spiritual marriage between Christ and the church was the model earthly couples strove to emulate in their own marriages, and through their own domestic relations, couples learned the meaning of genuine faith. As a godly wife should humbly submit to her husband's authority as head of the household, so all believers should embrace Christ's headship over his church. "Spousal metaphors,"

> ### Christ as a Loving Husband to His Church
>
> The love that is between Christ and his church is an electing and distin-guishing love as the love ought to be between husband and wife. They ought, each of them in their affec-tions, to forsake all others for the sake of one another. They should choose one another above all and should give their hearts to each other, rejecting all others.
>
> —Jonathan Edwards, "Sermon on Matthew 25:1" (November 1737), Jonathan Edwards Collection, Beinecke Rare Book and Manuscript Library, Yale University.

notes Richard Godbeer, "envisaged all believers, male and female, as prospective brides of Christ." When Edwards, in his sermon on Matthew 25:1, exhorts his congregation "to harken to the invitations of Jesus Christ" to make "an espousal with him," he figures both men and women as wives. In their devotional lives, all persons should adopt the passive and subordinate posture best expressed by the feminine virtues of humility, submission, and obedience. This ideal of "female piety," according to Porterfield, "functioned similarly for both men and women by representing the loving disposition and deference to authority that all Puritans associated with grace." As a consequence, it, too, elevated the status of women and provided a religious and moral unity to colonial New England society.[11]

SIGNS OF DISCONTENT

New England was not, however, perfectly united in its devotion to either God or the family. To assume all persons embraced the domestic ideal of female piety attributes to colonial life a cohesiveness it lacked. Although all could aspire to this ideal, not all did, in either their inner spiritual lives or their external actions. Assessments of the range of religious adherence should not underestimate the number of godly people in colonial New England, but their numbers also should not be exaggerated. After the first decades of settlement, which were marked by high rates of religious adherence, less than half the population ever qualified for full church membership. These laypeople were not atheists. Some colonists did choose to live "profane" lifestyles, but as Richard Gildrie observes, "'profane' did not mean 'secular,' but rather denoted a contempt, irreverence, or flagrant disregard for things sacred." Most likely, those who never came forward to give a conversion relation were halfway members who attended church, had their children baptized, and generally lived moral lives, but who preferred, according to Hall, "a mode of religious response less taxing than the extremes of an ideal faith."[12]

Near-universal literacy meant that the laity read the Bible and other devotional books and developed their own independent interpretations. Although radical or heretical beliefs were uncommon, they sometimes decided "that Scripture did not coincide with what the minister had said." For example, laypeople freely placed their own meanings upon the sacraments, embracing the family-centered ritual of baptism while fearing Paul's warning to those who "eateth and drinketh unworthily" the elements of the Lord's Supper (1 Cor. 11:29 KJV). And as David Hall and Jon Butler have shown, popular culture also supported a widespread belief in occult and magical practices. The more than two hundred episodes of witchcraft that occurred in New England before the massive outbreak in Salem were only the most dramatic examples of the colonists' belief in the supernatural. People looked for wonders and portents in nature and read almanacs for interpretations of meteorological and astrological signs. Towns were commonly inhabited by a number of "cunning folk" who claimed to cure illness, find lost objects, and make love potions. And although clergy began in the eighteenth century to preach against such practices from the pulpit, they too inhabited this "world of wonders," regularly interpreting surprising natural events, such as an earthquake or a "monstrous" birth, as manifestations of divine providence.[13]

In the latter seventeenth century, the clergy grew increasingly uneasy as the numbers of moderately pious Christians multiplied. Rates of church membership among men dropped, and women emerged as the majority of full communicants in all congregations. Condemning their parishioners for this apparent declension, pastors prophesied God's judgment on his people for their sins and called for a new dedication to the Puritan devotional ideal through covenant renewal and moral reform. As an extension of this jeremiad form, some also began to employ a more evangelical style of preaching, which emphasized conversion and the revival of piety through an emotional experience of saving grace. Revivals became more common in the eighteenth century, fueled not simply by evangelical preachers but by laypeople who found spiritually satisfying their dramatic oratory and its focus on heart religion. During one period of awakening that swept the Connecticut River Valley in the 1730s, for example, Jonathan Edwards reports that in Northampton "more than 300 souls were savingly brought home to Christ . . . in the space of half a year." Edwards and other local ministers preached the new birth from their pulpits, but according to Harry S. Stout's analysis, "the primary momentum was generated from beneath," among the laity.[14] Although conversions occurred among the "very young" and those "past middle age" and affected "about the same number of males as females," the revival's principal energy was supplied by the town's "young people," who "divide[d] themselves into several companies to meet in various parts of the town" to speak among themselves of "the gloriousness of the way of salvation." The revival that enflamed Northampton in the early 1740s as part of a general colonywide awakening was again driven by the young people. Early on, Edwards observes, "a very considerable work of God appeared among those that were very young," and from this beginning, "the revival of religion continued to increase" (*WJE* 4:158, 148, 151–52, 545).

AN OUTBREAK OF SEXUAL FREEDOM

This youthful religious zeal was a hopeful sign of renewed commitment to the ideal of Puritan piety, but other adolescent actions in Northampton clearly displayed how far New England society had by the mid-eighteenth century moved away from the worldview that had initially supported that ideal. Revival increased devotional practice, but the godly conversation of the Puritan saint, which began with acts of personal piety and public worship, also encompassed moral behavior in daily life. "Puritanism," Hambrick-Stowe explains, "was a devotional movement dedicated to the spiritual regeneration of individuals and society."[15] This double regeneration expressed two aspects of the same process, for inner spiritual transformation manifested itself in external submission to God's moral law. "Christian practice" was, according to Edwards, "the chief of all the signs of grace"; no one, he insisted, can "pretend that they have a good heart, while they live a wicked life." During periods of revival, Northampton's young people met this standard. "[T]here has been a very great alteration among the youth of the town," Edwards reported in 1743, "with respect to reveling, frolicking, profane and unclean conversation, and lewd songs; instances of fornication have been very rare" (*WJE* 2:406, 428; 4:544). As the religious excitement decreased, however, "unclean conversation" increased, and Edwards employed all the powers of his office to correct this growing disjunction between piety and practice.

The family was the first bulwark against immorality. Parents were responsible for training their children in both godly habits and moral behavior. Pious children were orderly in their actions; when they failed to respect the commonwealth's laws, it was their parents' duty to correct them. Fathers, the principal disciplinarians, considered the birch rod a biblically sanctioned punishment but used it only as a last resort. "Though it was better to be whipped than damned," Morgan notes, "it was still better to be persuaded than whipped."[16] Although interference in family discipline was rare, parents who inflicted cruel or excessive punishment could be sanctioned by the state, as could children who violated the Fifth Commandment. More problematic than overzealous discipline was lax family government. Disorderly families meant a disorderly society, and both the churches and the courts stepped in where families failed. Church and state operated in two separate but overlapping jurisdictions. The reach of church discipline extended only to its members, and unlike the state, it had the power to excommunicate but not to inflict punishments. The courts could not meddle in internal church affairs, but they could sanction lawbreakers with punishments ranging from monetary fines and whippings to banishment and death. Through much of the colonial period, these two institutions worked together to maintain social order, but in the latter part of the seventeenth century, as New England entered a period of rapid social transformation, the interests of the legal system began to diverge from those of the religious establishment. Edwards's effort to discipline the wayward young people in his congregation ran against this tide of social change.

Edwards's surveillance of the boundary separating licit from illicit sex was a constant source of conflict in postrevival Northampton. "Our way of managing church discipline," he observes in a series of lectures preached in 1748, "has been the greatest wound." "No one thing has been the occasion of . . . [so much] contention," leading the people to quarrel "with their minister" and quarrel "one with another." It has been, he concludes, "worse than all the scandals."[17] Although church records are scant, four controversial discipline cases can be identified: the so-called bad book affair of 1744, in which Edwards censured several young men in his congregation for reading illicit books and harassing young women, and three fornication cases. The church censured Samuel Danks in 1743, Thomas Wait in 1747, and Elisha Hawley in 1748, each for his persistent refusal to confess to a charge of fornication and for his contempt for the authority of the church. This last, more fully documented, fornication case clearly reveals how the newly developing values of privacy and individual self-assertion conflicted with the domestic piety of earlier generations.

Sometime in the fall or winter of 1746, Elisha Hawley, the twenty-year-old son of one of Northampton's most prominent residents, and a young unmarried woman named Martha Root, committed what according to Massachusetts law was a crime and Congregational church rule was a sin. They had sex, probably on more than one occasion, for Martha became pregnant and gave birth to twin girls, one of whom died in September 1747.[18] Contrary to the common stereotype, Puritans were passionate lovers. As Godbeer observes, they "sought not to repress their sexual instincts but to keep them within ordained borders." Only marital sex was officially sanctioned, but within these bounds sexual passion was encouraged. The condemnation of celibacy and the elevation of the domestic life transformed the traditional Christian association between sexuality and sin. Sex was celebrated not simply as a means of procreation but as an end in itself, reflecting the spiritual union all saints hoped to experience with the heavenly bridegroom after death. Impotence, therefore, invalidated the marriage covenant, for a mutually satisfying sex life was part of the very definition of marriage. Even beyond the years of procreation, refusal or inability to give "due benevolence" (1 Cor. 7:3 KJV) to one's spouse was grounds for divorce, as was adultery, which signified a sinner's spiritual betrayal of Christ's perfect love.[19]

Couples like Elisha and Martha show, however, that Puritans did not always confine their sexual passions to the marriage bed. The choice to have sex without the sanction of marriage certainly expressed a disregard for the dominant moral value structure, but Elisha and Martha and the many other couples like them were probably not just flaunting the rules. Elisha may have been a cad who sought sexual pleasure as an end in itself, and Martha may have been a scheming spinster who used sex to ensnare one of the town's most eligible bachelors. More likely, their choice reflected an alternate value structure, which flourished in English popular culture and was transported to New England by the colonists. As Godbeer has demonstrated, there was no consensus in England or the colonies on what constituted the boundary between licit and illicit sex. The law defined this boundary to be marriage, and this definition was supported not only by social elites, such as magistrates and clergy, but also by a majority of the population. It competed, however, with an alternate view that identified commitment—expressed either publicly in the formal declaration of banns or privately in promises to marry and professions of love—as the boundary. In the eighteenth century, as the traditional institutions of family, church, and community loosened their controls on individual behavior, expression of this popular sexual ethic increased. County court records show that bastardy rates steadily grew in this period, with bridal pregnancies rising to a high of nearly 40 percent in some New England towns in the second half of the eighteenth century.[20]

Martha and Elisha's sexual escapades reflect this demographic trend, but unlike most couples in this delicate situation, they did not marry. The high rate of bridal pregnancies in this period—that is, women who gave birth within seven months of marriage—indicates that most couples honored the commitment they believed justified their premarital sexual activity. But Martha and Elisha, if they had made such a commitment, failed to fulfill it. Instead, Elisha was commissioned a lieutenant in the colonial militia and sent in March 1747, when Martha was only a few months pregnant, to Fort Massachusetts, a dangerous outpost on the western frontier, to wait out the scandal. The records of the case do not reveal why Elisha chose not to marry his pregnant lover. It was a suitable match. She was a church member like him, and although the Roots were not the Hawleys' social equals, they occupied only a slightly inferior position in the social hierarchy. But informing this choice was surely the understanding that refusal would not significantly damage the family's social standing. In the first century of settlement, Massachusetts courts, like the churches, treated fornication as a serious offense; a 1642 statute stipulated that the appropriate punishment for a man convicted of fornication with a single woman was "Marriage, or Fine, or Corporal punishment, or all, or any of these" at the court's discretion. Disenfranchisement was added to this list of possible punishments in 1665. But in practice men routinely confessed their crime and married their pregnant lovers, which allowed judges to impose more lenient sentences. A man who did not confess, moreover, could be held liable for the bastard child's maintenance if, as stipulated in a 1668 law, the mother consistently named him as the father of the child, especially during the labor of childbirth.[21] Following the provisions of this law, Martha identified Elisha Hawley as the father of her twins probably well before their delivery. But when she appeared in court, she did not name him the father, an act necessary to initiate criminal child-support proceedings. Like many pregnant single women in the mid-eighteenth century, she assumed the whole guilt for their criminal action. She appeared at the November 1747 sitting of the Hampshire County Court of General Sessions, "confess'd herself guilty of the crime of fornication," and was "ordered to pay a fine of 25 shillings . . . and costs."[22] Elisha's name appears nowhere in the court records of the case.

> ### A Law against Fornication
>
> It is ordered by this Court and the Authority thereof; That if any man Commit Fornication with any single Woman, they shall be punished by enjoyning Marriage, or Fine, or Corporal Punishment, or all, or any of these, as the judges of the Court that hath Cognizance of the Cause shall appoint.
>
> —From The General Laws and Liberties of the Massachusetts Colony (1672).

A DOUBLE STANDARD TAKES HOLD

Elisha's ability to avoid criminal liability reflected a more general transformation of the legal system occurring throughout New England in the eighteenth century. The Anglicization of court procedures and the growth of the legal profession made for a more litigious society, while an increasingly complex economy filled the courts' dockets with financial disputes. Less concerned with moral regulation, judges became more concerned with standards of evidence. As Cornelia Hughes Dayton has shown, men commonly refused to confess their crimes, preferring instead to hire a lawyer to contest the charges or to formulate grounds for an appeal. Most often, men contested fornication charges by portraying themselves as the innocent victims of unscrupulous women's lies and schemes. Judges, who had once tried to implement a "single standard" of conduct for both men and women, a standard that held "that godly behavior should be the measure for *all* inhabitants" and that punished both men and women equally for their sexual and moral transgressions, became increasingly skeptical of a woman's word. Without this foundation, criminal prosecutions of men for fornication virtually disappeared from the courts, so that by the mid-eighteenth century, a double standard had emerged that shielded male impunity with women's sole culpability. As Ulrich observes, "Fornication had become a woman's crime."[23]

This transformation of the legal system was, notes Dayton, facilitated by a reconfiguration of the boundary separating public from private space, which increasingly sheltered middling and elite families like the Hawleys from "public scrutiny, humiliation, and penalty" and allowed them to claim "the right to keep private the premarital sexual lapses of their young people."[24] Although the Hawleys surely were not successful in keeping Elisha's indiscretion secret—such newsworthy gossip would have quickly spread throughout the town—they did keep it private. Joseph Hawley, Elisha's brother and a young lawyer eager to make a reputation for himself, negotiated privately a settlement with Martha for the child's maintenance. In May 1748, she signed an agreement accepting "One Hundred and fifty five pounds Old Tenor in full Satisfaction for and towards the Support and maintenance of a Bastard Child born of my Body Now living." A local justice of the peace probably arbitrated this agreement, but no trace remains in the court documents. Only Martha's crime and only Martha's confession are visible in the public records.

When Martha accepted the Hawleys' settlement offer, the court's interest in this routine fornication case came to an end, but Edwards's was just beginning. Although the Hampshire County Court was getting out of the business of moral regulation, the Northampton Congregational Church remained—like many evangelical churches at the time—committed to it. Edwards objected to the new double standard, which allowed men to escape their responsibilities and brought the colony's ecclesiastical establishment into conflict with its legal system. He, like other evangelical pastors after the Awakening, upheld the older single standard, in which courts encouraged men to confess their sins and marry their pregnant lovers, and punished equally both men and women guilty of fornication, sometimes even enjoining an errant couple to marry, as the law allowed. This single legal standard reflected the traditional image of Puritan piety, in which both men and women were expected to humbly submit to the authority of their heavenly bridegroom. But like the legal system, this Puritan religious ideal was also changing in eighteenth-century New England. Although women continued to uphold the ideal of female piety, men moved away from it, embracing instead, as Porterfield observes, "a new appreciation of manhood and its virtues of independence and self-confidence."[25]

As this new construct of masculinity developed, Edwards used the power of church discipline to uphold traditional Puritan values of piety

and practice. Wayward members had been responsive to the church's authority in the past. In March 1731, for example, not long after Edwards became full pastor of the church in Northampton, Hannah Graves of Hatfield was presented for fornication in Hampshire County Court, and at her confession she named Eleazar King the father of her child. King was a member of Edwards's congregation, but he pled not guilty to the charge and was convicted and ordered by the court to pay Hannah four shillings a week for maintenance. Uncertain how to proceed, Edwards apparently asked his colleagues at a meeting of the Hampshire County Ministerial Association in October 1731 to address three questions related to his

Fig. 8.4. The Reverend Jonathan Edwards, painted by Joseph Badger circa 1750–1755. Reproduced by permission, Jonathan Edwards Center and Jonathan Edwards College, Yale University.

church's disposition of the King case. At this time the ministers agreed that the Scripture rules (Exod. 22:16-17; Deut. 22:28-29) requiring a man to marry a virgin whom he has humbled are "moral" rules and so "of perpetual obligation"; that a man who confesses to the sin of fornication cannot be judged truly repentant by his church so long as he refuses to marry; and that these rules applied to Eleazar King. Not long after this meeting, King married Hannah Graves, presumably at the insistence of Edwards and the church.[26]

Nearly twenty years later, Edwards proceeded against Elisha Hawley as he had Eleazar King. A letter written by Joseph Hawley to his brother Elisha on December 23, 1748, more than six months after the private settlement, indicates the Northampton church had disciplined Elisha, apparently excommunicating him for his persistent refusal to confess his sin and to marry Martha. But unlike his more compliant predecessor, Elisha Hawley did not humbly submit to his church's censure. Appealing its judgment to a council of ministers, Joseph Hawley employed in the ecclesiastical context the legal maneuvering that had proved unnecessary for him to use in the courtroom. Convening in the Northampton meetinghouse on June 29, 1749, the council heard arguments from both sides. Hawley argued that the Scripture rules requiring a man to marry a virgin whom he had humbled did not apply in this case because Martha Root had been "of a grossly lascivious character" before her acquaintance with his brother and had been the aggressor, enticing him into the entanglement. By his own later admission, Hawley exaggerated the evidence against Martha, but his arguments were evidently successful at the time. Although the council of ministers judged Elisha guilty of fornication and believed he was "bound in conscience" to marry Martha—judgments the county court had been unwilling to make—they ruled it not his "duty" to marry her. The church should receive him back into their fellowship "upon his making a penitent confession of the sin of fornication," and unlike Eleazar King, Elisha's unwillingness to marry Martha should not impugn the sincerity of this confession.

> **Men's Responsibility for Sex**
>
> If a man find a damsel that is a virgin, which is not betrothed, and lay hold on her, and lie with her, and they be found; then the man that lay with her shall give unto the damsel's father fifty shekels of silver, and she shall be his wife; because he hath humbled her, he may not put her away all his days.
> —Deuteronomy 22:28-29 KJV.

This council's judgment revealed the limits of Edwards's support as he struggled in the 1740s to maintain the traditional Puritan ideal of disciplined devotion to God. In this effort he did have allies. He could not have initiated disciplinary action against a series of sexually profligate parishioners without the support of a church majority. Many must have agreed that although their exploits were only minor infractions, the irresponsibility of these young men was inexcusable. The domestic piety of earlier generations had identified faith with family formation and manliness with a robust profession of faith, a sincere repentance of sin, and a willingness to accept responsibility. By the mid-eighteenth century, although women continued to embrace the ideal of female piety, the wider culture offered men the competing value of individual self-assertion. Realizing church discipline was insufficient to keep his congregation free from such corruption, Edwards devised a more radical strategy to achieve the same end. He closed communion to all but those who through profession of faith and confession of sin visibly demonstrated their spiritual regeneration.

In this final struggle with his Northampton congregation, several of the same figures who had blocked Edwards's action against Elisha Hawley reemerged to force him to relinquish his pastorate. In particular, Joseph Hawley was chosen, perhaps because of his recent success in arguing his brother's appeal, to present the case for dismissal before the council of ministers that would ultimately decide Edwards's fate. But more interestingly, when Edwards himself defended his new church-membership policy, he voiced substantially the same position as in the earlier fornication case. Elisha was morally obligated to marry Martha, he had argued, for it is "fit and suitable" for couples who have "united and become one flesh" to be legally joined. They are "one flesh *de jure*, or in obligation," he had asserted; and so it is unsuitable for them to "see one another from time to time and be seen by others remaining separate, not united as one flesh." Similarly, it is unsuitable for church members, who are in *foro ecclesiae* espoused to Christ as their heavenly bridegroom, to be in reality separate from him. The Lord's Supper, Edwards stated in the treatise he wrote to justify his new communion policy, is a sign of that "which is spiritually transacted between Christ and his spouse in the covenant that unites them." When a person takes the bread and wine, it "is as much a professing to accept of Christ . . . as a woman's taking a ring of the bridegroom in her marriage is a profession and seal of her taking him for her husband"(*WJE* 12:257). Hypocrites, who join the church without an experience of saving grace, wear the ring but have not consummated the marriage. Fornicators consummate their union but do not wear the ring. In both cases the offending parties are engaged in a fraudulent marriage. The bride is either legally separate from him to whom she is actually joined in physical union or spiritually separate from him to whom she is visibly joined in gracious union. Edwards objected to this gap between appearance and reality, but in neither case could he sustain within his church a unity the wider society was no longer willing to support.

The family was the central organizing principle of Puritan society. As both a "little church" and a "little commonwealth," it was the foundation of the twin institutions of church and state. The authority conferred upon parents by the Fifth Commandment also legitimated the claims to authority made by both church and state. And it was within the family that children learned the habits of piety and obedience necessary for adult lives as righteous Christians and law-abiding subjects. In the eighteenth century, with the growth of a more diverse population and the introduction of a market economy, this organic unity began to fragment. With the increasing separation of private from public space, the family and the state became, as Mary Beth Norton observes, "different, diametrically opposed institutions."[27] Men championed the public virtues of equality, individualism, and independence, while women upheld the domestic virtues of piety, humility, and self-sacrifice. Caught between these separate spheres, the church maintained a quasi-public role in society but was increasingly identified with women—a growing majority in the churches—and the family. Domestic piety continued to flourish in the transition from Puritan congregationalism to Protestant evangelicalism, but the nature of the domestic realm changed. Women, now considered innately more pious and more virtuous than men, became the guardians of this little church, responsible not only for their children's religious education but also for their husbands' virtue, which was threatened from without by the competitive marketplace and from within by moral frailty. The pious housewife used the power of her passionless and selfless nature to construct her home as a refuge from these sinful forces. In this domain she preserved the ideal of female piety, but by the time of the establishment of the new republic, the erotic spousal imagery that had defined the domestic theology of both men and women in Puritan New England had given way to a gendered ideology of virtue.

When Sarah Edwards learned of her husband's death in March 1758, she sent a letter of consolation to her daughter Esther, whose husband, Aaron Burr, past president of the College of New Jersey and Edwards's close ministerial colleague, had died the previous fall.

Struggling to submit to God's will in this time of trial, she writes, "The Lord has done it. He has made me adore his goodness, that we had him so long. But my God lives; and he has my heart. Oh what a legacy my husband, your father, has left us!" The referent of the masculine pronouns in this cry of bereavement is ambiguous. It could be either God or Edwards himself—either Sarah's heavenly or her earthly spouse—who has her heart and whose goodness she adores. This conflation of the domestic and the spiritual is one of the legacies of Puritanism in America. But for Sarah, who had spent her life in disciplined service to both God and her husband, there was no real confusion in the proper order of loves. "We are all given to God," she unambiguously states in the closing line of the letter, "and there I am, and love to be."[28] Through daily acts of private devotion and weekly Sabbath worship, Puritans cultivated this sense of belonging not to the world but to God. Although the family was the proper context in which to live the religious life, it was not the saint's proper home. Even the loss of a beloved spouse was a timely reminder that only after death was the fullness of domestic bliss achieved.

Fig. 8.5. Mrs. Jonathan Edwards (Sarah Pierpont) painted by Joseph Badger circa 1750–1755. Reproduced by permission, Jonathan Edwards Center and Jonathan Edwards College, Yale University.

FOR FURTHER READING

Dayton, Cornelia Hughes. *Women before the Bar: Gender, Law, and Society in Connecticut, 1637–1789.* Chapel Hill: University of North Carolina Press, 1995.

Godbeer, Richard. *Sexual Revolution in Early America.* Baltimore: Johns Hopkins University Press, 2002.

Hambrick-Stowe, Charles E. *The Practice of Piety: Puritan Devotional Disciplines in Seventeenth-Century New England.* Chapel Hill: University of North Carolina Press, 1982.

Morgan, Edmund S. *The Puritan Family: Religion and Domestic Relations in Seventeenth-Century New England.* 1944. Reprint, New York: Harper & Row, 1966.

Porterfield, Amanda. *Female Piety in Puritan New England: The Emergence of Religious Humanism.* New York: Oxford University Press, 1992.

Ulrich, Laurel Thatcher. *Good Wives: Image and Reality in the Lives of Women in Northern New England, 1650–1750.* 1982. Reprint, New York: Vintage Books, 1991.

RACE AND GENDER

Part 3

GENDERING CHRISTIANITY

MARILYN J. WESTERKAMP

CHAPTER NINE

> There is no longer Jew or Greek, there is no longer slave or free, there is no longer male and female; for all of you are one in Christ Jesus. And if you belong to Christ, then you are Abraham's offspring, heirs according to the promise.
>
> —Galatians 3:28-29

Throughout the epistles included in the New Testament, Paul espoused many visions of the Christian and the Christian community, yet no passage of Paul has resonated among feminists as has this one. It is almost a proclamation of spiritual equality for all, and feminist Christians have argued for the universal soul unmarked by race, class, or gender. From the 1960s forward, during the second wave of the feminist movement, this vision of God and Christianity has been invoked repeatedly as feminist theologians have battled Christian churches for increasing power and authority for women. In fact, these verses were cited as early as 1838 by Quaker Sarah Grimke, in her *Letters on the Quality of the Sexes*, as she fought the efforts of New England's ministerial association to silence her as she proclaimed her right (and her duty) to speak out against slavery. As a political slogan, the text is marvelous, as a theological concept inspiring. As a historical description of the Christian community, however, the text is, at best, unfulfilled prophecy and woefully inaccurate.

Gender is not merely incidental to the development of Christianity; gender sits at the heart of its theology, cosmology, and praxis. The importance of male and female as a means by which societies organize production, reproduction, leadership systems, and thus cultural values forces historians to see gender as a primary principle constructing different societies. From the intellectual elites through to the least educated, men and women have understood themselves and others, their roles and responsibilities, in terms of sex identity. Christianity, like other religious systems, has been produced within and influenced by specific social and cultural climates. The centrality of gender means that despite universalistic claims, Christian institutions must to some extent have treated and impacted men and women differently. I argue, however, that this is at best an understatement, for Christian theologians and communities have been active partners in the changing ideologies that construct gender identities. Christianity is founded upon an incarnational theology; Christians believe that God became human, was embodied, in the historically male person of Jesus Christ. Theologians might say that God is neither male nor female, but most practitioners are not so sophisticated, and truthfully, neither are most theologians. In this direct connection between humanity and God in the historical person of Jesus, God became male.

Here, Christianity must be understood as a network of religious systems organized in part through gender identities and relations and whose theology, embodied in Jesus, is gendered at its core. This gender system is not eternally unchanging but is tied to the historical societies it inhabits. This chapter examines Christianity, primarily in the Anglophone world, as it has developed and shifted in response to the gender politics and culture that accompanied the Western world's two-century movement toward the modern era. This focus upon the gender structure of social and ideological systems not only illuminates particular corners of Christianity but changes the very questions that are asked about theology, institutional development, practices, and the processes of expansion. Obviously, gender systems limited the religious elite and determined access to power and authority; they also structured the relationship between established leaders and followers, between missionaries and converts, and among ordinary believers themselves. Even more, at the most basic level, the changing constructions of gender affected spirituality, that is, the way that believers developed their individual relationships to a personal, gendered God. Yet while the gender politics of Christianity established a system of inequality that shut women off from positions of power and influence, many Christian theologies and religiosities opened, perhaps inadvertently, avenues to spiritual experience that empowered many female believers to challenge their churches and their societies and to develop a spiritual charisma recognized as godly by others around them.

The two centuries that began in the mid-seventeenth century might be envisioned as a series of aftershocks following upon the upheavals of the Protestant Reformation and responsive Roman Catholic Counter-Reformation. Alongside these processes of institutional stabilization of the churches, the Western European and American worlds changed radically in terms of politics and economics, and, as recounted elsewhere in this volume, the theology and praxis of Christianity changed with it. The rise of the American republic was echoed by a growing democratization among Protestant denominations in the United States and, following this, the Anglophone world. The expanding reach of the British Empire into Asia and, later, Africa was fueled by the rise of mercantile and, in the nineteenth century, industrial capitalism: a somewhat brutal free-market system that replaced the moral economy of social duty and obligation with the commoditization of labor and the maximization of profit. These empires enrolled Protestants into serious missionary activity, and ministers and their wives went out from Britain, as agents of empire, to proselytize among non-Christians in the Pacific, South and East Asia, and Africa. Anglo-American Protestants would also, in the eighteenth century, begin serious work among African American slaves and North American indigenous people as well as, in the nineteenth century, join British efforts in the Asian and African mission fields.

This expansion of the empires and growing awareness of non-Christians living in foreign places occurred at the same time that dissonances ignited by the scientific revolution brought the Enlightenment, an intellectual culture identified primarily through the major epistemological changes that would transform Western society and ideology. These 250 years were years of major transitions, and every juncture meant changes for Christian communities and networks as they responded to and reacted against the range of social and ideological changes in the larger society. Christians were rarely ahead of the curve, sometimes with it, but most frequently behind. Nowhere was this more apparent than in the limited roles allotted to women in Christian organizations, the approaches taken by missionaries to spread the gospel and garner male and female converts, and especially the developing theology that still maintained an embodied male God, a humanity created in God's image, and a personal relationship between believer and God.

PROTESTANT INNOVATIONS

The Reformations of the sixteenth century brought changes in liturgical and theological structures and consequent changes for men and women in their relationships with each other and with God. Medieval images of Jesus and God as nurturing mother disappeared as God became unequivocally male. Protestant theologians were suspicious of devotions to saints, including Mary, the mother of Jesus, as idolatrous, and the emphases of worship, prayer, and theology moved entirely to God in his trinitarian personhoods. One new theological thrust was the "priesthood of all believers," a conviction that no person required a mediator, on earth (priest) or in heaven (saint), in his or her relationship with God. All people could pray directly to God, the Father, and Jesus, the Savior. It might be argued that this view cut across gender lines because male as well as female saints were either dismissed outright as too modern or retained as biblical models, such as Paul or Mary, or exemplary theologians, such as Augustine of Hippo. With the loss of prayers through saints, however, especially Mary, who was perceived by Roman Catholics as a powerful mediator, the feminine was removed from the divine.

Protestants also lost the convents, all-women religious communities that offered a haven to women who scorned the economic dependence and subordinate position of marriage. For Roman Catholic men and women, marriage was the common choice, and judged a good one, but the medieval world had placed a premium on the holiness that women as well as men could achieve through chastity, poverty, and prayer. Women such as Catherine of Siena and Julian of Norwich were highly respected and influential, and they exercised an authority over abbots and bishops as well as ordinary believers through their exemplary lives and connections to God. Protestant Reformers challenged the privileged status of celibacy, arguing that marriage was superior because of its role in promoting God's providence. All Protestant women and men, including ministers, were expected to marry.

Among English Protestants, the family was elevated to an almost sacred status, a little church. Theologians produced copious domestic manuals with hundreds of pages dedicated to descriptions of utopian households. The vocation of spouse and parent was spiritually elevated, and each man would become a ruling Abraham-like patriarch in his own household, while his wife, in her domestic labor and complete subordination, could aspire to emulate the good wife honored in Proverbs 31. Housewives did provide extensive, essential labor in the household, rearing godly children as well as preparing the family's food, and some undoubtedly exercised great influence there. This vision articulated in the domestic manuals was reflected in countless eulogies and memorials, such as Anne Bradstreet's praise of her mother Dorothy Dudley. Loving, charitable, awful, and wise, she ordered her family. Still, whatever the honor, housewifery did not bring autonomy. Dorothy Dudley was also honored as an "obedient wife."

PERCEPTIONS OF FEMALE DIFFERENCE

The New England Puritan community in which Dorothy Dudley lived undoubtedly believed that she had reached her full potential, limited as it was by her gender. Prescriptive domestic manuals echoed other theological, scientific, and literary texts that articulated in explicit detail the differences between men and women. Women were physically smaller and weaker than men, and their bodies were frequently overwhelmed with fluids, creating a physical disorderliness. This weakness and disorder was echoed in every aspect of their being. Women were unable to control their emotions; their disordered minds were unable to think clearly or control their will. Such infirmities also led them into petty little sins: envy, spite, greed. Gossip and slander, as words out of control at the service of petty malice, were the quintessential feminine sins.[1]

It is within this framework that good and evil became more starkly gendered. Sin was increasingly understood as the individual's

---

An Ideal Seventeenth-Century Wife

Here lies,
A worthy matron of unspotted life,
A loving mother and obedient wife,
A friendly neighbor, pitiful to poor,
Whom oft she fed and clothed with her store;
To servants wisely awful, but yet kind,
And as they did so reward did find.
A true instructor of her family,
The which she ordered with dexterity.
The public meetings ever did frequent,
And in her closet constant hours she spent;
Religious in all her words and ways,
Preparing still for death, till end of days:
Of all her children, children lived to see,
Then dying, left a blessed memory.
—Anne Bradstreet, "An Epitaph
on My Dear and Ever-Honoured Mother,
Mrs. Dorothy Dudley, Who Deceased
December 27, 1643, and of Her Age, 61"
(1678), in The Works of Anne Bradstreet, ed.
Jeannine Hensley (Cambridge:
Harvard University Press, 1967), 204.

---

conceding to the unwarranted demands of the disordered body and spirit, either the successful pursuit of wicked desires or the grudging resentment of the inability to fulfill them. Christian theology at this time proclaimed that all persons were depraved sinners. Yet because women were considered particularly at risk to lose control of their bodies and thus their desires, they were *by nature* more likely to be sinners. And since so much of physical desire was tied to sexual drives, and women were afflicted with bodily disorder and weakness, women were perceived to be the more sexually driven gender. From flirtation to vulgarity to fornication to adultery, women traveled the gamut of sexual excess in egregious efforts to satisfy their cravings. Uncontrolled sexuality became the metaphor for all descriptions of sin, including heresy and witchcraft. Heretics were described as "gadding after" false preachers or failing to be "faithful" to their pastors and to orthodoxy. Witches were portrayed as having perverse sexual relations with animals and the devil, producing imps and nursing familiars from teats that were frequently found near genitalia. Since women were the more sexual beings, one might even say *the* sexual beings, they were more likely to be witches and heretics. Weak, fickle, and unable to control themselves, women needed to be protected from the seduction of evil; but once seduced, women became seductresses and were, like Eve, a danger to all men.[2]

An alternative way of looking at the concept of women's sexual proclivities would be to envision a woman as passively open to a greater range of supernatural experiences. If she has less control, if she is easily seduced and led, might she not be seduced by God? Many Protestant communities had religious space, if not downright encouragement, for the individual to develop a close union with the divine. This space was frequently created through a lack of (or imperfectly developed) institutionalization. With few exceptions, Christian institutions at this time were built along the patriarchal lines that structured European society, reinforcing an authority of male ministers achieved through formal education and institutional appointment. In their early years, the New England Puritans, the Quakers, the Baptists, and the Methodists all lacked the established processes and buttressed hierarchies that successfully limited the leadership. These communities all found the role of grace through the Holy Spirit to be of immense importance to the spiritual health of the believer, and believers respected those members, male or female, who had experienced this union and were filled with this grace. At its most intense level, this union was frequently described in the sexual language of the marriage bed. God retained his maleness and stood as the loving, urgent, gentle bridegroom, while the soul (whether the believer was female or male) became the weak, passive, welcoming feminine mate. A man's experiencing himself as female in his relationship with the male God may have created personal stress. Certainly Puritan men, with their short hair and athleticism, appeared to strive to demonstrate their masculinity to all, including themselves.[3] By the beginning of the eighteenth century, however, Puritans were moving away from God the bridegroom/lover to God the Father, articulating their relationship with God as father/child and, incidentally, further justifying men's superior authority as derived from their reflecting a closer image of God than women.[4]

Among the most interesting groups that arose in the late seventeenth century, and one that would come to have an enormous impact upon the United States, was the Quakers. They certainly emphasized the connection of the individual with God and articulated the believer's relationship with the Spirit through the concept of the "inner light," the voice of the divine in one's soul. Because all souls had such a light, and because all persons had the potential to develop a relationship with God, all were equal, regardless of rank, wealth, education, or sex. Initially, the early lack of an established structure and leadership core may have opened the Quakers to this equality, but the Quakers, or Society of Friends, would build a strong community undergirded with hierarchically organized assemblies, or meetings. Yet their commitment to the importance of the inner light combined with a refusal to grant worldly status to any person kept the community open to recognizing grace wherever it appeared. As the Society developed meetings to manage the business as well as the spiritual affairs of the community, women held meetings parallel to the men's meetings, although the meetings managed different tasks. Moreover, in the spiritual meetings, women were as fully active as men, and many women were themselves called to travel the country and beyond. Initially, they carried the Quaker message to others, but by the eighteenth century, when Quakers focused their activities on their own community, charismatic women preached to community meetings. The community took its rejection of what they termed "the arbitrary hierarchies of society" quite seriously. In her spiritual autobiography, Elizabeth Sampson Sullivan recounted the pathway by

Fig. 9.1. American Quaker Meeting, engraving after Maarteen van Heemskerek, c. 1640. Photo: © Stapleton Collection / CORBIS.

which she, an indentured servant woman, could convert to the movement and later marry the wealthiest man in Chester County, Aaron Ashbridge, who was attracted to her godliness.[5]

During the eighteenth century, the model of the sacred household and the piety within began to change. Barry Levy has argued that the centrality of the *domus* as a center of piety was taken up and transformed by the Quakers. As a community that rejected many of the trappings of institutionalization, and a community always in the minority, even within their own Quaker-founded colony of Pennsylvania, Quakers turned to the home as a way to maintain the purity of their community. The household's responsibility to rear children and foster their spiritual growth became a primary duty, and Quakers were among the first to grant to women the responsibility for maintaining the godly community through their household management. In fact,

Fig. 9.2. Anne Hutchinson preaches, twentieth-century painting after Howard Pyle. Photo: © Bettmann/CORBIS.

one can see the housewife becoming the mother, reaping praise and shame depending upon the ultimate performance of her children. Soon this model of domestic piety would be taken up by Protestant Christians across the United States and Britain.[6]

By the end of the eighteenth century, the scientific community had developed a somewhat more sophisticated understanding of human anatomy. Gone was the perception that men and women were basically the same, that the reproductive organs of women were simply an internal version of those of men, and that sex identity was determined by fluids. Gone was the belief that gender was the product of action and that masculinity was dependent on the performance of activity while femininity would be the natural result of passivity. Now, science had determined that women were essentially different from men, from their reproductive organs to their nurturant mammary glands to their reproduction-adapted skeletal systems to their smaller skulls and brains. These essential differences would construct, or at least rationalize, the future status of women, for despite the new rationalist gender model empirically based in anatomy, mental capacities and psychic strength were still tied to the physical body.[7]

NEW OPPORTUNITIES, NEW RESTRICTIONS

Because women were judged less intellectually competent, it was accepted without debate that women would not be political participants in governments that were increasingly democratic. As the political realm in the United States became democratic, so, too, church politics became democratic as the Methodists and Baptists, with their focus on the call of the spirit and their rejection of the privileges of birth and education as markers of leadership, opened up their pastorates to all men. As the rights and privileges of citizenship extended beyond the highest classes to all free white men, citizen-participant activities became identified with manhood, and masculinity was one characteristic of a citizen and church member. Thus entered new language for disallowing women to move into religious leadership. During the earlier years of the century, for example, the Baptist Church had grown exponentially in the wake of the revivals sweeping the British colonies. This revivalistic, evangelical culture had placed great reliance on the work of the Spirit, and men and women who seemed touched by grace were honored for their gifts. According to Susan Juster, women had important roles in congregational administration and disciplinary processes. She found that by the early nineteenth century, however, Baptist churches had been structured on firmer bases, the surrounding communities no longer scorned their existence, and the members strove for respectability. In their efforts to model themselves on the society around them, and despite the numerical predominance of women among them, the Baptists silenced women's voices and turned the leadership over to men. Most Baptist men now judged that women had no authority to preach, teach, or pray aloud. One anonymous writer in the *Baptist Magazine* claimed that the prohibition on women's speech was "unlimited."[8] Women's speech and action was again judged disorderly, now the result not of a disorderly body but of a weak, uncontrolled mind.

Methodists also benefited from the early-eighteenth-century revivalism and adapted to the political and economic changes of the nineteenth. John Wesley, an Anglican minister who found the established church spiritually dead and unconcerned with the gospel, began his reform work during the first half of the eighteenth century. He toured England, bringing his Christian message to the working classes, whom he claimed were ignored by the established church. In this early work, he was assisted by a very few ordained ministers, so that as he traveled from preaching site to preaching site, he was dependent on the people he met and drew into his circle to continue his work in the community. Methodism, then, was a network whose stability depended on the work of its converts, and Wesley recognized at the outset that women, as well as men, were called by the Spirit to this work. Women were, indeed, of central importance to the spread of Methodism in Britain and the United States, serving as local leaders. Before Wesley's death, there remained a kind of equality between male and female Methodists since both were local lay leaders and neither could achieve ordination in the Anglican Church. Upon Wesley's death, however, the Methodists separated from the Church of England and began to ordain their own clergy; a similar institutional structure arose among American Methodists. Women's official authority did not move up to the level of ordination. The example for women remained Susannah Wesley, John Wesley's mother, who had become known for her spiritual leadership of the household and the neighborhood; domestic piety and clerical hospitality became the vocation of Methodist women.

The increased value on domestic piety stands as an indicator that good and evil were now gendered differently. The seventeenth-century conviction that all people were born innately depraved was passing; John Locke had articulated the notion that people are, at birth, blank slates—*tabula rasa*—upon which all aspects of their character, personality, and will would be inscribed. By the early nineteenth century, some began to suggest that at their core people are essentially good. Similarly, in the seventeenth century, passivity and innocence were characteristics of weakness, opening the way for sin to march in; in the nineteenth century, innocence and passivity became markers of goodness. The active male was now perceived as sexually driven; he was continuously on the verge of evil, while the passivity of the woman kept her out of harm's way. The body politic would begin to honor women as mothers of the republic, mothers of the nation. Women would be rearing the next generation of citizens, and by extension the next generation of Christians, and there were calls for the education of women so that they could fulfill their destiny as mothers.

All of the Protestant churches, not merely the Methodists, turned to women as the natural spiritual leaders in the home. Women were understood to have superior piety and ethical purity and therefore to be the guardians of holiness and goodness in the home. Women extended this role to the churches, where they sponsored Sunday schools, missionary societies, the publication of tracts, and fundraising for ministerial candidates. They became active in reform movements that befitted their superior ethical purity and their concern for the family. They promoted temperance and sabbatarianism to fight the drunkenness that was so destructive of family life and to close the taverns and shops that kept men away from home on Sundays. The more daring worked on moral reform, challenging the sexual license of men and hoping to find alternatives for prostitutes dependent on illicit sexual activity to support themselves. In fact, unlike male members of moral-reform societies, female moral reformers held the prostitutes to be victims and blamed the licentiousness and uncontrolled carnality of men, calling for male patrons of brothels to be publicly shamed.[9] The Spirit continued to breathe religious fervor into women, and in many areas of the new nation, women took the lead as converts during the revivals and became active agents effecting the conversion of their husbands, fathers, and sons.[10] Women were extremely important to the expansion of the evangelical movements and the expansion of reform activities, particularly those that could be connected to the home.

When considering the vast impact that domestic piety had on the perception and position of women in the nineteenth century, it is important to keep one caveat in mind. While women were now described as innocent, pure, and pious, these qualities were restricted by race and class. Anglo-American and British bourgeois women were judged capable of extraordinary piety and virtue, but African American women continued to be perceived as sexual, promiscuous persons who lured men into danger. So, too, working-class women were denied the same virtuous femininity as their bourgeois counterparts. Rather than give up the disorderly coquette or predatory seductress, the dominant culture reconstructed womanhood by race and class, placing one group on a pedestal while keeping others in the mire—the well-known Madonna and whore trope with a racist and classist slant. This permutation on gender was supported by science, in which naturalized racial inferiority rationalized white men's ownership of slaves and their sexual exploitation of unprotected women. In the cities, the unwomanly depravity of poor women, working as prostitutes or afflicted with alcoholism, might shock the sensibilities of middle-class women, who, as noted above, blamed the depravity of the cities. But the very existence of prostitutes pointed up the nature of virtuous womanhood even as they became the appropriate focus of middle-class Christian benevolence. As Christine Stansell has explained, "the language of virtue and vice" had become a "code of class."[11]

WOMEN PREACHERS

Additionally, despite the limitations with which domestic ideology bound women, not all women accepted the roles of household pastors, children's mentors, and ministers of hospitality. Some women did become preachers. The revivalist culture that continued into the early nineteenth century was far more democratic and anticlerical than that of the mid-eighteenth century, and educated, ordained ministers were often ignored in favor of the enthusiastic preaching of ordinary laypersons filled with the Spirit. The power of charismatic speaking was cherished, and during these decades networks of religious seekers would organize multiday meetings at which people could hear the voice of God. Within a culture that privileged the breath of the Spirit, many women found themselves called to preach, and many of these women had followers and disciples. They did not serve as pastors of congregations or as ordained officials in churches; they had no licenses from denominations. Rather, they felt the call to travel as itinerants, appearing in private homes, women's meetings, socials, and giant revival meetings, preaching the gospel and drawing people to God. Harriet Livermore, for example, enjoyed a twenty-five-year career on the revival circuit; she even preached before Congress four times, warning of the spiritual decline of the nation. Historian Catherine Brekus has identified some sixty women who established preaching careers between 1820 and 1845.[12] While they were not able to attain the prerequisites necessary to acquire an official sanction of ordination, these women were all empowered by their personal experience of the Holy Spirit. Despite the position of organized denominations that the role of pastor and preacher was not appropriate to the delicate sensibilities and limited skills of women, preaching women, most of whom had been raised within congregations, accepted their position as outsiders, convinced that they had no choice but to follow their call. This authority grounded in passivity was also exemplified by a new, though ephemeral, group of women, trance speakers, who dared to appear on public platforms not speaking in their own voices but channeling the spirits of the dead. Ann Braude has found that while they began their oratorical careers speaking for others, these women were among the first to discover their own voices and express themselves politically.[13]

Moreover, from the time that African Americans joined the evangelical churches in significant numbers, in the 1780s onward, black women felt called to preach. The number of black women who developed serious reputations as preachers is impressive. They converted in a flash of light, heard voices that summoned them to the preaching desk, and felt irresistibly drawn to the itinerant trail, sometimes at great personal risk. In the first decades of the nineteenth century, many of these women were members of the African Methodist Episcopal (A.M.E.) Church. This separatist black Methodist community had come into being in the wake of racial discrimination that had split the mixed Methodist community. Methodists, committed as they were to the common man, were unwilling to grant autonomy to African American congregations or to ordain black men to the pastorate. In response, the black communities built strong, separate church networks. Within the first decade of its establishment, the A.M.E. Church had to face the gender question, and the leadership's position was mixed. Initially, Pastor Richard Allen tried to discourage Jarena Lee from preaching, although he did allow her to hold private meetings and exhort; he later came to recognize the presence of the Spirit in Lee's call and was drawn into her circle of admirers. This ambivalence was acted out institutionally as well. At the annual AME Church conference of 1850, women who believed themselves called to preach were so numerous that they formed an organization. Just two years later, a resolution to license women preachers was defeated by the significant majority of delegates, all of whom were male.[14]

The success of African American women preachers (they attracted large mixed-race audiences and earned conversions and praise) underscores some significant spiritual differences between white and black women in the United States. Although a bit more subdued, the leadership of the AME behaved no differently than the white Methodist system, but many black women who heard the Spirit's call followed, while white women accommodated themselves to their pastors or left their denominations. While there may have been differences in the way that women and men, white and black, understood evangelical religiosity, I argue for the importance of the gender politics of this era. White women were enmeshed in a habit of obedience to male authority. The natural inability of women to serve as political citizens had remained largely unchallenged, and society rewarded women for their peculiar female contributions to the male citizenry.

African American women lived in a space in which their fathers and husbands had no social or political authority; power lay in the hands of the white elite. The manhood of citizenship had no personal meaning for them, since black men were, because of their race, excluded from citizenship. White men held the power, but the relationship was one of force rather than consent, and African American Methodists separated themselves rather than accept the domination of the white Methodist Conference. Once separate, the AME Church established its own hierarchy, with male leaders claiming the same privileges exercised by white men in the Methodist church. Out of habit of distrusting authority, black women may have challenged those privileges. Men only were ordained and controlled the lines of church power, but women were called as preachers, and preach they did. Add to this the reality that the rewards of domestic piety were not available to black women. The goodness attributed to femininity was understood to be restricted to white women, and black families did not have the economic ability to allow the male householder to work while his wife filled the role of nonproductive household guide and church volunteer. It was not that these women rejected the traditional family; in fact, Zilpha Elaw spoke strongly about women's place in the household and recognized the key roles that women filled there. Yet for Elaw, the work of mothering could not replace the satisfaction felt when she successfully navigated a preaching engagement. If she did not follow the call of the Spirit, she became ill. No wonder that she put her children under the care of another so that she could follow the insistent call to preach.[15]

PREACHERS' WIVES

For many white women, the call that they felt drawing them toward ministry could be realized through the aura of domestic piety. During the first half of the nineteenth century, white bourgeois women were able to establish ministries as pastors' and missionaries' wives. The concept of a pastor's wife came to be seen as a vocation in and of itself, developing in emulation of the example of Susannah Wesley, John Wesley's mother. The experience of this domestic role as a vocational call was exemplified by Catherine Livingston, Freeborn Garretson's wife. As a woman of excellent social connections and wealth, she had a high status within her community, and she built on her position to achieve her goals. She guided her domestic congregation, supported her husband in his work, and provided hospitality to itinerant circuit riders. Unquestionably she felt the Spirit deeply and found spiritual authority there. In a letter to a friend, she described a dream in which she identified with the embodied divinity, crucified and resurrected.[16] A most impressive example of the preacher's wife, also Methodist, was Fanny Newell, who traveled with her circuit-riding husband and became known for her public prayers, exhorting his congregations after his sermon had been completed. She consistently defended her work as a response to a call that she dared not refuse, and referred to her public speaking as her "cross."

Women prepared themselves for this role through prayer and meditation, focusing their attention throughout their early lives on virtuous behavior, spiritual growth, and theological learning. Early in the nineteenth century, Americans had responded to the ideal of republican motherhood by providing opportunities for women to be educated so that they could rear good citizens. As institutions of higher learning were constructed for women, seminaries and academies that aimed to prepare women for their vocation of motherhood sometimes turned to the need to produce pastors' wives.[17]

MISSIONS

As knowledge of the world at large grew and the lure of the foreign mission field arose, some of these women envisioned careers as missionaries through their vocations as wives and mothers. Sarah Lanman Huntington had evidenced a long-term commitment to missionary work long before she joined the work. Three years before she went to Syria, she saved up her money for the missionary cause, subscribed to the *Missionary Herald*, joined the Foreign Missionary Society, and taught Sabbath school among the Mohegans.

Throughout the nineteenth century, American mission societies sent and supported missionaries to work throughout Asia, in parts of Africa, and among Native Americans at home. Missionary societies funding overseas missions had decided that it wasn't safe to send young ordained men into the mission field unmarried, for the temptations of the exotic women in the field would be overwhelming (and disastrous). They believed that no man, however godly, should be subjected without protection against the seductive power of sexually active, exotic native women. And since these societies, at least in the first half of the nineteenth century, had also decided that single women should not be in the foreign mission field at all, women who felt called to missionary work necessarily connected themselves to promising men. Many young women drawn to ministry set their goals deliberately on marriage to a likely candidate; in fact, despite language of marriage for love, men and women both found themselves pulled toward brief courtships and immediate marriages.

Sarah Lanman Huntington to her father, March 1833, requesting his consent to her marriage to missionary Eli Smith

You know, my dear father, that I have long regarded the missionary cause with deep interest; but how deep, no being but the God of missions, has known. My sincerity is now put to the test; and the question is to be decided whether I will forsake home and country, to dwell as a laborer in that land which was the "cradle of Christianity"—is continuous to the scene of our Saviour's sufferings—and where he promised peculiar blessings upon those who should be made partakers of the same. I have not now to decide upon the single question, Am I willing to become a Missionary? That has been long settled in my own mind. But it involves another—Will I go in the way which Providence now seems to point out? This last depends upon the course which my feelings shall take towards the individual who has presented the inquiry, —in case your approbation be obtained . . . .

And now, my dear father, to you, who are the Earthly idol of my heart, is submitted the sole responsibility of deciding this interesting question, interwoven with the concerns of eternity. Were I invited to unite my destiny with a merchant, whose business called us to the shores of the Mediterranean, I think you would not hesitate to resign me, and would feel that you and my mother would be kindly provided with every attention. Will not He, who has required, as a test of discipleship, that all should be willing to forsake father, mother, and children for him, be true to his own promise? . . . I feel impelled to venture upon these and other trials, if I may go with your blessing. I want, my dear father, that you should enjoy the satisfaction of giving me up, as it were, voluntarily, to this work, in the spirit with which you renewed the dedication of all your children to God, in that hour when the soul of one was hovering near the gate of heaven.

—From Edward W. Hooker, Memoir of Mrs. Sarah Lanman Smith, Late of the Mission in Syria (Boston: Perkins and Marvin, 1839), 127–28, 130–31.

Prefabricated social situations, such as ordinations, were arranged so that appropriate women could meet the men who needed wives, and together they would embark on their missionary careers. Asa Thurston heard of an eligible schoolmate's cousin, arranged a meeting, and married schoolteacher Lucy Goodale eighteen days later. Hiram Bingham, at his own ordination, met Sybil Mosely and married her one week later. Charlotte Fowler, known locally for her charitable work in New York and New Jersey and for her support of missions, was "courted" by a medical doctor going to the Sandwich Islands. Fowler checked out a reference from one of his professors and at the end of a week agreed to marry him. Such efforts can only be understood within the context of individuals believing that the Spirit called them to missionary work. Many of the women who would travel to Burma, the Mediterranean, and the Pacific islands wrote of their own experience of the Spirit's voice, and they believed that the truth of the call was attested by the ease of their courtships and marriages. The climate, the diseases, the politics, and the economics of these lives were often brutal and literally life destroying, yet one finds that upon the death of a spouse, missionaries often found a new wife or husband among others widowed in the field.

It made sense for churches to use women in the mission fields. Many of the communities to which missionaries traveled were sex-segregated societies, and the men would have no opportunity to work with the women. Like pastors' wives, missionary wives could fill roles particular to women in bourgeois culture—somewhat like the pious leader of the household writ large. Wives might serve as teachers of young children in makeshift classes of religion; they might carry the domestic nursing and practical housewifery skills into the wilderness. They would also be able to go among women to teach the Bible along with the values of monogamous marriage, fidelity, and orderly housekeeping. In these efforts women were members of a team working not only to evangelize but also to civilize communities that had hitherto been beyond the reach of the Christian message. Yet their work was particularly difficult and perhaps less welcome than the efforts of a pastor's wife at home. These men and women of the first waves of missionary activity had embarked in the simple faith that the heathen would welcome the missionaries and embrace the gospel once it was preached. And while physical hardships were expected, the indifference and hostility of those they hoped to convert were not. Many of the "heathen" were followers of religious systems, especially Buddhism and Islam, that they found quite satisfactory. Ann Judson, for example, noted that she was in Burma seven years before she felt the joy of her first convert.[18]

Early missionaries were disadvantaged by their simplistic view of themselves, their purpose, and the people they sought to convert. An uncomplicated Christian ethnocentrism and an inherent sense of sacrificial virtue and superiority supported them in their efforts even while rendering them unable to understand and adapt to the social and ideological worlds that they entered and tried to alter. Missionary descriptions of the heathens as intellectually weak, less capable of understanding, did not bode well for cross-cultural exchange. Yet one can see that language once used to describe women was now redirected at the subjects of conversion efforts. The native women represented sexual temptations for godly men, the men sexual excess. Their marriage systems of multiple wives, disorderly marital relations, and disordered families marked them as less sophisticated and less moral.

Among the most difficult tasks that some missionaries would set for themselves and the communities would be the eradication of polygamy and the unequal status accorded women. Paradoxically, Western societies that restricted their own women to domestic tasks could yet look down on another community and call for reforms because of the restrictions placed on women. Missionaries were not interested in changing the status and identification of women as domestic beings, however; instead, they were focused on changing the nature of the domestic role among foreign populations.

SISTERS

Oddly enough, although Protestant and Catholic missionaries were, in the nineteenth century, in desperate competition with each other, among women's efforts it is difficult to see any differences. The work of pastors' wives was not unlike that of Roman Catholic nuns who provided educational and social services throughout the church's mission fields, which, in the nineteenth century, included the United States. Catholic women who felt a vocational call to the ministry could join an active religious order and there find plenty of space for serving the community as religious support. The pervasive image of the Catholic priest leading parishes is not false, but it is woefully incomplete. In addition to their primary, sacramental work, priests were vested with authority over church finances and administrative operations. In many parishes, however, the religious representatives of the Catholic Church with whom parishioners interacted most often were nuns. Some might argue that, like the status of the pastor's wife, the status of sisters was under and subordinate to ordained male ministers, in this case priests, but that would not be correct. Nuns lived in women-centered communities led by women; the institutions they established were also administered by nuns. It would be more accurate to say that sisters, like priests, served under the bishops, although even in this case, sisters had ways of claiming their authority over their lives and their ministries.[19]

Sisters worked among families in early forms of social services, and although the word "pastor" would be deemed inappropriate by the magisterium, many nuns provided the domestic counseling and assistance needed within families. Similar to ministers' wives, nuns would often know the names of the children and women living in the parish. Most of the tasks nuns performed fell under the traditional rubrics of domestic labor, but nuns lived in a women's community instead of a nuclear household, and they generally served a much larger population than a pastor's wife. In Los Angeles, for example, the Daughters of Charity arrived in 1855, and within five years they had established an academy for girls, an orphanage, and a hospital. Unlike the parish priests whose labor was concentrated among Catholics, sisters frequently worked among people of different religious affiliations, cultures, and classes.

Fig. 9.3. Sister of Charity.

The Daughters of Charity in Los Angeles, most of whom were Irish Americans, worked among Mexican Americans and Indians as well as European Americans, and they actively worked to learn Spanish and adapt themselves to the cultures they found. In fact, the Daughters of Charity had a community in Mexico that sent several sisters to work in Los Angeles, and while the Spanish and Irish American priests there were unable to recruit local men into the priesthood, the Daughters of Charity attracted several local women, including Latinas, into their order.[20] In fact, in the extension of their work to the community, Catholic sisters were much more like the settlement-house workers of the late nineteenth century, at ease with their surroundings in distressed neighborhoods, comfortable with the variety of people in the cities, and successful in recruiting workers.

While schools for children had always been a key component of Protestant and Catholic missionary programs, hospitals, orphanages, and other institutions of social service were clearly the product of the late nineteenth century. Building on the philosophy of the eighteenth-century Enlightenment and scientific developments in the nineteenth, Western society became more convinced of the benefits that science could bring to all aspects of life. If the seventeenth and eighteenth centuries were the decades that opened astronomy and physics to human understanding, the nineteenth century added geology and biology to the frame, with Charles Darwin's theory of evolution becoming the new paradigm through which scientists and educated readers understood the history of the earth and life upon it. What pushed society into a radically new framework was the application of scientific principles to the political, social, and economic organization of society. Political theory as grounded in the philosophical understanding of humanity gave way to the social sciences, in which human beings could be understood through scientific observation, social organization could be analyzed in terms of appropriate roles, and social problems could be solved through objective, scientific methods.

MEDICAL INTERPRETATIONS OF GENDER

Within this increasingly modern world, the medicalization of gender resulted in new ways of understanding the nature of gender difference. Women and men were still understood to be essentially different from each other, with anatomical differences, particularly women's reproductive capacity, working to define the essence of femininity. While motherhood continued to define woman's capacity, ideologically she remained explicitly tied to her physicality. In the seventeenth century, with its concentration on spiritual strength, women had been considered feeble and inclined to sin because their biology created disordered bodies that opened their souls to temptation and undermined the ability of their minds to perceive and their wills to choose good. A century later, when society emphasized the ability to think, women's anatomical differences, including their relatively small skulls and brains, marked them as less capable of learning and reason and therefore unable to serve as ordained ministers. Now, in the middle of the nineteenth century, society's focus, including women's own attention, had turned explicitly to women's health and the connection of physical to psychological pathology.

Significant numbers of white bourgeois women suffered from fatigue, respiratory and digestive disorders, and depression or melancholia. In hindsight, many scholars have persuasively argued that some of this sickness was due to the poor diet and constricting clothing of women, as well as their restricted, sedentary lives spent mostly indoors rather than outdoors, and some health reformers argued this position at the time, calling for fresh air, exercise, healthy eating, lighter-weight clothing, and the eradication of corsets. Other scholars have suggested that the significant levels of what might today be called clinical depression resulted from social prescriptions of inactivity. Physicians were so convinced of the ultimate significance of gender differences that they developed radically different diagnoses for the same medical problem in men and women. While men might be diagnosed with infections in their stomachs, hearts, or lungs, women were usually diagnosed with a disordered uterus and were treated accordingly through physical manipulation or removal of the uterus, restriction to the female space of the home, and prescriptions to adhere to the feminine roles of housekeeping and motherhood.

With this new focus on physical health and women's increasing awareness of their own sickness, some Christian women began to tie their spiritual well-being to physical health, and they tied their physical health to their spiritual well-being. During the 1860s, Ellen Gould White, a former follower of the millennialist William Miller, began to have visions calling her to turn away from gloom and embrace good health. People were urged to give up intemperance in eating, drinking, and drugging and to return to the basics of good health. She opposed medical practitioners who prescribed drugs, embraced a vegetarian diet, and supported abstinence from alcohol. The remnant followers of Miller reconstructed themselves under her leadership as the Seventh-day Adventists, and for the rest of her life, she and the church were directed by her visions calling for church members to take on healthy lifestyles and to provide institutional health care to the sick. The Adventists believed that a healthy body was prerequisite to spiritual health, and White traveled the world establishing health sanitariums founded on health-reform principles.[21]

At the same time, Mary Baker Eddy noticed the connection between spiritual strength and physical health, but unlike White, whose visions called her to foster physical health for the sake of the soul, Eddy's vision led her to nourish the spirit in order to cure the body. The Church of Jesus Christ, Scientist and her Metaphysical College grew out of Eddy's own explorations of experimental mental healing, marking her efforts to share her knowledge and train practi-

Fig. 9.4. Mary Baker Eddy, May 4, 1916.

tioners in her methods. She too rejected contemporary medical practice, particularly its dependence on opiates and other drugs, as misguided and called on her followers to cure their bodies by healing their spirits. Eddy's movement resembled the rising psychoanalytic movement that had begun to tie physical disorder to psychic disorders, but unlike the secular scientists of the mind, Eddy believed that a person could be trained to focus the mind, transform the spirit, and achieve good health, essentially through individual effort.[22]

Significantly, both Ellen Gould White and Mary Baker Eddy established their authority through their passivity, a traditionally feminine characteristic. They opened themselves to the Spirit and the Spirit came. Equally important, however, is the way that both religious communities adapted to the imperatives of modernity. The

Christian Scientists would argue for an active role on the part of religious leaders, women as well as men. The Metaphysical College trained them in prayer and in the ability to assist the ailing, usually women, to open themselves to the power of the Spirit. At the turn of the century, the Adventists remained a refreshing alternative to the painful health care of the time. Following the death of White and the development of medicine in the twentieth century, however, the Adventists would transform their sanitariums into high-powered, mainstream, though generally osteopathic, medical facilities.

WOMEN'S REFORM MOVEMENTS

Medicine and psychology were but two of the professions that developed at this time to explore the nature of human persons, their societies, and the world around them. Scientific historical criticism arose during this period, pushing scholars to develop professional methods of biblical criticism. In the lead were German and British specialists, but progressive American theologians embraced the new modern methods. Political philosopher and activist Elizabeth Cady Stanton had never accepted the premise that gender made men and women essentially different, and she argued in the language of the Enlightenment that as persons with human minds, women were essentially the same as men who had merely learned the habits, emotions, and inferior intellectual capacity of womanhood. Cady Stanton had watched and read some of the new scriptural interpretations with great interest and concluded that Christianity in general, and certain passages in the Bible in particular, had provided the foundations of women's political and educational inequality. She therefore decided to apply the new scientific scholarship methods to her own exploration of the Bible and produced *The Woman's Bible*, a scholarly, bitterly feminist interpretation of particular passages in the book.[23]

Most women, however, vehemently rejected Cady Stanton's attack on the Bible, finding in Christianity fulfillment and authority to pursue labor in the world. The new social sciences confirmed scientifically previous understandings of gender roles, so that women were still most useful in roles of caretaking, nursing, and general social service.

By the end of the nineteenth century, however, women had extended the definition of household to the neighborhood, the city, the nation, and the world, and women began to fill roles that historians have called social housekeepers and social mothers. Combining women's feminine sensitivities and moral perspicacity with the new emphasis on institutionalization and order, bourgeois women in England and the United States established settlement houses, orphanages, and women's schools and embarked once again on multitiered reform efforts.

Unlike reform efforts at the beginning of the century, however, women did not necessarily organize themselves through their churches but were permitted to work toward changing society through separate women's organizations. The Women's Christian Temperance Union, for example, built an extraordinary network that mobilized American female Protestants throughout the nation to keep their families from consuming alcohol and to work against its sale and consumption. Portraying alcohol as a male vice that undermined the family and left women and children penniless, women were empowered to protest, hold rallies, and ultimately destroy saloons.[24] Maintaining separation from men meant that women were kept pure from the dirt necessarily involved in politics and other forms of leadership; it also meant, of course, that women were excluded from leadership in the state and the church. In fact, the work of women increasingly focused on cleaning up the literal dirt of the city streets and the hospitals, the metaphorical dirt of capitalism and politics, and the international dirt of the undeveloped world.[25] Still, in the midst of this separatism, women found impressive power to work, network, and change the world.

Among Christian workers, especially missionaries, this separatism proved to be immensely empowering for women called to service. Women themselves first pushed for the change, realizing that in sex-segregated societies, missionaries' wives had brought the gospel to unconverted women, and despite initial resistance by church denominations, American and British women established their own boards to support the work of women missionaries. At midcentury, missionary boards adapted their policies to changing perceptions of women's strength and dedication and began recruiting unmarried women to join male ministers and their wives in the mission field. Women from Europe and the United States traveled to China, Japan, South Asia, and Africa to fill the peculiarly feminine roles of teaching women and children. Following trajectories established at home, women established institutions such as children's schools, academies for young women, orphanages, and even health-care facilities.[26] Initially, missionaries had been caught in a dualistic vision of uncivilized heathens and civilized Christians. Women's missionary societies published periodicals titled *Life and Light for Heathen Women* and *The Heathen Woman's Friend*. Both British and American Protestant missionaries accepted the need to provide the benefits of civilization and train the people in the ways of the Protestant ethic and bourgeois domesticity. In the British colonial territories, missionaries were often seen as agents of the nation, serving the empire and the colonized at the same time. Thus missionaries believed that the function of schools for girls and young women was to teach them the role of Christian housewife so that native women could fill their ordained role as a Christian guide to convert the household and further the process of civilization by joining efforts to clean up village and nation.

By the end of the century, however, a change had taken place in women's schools. Many missionary women wanted to build the kind of schools in which they had been taught, and soon academies for native women were opened, educating women not for domesticity and motherhood but for education and ministry itself. When the annual report of the Congregationalist American Board asserted that priority should be placed on preaching rather than teaching, the outraged editor of *Heathen Woman's Friend*, Harriet Warren, decried this attitude, noting that in the Bible, all forms of communication are part of evangelism. She argued that the attack on the educational mission was in fact an attack on women's work in the missions.[27] Of course, the male-administered missionary boards had felt the loss of financial support when separate women's associations had siphoned off an increasingly significant segment of donations. Yet while the women at home continued to see the need to support young men for the ministry, they had also come to realize, in their separate sphere, that male leaders did not always recognize or fill women's needs.

Moreover, as missionary women developed some familiarity in Asia and Africa, as they came to understand the sophisticated societies in which they worked and grew in appreciation of the local women, they moved away from that dualistic vision and called for an end to the use of the language of "heathen." In fact, these women and the reports they published in American and British missionary publications did much to educate the metropole about the foreign civilizations that thrived in Asia, the Pacific, and Africa. At the very end of the century, at their behest, the Women's Missionary Board agreed to change the title *Heathen Woman's Friend* to *Woman's Missionary Friend*. By the end of the century, many missionary women would set themselves up in alliance with native women, calling attention to the inequities and violence that afflicted their lives and working to bring change, through the empire and through Christian conversion, to these communities. These efforts, which were often characterized by a continued condescension, were sometimes successful in gaining trust, sometimes not. It was truly not until the twentieth century that the benefits of the Christian missions took hold, possibly as the missionaries' positions changed from aloof sympathy to full identity and empathy as they began to oppose imperial designs and support nationalist movements.

Fig. 9.5. Two Lakota women endure sitting for a missionary photographer. Another Lakota woman, probably Elizabeth Winyan, holds a child and appears more trusting and more affluent. Photo © Denver Public Library, Western History Collection, Photo by Thomas L. Riggs. X-31715.

At the close of the century, women had moved closer to positions of serious power, or at least influence, in the churches. They filled the pews and did the majority of church work, including the social-outreach programs and much of the financing of church efforts at home and abroad. In

Fig. 9.6. American missionary Emily Hartwell with the Chinese Bible Women of Fuzhou, Fujian Sheng, China, 1902.

this work they may have been guided by the principles of order, structure, and accountability that had come into play as the cities and the empires embraced modernity, but they remained focused on the need to take care of the congregation, the town, and the world: evangelizing through Christian housekeeping. A development that had progressed across two centuries, Christian churches were now firmly established as women's spaces. Some historians, pointing to the sentimentality of liturgy and the central role women played in the increasingly important institution of children's Christian education, have written of this era in terms of the feminization of Victorian Christianity, despite the fact that the leadership remained firmly in men's hands.[28] More important, some women were beginning to speak in terms of their own active choices, particularly to go out into the mission field, rather than seeing and portraying themselves justified as the passive followers of the Holy Spirit.

Whether in response to the gentility of Victorian Christianity or to the growing authority of women reformers and missionaries, the beginning of the twentieth century would see the rise of a stark, fundamentalist, muscular Christianity.[29] Mirroring so many efforts at this time to build up the social fabric by building up the physical body, some Christian men began to promote Christianity to men through social clubs for boys and young men, such as the Boy Scouts and the YMCA, and through popular preachers such as baseball player Billy Sunday. Many Christian women entered the twentieth century focused on the need to care for the powerless; their favorite parable was the Good Samaritan, and they followed as their guide the example of Jesus as he fed the hungry and healed the sick. For others, the face of Jesus, the gentle teacher, healer, friend of children, and self-proclaimed servant, faded as the specter of God, the masculine father and judge, returned triumphant. At this turn of the century, gendered ideologies and sexual politics continued to inform the experiences and identities of individuals in their relationships to God and their ever-expanding community.

FOR FURTHER READING

Brekus, Catherine. *Strangers and Pilgrims: Female Preaching in America, 1740–1845.* Chapel Hill: University of North Carolina Press, 1998.

Ginzberg, Lori D. *Women and the Work of Benevolence: Morality, Politics, and Class in the Nineteenth-Century United States.* New Haven: Yale University Press, 1990.

Juster, Susan. *Disorderly Women: Sexual Politics and Evangelicalism in Revolutionary New England.* Ithaca, N.Y.: Cornell University Press, 1994.

Porterfield, Amanda. *Mary Lyon and the Mount Holyoke Missionaries.* New York: Oxford University Press, 1997.

Robert, Dana. *American Women in Mission: A Social History of Their Thought and Practice.* Macon: Mercer University Press, 1996.

Taves, Ann. *Fits, Trances, and Visions: Experiencing Religion and Explaining Experience from Wesley to James.* Princeton: Princeton University Press, 1999.

Westerkamp, Marilyn J. *Women and Religion in Early America, 1600–1850: The Puritan and Evangelical Traditions.* London: Routledge, 1999.

SLAVE CHRISTIANITY

CHARLES H. LIPPY

CHAPTER TEN

Slavery has exerted an enduring impact on the religious life of the American people, African American and Euro-American alike, from the arrival of the first slaves until long after the legal end of slavery in the mid-nineteenth century. One strand is the history of a profound religious culture nourished among the slaves themselves, for those forced to come from Africa as slaves brought with them a range of understandings of how to make sense of the world. Much was shaped by the rich tribal heritage that flourished in areas of West Africa that were the ancestral homes to thousands of slaves. Some slaves had worldviews formed by Islam, which had already spread from its Arabian birthplace through much of Africa. And on the west coast of Africa, Europeans had planted versions of Christianity that had by the seventeenth century interacted with tribal patterns to generate yet another cluster of ways of being religious for those who came to North America as slaves.

For generations, however, analysts of slave religion presumed that the conditions of slavery, beginning with the moment Africans were forced onto slave ships and continuing through their experience in the Americas, were so destructive of cultural identity that few, if any, African elements survived. That hypothesis seemed more plausible when examining slavery in North America, for by the time of emancipation, Christianity had been introduced into the slave culture, and thousands of slaves identified in some fashion with strands of evangelical Protestantism. The groundbreaking work of Melville Herskovits, *The Myth of the Negro Past*, which appeared in 1941, began to

291

dispel this misconception. Later commentators offered some correctives to Herskovits's contention about the survival of aspects of the African religious heritage despite the efforts of slave owners to quash any indigenous cultural life in order to increase their control over slaves, and despite the movement of African Americans into Christian groups, particularly in the half century before the end of chattel slavery in the United States.[1] Nonetheless, few today examine slave religion without recognizing significant, enduring African dimensions that have been central to the story since the arrival of the first slave ship in Virginia in 1619.

In the 1960s, when a distinctive black theology began to emerge, some early theorists raised serious criticism about the very character of Christian expression that Euro-Americans had proffered to slaves. Some argued that the emotion-laden style of the Protestant Christianity Baptist and Methodist evangelists presented to slaves, with its emphasis on enduring suffering and being submissive in anticipation of heavenly reward, represented a skewed version of Christianity. Others claimed that there had been a fusion of things African and things Christian in slave religion, so that the result was a syncretistic amalgamation that was neither authentically African nor authentically Christian.

If scholars of religion were slow to appreciate the ongoing presence of African qualities in the culture that developed among American slaves, others—particularly anthropologists and students of what many have called "folk culture"—acknowledged at least the African roots of some practices among African Americans. At the same time, however, by classifying such phenomena as folklore, they tended to dismiss their significance and lump them with other quaint remnants of a prescientific way of life that would naturally fade as African Americans learned to imitate the presumably more civilized ways of Euro-Americans. Included here were many features of spirituality that seemed anachronistic to rationalistic thinkers smitten with post-Enlightenment approaches.

None of these perspectives provides the model for understanding the intricate connections between slavery and Christianity that undergirds this essay. Here I shall argue that the lived experience of slavery sustained a religious culture among African Americans that was not simply a patchwork combination of African and Christian elements resulting in a hybrid that was neither African nor Christian. Rather, African slaves demonstrated extraordinary cultural creativity in developing religious forms that had their own internal integrity. This approach requires jettisoning European models of Christianity as the norm against which to evaluate the contours of African American religious life; it also requires abandoning African tribal religiosity as the standard for scrutinizing whether Africanisms managed to survive the dehumanizing conditions of slavery itself. There may be correspondence between aspects of African religious life and the religious life of slaves in the United States, but the product is unique and demands attention as a religious style that is *sui generis*. Gone, too, are assumptions that scientific, "modern" approaches to spirituality wedded to urban, industrial societies are qualitatively superior to other forms of religious expression.

At the same time, this approach entails moving beyond European models for looking at the religious culture that prevailed among slave owners. It assumes that the experience of slavery had ramifications not only for the Africans relegated to the status of property but also for the Euro-Americans who exercised power over them. That relationship likewise echoed through the Christianity of white slave owners, transforming it into a religion of its own. Although most of this chapter will explore the emergence of slave Christianity as a religious style with internal coherence and integrity, the last section will examine how the experience of slavery also generated a distinct religion or at least a distinctive religious style among white slave owners.

AFRICAN ETHOS

Salient features of African spirituality provide a foundation on which to see the building of a distinctive religious style among African Americans that provided for individual and corporate identity even as it adapted to the cultural and religious conditions of slavery. Africans forced to come to North America as slaves did not bring with them a single religious understanding. Although the majority may have shared some patterns and behavior common to all tribal cultures, some of the slaves had their religious identity shaped by strands of Islam that had already penetrated into those areas of West Africa that were the primary sources of slaves during the colonial period. African Islam had obvious distinctions from more traditional tribal understandings of spirituality and religion, but some continuities prevailed. For virtually all of the Africans sold as slaves, the world as they knew it was not neatly divided into realms of the sacred and the secular. That division was taking hold among Europeans, largely in the wake of the Enlightenment and scientific revolution, but not among Africans. Rather, for Africans all of life was sacred; all of life had a spiritual quality. Hence religion was not a separate sphere of life but a facet of every aspect of life. Thus there were no social institutions per se that were religious, while others were not. Every institution was religious.

Figs. 10.1 (top) and 10.2 (bottom). Grave decorations. 10.1: African grave decoration, Congo. Reprinted from Century Magazine 41, no. 6 (April 1891): 827. 10.2: African American grave plot.

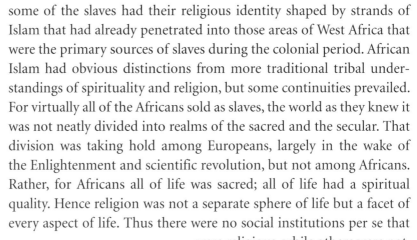

Behind this understanding lay a variety of West African cosmogonies. Unlike the biblical cosmogony that attributed creation to the work of God *ex nihilo*, some West African cosmogonies saw human life echoing the realm of the heavens, with offspring of the gods responsible for the emergence of human life and human society mirroring life in a heavenly sphere. Although it became fashionable for interpreters to designate a supreme deity as a "high God" resembling the Creator God of Christianity, that categorization represents the imposition of an alien understanding on a more fluid tribal consciousness. Rather than having a "supreme" God who was like the God of the slave traders and owners, many tribal cosmogonies posited a God whose providence buttressed the common life of the people. Hence there was a moral quality to divinity that was thought essential to the corporate life of the people. Concomitant with those providential and moral qualities was the perception that injustice was incompatible with the ways of God and that whatever disrupted the moral life intended for humanity was evil.

Most vital, though, was the ongoing sense that all of life is sacred, that nothing is without spiritual value, that every action and behavior thus has a spiritual quality. Put another way, what was basic to the African spirituality that served as the foundation for African American religion and the type of Christianity linked to it was a sensibility of the supernatural and its presence in every niche of life. Equally important was the means by which this penetrating sense of the sacred, this supernatural power, could be experienced. Anthropologists such as Anthony F. C. Wallace and I. M. Lewis have accented the role of ecstatic experience, or what many also call possession, in many tribal societies. Ecstatic religious expression was central to the tribal cultures in places such as Nigeria and Dahomey that provided the source for much of the slave population of the United States. But if possession suggests that for a time a spiritual presence seizes control of an individual or even a group of individuals and becomes an operative power manifested through unusual physical action and/or verbal expression, in the African context possession was even more profound. It was as if for a time the individual actually became one with the divine power, not just a transient vehicle through which the supernatural became evident.

In Africa, as elsewhere, ecstatic possession that linked the empirical realm with the supernatural generally occurred in ritual contexts where both song and dance were prominent. In West Africa, such dance involved the whole body, not just simple motion. Moreover, dancers almost always moved in a circular pattern, usually counter-clockwise. The singing that accompanied ritual dance, like the movement of the dancers, often involved lengthy repetition. The repetition, percussive quality, and rich use of syncopation in the ritual could dramatically alter the moods and feelings of participants.

One result of this dynamism was the creation of strong social bonds on many levels. On the one hand, the shared ritual experience joined together in one community all those who had participated and been drawn into intimate contact with supernatural power. On the other hand, it forged an organic connection between contemporary singers, dancers, and even observers with all those who had themselves entered a realm of supernatural ecstasy across generations. Euro-Americans often commented on how Africans and African American slaves were attracted to ancestor worship. It was not so much worship of ancestors as it was a sense of solidarity with all who came into the arena of sacred power through ritual song and dance, whether living or dead. But the conviction that previous generations were also spiritually present meant that funeral and burial practices would also have import, for one was dealing not only with physical remains but also with a sacred power with which one's own identity was entwined. (See plate D in gallery.)

Despite the dehumanizing effects of slavery, African Americans forced to come to the Americas never lost this sense of an abiding spiritual presence that could be more directly actualized through ritual song and dance. If traders and owners attempted to separate slaves who could communicate with one another verbally in order to enhance their control over them, they could not quash the communal bonds forged by the shared experience of the supernatural in moments of ecstasy. Then, too, Euro-Americans often misconstrued the vitality of slave spirituality, mistaking ritual song and dance for mere recreation. When evangelists sought to present their version of the Christian message to slaves, African Americans demonstrated their own genius in mining the depths of tribal spirituality to create a unique Christian expression.

CHRISTIANIZATION

From the arrival of the first slave ship in Virginia in 1619 until the Civil War that brought an end to legalized chattel slavery in the United States, Euro-Americans demonstrated an ambivalent attitude with regard to efforts to evangelize among the slave population. Much of the ambivalence stemmed from tacit efforts to avoid the moral issues surrounding slavery. If Euro-American preachers and missionaries succeeded in their evangelizing endeavors and slaves became baptized Christians, had they in effect become social and religious equals of those who kept them as property? Fears of having to acknowledge slaves as equals in the eyes of God, should they become fellow Christians, raised the thorny issue of whether conversion and baptism brought emancipation from the bonds of slavery. After all, it was difficult to assert equality in the eyes of God if one human being held another human being as property, thus asserting a social inequality of the most basic sort. It was easier for many Euro-Americans simply to regard African American slaves as hopeless heathens, perhaps even without souls, than to wrestle with their own internal demons about holding humans as property.

Then, too, when Euro-Americans observed the contours of slave life, they generally remained blissfully ignorant of the ways in which a profound religious consciousness and spiritual sensibility cascaded through slave culture. Because the worship structure of Euro-American Protestant Christianity was marked by order and decorum, few who witnessed the song and dance that marked slave "leisure" time saw anything other than amusement and entertainment, a diversion from the horrendous rigors of slave labor. Such exuberance, from the Euro-American point of view, had nothing to do with religion. Indeed, some could actually point to the frenzy of such activity as proof that efforts to present the Christian gospel to slaves was fruitless; none whose behavior was so "uncivilized" could appreciate the nuances of Christian affirmation.

Some of the ambivalence was mitigated by legal machinations that addressed the issue of whether slave conversion brought automatic emancipation. It was a simple matter for colonial legislative assemblies to insert in the codes that regulated slavery statements indicating that conversion and even baptism did not alter the slave status of one born a slave. By the early eighteenth century, such provisions were part of virtually every slave code. Legal maneuvering thus removed one of the messy questions that may have worked against Euro-American attempts to bring the Christian message to African American slaves. But there were other underlying problems. Slave codes also generally forbade teaching slaves to read; essential to the style of Protestantism that came to prevail in the colonial United States, even in the areas where a more genteel Anglicanism held sway, was the reading of

Scripture. Regular reading of the Bible not only brought many men and women to discern whether they could detect the work of grace in their own lives; it also nurtured spiritual growth. Those who could not read were thus denied access to one of the most important tools for spreading the Christian message.

Regardless, there were no sustained missionary ventures directed toward African American slaves in the seventeenth century. Any significant endeavor waited until the evangelical revivals of the eighteenth century, collectively known as the Great Awakening. These revivals stirred preachers to take the Christian gospel directly to the slaves. Samuel Davies of Virginia, whose evangelical efforts are among the more well known, reported preaching to slaves and witnessing many conversions. He also commented on the deft use of musical forms among his slave converts to give voice to their religious experience. When Baptist preacher Shubal Stearns made his way to Virginia in 1754 and 1755, he too labored among the slave communities. As a Baptist, he offered baptism by immersion to adults, rather than infant baptism, and found slaves more directly drawn to immersion. Indeed, he noted the emotional testimony and often ecstatic expression that slaves evidenced prior to immersion.[2]

What Davies and Stearns saw were slaves joining their masters in worship and the emergence of many biracial congregations, along with a handful that were nearly exclusively African American in their constituency. What neither appreciated was the extent to which the evangelical approach to the Christian gospel was reworked by the slaves, filtered through their African religious sensibilities until it emerged as a religious form with its own integrity and momentum. Nor did Davies, Stearns, and other evangelically inclined preachers realize the extent to which their own brand of Christian expression from then on would become something different, thanks to its interaction with things African American. Nor did they understand that what was emerging in many places was what Ira Berlin called a "new African-American culture" that involved considerable reformulation of the Christian message with a texture that was distinctly African.[3] If the result was sometimes hostile to the Christianity presented by Euro-Americans, it was also a becoming a religious phenomenon with a character and style all its own.

These dynamics were by no means limited to slave Christianity as it emerged in the American South. An African American subculture also developed in eighteenth-century New England, with its religious dimensions flowing as well from the revivals associated with the Great Awakening. If New Englanders had been less reluctant in theory to evangelize among African American slaves, the religious style of Puritanism, with its emphasis on reasoned preaching and the singing of psalms, impeded the development of a distinctive slave religion that accommodated elements both African and Christian. The enthusiastic preaching associated with the Great Awakening, especially the preaching of George Whitefield, provided a better opportunity, for often even among the traditionally more staid white Puritans, there were physical responses akin to spirit possession. As several analysts have argued, the evangelical tone of Awakening revivalism was simply better suited to the oral culture and more ecstatic spirituality that were part of the African heritage than were other forms of Christianity. From the mid-eighteenth century on, a distinctive African American religious culture began to take shape in New England as in the South, a religious culture that was neither fully Euro-Christian nor African, but an entity in its own right.

THE RING SHOUT

Central to slave Christianity, as to African religious expression, were a profound sense of the supernatural and a conviction that supernatural power could be experienced and accessed here and now. Almost as soon as Euro-Americans started commenting on the distinctive character of slave Christianity, they pointed to the ring shout as its most notable feature. The ring shout was a metamorphosis of the exuberant song and dance at the heart of tribal celebration. If there were obvious Christian elements, the performance style was, as Sterling Stuckey has noted, distinctly African. In many areas of Africa that provided the source for much of the slave population, movement in a counterclockwise circle (the direction the sun moves south of the equator) was a metaphor for the life-process itself and thus a key element of those ceremonies, such as burial, in which ancestral spirits were honored. The shout was a reciprocal dialogue between the living and the dead. In the developing African American religious culture, dance became a medium of prayer, a link between the empirical realm and the spiritual realm, with the accompanying shout a means of conversation or access to the sacred power addressed.

Historians of slave culture remind us that some who were tribal priests or shamans (in Mircea Eliade's sense of being technicians of ecstasy) were included among those forced to migrate to the Americas and sold into slavery. Their identity was no doubt unknown to Euro-Americans, yet many of them readily became the exhorters and religious leaders of presumably converted Christian slaves and vital actors in transforming the ring shout into a central ritual of slave Christianity. In the execution of the ring shout, possession frequently occurred, although with a somewhat different quality. In West Africa, drums would have set the rhythm; in the evangelical ethos, an equally rhythmic preaching may have supplemented or replaced the drumbeat. In West Africa, ecstasy meant that those possessed became actual carriers of the gods, while in slave Christianity the experience may have been more one of the presence of God within. And within slave Christianity, the ring shout embraced many different sorts of religious occasions when it was important to bridge ordinary reality with sacred reality: funerals, praise meetings, worship, and in time, revivals and camp meetings. As late as 1878, the year of a "bush meeting" described by African Methodist Episcopal bishop Daniel Alexander Payne in his autobiographical recollections, the ring shout was still so embedded into the soul of African American Christianity that, Payne noted, some believed that the shout was a necessary precondition for the occurrence of both conversion and any genuine experience of the presence and work of the Spirit.[4]

In his classic study of slave religion, Albert Raboteau summarizes well:

> In the ring shout and allied patterns of ecstatic behavior, the African heritage of dance found expression in the evangelical religion of the American slaves. . . . [S]imilar patterns of response—rhythmic

clapping, ring-dancing, styles of singing, all of which result in or from the state-of-possession trance—reveal the slaves' African religious background. . . . While the North American slaves danced under the impulse of the Spirit of a 'new' God, they danced in ways their fathers in Africa would have recognized.[5]

In the process, they were creating a new religion, the religion of African American Christianity.

The ring shout, the unique combination of dance and song marking slave Christianity, was by no means limited to the evangelical awakenings of the eighteenth century, as the comment by Payne suggests. It continued to be vital to African American religious expression even when Euro-Americans began to question whether efforts to evangelize among the slaves created problems. In the early nineteenth century, for example, Euro-Americans again became ambivalent about evangelizing among the slaves. The issue then was a growing awareness of the potential association of Christian converts with the leadership of slave revolts and other efforts to end the oppressive system of chattel labor. Slaves who were worked into a frenzy through presumably

Fig. 10.3. African American camp meeting, 1872. Wood engraving by Sol Eytinge Jr. Illustration in Harper's Weekly, v. 16 (August 10, 1872), p. 620.

Christian experience, such as the ring shout, were more likely to be poised to rebel, and slave preachers were often assumed—often rightly so—to have the influence to transfer their religious authority into political leadership. Perhaps Euro-Americans also were beginning to understand not only that religion could be a potent force for justice and the end of oppression but also that the developing spirituals, the songs born in the slave experience that are explored elsewhere in this volume, were much more than a retelling of biblical narratives. They were also calls for freedom.

Yet the ring shout endured, for it had become more than just a central feature of the "invisible institution" that prevailed in the slave quarters and in late-night gatherings outside the watchful eyes of masters and owners. It was also a key ingredient in fostering a sense of corporate identity and a communal bond among slaves that transcended other ties. Those calling for abolition railed against the failure of states to grant legal status to marriages between slaves and attacked the ways in which slavery undermined the biological ties of family. When owners could sell a slave's spouse or child at any moment, family ties were always fragile and unstable. The larger slave community in some ways became the social unit that provided a corporate identity, strengthened by such ritual activity as the ring shout.

PREACHING AND PRAISE

After 1830, slave owners again manifested an interest in Christianizing slaves, albeit because many became convinced that Christian slaves would be easier to control and also because many slave owners in desperation believed the propaganda that asserted the compatibility of Christianity and slavery. Historians have documented the dramatic increase in the religious instruction offered to slave children by whites in the two or three decades immediately prior to the Civil War. Through it all, the ring shout continued as a principal component of African American religious expression. And where slaves and free African Americans built praise houses, the ring shout became the focus of much worship.

Even in services in which dance did not predominate, the rhythmic element that could be almost hypnotic came through in the preaching style of African American exhorters, often leading to some physical response on the part of hearers that echoed the movement of the ring shout. Indeed, the call-response pattern that came to characterize African American preaching parallels the ring shout, albeit without the structured counterclockwise movement. As the tempo and cadence of the preaching picked up, like the rhythm and movement of the ring shout dance, the response of the congregation became more exuberant. The more the intensity built, the more a spiritual power was apt to seize control of both preacher and responder. Such preaching is itself a form of ecstatic religious expression. The preaching that distinguished slave Christianity was thus a verbal counterpart to the ring shout.

The contagious power of black preaching and the ring shout aroused the interest of white observers, lured by their palpable spiritual vitality. Three well-known accounts by white eyewitnesses illuminate the discernable spiritual energy unleashed in African American Christian religious gatherings. European observer Fredrika Bremer, writing in late January 1851 about an African church service she attended in New Orleans, commented about how different the "sermon" was from that to which she was accustomed. Not confined to preaching from a pulpit, the exhorter moved among the people, with those congregants moved by the Spirit bursting into verbal response. As the noise level mounted, Bremer noted, many of the people leapt to their feet, moving their bodies in a twisted, contorted fashion. It was, she said, "regular bedlam." In one case, a woman who was in the throes of conversion remained in an ecstatic state for at least a quarter of an hour.[6] As Sterling Stuckey commented, "What Bremer witnessed was Christianity shot through with African values."[7] It was not mere syncretism or fusion of Christianity with elements drawn from an African religious subconscious; it was a manifestation of a religious phenomenon all its own.

Sing and Shout

In the blacks' quarter the coloured people get together, and sing for hours together, short scraps of disjointed affirmative pledges, or prayers, lengthened out with long repetition choruses. . . . "Go shouting all your days," in connection with "glory, glory, glory," in which the shouting is repeated six times in succession.

—John E. Watson, Methodist Error, or Friendly Advice to Those Methodists Who Indulge in Extravagant Religious Emotions and Bodily Exercises (Trenton: n.p., 1819), 30, 122.

In 1860, Frederick Law Olmsted first published his account of a journey across the South that took him through cotton country to New Orleans. There he witnessed a gathering much like that which had aroused Bremer's interest, although this time the service was led by a white preacher whose style was, Olmsted commented, "nearly black." As in the service that Bremer attended, the congregational response was dramatic. Some seemed to be seized by convulsions; others began to shriek and groan. Olmsted described in detail one woman who was sitting in the gallery. When there was relative quiet near the end of the sermon, she stood and began to shout. Soon spontaneous singing began, accompanied by swaying that continued long after the singing itself had stopped. Olmsted had seen supernatural power came alive as it brought ecstatic experience to this African American congregation.[8]

The third account comes from plantation mistress Mary Boykin Chesnut. In her diary entry for October 13, 1861, Chesnut recounted attending a service conducted by slaves in the praise house on her Camden, South Carolina, plantation. The Methodist exhorter, Jim Nelson, was himself a slave. She noted that while Nelson prayed, his voice began to rise until it reached a shrill musicality. He and the slaves present began to clap their hands in a steady rhythm. Chesnut herself was moved by the obvious spiritual power of the occasion. "I wept bitterly," she wrote. Then, she remarked, "the Negroes sobbed and shouted and swayed backward and forward, some with aprons in their eyes, most of them clapping their hands and responding in shrill tones: 'Yes, God!' 'Jesus!' 'Bless de Lord, amen,' etc. It was a little too exciting for me. I would very much have liked to shout, too."[9] Chesnut knew she was on holy ground

Fig. 10.4. A plantation preacher exhorts the slaves. Courtesy of the Billy Graham Center.

where spiritual power was present. Others noted how, in a presumably Christian context, sometimes in response to preaching and sometimes in response to song, African Americans would beat their breasts, an action that resonated with the Dahomey way of keeping time with music. Little wonder that years later Zora Neale Hurston remarked that African Americans were never as "Christianized" as many thought, if being Christianized meant simply adopting the religious ways of Euro-Americans.[10] In essence, African Americans had created their own Christianity.

One cannot underestimate the importance of supernatural power in the ecstasy of the ring shout, call-response preaching, and other manifestations of slave Christianity. The shared experience created social bonds among slaves, to be sure. But it went well beyond that. Religious ecstasy was itself an empowering experience, giving one access to a transcendent realm where the Spirit reigned supreme. It was this power that propelled and sustained the cry for freedom, for its incomparable quality nurtured hope for change and carried with it an assurance that such change would indeed become lived reality in this world, not just in a world to come after death.

WADE IN THE WATER

The dynamic of the transcendent entering into lived reality came to powerful expression in the ritual of baptism as it took shape in slave religion, reflecting a development of religious practice that fused traditional African and traditional Christian elements. Although the New Testament speaks of baptism as "dying and rising with Christ" (Romans 6), the notion of water burial was also a feature of some African tribal initiation rites, particularly those associated with something akin to secret societies. In his debunking of the myth that African elements vanished from slave religion, Herskovits drew attention to parallels between baptism by immersion and water rituals among the Niger and Dahomey.[11] These parallels help explain why African Americans always insisted on baptism by immersion, even when the Christian influence came from Methodists and others, whose normal practice was sprinkling, not immersion.

In entering the water, one gave up a former identity altogether; emerging, one became a new being with a new status in the world. After undergoing such a water lustration, the initiate was recognized as a full member of the community. The practice of baptism as communal initiation allowed for a particularly rich interplay of things African and things Christian. In some cases, baptism was also a prerequisite for participation in the ring shout.

But baptism by immersion in slave religion involved more than taking on a new identity. It was also another venue for experience of transcendent power. The spiritual "Wade in the Water," with its telling words "God's a-gonna trouble that water" as a refrain, helped create a sacred space that elevated and transformed the meaning of the troubled passage Africans made across the Atlantic to the Americas. The sacred space of baptismal waters also elevated and transformed the troubled waters of slavery itself, creating a sacred space where one was not only reborn but also filled with spiritual power. Baptism linked one to the ancestors whose spiritual presence remained a sustaining force, and also to future generations and to the promise of freedom for them. As the African past and God's apocalyptic future merged in the ecstatic movement of the water over the body, the officiant, often a fellow slave who might hold standing as a deacon, was a fresh

Fig. 10.5. Baptismal ceremony. Photo © Schomburg Center / Art Resource, N.Y.

manifestation of the tribal priest who introduced the one being baptized not only to the ancestral spirits but also to the power that would lead to a sacred future.

Just as those who participated in the ring shout were imbued with the power of the Holy Spirit, so, too, those who entered the waters of baptism could experience the same sort of transformative possession. And just as those who responded with shouts and swaying to the preached Word when the Spirit moved within their souls and bodies, so, too, those who presented themselves for immersion were open to the uplifting presence of the Holy Spirit.

> **"Wade in the Water"**
> Look over yonder, what do I see?
> God's a-gonna trouble the water.
> The Holy Ghost a-coming on me.
> God's a-gonna trouble the water.
> —Like many spirituals, "Wade in the Water" has many versions; see http://www.negrospirituals.com /news-song/wade_in_the_water .htm (accessed 2/7/07). Also see Songs of Zion, Supplemental Worship Resources (Nashville: Abingdon Press, 1981), no. 129, n.p.

Euro-Americans often marveled at the spiritual power slaves evidenced in baptism, a power far superior to what they had themselves found in baptism. If baptism among white Christians was more a solemn sacrament, among African Americans it was a cognate to the ring shout, to burial rites, and to preaching and praise. All provided opportunities to affirm the presence of the divine and its power to transform human experience. Baptism was a bridge that connected slaves to the freedom of an African tribal past, on the one hand, and to the freedom of a future when slavery had been destroyed. Hence "Wade in the Water" linked participants to the Israelites moving through the troubled water of the Red Sea from slavery in Egypt to freedom in a promised land, as well as to the baptism of Christ in the Jordan River. Little wonder, then, that white Christians were often apprehensive about allowing slaves to be baptized, for at some level they understood that the act of baptism undermined all of the props that supported the system of slavery. Baptism represented experiences of emotional empowerment that defied white control.

PREACHER, PRIEST, AND CONJURER

As W. E. B. Du Bois pointed out long ago, the slave preacher stood in a direct line with the African tribal priest and shamanic healer. Like African priestly predecessors, slave preachers presented themselves as mediators between a realm of power and ordinary reality. As slave communities on plantations came to supplant clan and tribe as the locus for social bonds and corporate identity, preachers gained increasing responsibility for religious life. While the slave owner took on the role of the tribal chief, albeit with more despotic and arbitrary power, the slave preacher functioned more clearly as the tribal priest. The preacher was one who in human form represented what baptism did in ritual form, namely, bridging the world of the ancestors (the world of the dead) and the world of daily life (the world of the living).[12]

This singular status also meant that slave preachers took on roles that to Euro-Americans had no religious element at all. Yet within slave Christianity, the boundaries between the religious and the non-religious were never as clearly delineated as they were for the slave owners. For example, Charles Joyner's careful examination of the slave community that developed on a Waccamaw rice plantation in South Carolina revealed that slave preachers, in addition to exhorting and moving slaves to spiritual ecstasy as they proclaimed their understanding of the Christian gospel, also often served as agents who would mediate disputes between slaves.[13] Of course, this posi-

Fig. 10.6. African American prayer meeting in the Antebellum North. Courtesy of the Billy Graham Center.

tion of leadership, as Joyner also argued, poised slave preachers to sow seeds of discontent with the horrors of chattel slavery and to fuel desires for freedom.

In Africa, tribal priests were often called on to conjure, or summon spiritual powers to heal or alter the events in a person's life. There are numerous examples as well of slave preachers in the United States who were regarded as much adept at conjuring as they were at arousing the power of the Holy Spirit in their listeners. As with African conjurers, some slave preachers were renowned for their knowledge of magical substances, such as herbs that had healing powers. Because of this ability to play dual roles, preacher and conjurer, slaves often took their problems to the preacher. Euro-Americans may have been aware of this dimension of slave religion but like much else consigned it to folk belief and superstition. After all, Euro-American Christians

> ### Leadership
> The Negro Church is the only institution of the Negroes which started in the African forest and survived slavery; under the leadership of the priest and medicine man, and afterward of the Christian pastor, the Church preserved in itself the remnants of African tribal life.
> —W. E. B. Du Bois, "Of the Faith of the Fathers," in The Souls of Black Folk (1898); also in African American Religious Thought: An Anthology, ed. Cornel West and Eddie S. Glaude (Louisville: Westminster John Knox, 2003), 7.

Fig. 10.7. Meeting in the African Church, Cincinnati, Ohio. Photo © Schomburg Center / Art Resource, NY.

themselves entertained beliefs and practices involving fortune-telling, magic, and witchcraft.

The slave preacher thus exercised a central role in the emergence of a distinctive slave Christianity that fused together elements that many would recognize as unabashedly Christian with those that were equally rooted in African life and culture. As shamanic technicians of ecstasy, they were adept at bringing the power of the spiritual realm into the daily realities of the slave community. Their proclamation lifted their hearers to a plane of power where they could transcend the vicissitudes of slave life, assured of an individual and corporate identity that was at least partially free from white control. Sometimes the skills of the preacher had very practical consequences as they brought both physical and spiritual healing to other slaves on the plantation, summoned divine power to resolve disputes, called on the Spirit to quash enemies, and thus became symbols of the cohesiveness necessary for slaves to affirm themselves as a people. Sometimes, however, the power of the preacher moved into a zone of danger, for many of the nuances of power associated with the preacher were also central to the practice of voodoo.

VOODOO

The mix of beliefs and practices known as voodoo emerged in the West Indies, especially in Haiti, through the stunning interaction of African ways indigenous to those who were brought to the Caribbean as slaves with Native American traditions and Christianity, particularly in its Roman Catholic form. In Haiti, some voodoo ceremonies began with traditional Roman Catholic prayers, although the final result is something rather different from traditional Catholicism. The religious ethos of Roman Catholicism, with its panoply of saints and rich liturgical heritage, resonated with African tribal understandings of a sacred universe where spiritual forces were omnipresent and where the living were linked with ancestors through the repetition of tribal rites. The starker character of Protestantism that prevailed in some areas of North America lacked some of the luster of Catholicism and its ability to serve as a counterpoint to the tribal ways of African and Native American peoples.

In Haiti and Jamaica, where the particular amalgamation that generated religious voodoo took shape, one finds elements that are clearly at odds with a Christian orientation, but also elements that reflect the same sense of spiritual power and sacred reality that nourished virtually all slave religion. From the West Indies, the religion of voodoo came to Louisiana, especially the area around New Orleans, and remained an integral part of slave religious culture until well into the nineteenth century. Indeed, there are a few accounts of nineteenth-century voodoo worship that have survived.[14] Voodoo, as a system of magic, has had a more enduring influence, with some continuing to appropriate this dimension of voodoo into the twenty-first century as part of their own lived religion.

Perhaps the most obvious areas where religious voodoo reveals departures from Christianity are the regard for the snake as a divine being and practices of animal sacrifice. But voodoo cultic practice that relied on dancing accompanied by drumming and singing, often leading to possession by spiritual powers, was clearly akin to the song and dance of the ring shout and manifestations of ecstatic experience that cascaded through slave Christianity. Like the ring shout, the ecstatic dance associated with voodoo signified freedom in at least two ways. It brought freedom from the oppression of slavery for the moment in its ecstatic release from things of this world. And in so doing, it brought the hope of freedom from that oppression when spiritual power at some future point had replaced the empirical power of slave owners and masters.

In this sense, then, religious voodoo offered access to a realm of supernatural power that was superior to anything in the empirical world. Slave Christianity also offered access to a realm of supernatural power that was superior to anything in the empirical world. Hence there was a congruence that meant many slaves drawn to voodoo did not themselves see voodoo as contradictory to Christian affirmation but rather complementary to it. It is also precisely here that voodoo as magic tied in, for magic suggests an ability to manipulate or control powers that transcend the ordinary. Being able to control such powers at one's will was rather different from responding to the invasion of life by the Spirit of God; hence some slave preachers who identified themselves more directly as Christian rejected voodoo and other practices that resembled it. But even then, most slave Christians did not reject the worldview that sustained voodoo either as a religion or as a form of magic. Slave Christianity and voodoo both presumed that the world was a place of spiritual power and energy. In Christianity, that power came into human life in ways that could be overwhelming and transformative, even if certain ritual activity such as the ring shout could create the conditions in which divine power was more likely to manifest itself. In voodoo, particularly as its practice moved from the arena of religion to that of magic, one could summon that power and use it for personal ends. Regardless of this difference, the world remained a venue where spiritual power prevailed.

TRANSFORMING AMERICAN CHRISTIANITY

Slave religion not only yielded a unique form of Christianity among African Americans but also had an enduring impact on the shape of Christianity among Euro-Americans. The most obvious impact is the contortions in Christian thought that came with ongoing efforts to justify the support of individuals and churches for maintaining a system of slave labor. Those contortions became more pronounced as antislavery sentiment mushroomed in the United States in the decades between 1830 and the Civil War. During that epoch, the most virulent defenses of slavery came from Christian writers, often southern Protestant clergy. Rather than focusing on that often-told story, here we shall look at two ways in which the development of African American Christianity, the lived religion of slaves themselves, altered the character of Euro-American Christianity. The first will highlight how African American Christian religious expression transformed Euro-American religious expression; the second will examine how the interaction with slave Christianity produced an understanding of doctrine that left a lasting imprint on Christian ethics in those areas of the South where slavery was most firmly entrenched.

Almost from the beginning of efforts to evangelize among the slaves, white observers were impressed by the power evident when slave exhorters began to preach. As slave Christianity began to take shape as a lived religion that drew from African sources and Euro-American Christian ones, whites were drawn to the ecstasy that prevailed in the black praise houses. As noted previously, the spiritual dynamism of the ring shout and song, the call-response form of preaching, and other physical demonstrations of the presence of the Spirit offered Euro-American Christians and other onlookers a glimpse of a religious potency that made their own religious styles seem anemic.

Slave Christianity proved to have elements that made their way into some strands of the developing Euro-American evangelical Protestant style, particularly because worship and other religious gatherings, such as frontier camp meetings, were frequently biracial affairs. Even if, for example, those attending a frontier camp meeting were likely to be separated by race in terms of where they gathered in the forest clearings for preaching services, they were able to observe each other. The natural ecstasy that characterized slave religion quickly became almost the norm for Euro-American camp meeting religion as well. When camp meeting revivalists, such as the well-known Methodist evangelist Peter Cartwright, wrote about such physical evidences of the Spirit as the barking exercise or the jerking exercise, they were describing Euro-American ecstatic experience that now seemed appropriate, no doubt because white folks had seen the ecstasy that marked slave religion and made it their own.

Over generations, even when the enthusiasm of the frontier camp meeting became more domesticated, there remained in white evangelicalism a form of Christian expression that was open to ecstatic experience. It came to the fore again in the Pentecostal explosion traced to the 1906 Azusa Street revivals in Los Angeles, which were also biracial in composition and which relied on the charismatic preaching of an African American, William J. Seymour. Although the Azusa Street revivals are not the sole source of the Pentecostal movement that swept through American Protestantism in the opening decades of the twentieth century, the ecstatic element that African Americans celebrated from the heritage of slave religion became a hallmark of twentieth-century Pentecostal expression.

Moreover, the song that was central to slave worship penetrated white Christianity as those influenced by spirituals and then the blues formulated a "white gospel" musical heritage that paralleled developments in African American religion. By the twenty-first century, with the popularity of praise choruses and other religious music relying on the percussive rhythm and cadence of slave music, the transformation of white Christianity by worship forms that were anchored in slave religion continued apace.

There were other ways in which slavery, if not slave religion, altered the character of much Euro-American Christianity and transformed it to such an extent that for all practical purposes it became a different religion. Euro-American Christianity had to remake itself in order to allow individuals to proclaim themselves as devout Christians while they oppressed other humans and held them as property. The so-called justification of slavery thus caused much white Christianity to change its very nature. One example, most obvious among southern evangelicals who sought to affirm both the legitimacy of slavery and their espousal of Christianity, is the idea of "the spirituality of the church" that emerged in southern Presbyterian circles.

As articulated by Benjamin Morgan Palmer and others, this doctrine built on the idea that human life was divided into sacred and secular spheres. In this case, however, one had little to do with the other. In particular, it asserted that the primary focus of the church was on matters of salvation, on things of the spirit. It should not interfere with—indeed, it really had nothing to say about—affairs of politics and government, which had their own divine imprimatur. Hence so long as slavery was legal according to government, the church had no right to condemn it or even to criticize it. Doing so would involve abrogating concern for things spiritual. In retrospect, it is easy to understand that this strict separation of spheres was a useful ploy to buttress justification for the maintenance of the institution of slavery. Even raising moral and ethical questions about slavery was trespassing on territory that was not the divinely ordained responsibility of the church as a spiritual institution.

An unintended consequence of the idea of the spirituality of the church for much southern white Protestantism was the definition of ethics almost exclusively in individualistic terms; since spirituality concerned the individual soul, ethical behavior as a reflection of one's spiritual state was likewise a matter of individual conduct. To think of social ethics or ethical dimensions of institutions such as slavery or other governmental economic and political policies was to misconstrue the very nature of spirituality itself. By sidestepping social ethics in this way, the idea of the spirituality of the church allowed Euro-American southern evangelical Protestants to avoid the thorny questions of the immorality of slavery and begin to see ethics as concerned almost exclusively with matters of individual choice, such as consuming alcoholic beverages, engaging in leisure activities such as dancing or playing cards, or even wearing makeup. A century after amendments to the U.S. Constitution outlawed slavery, variations of the idea of the spirituality of the church became part of the religious critique of religious involvement in the civil rights movement and the condemnation of clergy and religiously committed laity who sought to secure equal rights for all humans. Civil rights were a matter for the government to determine, not for the churches or its leaders.

Slave religion thus had a significant impact on Euro-American Protestant Christianity. Its appreciation for the ways the presence of the divine evoked physical and emotional responses helps illuminate the sometimes dramatic character of white behavior at frontier camp meetings in the early nineteenth century. It also was one thread in the tapestry that created the Pentecostal movement in its many manifestations in the twentieth century. In other words, slave Christianity helped assure a place for ecstatic expression in forms of white Christianity. At the same time, the efforts of some Euro-American Protestants to avoid dealing with the moral and ethical dilemmas surrounding chattel slavery led to some extraordinary doctrinal formulations, such as the idea of the spirituality of the church as something disconnected from social ethics and responsibility. The Euro-American Protestantism infected by those ideas became something new and different. Like slave Christianity, it became a new religion, one with some roots in the larger Christian tradition and others in the immediate culture. Like slave Christianity, it became a religion with a life of its own.

FOR FURTHER READING

Frey, Sylvia R., and Betty Wood. *Come Shouting to Zion: African American Protestantism in the American South and British Caribbean to 1830*. Chapel Hill: University of North Carolina Press, 1998.

Genovese, Eugene D. *Roll, Jordan, Roll: The World the Slaves Made.* New York: Pantheon, 1974.

Levine, Lawrence W. *Black Culture and Black Consciousness: Afro-American Folk Thought from Slavery to Freedom.* New York: Oxford University Press, 1987.

Raboteau, Albert J. *Slave Religion: The "Invisible Institution" in the Antebellum South.* New York: Oxford University Press, 1978.

Sobel, Mechal. *The World They Made Together: Black and White Values in Eighteenth-Century Virginia.* Princeton: Princeton University Press, 1987.

Stuckey, Sterling. *Slave Culture: Nationalist Theory and the Foundation of Black America.* New York: Oxford University Press, 1987.

SPIRITUALS AND THE QUEST FOR FREEDOM

CHERYL A. KIRK-DUGGAN

African American spirituals are "chants of collective exorcism" that delivered souls of black folk from total despair during the pre–Civil War era in the United States. Sung a cappella (without instrumental accompaniment), spirituals emerged as a distinctive form of Christian practice among African American slaves. This practice pervaded slave culture in North America; one historian estimated that as many as six thousand different spirituals may have been sung prior to emancipation.[1]

African Americans practiced spirituals while working in the fields of a plantation or over a hot stove in the kitchen of the master's big house. They chanted on caravans moving from station to station on the Underground Railroad. They chanted in hush arbors away from white oversight, sharing old songs and improvising new ones in collective expressions of hope and solidarity. By examining some of these songs, we can glimpse the dynamics of slave existence and begin to uncover the rich aesthetic tradition that characterized African American Christianity in the eighteenth and nineteenth centuries. Blending African, Euro-American, and African American ideas, harmonies, and rhythms in a new form of Christian practice, spirituals helped a people grapple with the social evils of oppression and contributed to a vital black aesthetic of justice and freedom that persists in African American gospel music today.

The lyrics of spirituals derived from biblical stories. Slaves drew upon biblical lore, from the story of creation in Genesis to that of John at Patmos naming names in Revelation. Slaves recast these stories in

Fig. 11.1. Ring shout. Image from *Singing the Master: The Emergence of African-American Culture in the Plantation South* by Roger D. Abrahams (Penguin, 1994), 44. Origin of image unknown.

the terms of their own existence, emphasizing themes of freedom from bondage, divine justice, and redemption of suffering. Many biblical stories did not get included; others were repeated again and again, sometimes merged with different stories in innovative ways. The exodus of God's people from bondage in Egypt was a favorite story and often was linked with other stories from the Old and New Testaments in ways that drove home their relevance for African American people. Spirituals invoked specific characters from the Bible, making them come alive as slave heroes or commentators on the system of slavery that African Americans inhabited. Noah, Moses, Joshua, Samson, Jonah, Lazarus, and Mary appeared in numerous spirituals, along with Jesus, who made his presence known in various roles as infant, Savior, brother, friend, and composite of God/Lord/Holy Spirit all in one. As a subject of many spirituals, Jesus' suffering resonated powerfully with the suffering slaves knew from their own experiences. His ultimate triumph over evil represented their hope for themselves.

Slavery was big business, involving systematic kidnapping, marketing, and breeding of people for labor and servitude. In response to this system of exploitation, slaves relied on spirituals to invoke a cosmology that celebrated divine justice, championed freedom, and held human beings responsible for the sins they committed. In the cosmology represented through spirituals, oppression ultimately could not thwart the triumph of freedom. Spirituals proclaimed the existence of a larger order of justice that framed ordinary reality and passed judgment on human crime. In this larger order of justice, evil was real but ultimately was vanquished through the power of God and the fortitude of his people.

By conflating biblical stories with the sufferings and hopes of black people, spirituals made Christianity a liberating religion that challenged the moral authority of masters who claimed to be Christian and disputed their interpretations of slavery as a Christian institution. In many references to Jesus as a presence in the midst of slave life, spirituals implied that Jesus was on the side of slaves and that slaves were God's children, made in the image of God. As *imago Dei*, or the image of God, slaves stood at the center of a powerful story of divine justice.

Through the practice of singing spirituals, this cosmology of divine justice took on a life of its own. Ironic juxtapositions between divine truth and the degradations of slave existence provided scaffolding that enabled singers to climb from feelings of sorrow to feelings of joy. Through their practice of chanting, people could throw off some of the ill effects of slavery. In this respect, spirituals were "chants of exorcism" that named the forces of evil, strengthened people to resist those forces, and encouraged them to seek freedom and justice.[2]

In their structure and meaning, spirituals turned on the ironic tension between spiritual reality and physical appearance, juxtaposing the real strength and dignity of African Americans and their apparent poverty and inferiority. They also called attention to the moral superiority of slaves over their white masters, exposing that superiority in juxtaposition to the legal rights of white masters to rule over their slaves.[3]

Analysis of particular spirituals illustrates the use of biblical stories as a means of constructing ironic tension between the hierarchy of oppression under which slaves lived and the larger spiritual reality of divine justice. Such analysis enables us to understand how irony could work as a means of warding off some of the demoralizing and degrading effects of slavery. For example, two spirituals, "Oh Freedom" and "I Shall Not be Moved," employ irony to invoke the cosmology of final justice, identifying slaves as true Christians and the ones who will ultimately be free. Both of these spirituals are songs of resistance, good examples of how chanting could enable slaves to summon strength to resist or transcend the difficulties of their lives.

Sung with the slow-paced majesty of a processional hymn, "Oh Freedom" proclaimed the reality of divine justice, championed a merciful, freedom-loving God, and denied final authority to the forces of bondage. As well as being sung in fields and hush arbors, "Oh Freedom" was a marching song of black regiments during Civil

"Oh Freedom"

Vs. 1: Oh Freedom, Oh Freedom,
Oh Freedom, Oh Freedom over me;
And before I'd be a slave
I'd be buried in my grave
And go home to my Lord, and be free.

Vs. 2: No more moanin', no more
      moanin',
No more moanin' over me. . .
Vs. 3: No mo' weepin' . . .
Vs. 4: There'll be singin' . . .
Vs. 5: There'll be shoutin' . . .
Vs. 6: There'll be prayin' . . .

—From Songs of Zion,
Supplemental Worship Resources 12
(Nashville: Abingdon,
1981, 1982), 102.

War skirmishes, a cry of victory after emancipation, and a sustaining psalm during the travails of Reconstruction.

To some of the overseers who heard them, the words might have seemed to deny reality or simply be meaningless jargon. But for participants, the words might have represented engagement with the structure of society and unwillingness to accept the moral authority of the slave system. In other words, the one who appears headed for burial as a slave might really be headed for a life of freedom and already possess elements of freedom internally. The music of these chants contributed to these underlying meanings; the music carried the words, engaged the bodies and emotions of singers, and united people into a community that shared meaning and created emotional distance from the injustice that surrounded them.

"I Shall Not Be Moved" is a second example of how spirituals expressed resistance. The rocking, ballad style of this chant dovetailed with its imagery of moving water. The call and response between leader and chorus highlighted the tension between a tree planted on the shore and the boat holding steady on the one hand and the force of the moving waters on the other. As a grammatical phrase, "I shall not be moved" is an independent, declarative clause, conveying choice as well as certainty. The song echoes the messages of Psalm 1:3, "They are like trees planted by streams of water, which yield their fruit in its season," and Jeremiah 17:8, "They shall be like a tree planted by water, sending out its roots by the stream. It shall not fear when heat comes, and its leaves shall stay green."

After emancipation, singers changed the "I shall not be moved" of the song's early version to "We shall not be moved" perhaps as a way to reaffirm the existence of African American community and to acknowledge solidarity with an earlier generation of slaves.

"I Shall Not Be Moved" is a refusal to give in; the person to be moved refuses to move. The juxtaposition between movement and nonmovement mirrors that between the tran-sience of evil and the final certainty of justice. At another level is a reversal of meaning with respect to movement—the singers choose to move them-selves in choosing not to be moved by their owners. Along this line, the real momentum of the song is the movement from slavery to free-dom. The moving voices of the singers lift up the underlying, ironic message—the one who moves the world is the one who will not be moved.

The meaning of this song unfolds and touches us through the language of irony and paradox. The slaves would sing, "I shall not be moved," even when they were bought and sold as chattel; they "were moved" as merchandise at the whim of their owners. While slaves could be physically moved around by others at will, they had a reli-gion that held them apart from the system and held them together emotionally.

The irony of spirituals such as "I Shall Not Be Moved" illustrates the duality of being that African Americans expe-rienced as slaves. As described by W. E. B. Du Bois, African Americans often had a sense of themselves as at once hidden and visible, as if they were living a veiled existence.[4] Du Bois's metaphor of the veil symbolized the double consciousness of African Americans as persons of dignity hidden behind roles imposed on them as lowly and often despised members of a racist society. This duality of being existed in a state of tension; chanters of spirituals proclaimed the underlying mes-sage that they themselves were saints, even as they labored as chattel under the white man.

Spirituals reveal a distinctive black aesthetic that involves playing with words, revising and reversing them and using humor and double meaning to turn messages around. In the word games played through spirituals, people sang as a way of taking some authority in their own lives, using irony and oral shorthand mixed with mysticism and knowledge of biblical texts to communicate the complexity of their situation as double beings and Christians enslaved.

> ## "I Shall Not Be Moved"
>
> Vs. 1: I shall not, I shall not be moved.
> I shall not, I shall not be moved.
> Just like a tree that's planted by the water
> I shall not be moved.
>
> Vs. 2: The church of God is marching;
> I shall not be moved. . . .
> Vs. 3: Come and join the army. . . .
> Vs. 4: King Jesus is our Captain. . . .
> Vs. 5: Satan had me bound. . . .
> Vs. 6: On my way to heaven. . . .
>
> —"I Shall Not Be Moved,"
> arr. Betty Gadling, African
> American Heritage Hymnal
> (Chicago: GIA, 2001), 479.

Fig. 11.2. W. E. B. Du Bois.

A third spiritual, "Mary, Don't You Weep," illustrates some of the ways slaves used their knowledge of biblical texts, especially their knack for editing biblical texts to serve their needs, combining themes and characters from several different texts. "Mary, Don't You Weep" proclaimed ownership of biblical stories and characters and exuded confidence about using them to convey the complexity and contradictory nature of their slave existence. Two early versions of the spiritual invoked several Marys, including Mary the mother of Jesus (Matthew 1, 2; Mark 6, 15, 16; Luke 1, 2, 24; John 2, 19; Acts 1), Mary the sister of Martha and Lazarus (John 11), and another Mary and Martha who appear in Luke 10:38-42. The Mary who weeps can be both Mary the mother of Jesus at the death of her son and Mary the sister of Lazarus at the death of her brother, before Jesus resurrects him. In verse 3, the "Cheer up, sisters" could indicate the Mary and Martha connection as well as the cross (Mark 15:40; Matt. 27:55; Luke 23:26-31; John 19:25-27) and the empty-tomb experiences of Mary Magdalene, sometimes alone, sometimes with other women, thus sisters (Mark 16:1-8; Matt. 28:1-8; Luke 24:1-7; John 20:1-12. Both versions signal the destruction of Pharaoh's army in Exodus 3–15 and conflate that Old Testament event with the Mary stories of the New Testament, making the Old Testament event the explanation for why Mary need not weep.

Sung in an upbeat manner, "Mary, Don't You Weep" was meant to cheer African American women, lift their spirits, and dry their tears. Directed specifically to women, this chant acknowledges that slavery gave women many reasons to weep—enforced labor, separation from children, and rape by white owners who had legal rights to handle female property any way they chose. This chant of endurance made the linkages between ordinary women and their biblical counterparts completely explicit. In both versions of the spiritual, the Marys are obviously African American women as much as they are legendary heroines from the Bible.

A fourth spiritual focuses on Mary the mother of Jesus and goes even further in this process of identification by linking slave women to the most sacred female figure in the history of Christianity. "Mary Had a Baby" represents the lives of slave women in the terms of the biblical story of Mary and her baby Jesus. All of these women faced the joy—and the difficulties—of

---

"Oh, Mary, Doncher [Don't You] Weep"

Chorus: Oh, Mary, doncher you weep, doncher moan.
Oh, Mary, doncher you weep, doncher moan.
Pharaoh's army get drownded?
Oh, Mary, doncher you weep.

Vs. 1: Gladsome o' dese mornin's 'bout nine o'clock.
Dis ol' worl' ago'n'ter reel an' rock.
Pharaoh's army get drownded.
Oh, Mary, doncher weep.

Vs. 2: Some o' dese mornin's bright an' fair,
Take my wings an' cleave ce air. . . .

Vs. 3: When I git to Heav'n go'n'ter sing an' shout
Nobody dere for to turn me out. . . .

Vs. 4: When I git to Heavn'n go'n'ter put on my shoesd.
Run about glory an' tell de news. . . .

—"Oh, Mary, Doncher Weep,"
arr. Hall Johnson,
The Hall Johnson Collection:
Over 50 Classic Favorites
for Voice and Piano
(New York: Carl Fischer,
1930, 2003), 26–27.

---

birthing, naming, loving, and caring for their children. To all outward appearance, Mary and her African American counterparts are poor women, disgraced and giving birth in conditions fit for animals. In reality, of course, Mary gives birth to the Savior of humanity, the Lord unto whom all the world will eventually pay homage. The song imputes some of the same joy and expectation to the slave mothers who loved their babies. Along the road to salvation, however, humiliation, suffering, and death await the children of slaves, just as they did

---

Mary's child. A necessary relationship between sorrow and joy, and between scorn and glory, defines them all.

The refrain "People keep a-comin' an' the train done gone" is as persistently ambiguous as its message of sorrow and joy. If "the train" refers to the Underground Railroad, and "the train done gone" means one group of slaves has left the station or safe house and moved on to another, are the "people" who "keep a-comin'" authorities hounding the fugitives who just escaped capture? Or slaves who arrived too late to join the caravan, who are now more vulnerable than ever to getting caught and punished? Or the persistent slaves in search of freedom who will continue to form trains and find more passageways out? Is the train a fleeting image, a missed opportunity, or a sure promise for the future? Holding all of these ambiguities in the clear framework linking slave mothers to the mother of Jesus, "Mary Had a Baby" expressed the instabilities and some of the deep textures of that existence with great deftness and originality.

"I Got Shoes" is a masterpiece of irony and humor. The singers claim to have something that, in many cases, everyone around them could plainly see they did not have—shoes. The same goes for wings, a crown, and a harp. But the invisibility of these signs of high status now is the certain indicator of their reality later on, or in a spiritual realm up above. The words of the song affirm without equivocation that African American Christians will walk, fly, shine, and play all over God's heaven. Their freedom will be manifest in their supernatural mobility in heaven, a realm juxtaposed to the realm of bondage and forced mobility they now inhabit. In addition to playfully expanding on the ironic relationship between the appearance of no shoes, wings, crown, or harp and their heavenly reality, the spiritual seems to take a humorous view of the irony itself, perhaps gently poking fun at the reliance on irony in slave Christianity and its enthusiastic assertions of good fortune.

"Mary Had a Baby"

Mary had a baby, yes, Lord,
Mary had a baby, my Lord,
Mary had a baby, yes, Lord,
De people keep a-comin' an' the train done gone.

What did she name him? Yes, Lord,
What did she name him? My Lord,
What did she name him? Yes, Lord,
De people keep a-comin' an' the train done gone.

She name him King Jesus, yes, Lord,
She name him Jesus, my Lord,
She name him Jesus, yes, Lord,
De people keep a-comin' an' the train done gone.

She name him Mighty Couns'lor, yes, Lord!
Name him Mighty Couns'lor, yes, Lord
Name him Mighty Couns'lor, yes, Lord
De people keep a-comin' an' the train done gone.

Where was he born? Yes, Lord,
Where was he born? Yes, my Lord,
Where was he born? Yes, Lord,
De people keep a-comin' an' the train done gone.

Born in a manger, yes, Lord,
Born in a manger, yes, my Lord,
Born in a stable, yes, Lord,
De people keep a-comin' an' the train done gone.

—"Mary Had a Baby,"
in The Books of American Negro Spirituals,
ed. James Weldon Johnson and
J. Rosamond Johnson (New York:
Viking Press, 1925), 124–25.

"I Got Shoes"

I got shoes you got shoes all of God's childrens got shoes
When I get to heaven gonna put on my shoes
I'm gonna walk all over God's heaven (heaven) heaven
    (heaven)
Everybody talkin' 'bout heaven ain't a-goin' there heaven (heaven) heaven
    (heaven)
 I'm gonna walk all over God's heaven (I'm gonna fly)

I got wings you got wings all of God's childrens got wings
When I get to heaven gonna put on my wings
I'm gonna fly all over God's heaven (heaven) heaven (heaven)
Everybody talkin' 'bout heaven ain't a-goin' there heaven (heaven) heaven
    (heaven)
I'm gonna fly all over God's heaven (it's gonna shine)

I got a crown you got a crown all of God's childrens got a crown
When I get to heaven gonna put on my crown
I'm gonna shine all over God's heaven (heaven) heaven (heaven)
Everybody talkin' 'bout heaven ain't a-goin' there heaven (heaven) heaven
    (heaven)
I'm gonna shine all over God's heaven (I'm gonna play)

I got a harp you got a harp all of God's childrens got a harp
When I get to heaven gonna play on my harp
I'm gonna play all over God's heaven (heaven) heaven (heaven)
Everybody talkin' 'bout heaven ain't a-goin' there heaven (heaven) heaven
    (heaven)
I'm gonna play all over God's heaven
(I'm gonna walk fly shine play) walk all over God's heaven.

—"I Got Shoes,"
arr. Johnny Cash,
http://www.lyricsdepot.com
/johnny-cash/i-got-shoes.html.

A final example takes a more plaintive approach to the interplay of bondage and freedom at the heart of the spirituals of slave Christianity. The music of "You May Bury Me in the East" is dirgelike with a minor tonality that signals solemnity and a sense of finality. We can imagine people chanting this mournful song at burials and wakes or on occasions when people gathered together to remember the dead. The song's expression of hope and intimacy with God deepens the solemnity of the tune. Here, too, the juxtaposition of contradictory realities—the sadness and finality of death in tension with the promise of freedom, justice, and glory and the satisfaction of life lived without the extinction of goodness—defines the spiritual and its profound beauty.

The spirituals examined in this chapter provide a glimpse into the complexities of slave existence. They all speak of adherence to a cosmology of divine justice involving faith in God, human responsibility, and desire for freedom. They all reflect an ironic sensibility that juxtaposed the difficulties of physical existence with moral authority and spiritual rewards. They proclaim ownership of great characters and stories of the Bible and freedom to interpret those characters and stories in relation to the singers' daily experiences. The chants came alive when workers practiced them in the fields and kitchens of slave plantations, when fugitives sang them on the Underground Railroad, and when slaves gathered in hush arbors as persecuted Christians. During the antebellum era, these "chants of collective exorcism" strengthened people and enabled them to ward off some of the evils of slavery. We will never know how many people's lives were saved by singing spirituals. We do know that these chants inspired endurance, resistance, and hope of freedom.

"You May Bury Me in the East"

You may bury me in the East
You may bury me in the West
But I'll hear the trumpet sound in a-tat morning
In-a that morning, my Lord
How I long to go
For to hear the trumpet sound in-a that morning

In that dreadful Judgement day
We'll take wings and fly away
But I'll hear the trumpet sound in a-tat morning
In-a that morning, my Lord
How I long to go
For to hear the trumpet sound in-a that morning

Good old Christians, in that day
We'll take wings and fly away
For to hear the trumpet sound in a-tat morning
In-a that morning, my Lord
How I long to go
For to hear the trumpet sound in-a that morning
—Traditional spiritual, http://www.negrospirituals.com/news-song/you_may_bury_me_in_the_east.htm (accessed 2/1/07).

FOR FURTHER READING

Cone, James, *The Spirituals and The Blues: An Interpretation.* New York: Seabury, 1972.

Davis, Charles T., and Henry Louis Gates Jr., *The Slave's Narrative.* Oxford: Oxford University Press, 1985.

Du Bois, W. E. B. *The Souls of Black Folk.* 1903. Reprint, ed. Henry Louis Gates Jr. New York: Bantam, 1989.

Kirk-Duggan, Cheryl A. *Exorcizing Evil: A Womanist Perspective on the Spirituals.* Maryknoll, N.Y.: Orbis, 1997.

Lovell, John, Jr. *Black Song: The Forge and the Flame; The Story of How the Afro-American Spiritual Was Hammered Out.* New York: Macmillan, 1972.

Starling, Marion Wilson. *The Slave Narrative: Its Place in American History.* 2nd ed. Washington: Howard University Press, 1981.

NOTES

Introduction. Expansion and Change

1. For an excellent overview of scholarly discussion of the term "modernization" and its relation to religion, see Michael Saler, "Modernity and Enchantment: A Historiographic Overview," *The American Historical Review* 111, no. 3 (June 2006): 692–716.

2. Thomas Paine, *Common Sense* (1776; New York: Penguin, 1976), 76, 98.

3. Gregory Evans Dowd, *War under Heaven: Pontiac, the Indian Nations, and the British Empire* (Baltimore: Johns Hopkins University Press, 2002); Michael Hittman, *Wovoka and the Ghost Dance* (Lincoln: University of Nebraska Press, 1997).

4. Amanda Porterfield, *Mary Lyon and the Mount Holyoke Missionaries* (New York: Oxford University Press, 1997), 68–86.

5. Amanda Porterfield, *Healing in the History of Christianity* (New York: Oxford University Press, 2005), 152–57.

Chapter One. New Ways of Confronting Death

1. Edward Shills, "Ritual and Crisis," in *Center and Periphery: Essays in Macrosociology, Selected Papers of Edward Shills*, (Chicago: University of Chicago Press, 1975), 2:154.

2. Saint Gregory, *Dialogues*, book 4, chap. 57, p. 266

3. Roland H. Bainton, quoting Johann Tetzel, in *Here I Stand: A Life of Martin Luther,* (New York: Abingdon, 1950), 78.

4 . Martin Luther, "On the Misuse of the Mass" (1521), in *Luther's Works*, vol. 36, *Word and Sacrament II,* ed. Abdel Ross Wentz (Philadelphia: Fortress, 1959), 191.

5. Joannis Calvini opera quae supersunt omnia, ed. By W. Baum, E. Cunitz, and E. Reuss (Braunschweig, 1863-1900), 59 vols. Hereafter cited as CO, by treatise, volume, and page number: Commentary on the Acts of the Apostles, CO 48.562.

6. John Calvin, *De christiani hominis officio in sacerdotiis papalis ecclesiae vel administrandis vel abiiciendis*, CO 5. 304.

7. John Calvin, *Institutes of the Christian Religion* (1559), 4.18.1 Translated by Ford Lewis Battles; edited by John T. McNeill, 2 vols. (Philadelphia, 1960). Cited by book, chapter, and subchapter.

8. Martin Luther, "First Invocavit Sermon," in *Luther's Works*, vol. 51, *Sermons I*, ed. Helmut T. Lehmann (Philadelphia: Fortress, 1959), 70.

9. *The Works of James Pilkington*, ed. James Scholefield (Cambridge: n.p., 1842), 318, 543. Quoted by David Cressy, *Birth, Marriage and Death: Ritual, Religion, and the Life-Cycle in Tudor and Stuart England* (Oxford: Oxford University Press, 1997), 399.

10. Robert Hill, *The Pathway to Prayer and Pietie* (1610), 197, 229.

11. Juan Eusebio Nieremberg, *De la diferencia entre lo temporal y lo eterno. Crisol de desengaños con la memoria de la eternidad, postrimerias humans y principales misterios divinos*, in *Obras escogidas del R.P. Juan Eusebio Nieremberg,* ed. Eduardo Zepeda-Henríquez, 2 vols, (Madrid: Ediciones Atlas, 1957), 2:223.

12. Diego Murillo, *Discursos predicables sobre todos los evangelios* (Zaragoza, 1611). Cited in Ana Martínez Arancón, *Geografía de la Eternidad* (Madrid: Tecnos, 1987), 79.

13. Jean Delumeau, *Sin and Fear: The Emergence of a Western Guilt Culture, 13th–18th Centuries,* trans. Eric Nicholson (New York: Palgrave Macmillan, 1990); Piero Camporesi, *The Fear of Hell: Images of Damnation and Salvation in Early Modern Europe,* trans. Lucinda Byatt (University Park: Pennsylvania State University Press, 1991).

14. François Rabelais, quoted in D. J. Enright, ed., *The Oxford Book of Death* (Oxford: Oxford University Press, 1987), 330.

15. Thomas Paine, *The Age of Reason*, being an investigation of true and fabulous theology (1794), part 2, chapter 3. Edited by Daniel Edwin Wheeler, *The Life and Writings of Thomas Paine: Containing a Biography by Thomas Clio Rickman* (New York, 1908), 274–75.

16. Denis Diderot, quoted by Paul Johnson, *A History of Christianity* (New York: Touchstone, 2005), 350ff.

17. Jonathan Edwards, "Sinners in the Hands of an Angry God" (1741), in *A Jonathan Edwards Reader*, ed. John E. Smith, Harry S. Stout, and Kenneth P. Minkema (New Haven: Yale University Press, 1995), 97–87.

18. Philipe Ariès, *The Hour of Our Death*, trans. Helen Weaver (New York: Oxford University Press, 1981), 506–56.

19. William Shakespeare, *Hamlet*, 1.5.9–13.

Chapter Two. Controlling and Christianizing Sex

1. Frances E. Willard, "A White Life for Two," in *The World's Parliament of Religions*, ed. John H. Barrows (Chicago: Parliament, 1893), 2:1230, reprinted in Richard Hughes Seager, ed., *The Dawn of Religious Pluralism* (La Salle, Ill.: Open Court, 1993), 88; Dennis B. Downey, *A Season of Renewal: The Columbian Exposition and Victorian America* (Westport, Conn.: Praeger, 2002), 74–78.

2. John Noonan, *Contraception: A History of Its Treatment by the Catholic Theologians and Canonists,* enlarged ed. (1965; Cambridge: Harvard University Press, 1986), 387–89; Daniel Scott Smith, "Family Limitation, Sexual Control, and Domestic Feminism in Victorian America," *Feminist Studies* 1 (Winter–Spring 1973): 40–57;

Jayme A. Sokolow, *Eros and Modernization: Sylvester Graham, Health Reform, and the Origins of Victorian Sexuality in America* (London: Associated University Presses, 1983), 19–27; Peter Laslett, Karla Oosterveen, and Richard M. Smith, eds., *Bastardy and Its Comparative History* (Cambridge: Harvard University Press, 1980).

3. Richard C. Trexler, *Sex and Conquest: Gendered Violence, Political Order, and the European Conquest of the Americas* (Cambridge: Polity Press, 1995); Albert J. Raboteau, *Slave Religion: The "Invisible Institution" in the Antebellum South* (New York: Oxford University Press, 1978), 183, 187. See also George Eaton Simpson, *Black Religions in the New World* (New York: Columbia University Press, 1978).

4. Alphonsus Marie de Liguori, *Praxis Confessarii* (1755; Graz, 1954), pars. 39 and 41; Alphonsus Marie de Liguori, *Theologia Moralis* (1748; Graz, 1954), book 6, par. 935; book 3, par. 427.

5. Rosalind Mitchison and Leah Leneman, *Sexuality and Social Control: Scotland 1660–1780* (Oxford: Basil Blackwell, 1989), 19–26, 140–47, 243; John Murrin, "'Things Fearful to Name': Bestiality in Early America," in *American Sexual Histories*, ed. Elizabeth Reis (Oxford: Basil Blackwell, 2001), 26; Piers Beirne, "Rethinking Bestiality: For a Nonspeciest View of Rights," available online at http://www.stthomasu.ca/~ahrc/conferences/beirne.html (accessed 1/24/07).

6. Sokolow, *Eros and Modernization*, 25–26 n. 2; Cornelia Hughes Dyson, "Taking the Trade: Abortion and Gender Relationship in an Eighteenth-Century New England Village," in *Sexual Borderlands: Constructing an American Sexual Past*, ed. Kathleen Kennedy and Sharon Ullman (Columbus: Ohio State University Press), 54.

7. Trevor Burnard, "The Sexual Life of an Eighteenth-Century Jamaican Slave Overseer," in *Sex and Sexuality in Early America*, ed. Merril D. Smith (New York: New York University Press, 1998), 171; Martha Hodes, "Adultery: Dorothea Bourne and Edmond," in Reis, *American Sexual Histories*, 159–63 n. 5.

8. Hendrik E. Niemeijer, "Slavery, Ethnicity, and the Economic Independence of Women in Seventeenth-Century Batavia," in *Other Pasts: Women, Gender, and History in Early Modern Southeast Asia*, ed. Barbara Watson Andaya (Honolulu: University of Hawaii, Center for Southeast Asian Studies, 2000), 182–84; Eddie Donoghue, *Black Women/White Men: The Sexual Exploitation of Female Slaves in the Dutch West Indies* (Trenton: Africa World Press, 2002), 96–98, 102–3.

9. Peter Gardella, *Innocent Ecstasy: How Christianity Gave America an Ethic of Sexual Pleasure* (New York: Oxford University Press, 1985), 130–31.

10. Otho T. Beall Jr., "Aristotle's Master-Piece in America: A Landmark in the Folklore of Medicine," *William and Mary Quarterly* 20 (April 1963): 22; Benjamin Franklin, *The Autobiography of Benjamin Franklin*, available online at http://www.ushistory.org/franklin/autobiography/page38.htm (accessed 1/24/07).

11. Reay Tannehill, *Sex in History* (New York: Stein & Day, 1980), 75; Shere Hite, *The Hite Report: A Nationwide Study of Female Sexuality* (New York: Dell, 1976), 59.

12. Richard Lewinsohn, *A History of Sexual Customs* (New York: Harper & Row, 1958), 317–18.

13. Michel Foucault, *The History of Sexuality*, vol. 1: *An Introduction*, trans. Robert Hurley (1976; New York: Pantheon, 1978), 17–23, 69; Horace Bushnell, *Christian Nurture* (1861; New York: Scribner's, 1892), 195–223; Elizabeth Blackwell, "The Human Element

in Sex: Being a Medical Inquiry into the Relation of Sexual Physiology to Christian Morality," in *Essays in Medical Sociology,* (London, 1902; New York: Arno Press, 1972), 2:77.

14. Horatio Bigelow, *Social Physiology, or Familiar Talks on the Mysteries of Life* (New York: Union Publishing House, 1891), 214–17.

15. R. T. Trall, M.D., *Sexual Physiology: A Scientific and Popular Exposition of the Fundamental Problems in Sociology* (1866; New York: M. L. Holbrook, 1881), 230–32; Bigelow, *Social Physiology,* 284 n. 14; 114–15; Beryl Sattler, *Each Mind a Kingdom: American Women, Sexual Purity, and the New Thought Movement, 1875–1920* (Berkeley: University of California Press, 1999), 136–38.

16. Charles Grandison Finney, *Lectures on Systematic Theology,* (Oberlin: James M. Fitch; Boston: Crocker & Brewster; New York: Saxton & Miles, 1846), 414; Bushnell, *Christian Nurture,* 2:278 n. 13.

17. Francis P. Kenrick, *Theologiae Moralis,* (Philadelphia: Eugene Commiskey, 1843), 3:306.

18. Elizabeth Blackwell, "The Influence of Women in the Profession of Medicine: An Address at the Opening of the Winter Session of the London School of Medicine for Women, October 1889," in *Essays in Medical Sociology,* 2:77 n. 13. On the number of women doctors in 1900, see Ishbel Ross, *Child of Destiny: The Life Story of the First Woman Doctor* (New York: Harper & Bros., 1949), 290.

19. Eileen Mary Brewer, *Nuns and the Education of American Catholic Women, 1860–1920* (Chicago: Loyola University Press, 1987); Jenny Franchot, *Roads to Rome: The Antebellum Protestant Encounter with Catholicism* (Berkeley: University of California Press, 1994). See also Peter Gardella, "American Anti-Catholic Pornography," in *Religions of the United States in Practice,* ed. Colleen McDannell (Princeton: Princeton University Press, 2001), 1:452–58; Gardella, *Innocent Ecstasy,* 25–32 n. 9; 95–129.

20. David Pivar, *Purity Crusade: Sexual Morality and Social Control, 1868–1900* (Westport, Conn.: Greenwood Press, 1973), 138; Tannehill, *Sex in History,* 356–57, n. 11.

21. Sigmund Freud, "The Aetiology of Hysteria" (1896), trans.James Strachey, in *The Freud Reader,* ed. Peter Gay (New York: Norton, 1989), 107.

Chapter Three. Economic Change and Emotional Life

1. William A. Christian Jr., "Provoked Religious Weeping in Early Modern Spain," in *Religion and Emotion: Approaches and Interpretations,* ed. John Corrigan (New York: Oxford University Press, 2004), 34.

2. Catherine Peyroux, "Gertrude's *furor*: Reading Anger in an Early Medieval Saint's *Life,*" in Corrigan, *Religion and Emotion,* 318.

3. Max Weber, *The Protestant Ethic and the Spirit of Capitalism,* trans. Talcott Parsons (New York: Scribner's, 1958), 26–27.

4. Karl Marx and Frederick Engels, "Manifesto of the Communist Party," in *The Marx-Engels Reader,* ed. Robert Tucker (New York: Norton, 1972), 337–38.

5. Joseph de Rivera, "Emotional Climate: Social Structure and Emotional Dynamics," in *International Review of Studies on Emotion,* vol. 2, ed. K. T. Strongman (New York: John Wiley & Sons, 1992).

6. Michel Beaud, *A History of Capitalism 1500–2000*, trans. Tom Dickman and Anny Lefebvre (New York: Monthly Review Press, 2001), 292.

7. Jane Schneider, "Spirits and the Spirit of Capitalism," in *Religious Orthodoxy and Popular Faith in European Society,* ed. Ellen Badone (Princeton: Princeton University Press, 1990), 182, 188–91, 184.

8. Richard Rogers and Samuel Ward, *Two Elizabethan Puritan Diaries*, ed. M. M. Knappen (Chicago: American Society of Church History, 1933), 105–9, 111, 120, 123.

9. *The Salem Witchcraft Papers*, ed. Paul Boyer and Stephen Nissenbaum (New York: Da Capo Press, 1977), 611, 584, 586, 855, 743.

10. William A. Christian Jr., *Moving Crucifixes in Modern Spain* (Princeton: Princeton University Press, 1992), 131–40. Quoted material from p. 126.

11. Christina Landman, *The Piety of Afrikaans Women: Diaries of Guilt* (Praetoria: University of South Africa, 1994).

12. William John Wright, *Capitalism, the State, and the Lutheran Reformation: Sixteenth-Century Hesse* (Athens: Ohio University Press, 1988), 246; Peter Blickle, *Communal Reformation: The Quest for Salvation in Sixteenth-Century Germany*, trans. Thomas Dunlap (London: Humanities Press, 1992).

13. Ralph Gibson, *A Social History of French Catholicism, 1789–1914* (New York: Routledge, 1989), 252.

14. Winnie Lem, *Cultivating Dissent: Work, Identity, and Praxis in Rural Languedoc* (Albany: State University of New York Press, 1999), 194.

15. Fyodor Dostoevsky, *The Brothers Karamazov*, Constance Garnett translation, rev. Ralph E. Matlaw (New York: Norton, 1976), 298–99.

16. William Penn, quoted in Ann Prior and Maurice Kirby, "The Society of Friends and Business Culture, 1700–1830," in *Religion, Business, and Wealth in Modern Britain*, ed. David J. Jeremy (New York: Routledge, 1998), 117; "The Testimony of William Penn concerning That Faithful Servant George Fox," in *George Fox: An Autobiography*, ed. Rufus M. Jones (Richmond: Friends United Press, 1976), 23.

17. John Corrigan, *Business of the Heart: Religion and Emotion in the Nineteenth Century* (Berkeley: University of California Press, 2002).

18. Gregor Dallas, *The Imperfect Peasant Economy: The Loire Country, 1800–1914* (Cambridge: Cambridge University Press, 1982), 46–53; 137–96; Charles Eldon Freedeman, *The Triumph of Corporate Capitalism in France, 1867–1914* (Rochester: University of Rochester Press, 1993), 20–29.

19. Gibson, *A Social History of French Catholicism, 1789–1914*, 181.

20. Raymond A. Jonas, "Anxiety, Identity, and the Displacement of Violence during the Annee Terrible: The Sacred Heart and the Diocese of Nantes, 1870–1871," *French Historical Studies* 21 (1998): 62–64; Jonas, *France and the Cult of the Sacred Heart* (Berkeley: University of California Press, 2000).

Chapter Four. Vulgar Science

This chapter is appearing simultaneously in Ronald L. Numbers, *Science and Christianity in Pulpit and Pew* (New York: Oxford University Press, 2007), where full documentation is provided. I am indebted to Stephen E. Wald for his assistance in tracking down sources used in this essay and for his critical comments. I also want to thank Ted Davis, Aileen Fyfe, Randy Maddox, Jon Roberts, and Mike Shank for their comments and suggestions.

Chapter Five. Tropical Christianity in Brazil

1. A. J. R. Russell-Wood, "Prestige, Power, and Piety in Colonial Brazil: The Third Orders of Salvador," *Hispanic American Historical Review* 69, no. 1 (February 1989): 61–68; quote is on p. 62.

2. Ibid., 67.

3. H. B. Johnson, "Portuguese Settlement, 1500–1580," in *Colonial Brazil*, ed. Leslie Bethell (Cambridge: Cambridge University Press, 1987), 22.

4. Thomas E. Skidmore, *Brazil: Five Centuries of Change* (New York: Oxford University Press, 1999), 17.

5. Jacob U. Gordon, "Yoruba Cosmology and Culture in Brazil: A Study of African Survivals in the New World," *Journal of Black Studies* 10, no. 2 (December 1979): 231–44; quote is on p. 238.

6. Sheila S. Walker, "Everyday and Esoteric Reality in the Afro-Brazilian Candomble," *History of Religions* 30, no. 2 (November 1990): 103–28; quote is on p. 125.

7. The brief information on the African Orisha hierarchy and their equivalency with Catholic saints comes from multiple sources, including J. Omosade Awolalu, *Yoruba Beliefs and Sacrificial Rites* (London: Longman, 1979); E. Carneiro, *Candombles da Bahia* (Rio de Janeiro: Conquista, 1961); J. O. Lucas, *The Religions of the Yoruba* (Lagos: C.M.S. Bookshop, 1942); Pierre Fatumbi Verger, *Orixas: Deuses Iorubás na Africa e no Novo Mundo* (Salvador, Bahia: Editora Corrupio, 1981).

8. Walker, "Everyday and Esoteric Reality," 112–13.

9. E. Bradford Burns, *A History of Brazil*, 2nd ed. (New York: Columbia University Press, 1980), 199, 201; Rollie E. Poppino, *Brazil: The Land and People* (New York: Oxford University Press, 1968); Emilia Viotti da Costa, "1870–1889," in *Brazil: Empire and Republic, 1822–1930* , ed. Leslie Bethell (Cambridge: Cambridge University Press, 1989), 161–213.

10. Viotti da Costa, "1870–1889," 166.

11. Antônio Mendonça, "Evolução histórica e configuração atual do protestantismo brasileiro," in *Introdução ao Protestantismo no Brasil*, ed. Antônio Mendonça and Prócoro Velasques Filho (São Paulo: Edições Loyola, 1990), 43–44.

Chapter Six. Iconic Piety in Russia

1. L. P. Rushchinskii, *Religioznyi byt russkikh po svedeniiam inostrannykh pisatelei XVI and XVII vekov* (Moscow, 1871), 72.

2. P. P. Pekarskii, "Spisok s Gosudarevoi Gramoty," in *Materialy dlia istorii ikonopisaniia v Rossii* (St. Petersburg, 1865), 16.

3. *Opisanie dokumentov i del khraniashchikhsia v archive Sviateishago Pravitel'stvuiushchago Sinoda*, vol. 2, part 1 (St. Petersburg, 1878), d. 743 (1722).

4. Iosif Vladimirov, "Poslanie nekoego izugrafa Iosifa k tsarevu izugrafu i mudreishemu zhivopistsu Simonu Fedorovichu," in *Drevne-russkoe iskusstvo, XVII vek* (Moscow: Nauka, 1964), 28; V. Illarionov, "Ikonopistsy-Suzdaltsy," *Russkoe obozrenie* 32 (March–April 1895): 735; N. Trokhimovskii, "Ofeni," *Russkii vestnik* 63 (June 1866): 577–78.

5. Rossiiskii Gosudarstvennyi Istoricheskii Arkhiv (RGIA), fond (f.) 796, opis (op.) 110, delo (d.) 866; P. Pankrat'ev, "O russkikh narodnykh kartinkakh," *Blagovest* 45 (1892): 1703; *Opisanie dokumentov i del*, vol. 2, part 2 (St. Petersburg, 1878), d. 1128 (1723); Aleksandr Malevinskii, *Instruktsiia blagochinnomu prikhodskikh tserkvei iz'iasnennaia ukazami sv. Sinoda, rasporiazheniiami eparkhial'nago nachal'stva, Svodom zakonov, i tserkovnoi praktikoi*, 3rd ed. (St. Petersburg, 1910), 7; S. V. Kalashnikov, *Alfavitnyi ukazatel' deistvuiushchikh i rukovodstvennykh kanonicheskikh postanovlenii, ukazov, opredelenii i rasporiazhenii Sviateishago Pravitel'stvuiushchago Sinoda, 1721–1901* (St. Petersburg, 1902), 165.

6. Archdeacon Paul of Aleppo, *The Travels of Macarius, Patriarch of Antioch*, trans. F. C. Belfour, vol. 2, part 6 (London: Oriental Translation Committee, 1835), 158–59; Iosif Vladimirov, "Poslanie," RGIA, f. 796, op. 110, d. 866, ll. 3–4; 34. For a description of the production of "native" Russian iconography as perceived by a nineteenth-century academic icon expert, see N. P. Kondakov, *Sovremennoe polozhenie o russkoi narodnoi ikonopisi* (Moscow, 1901).

7. I. M. Snegirev, *O lubochnykh kartinkakh russkago naroda* (Moscow, 1844), 4–5; O. R. Khromov, "Russkii religioznyi lubok v XIX stoletii," *Knizhnoe delo*, no. 4 (1993): 84–89; T. A. Voronina, "Russkii religioznyi lubok," *Zhivaia starina*, no. 3 (1994): 6–11.

8. For basic information about Blessed Ksenia of St. Petersburg, who was officially canonized by the Orthodox Church in Russia in 1988, see Nadieszda Kizenko, "Protectors of Women and the Lower Orders: Constructing Sainthood in Modern Russia," in *Orthodox Russia: Belief and Practice under the Tsars*, ed. Valerie A. Kivelson and Robert H. Greene (University Park: Pennsylvania State University Press, 2003), 105–24.

9. Rossiiskii Etnograficheskii Muzei, Tenishev Collection, f. 7, d. 1833, l. 4 (Iaroslavl Diocese); A. Zav'ialov, comp., *Tsirkuliarnye ukazy Sviateishago Pravitel'stvuiushchago Sinoda, 1867–1900* (St. Petersburg, 1901), 364–65; Paul of Aleppo, *Travels of Macarius*, vol. 2, part 5, 49.

10. N. F. Kapterev, *Patriarkh Nikon i tsar' Aleksei Mikhailovich* (Sergiev Posad, 1909), 1:155; K. V. Tsekhanskaia, *Ikonopochitanie v russkoi traditsionnoi kul'ture* (Moscow: Institut etnologii i antropologii RAN, 2004), 73–75; Zav'ialov, *Tsirkuliarnye ukazy*, 364.

11. *Opisanie dokumentov i del*, vol. 1 (St. Petersburg, 1868), d. 582 (1722).

12. Episkop Vissarion, "O sviatykh ikonakh," *Dushepoleznoe chtenie* (October 1901): 228–29.

13. *O chudotvornykh i mestno-chtimykh sviatykh ikonakh Tambovskago kraia* (Tambov, 1902), 29–33.

14. Eugene N. Trubetskoi, *Icons: Theology in Color*, trans. Gertrude Vakar (Crestwood, N.Y.: St. Vladimir's Seminary Press, 1973), 41. For a history of the icon setting or *riza*, see I. A. Sterligova, *Dragotsennyi ubor drevnerusskikh ikon XI–XIV vekov* (Moscow: Progress-Traditsia, 2000). For an Orthodox defense of icon ornamentation, see "Otvet

na nekotoryia vozrozheniia otnositel'no ukrashenii sviatykh ikon," *Rukovodstvo dlia sel'skikh pastyrei*, no. 22 (1899): 131–37.

15. RGIA, f. 797, op. 16, d. 37483; f. 796, op. 160, d. 1757.

16. "Slovo vysokopreosviashchenneishago Sergiia, mitropolita Moskovskago i Kolomenskago," *Kormchii*, no. 48 (1895): 620. For eighteenth-century legislation concerning icon veneration, see A. S. Lavrov, *Koldovstvo i religiia v Rossii: 1700–1740 gg.* (Moscow: Drevnekhranilishche, 2000).

17. Robert Muchembled, quoted in Thomas A. Kselman, *Miracles and Prophecies in Nineteenth-Century France* (New Brunswick: Rutgers University Press), 191. These concerns were not new to Russia and had precedents in the mid-seventeenth century.

18. Sv. Vasilii, "Sv. ikony," *Prikhodskaia zhizn'*, no. 2 (1917); RGIA, f. 796, op. 181, d. 2580.

19. RGIA, f. 796, op. 102, d. 75, l. 1.

20. Sergei Glagolev, "Chudo i nauka," *Bogoslovskii vestnik* (June 1893): 514. For other treatises on miracles, see Protoierei, Magistr Bogosloviia, Grigorii D'iachenko, *Dukhovnyi mir* (Moscow, 1900), iii; D. Sosnin, *O sviatykh chudotvornykh ikhonakh* (St. Petersburg, 1833); Sergii, Episkop Mogilevskii i Mstislavskii, *Pravoslavnoe uchenie o pochitanii sviatykh ikon* (Mogilev na Dnepre, 1887); Protoierei P. Smirnov, *Chudesa v prezhnee i nashe vremia* (Moscow, 1895); Protoierei S. Ostroumov, *Mysli o chudesakh* (Kiev, 1916).

21. Episkop Tikhon, "Slovo v nedeliu Pravoslaviia," *Eniseiskiia eparkhial'nyia vedomosti*, otdel neoffitsial'nyi, no. 5 (1887): 61–69.

Chapter Seven. Religious Experiences in New England

1. This chapter draws upon published church-admission narratives in Robert G. Pope, *The Notebook of the Reverend John Fiske, 1644–1675*, vol. 47, *Publications of the Colonial Society of Massachusetts* (Boston: Colonial Society of Massachusetts, 1974); J. M. Bumsted, ed., "Emotion in Colonial America: Some Relations of Conversion Experience in Freetown, Massachusetts, 1749–1770," *New England Quarterly* 49 (1976): 97–107; George Selement and Bruce C. Woolley, eds., *Publications of the Colonial Society of Massachusetts*, vol. 58, *Thomas Shepard's Confessions* (Boston: Colonial Society of Massachusetts, 1981); Kenneth P. Minkema, ed., "The East Windsor Conversion Relations, 1700–1725," *Bulletin of the Connecticut Historical Society* 51 (1986): 7–63; Mary Rhinelander McCarl, ed., "Thomas Shepard's Record of Relations of Religious Experience, 1648–1649," *William and Mary Quarterly*, 3rd ser., 48 (1991): 432–66; and Minkema, ed., "The Lynn End 'Earthquake' Relations of 1727," *New England Quarterly* 69 (1996): 473–99. In addition, I have relied on archival sources for relations from the West Parish Church, Barnstable, Mass. (Lemuel Shaw Papers, Massachusetts Historical Society, Boston); First and Old South Churches, Boston (Autograph Collection, Houghton Library, Harvard University, Cambridge, Mass.; James Davis Papers, Massachusetts Historical Society; Thomas Foxcroft Papers, Howard Gotlieb Archival Research Center, Boston University, Boston); First Church, Dedham, Mass. (Dedham Historical Society), East Parish Church, Granville, Mass. (Granville Public Library); First Church, Haverhill, Mass. (Haverhill Public Library); First Church, Medfield, Mass. (Amos Adams Papers

and Baxter-Adams Papers, Massachusetts Historical Society; Mvedfield Historical Society); First Church, Middleborough, Mass. (First Congregational Church); First Church, Rowley, Mass. (Mss. C52 and C77, New England Historic Genealogical Society, Boston); and First Church, Westborough, Mass. (Ebenezer Parkman Papers, American Antiquarian Society, Worcester, Mass.).

2. Williston Walker, ed., *The Creeds and Platforms of Congregationalism* (1893; reprint, with an intro. by Elizabeth C. Nordbeck, New York: Pilgrim Press, 1991), 206, 221–24.

3. Published seventeenth-century collections of English spiritual experiences and confessions include Vavasor Powell, *Spiritual Experiences, of Sundry Beleevers* (London, 1653); John Rogers, *A Tabernacle for the Sun* (London, 1653); and Samuel Petto, *Roses from Sharon* (London, 1654).

4. David D. Hall, ed., *The Antinomian Controversy, 1636–1638: A Documentary History*, rev. ed. (Durham: Duke University Press, 1990), 336–37. For a recent biography of Hutchinson, see Michael P. Winship, *The Times and Trials of Anne Hutchinson: Puritans Divided* (Lawrence: University Press of Kansas, 2005). Michael G. Ditmore examines the conservative impact of the Antinomian Controversy on New England church-admission practices in "Preparation and Confession: Reconsidering Edmund S. Morgan's Visible Saints," *New England Quarterly* 67 (1994): 298–319.

5. Thomas Shepard, *The Sound Beleever* (London, 1645), in Albro, *Works*, 316–17.

6. Shepard, *Parable of the Ten Virgins*, quoted in *God's Plot: Puritan Spirituality in Thomas Shepard's Cambridge*, ed. Michael McGiffert, rev. ed. (Amherst: University of Massachusetts Press, 1994), 20.

7. Walker, *Creeds and Platforms of Congregationalism*, 207, 222–24.

8. M. Halsey Thomas, ed., *The Diary of Samuel Sewall, 1674–1729*, (New York: Farrar, Straus, & Giroux, 1972), 1:39.

9. Gerald F. Moran, "Conditions of Religious Conversion in the First Society of Norwich, Connecticut, 1718–1744," *Journal of Social History* 5 (1972): 331–43; Moran, "Religious Renewal, Puritan Tribalism, and the Family in Seventeenth-Century Milford, Connecticut," *William and Mary Quarterly*, 3rd ser., 36 (1979): 236–54; Moran and Maris A. Vinovskis, "The Puritan Family and Religion: A Critical Reappraisal," *William and Mary Quarterly*, 3rd ser., 39 (1982): 38–49; Mary Mcmanus Ramsbottom, "Religious Society and the Family in Charlestown, Massachusetts, 1630–1740" (Ph.D. diss., Yale University, 1987); Anne Speerschneider Brown, "'Bound Up in a Bundle of Life': The Social Meaning of Religious Practice in Northeastern Massachusetts, 1700–1765" (Ph.D. diss., Boston University, 1995); Brown and David D. Hall, "Family Strategies and Religious Practice: Baptism and the Lord's Supper in Early New England," in *Lived Religion: Toward a History of Practice*, ed. Hall (Princeton: Princeton University Press, 1997), 41–68.

10. John Brown to John Cotton, November 24, 1727, quoted in Cotton, *A Holy Fear of God, and His Judgments* (Boston, 1727), 3–7.

11. Whitefield's career is chronicled in Harry S. Stout, *The Divine Dramatist: George Whitefield and the Rise of Modern Evangelicalism* (Grand Rapids: Eerdmans, 1991); and Frank Lambert, *"Pedlar in Divinity": George Whitefield and the Transatlantic Revivals, 1737–1770* (Princeton: Princeton University Press, 1994).

12. *New England Historical and Genealogical Register* 15 (1861): 58.

13. William G. McLoughlin, ed., *The Diary of Isaac Backus*, (Providence: Brown University Press, 1979), 3:1523–26; Jonathan Edwards, *The Works of Jonathan Edwards*, vol. 7, *The Life of David Brainerd*, ed. Norman Pettit (New Haven: Yale University Press, 1985), 100–153; Michael J. Crawford, ed., "The Spiritual Travels of Nathan Cole," *William and Mary Quarterly*, 3rd ser., 33 (1976): 89–126; Sue Lane McCulley and Dorothy Z. Baker, eds., *The Silent and Soft Communion: The Spiritual Narratives of Sarah Pierpont Edwards and Sarah Prince Gill* (Knoxville: University of Tennessee Press, 2006); Barbara E. Lacey, ed., *The World of Hannah Heaton: The Diary of an Eighteenth-Century New England Farm Woman* (DeKalb: Northern Illinois University Press, 2003), 3–25; Samuel Hopkins, ed., *Memoirs of the Life of Mrs. Sarah Osborn . . .* (Worcester, Mass., 1799); William McCulloch, *Examination of Persons under Spiritual Concern at Cambuslang*, 2 vols., New College Library, Edinburgh (I thank Roark Atkinson for sharing his copy of the Cambuslang narratives with me); Josiah Crocker, "An Account of the late Revival of Religion at Taunton," *Christian History* 2 (1744): 246.

14. Statement of Sarah Martin, Sturbridge Separate Congregational Church Papers, 1745–1762, Congregational Library, Boston; Samuel Hopkins, ed., *Life and Character of Miss Susanna Anthony* (Worcester, Mass.: Leonard Worcester, 1796), 27; William Pitkin, Diary, 1711–1756, Connecticut State Library, Hartford, Conn., 56; "Diary of the Reverend Stephen Williams," 1715–1782, 10 vols., typescript, Storrs Public Library, Longmeadow, Mass., 3:379; Lacey, *World of Hannah Heaton*, 26.

15. Douglas L. Winiarski, "Souls Filled with Ravishing Transport: Heavenly Visions and the Radical Awakening in New England," *William and Mary Quarterly*, 3rd ser., 61 (2004): 3–46.

16. Douglas L. Winiarski, ed., "A Jornal of a Fue Days at York: The Great Awakening on the Northern New England Frontier," *Maine History* 42 (2004): 70.

17. For analyses of Finney and the Second Great Awakening, see Paul E. Johnson, *A Shopkeeper's Millennium: Society and Revivals in Rochester, New York, 1815–1837*, rev. ed. (New York: Hill and Wang, 2004); and Charles E. Hambrick-Stowe, *Charles G. Finney and the Spirit of American Evangelicalism* (Grand Rapids: Eerdmans, 1991).

Chapter Eight. Domestic Piety in New England

1. William Shippen to Sarah Edwards, March 22, 1758; quoted in George Marsden, *Jonathan Edwards: A Life* (New Haven: Yale University Press, 2003), 494.

2. Charles E. Hambrick-Stowe, *The Practice of Piety: Puritan Devotional Disciplines in Seventeenth-Century New England* (Chapel Hill: University of North Carolina Press, 1982), 4.

3. Laurel Thatcher Ulrich, *Good Wives: Image and Reality in the Lives of Women in Northern New England, 1650–1750* (1982; New York: Vintage Books, 1991), 36, 38.

4. Jonathan Edwards, *The Works of Jonathan Edwards*, vol. 16, *Letters and Personal Writings*, ed. George S. Claghorn (New Haven: Yale University Press), 745, 751, 789–80. The ongoing multivolume series *The Works of Jonathan Edwards* will hereafter be cited in parentheses as *WJE* with volume and page numbers only.

5. William Gouge, *Of Domestical Duties* (1622; Amsterdam: Theatrum Orbis Terrarum, 1976), 18; Hambrick-Stowe, *Practice of Piety*, 156.

6. Ulrich, *Good Wives*, 154.

7. David D. Hall, *Worlds of Wonder, Days of Judgment: Popular Religious Belief in Early New England* (Cambridge: Harvard University Press, 1990), 155, 153; Edmund S. Morgan, *The Puritan Family: Religion and Domestic Relations in Seventeenth-Century New England* (1944; New York: Harper & Row, 1966), 173, 174.

8. Morgan, *The Puritan Family*, 162.

9. Jonathan Edwards, *Sermon on Math. 25:1* (November 1737), Beinecke Rare Books and Manuscripts Library, Yale University, New Haven, Conn.

10. Amanda Porterfield, *Female Piety in Puritan New England: The Emergence of Religious Humanism* (New York: Oxford University Press, 1992), 20, 15.

11. Richard Godbeer, *Sexual Revolution in Early America* (Baltimore: Johns Hopkins University Press, 2002), 79; Porterfield, *Female Piety in Puritan New England*, 6–7, 9.

12. Richard P. Gildrie, *The Profane, the Civil, and the Godly: The Reformation of Manners in Orthodox New England, 1679–1749* (University Park: Pennsylvania State University Press, 1994), 43; Hall, *Worlds of Wonder*, 137.

13. Hall, *Worlds of Wonder*, 119, 156–59, 71–116; Jon Butler, *Awash in a Sea of Faith: Christianizing the American People* (Cambridge: Harvard University Press, 1990), 67–97.

14. Harry S. Stout, *The New England Soul: Preaching and Religious Culture in Colonial New England* (New York: Oxford University Press, 1986), 188–89.

15. Hambrick-Stowe, *Practice of Piety*, 23.

16. Morgan, *Puritan Family*, 105.

17. Jonathan Edwards, *Sermon on Deut. 1:13-18* (June 1748), Beinecke Rare Books and Manuscripts Library, Yale University.

18. The materials documenting the Elisha Hawley fornication case are located in the Hawley Papers, New York Public Library, and the Jonathan Edwards Papers, Trask Library, Andover Newton Theological School, Newton Centre, Mass. Northampton Town Hall Records (Forbes Library) record that one of the twins, named Esther, died on September 14, 1747.

19. Godbeer, *Sexual Revolution in Early America*, 55, 60.

20. Ibid., 33, 228.

21. *The General Laws and Liberties of Massachusetts* (Cambridge, 1672), 54–55, in *The Colonial Laws of Massachusetts, Reprinted from the Edition of 1672* (Boston, 1890).

22. Court of General Sessions of the Peace, November 11, 1747 (Hampshire County, Court Records, 1677–1859, Forbes Library).

23. Cornelia Hughes Dayton, *Women before the Bar: Gender, Law, and Society in Connecticut, 1637–1789* (Chapel Hill: University of North Carolina Press, 1995), 31, 60; Laurel Thatcher Ulrich, *A Midwife's Tale: The Life of Martha Ballard, Based on Her Diary, 1785–1812* (New York: Knopf, 1990), 148.

24. Dayton, *Women before the Bar*, 12, 215.

25. Porterfield, *Female Piety in Puritan New England*, 153.

26. Court of General Sessions, March 2, 1731 (Hampshire County Ministerial Association Minutes, October 1731, Forbes Library).

27. Mary Beth Norton, *Founding Mothers and Fathers: Gendered Power and the Forming of American Society* (1996; New York: Vintage Books, 1997), 10.

28. Sarah Edwards to Esther Edwards Burr, April 3, 1758; quoted in Marsden, *Jonathan Edwards*, 495.

Chapter Nine. Gendering Christianity

1. Phyllis Mack, *Visionary Women: Ecstatic Prophecy in Seventeenth-Century England* (Berkeley: University of California Press, 1992), 24–27, discusses the seventeenth-century meaning of female wetness in some detail, not merely in terms of physiology but also in terms of personality and moral character.

2. Elizabeth Reis, *Damned Women: Sinners and Witches in Puritan New England* (Ithaca, N.Y.: Cornell University Press, 1997); Carol F. Karlsen, *The Devil in the Shape of a Woman: Witchcraft in Colonial New England* (New York: Norton, 1987).

3. Amanda Porterfield, *Female Piety in Puritan New England: The Emergence of Religious Humanism* (New York: Oxford University Press, 1992); Roger Thompson, "Attitudes Towards Homosexuality in the Seventeenth-Century New England Colonies," *Journal of American Studies* 23 (1989): 27–40.

4. Marilyn J. Westerkamp, "Engendering Puritan Religious Culture in Old and New England," *Pennsylania History* 64 (1997): 105–22.

5. "Some Account of the Fore Part of the Life of Elizabeth Ashbridge," ed. with an intro. by Daniel B. Shea in William L. Andrews et al., eds., *Journeys in New Worlds: Early American Women's Narratives*, Wisconsin Studies in American Autobiography (Madison: University of Wisconsin Press, 1990), 147–70.

6. Barry Levy, *Quakers and the American Family: British Settlement in the Delaware Valley* (New York: Oxford University Press, 1988).

7. Londa Schiebinger, *Nature's Body: Gender in the Making of Modern Science* (Boston: Beacon, 1993).

8. Susan Juster, *Disorderly Women: Sexual Politics and Evangelicalism in Revolutionary New England* (Ithaca, N.Y.: Cornell University Press, 1994), esp. 122–35.

9. Carroll Smith Rosenberg, "Beauty, the Beast, and the Militant Woman: A Case Study in Sex Roles and Social Stress in Jacksonian America," *American Quarterly* (1971): 562–84; Lori D. Ginzberg, *Women and the Work of Benevolence: Morality, Politics, and Class in the Nineteenth-Century United States* (New Haven: Yale University Press, 1990).

10. Mary P. Ryan, *Cradle of the Middle Class: The Family in Oneida County, New York, 1790–1865* (Cambridge: Cambridge University Press, 1981).

11. Christine Stansell, *City of Women: Sex and Class in New York, 1789–1860* (Urbana-Champaign: University of Illinois Press, 1987), esp. 19–30, 63–101; quote is on p. 66.

12. Catherine A. Brekus, *Strangers and Pilgrims: Female Preaching in America, 1740–1845* (Chapel Hill: University of North Carolina Press, 1998).

13. Ann Braude, *Radical Spirits: Spiritualism and Women's Rights in Nineteenth-Century America* (Boston: Beacon, 1989).

14. Carol V. R. George, *Segregated Sabbaths: Richard Allen and the Rise of Independent Black Churches, 1760–1840* (New York: Oxford University Press, 1973), 128–29; William L. Andrews, ed., *Sisters of the Spirit: Three Black Women's Autobiographies of the Nineteenth Century* (Bloomington: University of Indiana Press, 1986).

15. Zilpha Elaw, *Memoirs of the Life, Religious Experience, Ministerial Travels, and Labours of Mrs. Zilpha Elaw*, in Andrews, *Sisters of the Spirit*, 49–160.

16. Catharine Livingston to Catharine Rutsen, December 1791; quoted in Rosemary Radford Ruether and Rosemary Skinner Keller, eds., *Women and Religion in America: The Colonial and Revolutionary Periods* (San Francisco: Harper San Francisco, 1983), 363–64.

17. Amanda Porterfield, *Mary Lyon and the Mount Holyoke Missionaries* (New York: Oxford University Press, 1997); Joan Jacobs Brumberg, *Mission for Life* (New York: Free Press, 1980).

18. Marilyn J. Westerkamp, *Women and Religion in Early America, 1600–1850: The Puritan and Evangelical Traditions* (London: Routledge, 1999), 140–50.

19. See, for example, John J. Fialka, *Sisters: Catholic Nuns and the Making of America* (New York: St. Martin's, 2003).

20. See, for example, discussions of the sisters' work in Michael E. Engh, *Frontier Faiths: Church, Temple, and Synagogue in Los Angeles, 1846–1888* (Albuquerque: University of New Mexico Press, 1992), 139–63.

21. Ronald L. Numbers, *Prophetess of Health: A Study of Ellen Gould White* (New York: Harper & Row, 1976).

22. Ann Taves, *Fits, Trances, and Visions: Experiencing Religion and Explaining Experience from Wesley to James* (Princeton: Princeton University Press, 1999), esp. chap. 6.

23. Kathi Kern, *Mrs. Stanton's Bible* (Ithaca, N.Y.: Cornell University Press, 2001).

24. Alison M. Parker, *Purifying America: Women, Cultural Reform, and Pro-Censorship Activity, 1873–1933* (Urbana: University of Illinois Press, 1997).

25. Mary Poovey, *Uneven Developments: The Ideological Work of Gender in Mid-Victorian England* (Chicago: University of Chicago Press, 1988).

26. Deborah Gaitskell, "Rethinking Gender Roles: The Field Experience of Women Missionaries in South Africa," in *The Imperial Horizons of British Protestant Missions, 1880–1914*, ed. Andrew Porter (Grand Rapids: Eerdmans, 2003), 131–57.

27. Dana L. Robert, *American Women in Mission: A Social History of Their Thought and Practice* (Macon: Mercer University Press, 1996), 81–188; ref. is on pp. 132–33.

28. Ann Douglas, *The Feminization of American Culture* (New York: Farrar, Straus, & Giroux, 1977).

29. Betty DeBerg, *Ungodly Women: Gender and the First Wave of American Fundamentalism* (Minneapolis: Fortress, 1990), argues for the centrality of women's growing leadership as a central issue among the new strain of evangelicals.

Chapter Ten. Slave Christianity

1. Melville J. Herskovits, *The Myth of the Negro Past* (1941; Boston: Beacon, 1958); Albert J. Raboteau, *Slave Religion: The "Invisible Institution" in the Antebellum South* (New York: Oxford University Press, 1978), chap. 2.

2. Mechal Sobel, *The World They Made Together: Black and White Values in Eighteenth-Century Virginia* (Princeton: Princeton University Press, 1987), 184–88; Lawrence W. Levine, *Black Culture and Black Consciousness: Afro-American Folk Thought from Slavery to Freedom* (New York: Oxford University Press, 1987), 20–21.

3. Ira Berlin, *Generations of Captivity: A History of African-American Slaves* (Cambridge: Belknap, 2003), 74–75.

4. Daniel Alexander Payne, *Recollections of Seventy Years* (1886; New York: Arno Press, 1969), 253–56.

5. Raboteau, *Slave Religion*, 72.

6. Fredrika Bremer, *America of the Fifties: Letters of Fredrika Bremer*, ed. Adolph B. Benson (New York: Oxford University Press, 1924), 274–81; quote is on p. 277.

7. Sterling Stuckey, *Slave Culture: Nationalist Theory and the Foundation of Black America* (New York: Oxford University Press, 1987), 57.

8. Frederick Law Olmsted, *The Cotton Kingdom* (1861; New York: Knopf, 1953), 240–47; quote is on p. 241.

9. Mary Boykin Chesnut, *A Diary from Dixie*, ed. Ben Amos Williams (Boston: Houghton, Mifflin, 1949), 149.

10. Zora Neale Hurston, *The Sanctified Church* (Berkeley: Turtle Island, 1981), 103.

11. Herskovits, *Myth of the Negro Past,* chap. 7.

12. W. E. B. Du Bois, *The Souls of Black Folk* (1903; New York: New American Library, 1969), 216; Stuckey, *Slave Culture*, 255–56.

13. Charles W. Joyner, *Down by the Riverside: A South Carolina Slave Community* (Urbana: University of Illinois Press, 1984), 170.

14. Two of the three known accounts are cited in Robert Tallant, *Voodoo in New Orleans* (London: Collier-Macmillan, 1962).

Chapter Eleven. Spirituals and the Quest for Freedom

1. John Lovell Jr., *Black Song: The Forge and the Flame; The Story of How the Afro-American Spiritual Was Hammered Out* (New York: Macmillan, 1972), 637; Henry Louis Gates Jr., introduction, W. E. B. Du Bois, *The Souls of Black Folks* (1903; New York: Bantam, 1989), xix.

2. Cheryl A. Kirk-Duggan, *Exorcising Evil: A Womanist Perspective on the Spirituals* (Maryknoll, N.Y.: Orbis, 1997).

3. Russell Ames, "Protest and Irony in Negro Folk Song," *Science and Society* 14 (Summer 1950): 207–12.

4. Du Bois, *Souls of Black Folk*, 43–48, 56–65.

INDEX